ISBN: 9781313583602

Published by:
HardPress Publishing
8345 NW 66TH ST #2561
MIAMI FL 33166-2626

Email: info@hardpress.net
Web: http://www.hardpress.net

SX
718
12
5

p.1

NUEL

THE LIBRARY
of
VICTORIA UNIVERSITY
Toronto

# LETTERS

OF

# JOHN CALVIN

COMPILED FROM THE ORIGINAL MANUSCRIPTS AND
EDITED WITH HISTORICAL NOTES

BY

DR. JULES BONNET.

VOL. II.

TRANSLATED FROM THE ORIGINAL LATIN AND FRENCH.

EDINBURGH: THOMAS CONSTABLE AND CO.
LITTLE, BROWN, AND CO., BOSTON, U.S.
MDCCCLVII.

BX
1418
A2
E6
V.

**MMANUEL**

10,095
31/3/1903

EDINBURGH : T. CONSTABLE, PRINTER TO HER MAJESTY.

# CONTENTS.

## 1545.

| LETTER | | PAGE |
|---|---|---|
| CXLIV. | To Viret.—Unpopularity of Calvin—various advices, | 1 |
| CXLV. | To Monsieur de Falais.—Exhortation to glorify God amid poverty and persecution, | 2 |
| CXLVI. | To Madame de Falais.—Congratulations on the constancy manifested by her in the midst of trials—salutations from the suffering Idelette de Bure, | 5 |
| CXLVII. | To Monsieur de Falais.—Vanity of trust reposed in the princes of this world—confidence in God, | 6 |
| CXLVIII. | To Farel.—Captivity of Farel's brother—ravages of the plague in Geneva, | 8 |
| CXLIX. | To Viret.—Dispersion of the School at Geneva—contests at Neuchatel on the subject of church property—Calvin's opinion of Farel, | 10 |
| CL. | To Monsieur de Falais.—Prayers for his restoration to health, | 12 |

## 1546.

| | | |
|---|---|---|
| CLI. | To Farel.—News from Germany—journey of the French Ambassador to Geneva—details concerning the condition of the town, | 12 |
| CLII. | To Monsieur de Falais.—Calvin dedicates to him one of his Commentaries, | 15 |
| CLIII. | To John Frellon.—Rupture of the Relations between Calvin and Servetus, | 16 |
| CLIV. | To Farel.—Reply to various questions—terrible threat against Servetus—imprisonment of one of the leaders of the Libertins, | 17 |
| CLV. | To Farel.—Pacification of the Church at Neuchatel—report of the speedy arrival of the Emperor in Savoy—dangers at Geneva —withering mention of Francis I., | 20 |
| CLVI. | To Viret.—Election of a minister at Neuchatel—sickness of Viret's wife, | 22 |
| CLVII. | To Viret.—Calvin invites his friend to repair to Geneva after the death of his wife, | 23 |

| LETTER | | PAGE |
|---|---|---|
| CLVIII. | To VIRET.—Renewed and more pressing invitation to come to Geneva, | 24 |
| CLIX. | To THEODORE VITUS.—Indication of the various documents wherein are set forth the opinions of Calvin regarding the Lord's Supper—earnest desires for union and peace among the Churches—condition of Geneva, | 25 |
| CLX. | To VIRET.—Instructions to Viret about a journey to Geneva, | 28 |
| CLXI. | To MONSIEUR DE FALAIS.—Calvin's labours—the diet at Ratisbon—the Church of Metz—the reformation at Heidelberg—*Apology* for M. de Falais—opinion regarding the sermons of Ochino, | 29 |
| CLXII. | To MONSIEUR DE FALAIS.—Advice regarding the editing of the *Apology*—details of a loan contracted for M. de Falais—news from Germany and Italy—Farel and Viret at Geneva—death of Juan Diaz, | 33 |
| CLXIII. | To FAREL.—Troubles at Geneva—imprisonment of the several members of the family of Favre—account of the assassination of John Diaz at Neubourg, | 38 |
| CLXIV. | To AMY PERRIN.—Complaints regarding the conduct of Perrin—firm and courageous declaration by the Reformer of his resolution to persevere in his duty unto death, | 42 |
| CLXV. | To FAREL AND VIRET.—Requests in favour of the faithful in France, | 44 |
| CLXVI. | To MADAME DE FALAIS.—Expression of Christian sympathy and condolence on occasion of the illness of M. de Falais, | 46 |
| CLXVII. | To FAREL.—Excitement caused at Geneva by the Representation of a Play, | 47 |
| CLXVIII. | To MONSIEUR DE FALAIS.—Proposals of matrimony on behalf of Viret, | 49 |
| CLXIX. | To VIRET.—Account of the steps taken relative to his marriage, | 51 |
| CLXX. | To VIRET.—Fresh details regarding the projects for his marriage, | 51 |
| CLXXI. | To VIRET.—Same subject as the preceding, | 54 |
| CLXXII. | To VIRET.—Breaking off of the match treated of in the preceding letters, | 54 |
| CLXXIII. | To FAREL.—Violence of the family of Amy Perrin—declamations of the wife of Froment against the ministers of Geneva, | 56 |
| CLXXIV. | To FAREL.—Calvin's indisposition—literary labours—apparent reconciliation with Perrin and his family, | 58 |
| CLXXV. | To MONSIEUR DE FALAIS.—Recurrence to the matrimonial projects of Viret—explanations on various subjects, | 60 |
| CLXXVI. | To MADAME DE FALAIS.—Sad communication to be made to M. de Falais—promise to send several discourses, | 62 |
| CLXXVII. | To MONSIEUR DE FALAIS.—Congratulations on his convalescence—uncertainty of prospects in Germany—confidence in the all-powerful protection of God, | 63 |
| CLXXVIII. | To MONSIEUR DE FALAIS.—Excuses for Viret—uses of sickness—various rumours concerning the war in Germany—explanations on the subject of the Supper, | 65 |

| LETTER | | PAGE |
|---|---|---|
| CLXXIX. | To Monsieur de Falais.—Consolations on the death of his sister, . . . . . . . | 70 |
| CLXXX. | To Madame de Falais.—Assurances of affection for herself and her husband, . . . . . . | 71 |
| CLXXXI. | To Viret.—Statement of the expense of a visit to Lausanne, on the occasion of Viret's marriage—ecclesiastical difficulties at Berne, . . . . . . | 72 |
| CLXXXII. | To Monsieur de Falais.—Military movements in Switzerland—policy of the Cantons in reference to the Emperor, . | 74 |
| CLXXXIII. | To Madame de Bude.—Calvin exhorts this lady to leave France, and retire with her family to Geneva, . | 76 |

## 1547.

| CLXXXIV. | To the Avoyer Nœguely.—Complaints of the misconduct of several ministers in the Pays de Vaud, . . | 80 |
|---|---|---|
| CLXXXV. | To Farel.—Mission of Calvin in Switzerland—dispositions of the various Cantons, . . . . . | 81 |
| CLXXXVI. | To Monsieur de Falais.—Search for a house for that gentleman in Geneva—various details—mention of Charles V. and Francis I., . . . . . . . | 83 |
| CLXXXVII. | To Monsieur de Falais.—Instructions regarding the *Apology*—alarming rumours current at Geneva—Calvin's confidence, . . . . . . . | 86 |
| CLXXXVIII. | To Monsieur de Falais.—Disputes of M. de Falais with Valeran Poulain—reports of the expected arrival of the former in Geneva, . . . . . | 88 |
| CLXXXIX. | To Valeran Poulain.—Severe reprobation of his behaviour towards M. de Falais—reply to a calumny directed against the Reformer, . . . . . . | 90 |
| CXC. | To Viret.—Weakness of the Genevese magistracy—expectation of Viret's arrival in Geneva, . . . | 92 |
| CXCI. | To Wolfgang Musculus.—Anxiety regarding the Churches of Germany—advice to Musculus, . . . | 94 |
| CXCII. | To Monsieur de Falais.—Steps taken at Basle to retract a promise of marriage made to Valeran Poulain, . . | 96 |
| CXCIII. | To Francis Dryander.—Confused state of the Church—hopes and fears for the future, . . . . | 97 |
| CXCIV. | To Monsieur de Falais.—The sending of a minister—perplexities regarding anticipated events in Germany, . | 99 |
| CXCV. | To Monsieur de Falais.—Information in regard to a house—advice on the subject of a marriage proposed for a relative of Monsieur de Falais, . . . . . | 100 |
| CXCVI. | To Viret.—Interview of Calvin with a senator of Berne—advantage secured over the party of the Libertins, . | 102 |
| CXCVII. | To Monsieur de Falais.—Recommendation of John de Budé—uncertainty of the news from Germany, . . | 104 |

| LETTER | | PAGE |
|---|---|---|
| CXCVIII. | To Monsieur de Bude.—He exhorts him to follow the example of the rest of his family, and retire to Geneva, | 105 |
| CXCIX. | To Viret.—Citation before the Consistory of the wife of Amy Perrin—case of Gruet—news from Germany, | 108 |
| CC. | To Monsieur de Falais.—Solemn lessons afforded by the sad occurrences in Germany—troubles in Geneva—energetic attitude of Calvin, | 111 |
| CCI. | To Viret.—Indecision of the Seigneurs of Geneva—inflexibility of Calvin, | 114 |
| CCII. | To the Faithful of France.—State of Germany—details regarding the struggles of the Reformer in the cause of the truth at Geneva, | 115 |
| CCIII. | To Monsieur de Falais.—Thanksgivings for the happy deliverance of Madame de Falais—false reports concerning the state of Geneva—details regarding the publication of the *Apology*—indisposition of Calvin, and his regret at being separated from Monsieur de Falais, | 118 |
| CCIV. | To Farel.—False report of Calvin's death—proposition (query) by the wife of Amy Perrin—calumnious accusation against Idelette de Bure—journey of Farel to Geneva, | 123 |
| CCV. | To Viret.—Mention of a letter from M. de Falais—Emmanuel Tremellius—a book by Viret—journey of Budé and Nicolas des Gallars to Paris, | 125 |
| CCVI. | To Monsieur de Falais.—Dedication of the *Apology*—mention of M. de Mommor—sickness of Maldonado, | 127 |
| CCVII. | To Henry Bullinger.—Comments by Calvin on a work by Bullinger—state of Germany and Italy—policy of the Cantons, | 129 |
| CCVIII. | To Monsieur de Falais.—Return of Nicolas des Gallars—stay of Farel and Viret at Geneva, | 131 |
| CCIX. | To Monsieur de Falais.—Re-assuring intelligence on the state of Geneva—restoration of Maldonado, | 132 |
| CCX. | To Farel.—Sad state of the Republic—discouragement of the Reformer, | 133 |
| CCXI. | To Viret.—Rising at the Hôtel de Ville—heroic bearing of Calvin—trust in God alone, | 134 |
| CCXII. | To Monsieur de Falais.—Printing of *The Apology*—troubles at Geneva, | 136 |
| CCXIII. | To Viret.—Invitation to come to Geneva, | 137 |
| CCXIV. | To Farel.—Publication of *The Antidote*—statement regarding the condition of Geneva, | 138 |
| CCXV. | To the Family of Bude.—Consolations on occasion of the Death of one of its Members, | 140 |

### 1548.

| | | |
|---|---|---|
| CCXVI. | To Monsieur de Falais.—Cost of printing of *The Apology*—despatch of several copies, | 143 |
| CCXVII. | To Monsieur de Falais.—Particulars regarding his departure, and the purchase of a property near Geneva, | 145 |

| LETTER | | PAGE |
|---|---|---|
| CCXVIII. | To HENRY BULLINGER.—Brotherly explanations regarding the difference on the subject of the Communion, . . | 146 |
| CCXIX. | To MONSIEUR DE FALAIS.—Obstacles to his departure—delay of some months, . . . . . . | 148 |
| CCXX. | To FAREL.—Distressing condition of the Swiss churches, . | 150 |
| CCXXI. | To FAREL AND VIRET.—Disputes among the ministers of Berne—and Calvin's journey thither, . . . | 151 |
| CCXXII. | To VIRET.—Communications regarding affairs at Berne, .. | 152 |
| CCXXIII. | To VIRET.—Ecclesiastical tyranny of the Seigneurs of Berne—sojourn of Idelette de Bure at Lausanne, . . | 153 |
| CCXXIV. | To HENRY BULLINGER.—New explanations regarding the Supper—violence of some of the Bernese ministers—Calvinism and Buceranism, . . . . | 154 |
| CCXXV. | To MONSIEUR DE FALAIS.—Preparations for the marriage of Mademoiselle de Wilergy, his relation, . . | 159 |
| CCXXVI. | To FAREL.—Uncertainty regarding the disposition of the Cantons—stay of Monsieur and Madame de Falais in Calvin's house, . . . . . . . . | 161 |
| CCXXVII. | To VIRET.—Embarrassment occasioned to Calvin by the treacherous publication of one of his letters to Viret, . | 162 |
| CCXXVIII. | To A FRENCH SEIGNEUR.—Exhortation to come to Geneva, that he might there serve the Lord faithfully, . | 165 |
| CCXXIX. | To THE PROTECTOR SOMERSET.—Duties imposed on the Protector by the high office which he holds—plan of a complete reformation in England—preaching of the pure Word of God—rooting out of abuses—correction of vices and scandalous offences, . . . . . | 168 |
| CCXXX. | To FAREL.—Election of new magistrates at Geneva—troubles in France—letter from Bucer, . . . . | 184 |
| CCXXXI. | To JOHN STURM.—Evidences of faith and Christian steadfastness, amid the dangers that threaten the Church, . | 186 |

### 1549.

| | | |
|---|---|---|
| CCXXXII. | To MADAME DE CANY.—Exhortation to a courageous and honest profession of the truth, . . . . | 187 |
| CCXXXIII. | To MADEMOISELLE DE . . . .—Exhortations to steadfastness in the faith—acknowledgment of liberality, . | 191 |
| CCXXXIV. | To THE MINISTERS OF THE CHURCH OF MONTBELIARD.—Exhortations to discharge to the end their ministerial duties, | 194 |
| CCXXXV. | To HENRY BULLINGER.—Hope of union with the theologians of Zurich—dedication of several writings, . . | 196 |
| CCXXXVI. | To BUCER.—Consolations to be found in the study of divine and everlasting truth, . . . . . | 198 |
| CCXXXVII. | To THE PASTORS OF THE CHURCH OF BERNE.—Desire of union between the Churches of Berne and Geneva, . . | 200 |
| CCXXXVIII. | To VIRET.—Death of Idelette de Bure, the wife of Calvin, | 202 |
| CCXXXIX. | To FAREL.—Further details regarding the death of Idelette de Bure, . . . . . . . | 203 |

## CONTENTS.

| LETTER | | PAGE |
|---|---|---|
| CCXL. | To MADAME DE CANY.—Account of the instructive death of Madame Laurent de Normandie, | 205 |
| CCXLI. | To VIRET.—Various particulars—recommendation of Francis Hotman, Jurisconsult, | 209 |
| CCXLII. | To HENRY BULLINGER.—Pleading in favour of the alliance of the Reformed Cantons with France, | 211 |
| CCXLIII. | To MADAME DE LA ROCHE-POSAY.—He exhorts her and her companions to live in conformity with the law of God, | 215 |
| CCXLIV. | To BUCER.—Encouragements and consolations—desire for the conclusion of peace between France and England—excesses of the ultra-Lutheran party in Switzerland and Germany—agreement between the Churches of Geneva and Zurich, | 218 |
| CCXLV. | To LADY ANNE SEYMOUR.—Thanks to the Duchess of Somerset, the mother of Anne Seymour—exhortation to perseverance in the true faith, | 222 |
| CCXLVI. | To FAREL.—Reply by the Protector of England to a letter from Calvin, | 224 |
| CCXLVII. | To FAREL.—Imprisonment of two brothers of M. de Falais—persecution in the Low Countries and in France, | 225 |
| CCXLVIII. | To VIRET.—Negotiations in reference to the publication of the *Consensus*—George Count of Montbeliard, | 226 |
| CCXLIX. | To THE PASTORS OF THE CHURCH OF ZURICH.—Urgent recommendation of the adoption of a fixed formulary in the celebration of the Lord's Supper, | 227 |
| CCL. | To BULLINGER.—Revisal of the Formulary—persecutions in France, | 229 |
| CCLI. | To FAREL AND VIRET.—Letter concerning Vergerio—history of Francis Spira, | 231 |
| CCLII. | To FAREL.—Criticism on a work by Farel, | 232 |
| CCLIII. | To VIRET.—First mention of Theodore Beza—poverty of Calvin's colleagues, | 234 |
| CCLIV. | To JOHN HALLER.—A reformer's complaints on the malevolence of the Bernese ministers, | 235 |
| CCLV. | To WOLFGANG MUSCULUS.—Prohibition of the Vaudois Conferences—remonstrances on the intolerance of the Bernese ministers towards those of France, | 237 |
| CCLVI. | To MONSIEUR DE SAINT LAURENS.—Statement of leading articles of the Reformed Faith, | 239 |

### 1550.

| CCLVII. | To THE PROTECTOR SOMERSET.—Congratulations on the royal favour shown to the Duke of Somerset—use to be made of his influence for spreading the Gospel in England, | 243 |
|---|---|---|
| CCLVIII. | To FAREL.—Tidings from Germany and England—recommendation of a domestic, | 248 |
| CCLIX. | To FAREL.—Election of a new Pope, | 250 |

## CONTENTS.                                              xi

| LETTER | | PAGE |
|---|---|---|
| CCLX. | To Francis Dryander.—Counsels and encouragements—collection of Commentaries on Isaiah by Des Gallars, | 251 |
| CCLXI. | To Nicolas Colladon.—Settlement of the Colladon family at Geneva, | 252 |
| CCLXII. | To the Seigneury of Geneva.—Notice of a publication attributed to Gruet, | 254 |
| CCLXIII. | To Melanchthon.—Controversies excited in Germany by the establishment of *the Interim*—brotherly reproofs, | 256 |
| CCLXIV. | To Viret.—Hope of an early visit from Viret—projected excursions in the neighbourhood of Geneva, | 261 |
| CCLXV. | To Farel.—Opinion regarding Vergerio—intelligence regarding Bucer—letter to Melanchthon—disputes with Berne—literary publications of Calvin, | 262 |
| CCLXVI. | To William Rabot.—Exhortation to the study of the Scriptures, | 264 |
| CCLXVII. | To Farel.—Publication of the book on *Scandals*—persecution by the King of France—Bucer's discouragement, | 265 |
| CCLXVIII. | To Farel.—State of religion in England—Calvin's literary labours—arrival of Robert Stephens at Geneva, | 268 |
| CCLXIX. | To Monsieur de Falais.—Misconduct of a servant of M. de Falais, | 271 |

### 1551.

| | | |
|---|---|---|
| CCLXX. | To Haller.—Explanations on the subject of the abolition of the great festivals at Geneva, | 273 |
| CCLXXI. | To Richard Le Fevre.—Explanations regarding various points of doctrine in dispute between the Romish and the Reformed Churches, | 275 |
| CCLXXII. | To Viret.—Various particulars—literary labours of Theodore Beza, | 283 |
| CCLXXIII. | To the King of England.—He exhorts him to persevere in the work of the Reformation in his kingdom—enumeration of abuses, ceremonies, ecclesiastical elections—universities, | 284 |
| CCLXXIV. | To Bullinger.—He excuses the infrequency of his letters, and urges the publication of the *Consensus*, | 289 |
| CCLXXV. | To Bullinger.—Thanks for a document—dedication of two commentaries to the King of England—captivity of Bishop Hooper—movements of the Emperor in Germany, | 291 |
| CCLXXVI. | To Bullinger.—Mention of a letter to the Duke of Somerset—re-opening of the Council of Trent—symptoms of war in Europe, | 293 |
| CCLXXVII. | To Viret.—Death of Bucer and of Joachim Vadian, | 295 |
| CCLXXVIII. | To Farel.—Renewed expressions of regret for the death of Vadian and Bucer—controversies excited by Osiander—numerous migrations to Geneva—commencement of hostilities in Italy, | 296 |

| Letter | | Page |
|---|---|---|
| CCLXXIX. | To a French Gentleman.—Sickness of Theodore Beza—Calvin's grief, | 299 |
| CCLXXX. | To the Duke of Somerset.—Protestations of attachment—reforms required in the Church of England—squandering of the revenues of benefices and of the universities, | 300 |
| CCLXXXI. | To Viret.—Reply to the attacks of Pighius, and of George de Sicile, | 302 |
| CCLXXXII. | To the Ministers of Neuchatel.—Arrest of a minister from Neuchatel in France—steps for obtaining his release, | 303 |
| CCLXXXIII. | To Bullinger.—Edict of Chateaubriand, in France—attacks on Calvin in Geneva, | 304 |
| CCLXXXIV. | To the Ministers of Switzerland.—Statement of the controversy with Bolsec regarding Election, | 307 |
| CCLXXXV. | To Oswald Myconius.—Recommendations regarding the dispute with Bolsec—request on behalf of the Protestants of France, | 311 |
| CCLXXXVI. | To Christopher Fabri.—Calvin's dissatisfaction with the reply of the ministers of Bâle, and the conduct of Monsieur de Falais regarding the affair with Bolsec, | 312 |
| CCLXXXVII. | To Farel.—Recommendation of a schoolmaster—complaints against the ministers of Zurich, | 313 |
| CCLXXXVIII. | To Laelius Socinus.—Refusal to reply to the curious questions proposed to him by Socinus, | 315 |

## 1552.

| | | |
|---|---|---|
| CCLXXXIX. | To Bullinger.—Thanks for the zeal manifested on behalf of the faithful in France—complaints of the conduct of the ministers of Zurich in the affair of Bolsec, | 316 |
| CCXC. | To Farel.—Fresh complaints by Calvin against the ministers of Zurich and Berne—his unpopularity in the latter city—advices to Farel, | 320 |
| CCXCI. | To Madame de Cany.—Rigorous and inflexible spirit of Calvin against heresy—praise of Theodore Beza, | 323 |
| CCXCII. | To Bullinger.—Journey of Calvin and Farel in Switzerland—steps in favour of the Reformed in France—return to the affairs of Bolsec, | 326 |
| CCXCIII. | To Cranmer.—Agreement to the proposal for assembling a General Synod for the more close union of the Reformed Churches, | 330 |
| CCXCIV. | To Bullinger.—Fresh details regarding the persecutions in France, | 334 |
| CCXCV. | To the Five Prisoners of Lyons,—Martial Alba, Peter Escrivain, Charles Favre, Peter Navihères, Bernard Seguin.—Information on various doctrinal points, and assurances of Christian sympathy, | 335 |

## CONTENTS.

| LETTER | | PAGE |
|---|---|---|
| CCXCVI. | To EDWARD VI.—Dedication of a new work, and Christian exhortations, | 339 |
| CCXCVII. | To CRANMER.—Calvin exhorts him to prosecute with fresh zeal the reformation of the Church in England, by purging it of the relics of Popery, | 341 |
| CCXCVIII. | To JOHN LINER.—Thanks for the zeal manifested by him on behalf of the prisoners of Lyons, | 343 |
| CCXCIX. | To THE FRENCH CHURCH IN LONDON.—Exhortations to harmony—Is it lawful to call Mary the Mother of God, and to pray for the Pope? | 345 |
| CCC. | To THE SEIGNEURS OF GENEVA.—Reply of Calvin to the Syndics of Geneva in the case of Trolliet, | 348 |
| CCCI. | To FAREL.—Conspiracy of the Libertins—energy of the Reformer—struggles of Viret at Lausanne, | 355 |
| CCCII. | To VIRET.—Literary labours of Theodore Beza, | 357 |
| CCCIII. | To AMBROISE BLAURER.—Troubles at Geneva—sad intelligence from France and Germany—steady in the promises of God, | 358 |
| CCCIV. | To MELANCHTHON.—Earnest desires for the continuance of their mutual affection—disputes with Trolliet—longing for agreement in doctrine regarding the Communion and Election, | 360 |

### 1553.

| | | |
|---|---|---|
| CCCV. | To MATHIEU DIMONET.—Exhortation to patience and constancy under persecution, | 366 |
| CCCVI. | To CHRISTOPHE FABRI.—Congratulations on the subject of his approaching marriage—Calvin's regret that he cannot be present at the ceremony, | 369 |
| CCCVII. | To JOHN CHEKE.—Calvin apologizes for silence, and enjoins him to use his influence with the King for the advancement of the Gospel in England, | 371 |
| CCCVIII. | To THE FIVE PRISONERS OF LYONS.—Exhortations to constancy—mention of Oritz the Inquisitor, | 373 |
| CCCIX. | To EDWARD VI.—Recommendation of a French gentleman, a prisoner for the sake of the Gospel, | 375 |
| CCCX. | To FAREL.—Serious illness and unexpected recovery of Farel—Calvin's joy, | 377 |
| CCCXI. | To CHRISTOPHER AND TO THOMAS ZOLLICOFFRE.—Last steps in favour of the Prisoners of Lyons, | 378 |
| CCCXII. | To CRANMER.—He entreats his influence in favour of the person already recommended to the King, | 380 |
| CCCXIII. | To MONSIEUR DE MAROLLES.—Christian encouragement and consolation, | 381 |
| CCCXIV. | To VIRET.—Extinction of all hope in regard to the prisoners of Lyons, | 383 |
| CCCXV. | To BULLINGER.—Assurances of respect and fraternal affection, | 384 |

## CONTENTS.

| LETTER | | PAGE |
|---|---|---|
| CCCXVI. | To the Five Prisoners of Lyons.—He exhorts them to steadfastness unto the end, in the assurance of eternal joy reserved in heaven, | 386 |
| CCCXVII. | To Madame de Cany.—Expression of Christian sympathy under trial, | 390 |
| CCCXVIII. | To the Prisoners of Lyons.—He impresses on them the duty of maintaining their confession of the truth quietly and modestly, | 393 |
| CCCXIX. | To Bullinger.—Expression of regret for the death of the King of England—sad condition of the German Churches, | 396 |
| CCCXX. | To Farel.—Arrest of Servetus, and institution of the process against him, | 398 |
| CCCXXI. | To Denis Peloquin and Louis de Marsac.—Information regarding various controverted points—exhortation to fidelity, even unto martyrdom, | 400 |
| CCCXXII. | To his Dearly Beloved the Pastors of the Church of Frankfort.—Request for the destruction of the copies at Frankfort of the book of Servetus, | 404 |
| CCCXXIII. | To Viret.—Troubles at Geneva—Berthelier and the chiefs of the Libertins are refused admission to the Lord's Table, | 405 |
| CCCXXIV. | To Bullinger.—Deep anxiety on account of the condition of the English Churches—Conference of the Swiss Churches in regard to Servetus, | 407 |
| CCCXXV. | To Sulzer.—Statement of the errors of Servetus, and of the duty of the Christian magistrate to repress them, | 409 |
| CCCXXVI. | To a Captive Lady.—He consoles her under her trials, and exhorts her to use every means to secure her retreat to Geneva, | 412 |
| CCCXXVII. | To the Believers in the Isles.—Religious counsels, and announcement of the sending of a minister, | 414 |
| CCCXXVIII. | To Farel.—Acknowledgment of Farel's care for the Church of Geneva, | 416 |
| CCCXXIX. | To Farel.—Deliverance by the Swiss Churches regarding Servetus—vain efforts of Calvin to obtain a mitigation of his punishment, | 417 |
| CCCXXX. | To Madame de Pons.—He encourages her to come out of the spiritual bondage in which she is held, | 418 |
| CCCXXXI. | To Viret.—Recommendation of several English Refugees in Switzerland, | 421 |
| CCCXXXII. | To Bullinger.—Appeal to the Magistrates of Zurich in reference to ecclesiastical discipline — thanks for the aid afforded by the ministers of that Church in the affair of Servetus, | 422 |
| CCCXXXIII. | To the Pastors and Doctors of the Church of Zurich.—Account of the struggles at Geneva for the maintenance of ecclesiastical discipline—appeal to the Pastors of Zurich for their influence with the magistrates of that town, | 424 |

## CONTENTS.

| LETTER | | PAGE |
|---|---|---|
| CCCXXXIV. | To BULLINGER.—Fresh details regarding ecclesiastical discipline—hope of speedy realization—announcement of the publication of a book against the errors of Servetus, | 429 |
| CCCXXXV. | To FAREL.—Assistance afforded to the faithful refugees in Switzerland—reply of the Churches on the subject of ecclesiastical discipline, | 430 |
| CCCXXXVI. | To JOHN A LASCO.—Expression of sympathy under his trials—loud complaints of the intolerance of German theologians, | 432 |

ERRATUM.

Page 20, line 23, *for* in His authority, *read* unexpectedly.

# CALVIN'S LETTERS.

### CXLIV.—To Viret.[1]

*Unpopularity of Calvin—various advices.*

[Geneva, *September* 1545.]

When a crowd of the godly had come hither, and I heard some things which it was of great consequence you should know, I wished two of them at once to set out for you. You will understand that Satan seeks by every sort of artful contrivance to keep all men from thinking of succouring these people, and to give a keener edge to the ferocity of the king and courtiers, which is already more than sufficiently whetted against them. The Swiss also are uncommonly severe upon me, not only the pensionaries, but all those who have no other wisdom than that of Epicurus, because, by my importunity, I have drawn down upon their nation the hatred of the king. But may there be nothing of such moment as shall

---

[1] The letters of the Cantons to the King, in favour of the Vaudois of Provence, only served to irritate that monarch. He passionately replied,—" The Vaudois have but received the just punishment of their crimes. Besides, the Swiss have no more right to busy themselves with what passes in my kingdom, than I have to make inquiry into what they do at home."—*Histoire de la Confédération Suisse*, vol. xi. p. 289. The failure of those proceedings redounded to the discredit of Calvin with the people, as he had been the instigator of them. His adversaries went about reiterating everywhere that he had compromised the most valued interests of the Cantons, by drawing upon them the enmity of the King of France.

retard us in the discharge of our duty beyond what cannot be avoided.

Charles the schoolmaster, on whose account Sebastian abused me, has deserted his post, induced by what prospect I know not. We have appointed Francis his successor; but as he had received one month's payment out of the salary of your school, it seemed the more honourable course that he should previously request permission and his discharge from the Bernese Council, a matter in which, as I trust, there will be no difficulty. A maternal uncle also of our colleague Peter sought a recommendation [for him,] which he brings with him. If you think it called for, you will likewise lend the aid of your suffrage. We have always found him an excellent and ingenuous man, peaceable and modest. He is said, for instance, to have laboured faithfully, and with success, in the vineyard of the Lord in Provence.

Adieu; may the Lord be ever present with you.—Yours,
JOHN CALVIN.

[*Lat. orig. autogr.—Library of Geneva.* Vol. 106.]

## CXLV.—To Monsieur de Falais.[1]

Exhortation to glorify God amid poverty and persecution.

[*September* 1545.]

MONSIEUR,—Although I do not know the state of mind or body in which you are at present, nevertheless, I have good confidence in God that, whether in health or sickness, He gives you strength to overcome all the annoyance you may have to encounter. For you are no novice in the fight, seeing that for

---

[1] Letter without date, written at the same time as the following, (September 1545.) Summoned in the name of the Emperor to leave Strasbourg and return to Brabant, M. de Falais had not obeyed that command. This refusal, in stirring up the imperial displeasure against him, had exposed him, without defence, to the interested denunciations of his enemies. The butt of most calumnious accusations, he saw his character misunderstood, his name outraged, his property put under sequestration, while he pined away himself,—a prey to sickness and discouragement.

a long time past this good Lord has begun to prepare you for it; and nothing has happened to you which you had not looked for beforehand. But it is time to show in reality that when you have set yourself frankly to follow Jesus Christ, you have not done so without being resolved to hold fellowship with Him at the cross, since He has done us that honour to be crucified in us, to glorify us with Himself. And there is no doubt, even at the time when you were in your own mansion, and in the peaceable enjoyment of your property, you would have had the courage to quit everything had it so pleased Him, and that you were of the number of those who *use the things of this world as not abusing them*, (1 Cor. vii. 31.) But, forasmuch as it is very reasonable that one should be taught by experience discernment of what our affection is most set upon, you are to consider that it has been our Lord's will to give you to many others for an example, and, by this means, to glorify His name in you.

On the other hand, we know not what it is to part with everything for the love of Him, until He has brought us to the test. True it is, that he who has taken off his affection from the goods of this world has already sold all, and has made himself poor, so far as depends upon himself; but the fruit and the proof of this spiritual poverty are, patiently to endure the loss of worldly goods, and without any regret, when it pleases our heavenly Father that we should be despoiled of them. I do not set these things before you as to one who is ignorant, or who has need of lengthy remonstrances, but for the love that I bear you, of which God is my witness. I take comfort along with you, as I also suffer in your person.

The time then is arrived when you must manifest that you reckon all things no more than dung, that you may reach forward to Him who not only has bestowed on you all His benefits, but also Himself. And since God has permitted that you should be disburdened of a part of your worldly goods, you are to consider that He has clearly perceived that, for the present, they would prove a useless fardel for you. I say a part, albeit that, as it were, the whole has been snatched away from you, yet, so that there remains, as I hope, an abundance for your use. These whirlpools, however, which engulf the whole world, have daily greater want than those whose substance they have swallowed down.

In short, you have not been lessened one whit, seeing that our Lord, while teaching you that your inheritance is in Heaven, has made provision for what might be useful for the life of the body, by bestowing contentment upon you, and, as regards property, more than was needful to make you contented. If the whole should be taken away from you, there would yet remain the consolation to which we must chiefly betake ourselves, namely, to yield ourselves up entirely. It is certain, that having the Son of God, we suffer no injury in being deprived of all else : for thus highly ought we indeed to prize Him. But further, since this kind Saviour has so benignly upheld you, that while calling you to the fellowship of His cross, He has provided for your worldly comfort, it is quite fitting that you submit yourself to His good pleasure, and, besides, rejoice that in being minished, so far as the world is concerned, you are thereby so much the more exalted before Him and His angels. For howsoever the world strives, by all means, to bury Jesus Christ in ignominy, His burial cannot be otherwise than glorious, not only in Himself, but also in His members. Let us therefore endure personal humiliation, as shall seem good to Him. But my letters would never come to an end were I to follow out the drift of this discourse. Therefore, Monseigneur, after having humbly commended me to your kind favour, I pray our good Lord that He would so work in you now more powerfully than ever, to make you despise all that is in the world, and to make you breathe upwards direct to Him with your whole heart, without being turned aside by anything whatsoever, making you taste what is the worth of the hope which He reserves for us in Heaven ; and that it may please Him to lighten your burden as regards the body, in order that you may be all the better disposed, well to meditate upon the favours He has bestowed upon you, and to take delight in them, acknowledging the love which He has shewn you. My wife, who is sick in bed, begs also to be humbly commended to your kind remembrance. This bearer, who is of the better sort, and of the stamp such as you require, will inform you more at large concerning our state.

Your humble brother, servant, and assured friend,

JOHN CALVIN.

[*Fr. orig. autogr.—Library of Geneva.* Vol. 194.]

## CXLVI.—To MADAME DE FALAIS.

Congratulations on the constancy manifested by her in the midst of trials—salutations from the suffering Idelette de Bure.

FROM GENEVA, *this* 18*th September* [1545.]

MADAME,—I have not leisure to write at such length as I willingly would, on account of the state in which we are. The present letter shall be solely to praise our good Lord for the trust which He has bestowed on you, enlarging your heart in the midst of anxieties, by which it might have been tried, without your having His comfort from on high. Whatsoever may happen, if we have the patience to hearken to our Saviour, He will always give us wherewithal to rejoice our spirits, and will make us taste and feel, in a lively way, that it is not in vain that He has promised to make us unconquerable in tribulations. Now, then, learn in reality what that beautiful promise is worth, that we are indeed happy, when all the world shall speak ill of us, and shall hate us, and shall persecute us for His name's sake. Therefore it is, that He has prepared you, long before exposing you to danger. To this truth it is that you must now recur, that you may acquiesce in it; and, indeed, He is actually leading you thither by the hand.

Wherefore are we not together, to provoke Satan, by meditating upon the things which may well cause us spiritual rejoicing, and give us matter for glorying more than ever, even when we are utterly discomfited according to the world's estimation? But I am aware that you have no need of my fellowship in that; and besides, I say so, more to content myself than because of your necessity. Above all, understand that now the hour is come when you must shew what a helpmeet you are to Monseigneur your husband, in such a sort that he may always have occasion to bless God, as he has had hitherto, for having provided him with such a support. I say this, because I consider that it is the principal one that God has left him as regards the creature, without having deprived him of all. I see clearly, though absent, by what zeal you are urged forward to acquit yourself of duty, and what trouble you take to employ yourself therein. For which reason, what I now speak is not so much by way of exhortation as, while congratulating, to uphold you in that good courage which God has given.

I address to your care some reply which I have made to the sister of Monseigneur, who is at Mons, to a communication which she sent lately to the wife of Saint-André. If it seem good to you, you can cause forward it to her, with this which I send to the sister of Monsieur David. I submit the whole to your good discretion.

To conclude, Madame and very honoured sister, after having affectionately commended me to your kind favour, and having also presented to you the humble commendations of my wife, who lies sick in bed, I entreat our good Lord to fill you with all grace, daily to increase his glory in you, and to triumph in your constancy, in order that finally we may be also partakers of His glory which He has promised us.

Your servant and humble brother,

JOHN CALVIN.

[*Fr. orig. autogr.—Library of Geneva.* Vol. 194.]


## CXLVII.—To Monsieur de Falais.[1]

*Vanity of trust reposed in the princes of this world—confidence in God.*

MONSEIGNEUR,—I hope that, when these present shall reach you, they will find you, by the favour of our kind Lord, in such state of mind and bodily health as we desire, and likewise Madame your wife. The news, however, which we have had

---

[1] This letter, without date, seems to have been written at the same epoch, and under the same circumstances as the two preceding letters.

of the sickness of both have grieved us, and will do so until we receive others which may gladden us. Besides, there is reason indeed that we should live and that we should die to Him who has purchased, in order to be every way glorified in us, and that we shew practically that we are His, submitting ourselves entirely to Him in true obedience, which is not in our power to do without resigning and giving up our persons to Him, so that He dispose of them as shall seem good to Himself. That if it please Him to prolong life, we must prepare to see much poverty in the Christian Church. We see the dispersion and complete disorder there is in it at present. Hope of amendment there appears none on the side of the world; for to befool one's-self in relying upon princes, that is labour lost. They have, besides, so many hindrances, that they have not leisure to think about what ought to be the chief consideration of all. In short, they are entirely taken up with their civil state, for the sake of which they will persecute Jesus Christ, thinking that there is no other method of maintaining it. It will be nothing new, however, if, though only for shame's sake, they should make a pretence of applying a remedy for such horrible confusion, on account of which both heaven and earth cry out. Wherefore, it only remains for us to pray God that it may please Him to strengthen us with true constancy in the midst of these scandals, in such a way that nothing may seduce us, but that we may persevere always. And also, that He would look in pity upon His Church, and put forth the hand to lift her up again, fulfilling that which the prophet has said, that *seeing that he had no helper among men, he has put forth the strength of his arm,* (Isa. lix. 16.)

In conclusion, let us employ ourselves in His service, labouring without growing weary or losing courage, until that He call us away into that blessed rest where we have contentment in Himself, delighting ourselves in the labours we shall have undergone, receiving then the recompense of reward which shall be there revealed to us.

Now therefore, Monsieur, after humble commendation to your favour and that of Madame, I beseech this good Lord to uphold you in real prosperity, continuing His graces in you, so that to the end you may be instruments of His glory, and that He may be your sanctification.

Your servant and humble brother ever,
CHARLES D'ESPEVILLE.


CXLVIII.—To FAREL.[1]

Captivity of Farel's brother—ravages of the plague in Geneva.

[*September* 1545.]

You will hear sad news ; for this person will inform you that your brother Gautier[2] is lying in fetters, and in imminent peril of his life. The very thing that I always feared, and that I foretold would occur, has happened ; and in this I regret that I have not proved a false prophet. But of what avail are such complaints ? With regard to helping him, I do not know how far it is in the power of the Bernese to do so, nor what, at this time, they may be willing to undertake. You will know these things better than I. There is no hope of obtaining any seasonable assistance from Germany, unless by means of John Sturm, who, however well disposed he may be towards the cause, is not, so far as things have gone, friendly to your brother. Would that you had thought better, while there was time, of what it is to offend a friend who deserved well. Besides, you are not ignorant of the fact, that there are servile persons who wish, at this time of the day, to approve their obsequiousness to the princes. Yet, if you shall be of opinion that it will be useful to attempt something in that quarter, your influence with Sturm himself is great. You have, however, your own Bucer, to whom he never ventured to refuse anything ; but it is a long circuit. Let him, therefore, accelerate the movements of the Bernese, lest the remedy come too late.

We are surprised that we have had no announcement re-

[1] Letter without date, and without conclusion, written during the attack of the plague, under which the minister Geniston succumbed, that is to say, in September 1545.

[2] Gautier Farel, brother to the reformer. He was very soon afterwards restored to liberty, contrary to all expectation.

garding yourself. Viret made me aware of the resolution that had been come to by the brethren ; but, as far as I can gather from his letter, nothing has been done in the Council. How long, therefore, will the matter remain in doubt ? Here, as you know, we are in great straits : you are away from us ; Matthæus is occupied in the hospital for those who are suffering from the plague. In the meantime, while we are calling upon you to come, we have lost our very excellent brother and most faithful colleague Geniston.[1] What if the others should likewise be taken away ? What if one only should survive, [I myself ?] What if the ministers be shut up by themselves, through the absurd superstition of our townsmen ?—just as lately a large number was within a little of being so confined ? Consider, therefore, these our difficulties, lest you put us off longer than is right. But what Viret mentions that your people have added, viz., that you are conceded to us, on the condition of our being able to bring about the succession of Toussain, is certainly ridiculous ; for what can we do in that matter, or in what way shall we attempt the business ? The short of it is, we by no means prescribe a definite time, but we desire you to use your utmost diligence to disengage yourself from the place where you are, in order that you may forthwith repair to us unfettered ;[2] for we are now sadly in want of your presence, as you may judge from our condition. The wife of Geniston is, at the same time, in the death-throes, his little girl is wearing away, and his little boy is now given over. . . .

[1] The minister, Louis de Geniston, following the noble example of Pierre Blanchet, cut off by the plague in 1543, had, of his own accord, offered himself for the service of the hospital set apart for those afflicted with the plague. He fell under it, a victim of his devotedness, in September 1545. His wife and two of his children were carried off a few days afterwards by the scourge, which almost wholly depopulated several quarters of the city.

[2] There exists (Imp. Lib. *Recueil Hist. de France*, vol. xix.) a piece entitled *Lepida Farelli Vocatio*. In that letter Calvin vigorously urges his friend to repair to Geneva, by calling to mind the religious violence with which he was himself detained there, by the voice of Farel, at the time of his first entrance into that city in 1536. " Do you expect that I should thunder as you were wont to do, when you wished forcibly to draw me hither ?" The urgencies of Calvin were fruitless, and the Church of Neuchatel retained, for twenty years longer, the services and the indefatigable activity of Farel.

## CXLIX.—To Viret.

*Dispersion of the School at Geneva—contests at Neuchatel on the subject of church property—Calvin's opinion of Farel.*

*24th October* 1545.

We shall wait until you either restore Francis to us, or send Erasmus. As, meanwhile, the school is dispersed,[1] you must make haste. If both of these courses appear to you tedious, or attended with difficulty, briefly signify so to us; for I will send for a person from Strasbourg, who, in my opinion, will be suitable, although I would rather have taken one from this quarter. With regard to the *assistant-teacher*, I do not venture upon anything, because it will be more satisfactory that the person who has the superintendence of the school shall have the unfettered power of selecting whom he chooses.

I had excused myself to Farel, but he remains fixed in his purpose.[2] It would not only be ridiculous, but bordering on imprudence, to undertake to correct in the Neuchatelese a vice which here we are not able to cure. I had given it as my advice, that it would be better to draw up a memorial, in which the Princes should promise that they would be always ready to make restitution, if an agreement could be come to regarding legitimate administration. In the next place, I advised them, under this pretext, to put a stop to those profane alienations, in order that the matter might be left undecided until a more favourable time. Farel replies, that the authority of the Princes will not avail much. What confidence then will our letter produce? He further urges me to enter into communication with Bucer, in order to obtain from the Council of Strasbourg a letter to the Council of Berne to this purport:—That

[1] The plague had dispersed the regents and students of the College of Geneva, and Calvin was labouring at the re-organization of that establishment. He had already proposed to the Council, in March 1545, to call to Geneva the celebrated Maturin Cordier, *as president of the regents;* but this proposal ended in nothing, and Maturin Cordier remained at Lausanne.

[2] Farel was then at strife with the Seigneury of Neuchatel, on the subject of the administration of ecclesiastical property.

it had been pointed out to them that the Neuchatelese did very wrong in squandering the goods of the Church; and that it was the duty of the Bernese to check this license. He hopes that a letter of that nature would also do good at Berne. I, on the contrary, hardly think that the people of Strasbourg would write such a letter, as they would be afraid of increasing the sore. In the next place, if they should write, do we not know that their admonition would be laughed at? And, although the Bernese were in the highest degree desirous to remedy this fault of the Neuchatelese, with what face could they set about it? I have to implore that they will not venture to reprehend in others that which they pertinaciously defend as lawfully done by themselves. I may therefore say of Farel what Cicero said of Cato, " That he acts indeed with good judgment, but in counsel does not always shew the best." The cause of this is chiefly, that being carried away by the vehemence of his zeal, he does not always discern what is expedient, and either does not foresee dangers, or despises them; and there is to be added the evil, that he cannot bear with patience those who do not comply with his wishes. But what could I do? for I will not be induced to undertake anything which I think will be of injurious tendency.

Christopher will tell you about Champereau,[1] and I will write when the matter has come to an end. Adieu, most excellent brother, and most sincere friend. I have not yet had an opportunity of meeting Amédée. I will, however, fulfil your commission.—Adieu, again, including your wife, aunt, and brothers. The co-presbyters, my wife, and the neighbours respectfully salute you.—Yours,

JOHN CALVIN.

[*Lat. copy—Library of Geneva.* Vol. 111.]

[1] Rebuked on the ground of his morals, this minister had been banished to a country parish, and having refused to submit to the entire Consistory, he had received his dismissal.

## CL.—To Monsieur de Falais.

### Prayers for his restoration to health.

*From Geneva, this 26th of October* [1545.]

Monseigneur,— I hope that, according to what Antony Maillet has latterly informed us, you are better in body and mind than usual, for which I thank our good Lord, beseeching Him fully to confirm you; for I doubt not but the sickness has left a long trail of feebleness. But He who has begun to raise you up, will perfect, as I hope, what He has begun by His infinite goodness, as well to grant the prayers of His servants as to shut the mouth of the wicked, so that they take not occasion to say that you have been overcome by their temptation; for you are aware that they want not great colour for their blasphemy. Therefore, God will shew them that He has fitted you to receive still greater assaults, if there is need; and in the meanwhile, will grant us the favour to enjoy a longer time of you to our singular consolation. When we shall have tidings from yourselves, they will rejoice us still more.

In the meantime, Monsieur, after having humbly commended me to your kind favour and that of Madame, and having presented to both of you the kind remembrances of a woman brought back to life, I beseech our gracious Lord to have you always in His holy keeping, multiplying His graces in you daily, to the glory of His name.

Your humble brother, servant, and entire friend,

John Calvin.

[*Fr. orig. autogr.—Library of Geneva.* Vol. 194.]

## CLI.—To Farel.

### News from Germany—journey of the French Ambassador to Geneva—details concerning the condition of the town.

*Geneva, 26th January* 1546.

There is nothing from your brothers since they passed through this place. I briefly indicated my opinion to Viret about the choice of a colleague for you. I am afraid that further delay may involve a long train of inconveniences, which

I should wish to be guarded against. Feron, our brother,[1] so far as I see, will never have quiet of mind until he is translated elsewhere. I had made mention of him to Viret, but it will be for you to consider the matter.

My brother brought back no news from Germany, except that the Ratisbon Assembly pretends that our party continue their deliberations at Frankfort,[2] and the confident report of a league, or at least a friendly alliance, between your party and the King. The Emperor was also said to be laid up with gout in the feet or hands. The King's ambassador in that quarter, when passing through, supped with me. We talked together familiarly, for he acknowledges being under some obligation to me. I again, however, urge you to beware lest our friends prove too compliant. I point to the license that prevails over the whole kingdom, of taking cruel measures against the godly. We will await the issue. You are aware that the Pope is now busying himself that, by means of false pretences, a council may be held at Trent; we do not, however, hear that there is to be a full convocation.

I wish that even one day could be given to a conference on our affairs. As this, however, is for the present impossible, do not needlessly vex yourself, should many reports be spread abroad. There was, indeed, a time when we were on our guard, when our party appointed sentinels for the gates, and were usually more careful in keeping watch.[3] But they inconsiderately gave a signal of alarm, without my knowledge, however,

[1] Minister of the Church of Geneva; deposed, a few years afterwards, on account of the irregularities of his life.

[2] Alarmed at the first movements of the Council of Trent, and the perils to which the good understanding between the Pope and the Emperor might subject the Reformation, the Deputies of the League of Smalkald had reassembled at Frankfort. But their union was not so solid as the gravity of the occasion demanded. The Elector of Saxe and the Landgrave of Hesse were influenced by different political views; but they were both alike disposed to seek the alliance of the Kings of France and England, as well as of the Protestant Cantons of Switzerland, that they might withstand the storm that menaced them.—Sleidan, L. xvi., and Robertson, vol. iv. B. vii. p. 234. London, 1851.

[3] " Upon the intelligence that the Duke of Savoy has retaken two strongholds in Piedmont, and that he is collecting a body of troops, resolved to continue to work at the fortifications."—*Registers of Council*, 28th December 1545.

and when I had not the smallest suspicion that anything of the kind would take place.[1] Seizing the opportunity, our neighbours [the Bernese] run to our aid, and most unreservedly offer their assistance. No one had any suspicion of kindness so obliging. Our friends make no communication to me, and after speeches had been made backwards and forwards, an agreement is come to between the parties. Shortly afterwards, there arrives a new embassy with the most monstrous commissions. The captain of the garrison, proffered by the Bernese, with his proposals, having met with a refusal, has quitted the city.[2] I am now aware how many various reports are everywhere circulated, but I see no danger. Should you hear anything, deny confidently the existence of any sort of alliance between us. For presently, when they become ashamed of themselves, they will have recourse to the old arts, saying that they are unjustly defamed, &c. I can hardly persuade our friends that there is need of deeds on our side; nor is this wonderful, for in other things they act foolishly in spite of my remonstrances. Adieu, brother and most sincere friend. Salute for me, in the kindest manner, all your co-presbyters and your family. May the Lord direct all of you by His Spirit, and preserve you safe.

The impostor who had undertaken to carry Bucer's letter to you, stopped at Montbeliard, nor would he ever have conveyed it to you, had not my brother purposely set out for that place, because he had in his keeping another of far greater moment. He is a worker in gold by trade, but a fellow who is deserving of the gallows.

I am so far convalescent as to be able for preaching and lecturing, but am kept busy with arrears.[3]

[*Lat. orig. autogr.—Library of Geneva.* Vol. 106.]

[1] " Oath exacted of all private individuals, of fidelity to the Seigneury, and of their readiness to live and die for liberty."—*Registers of Council*, 7th January 1546.

[2] The Seigneurs of Berne, eagerly seeking every opportunity of establishing their influence at Geneva, had offered to guard the city, and to protect it against all foreign attacks. This proposal was discarded, as tending to compromise the independence of the Republic.—*Registers of Council*, 11th January 1546.

[3] We read, in the *Registers of Council* of the 29th January of this year :—" Calvin having been ill, the Seigneury present to him ten crowns. On his recovery, he returns the money to the Council, who cause it to be expended in the purchase of a tun of wine for him, thus leaving him no alternative but to accept it."

## CLII.—To Monsieur de Falais.[1]

*Calvin dedicates to him one of his Commentaries.*

[*January* 1546.[2]]

Monseigneur,—Since my written letter, I have changed my mind, touching the epistle dedicatory of my Commentary, because it is a great trouble and difficulty to be forced to fill up so many pages and no more ; I therefore send it altogether, nevertheless, with this condition, that it shall not be printed but by your command. Wherefore, I enclose it in the present letter, in order that Vendelin[3] may not have it but from your hands. Should it not appear fitting that I address it to you, I shall make a new one, on being advertised to that effect. As for the rest, do not be astonished if I speak with brevity of you, for I would fear to touch some thorns in entering further on the subject. But according as circumstances will bear it, we can, should it so please God, on a second impression, discourse fully and say all that there shall be need for. Howbeit, I would greatly desire, if it might so please God, to be with you for three or four days, to confer by word of mouth rather than by writing. Possibly it is folly on my part to think that my presence can be of any service to you. But why so ? while the power may be wanting, affection makes me speak thus. These wishes, however, are more easy to form than to fulfil. So let us be content with what God gives us.

Yesterday we had news here of the defeat of four thousand English by five hundred light horse. But it is from France.[4]

[1] Calvin had just dedicated to M. de Falais his Commentary on the First Epistle of St. Paul to the Corinthians. The epistle dedicatory is of the 22d January 1546. The name of M. de Falais—sad example of the fragile nature of human affections !—was effaced ten years afterwards from the preface of this Commentary, and replaced by the name of the Marquis of Vico.

[2] *On the back,* in the hand of M. de Falais—' Received the 6th February 1546.'

[3] Printer in Strasbourg.

[4] The French were then besieging the town of Boulogne, occupied by the English. The peace between the two rival monarchs of France and England, was signed the year following.—De Thou, lib. i. ii.

Monseigneur, after having humbly commended me anew to your kind favour, and that of Madame, I pray always our Lord that He would uphold you in His glory.

[*Fr. orig. autogr.—Library of Geneva.* Vol. 194.]

## CLIII.—TO JOHN FRELLON.[1]

Rupture of the Relations between Calvin and Servetus.

*This* 13*th of February* 1546.

SEIGNEUR JEHAN,—By cause that your last letter was brought to me at my going away, I had not leisure to reply to what was inclosed therein. Since my return, at the first leisure that I have had, I have been quite willing to satisfy your desire ; not that I have had great hope of late of being profitable to a certain person, judging from the disposition in which I see him to be ; but in order to try once more if there shall be any means of bringing him back, which will be, when God shall have wrought in him so effectually, that he has become entirely another man. Since he has written to me in so proud a spirit, I would fain

---

[1] The following is the address of this letter, taken from the original in the archives of the old Archbishopric of Vienne, and first published by the Abbé d'Artigny,—*A Sire Jéhan Frellon, marchand libraire demeurant à Lyon, en la rue Mercière, enseigne de l'Escu de Coulongne.* The mysterious personage who is pointed at in this letter, is no other than Michel Servetus—seven years before the trial which was to attach so fatal a celebrity to his name. Settled as a physician at Vienne, in Dauphiny, he kept up a correspondence with Calvin, under the cover of John Frellon, and he had just sent the Reformer an extract of the work which was in preparation under the title of *Christianismi restitutio,* expressing at the same time the desire of coming to Geneva. Then it was, that Calvin wrote to Farel the letter which has been so often cited, where this passage occurs, "Servet has lately written to me, and has added to his letter a large volume of his own delirious fancies. . . . *If it may be agreeable to me, he undertakes that he would come hither. But I will not interpose my assurance of his safety, for if he shall come, provided that my authority is of any avail, I shall not suffer him to depart alive.*"\*—Letter of the 13th February 1546. We know how that terrible threat was realized seven years afterwards.

\* Servetus nuper ad me scripsit, ac literis adjunxit longum volumen suorum deliriorum . . . Si mihi placeat, huc se venturum recipit Sed nolo fidem meam interponere, nam si venerit, modo valeat mea authoritas, vivum exire non patiar.

have beaten down his pride a little, speaking more harshly to him than is my wont; but I could scarcely do otherwise. For I do assure you that there is no lesson which is more necessary for him than to learn humility, which must come to him from the Spirit of God, not otherwise. But we must observe a measure here also. If God grants that favour to him and to us, that the present answer turns to his profit, I shall have whereof to rejoice. If he persists in the same style as he has now done, you will lose time in asking me to bestow labour upon him, for I have other affairs which press upon me more closely; and I would make a matter of conscience of it, not to busy myself further, having no doubt that it was a temptation of Satan to distract and withdraw me from other more useful reading. And therefore I beg you to content yourself with what I have done in the matter, unless you see some better order to be taken therein.

Wherefore, after my commendation to you, I beseech our good Lord to have you in his keeping.

Your servant and hearty friend,

CHARLES D'ESPEVILLE.

[Printed—*Nouveaux Mémoires de l'Abbé d'Artigny*, tom. ii. p. 70.]

### CLIV.—TO FAREL.

Reply to various questions—terrible threat against Servetus—imprisonment of one of the leaders of the Libertins.

GENEVA, 13*th February* 1546.

You will be at ease regarding your brothers since you received the letter of Claude. The messenger who brought it asked whether mine would be ready when I returned from sermon, after three o'clock. I replied in the negative; but I bid him dine at my house with my wife, as I myself had been invited to dine with Macrin. I promised to be with him immediately after dinner, to make a brief reply. He did not come [to my house,] but hurried away without waiting a moment, so that I was confounded by so sudden a departure. And yet the youth had not appeared to me to behave badly in general. I trust the reflection may occur to your brothers, that they have been thus extricated from all their difficulties by the hand of God, in order that they make the greater haste [in the work.] It did not become the Israelites, when a way was opened up to them, to show remissness in immediately girding themselves for flight.[1] Such would have been the burden of my epistle had not the messenger deceived me; but I am confident that they are burning with ardour of their own accord. I now come to your own contests.[2] If the ungodly still occasion you some trouble, when that letter shall arrive, I have briefly expressed in it what I think should be your mode of proceeding. I should wish, however, the matter to be discussed *viva voce;* and that, thereupon, the result, or something like it, be committed to writing. You will perhaps smile because I suggest nothing out of the common, as you looked for something recondite and elevated at my hands; but I do not wish, nor, besides, is it right to be fettered by your estimate of me. I had rather, however, be foolish by so writing, than by my silence lead you to suppose that your entreaties were neglected by me. If nothing can be effected by reasoning, and in this lawful way, the Bernese must be privately prevailed upon not to allow that wild beast to go out of its den. I do not sufficiently comprehend your meaning regarding a treaty, unless it be, as I conjecture, that you are turning your thoughts to some sort of alliance, with a view to your receiving the assistance of the Bernese; and that just as they guard the liberty of the people by the law of the state, so they may protect ministers in their office by some title which commands respect. If that be provided for, I do not disapprove of [the alliance.] Bear in mind, that recourse should be had to those extraordinary remedies only when there is the exculpatory plea of an ultimate necessity. In the next place, be very cautious

---

[1] Decimated by the most cruel persecution, the faithful of Dauphiné, the native country of Farel, had inquired of the ministers of French Switzerland, whether it was lawful for them to have recourse to flight, in order to escape the fury of their adversaries. Numerous refugees had already settled at Geneva. — See vol. i. p. 419.

[2] Ecclesiastical embroilments with the Seigneury of Berne.

lest anything you do be such as may injure your interests in time to come. You may have greater cause of regret in that you once received aid, and were parties to a compact, than if you were to remain in your original servitude. Marcourt has, without doubt, already promised a place for himself; for he publicly proclaims that he does not regard the consent of the brethren, since he is desired, both by magistrates and people, and he has no doubt but that they are indignant against you. Finally, since he prematurely discloses the wickedness of his character, he must be repulsed by all artifices, lest he rise to a position in which he is able to perform what he threatens. With regard to those who gave out that we were establishing here a permanent seat of despotism, under colour of defence, let us suffer this rumour to spread on both sides. Their impudence has been met with civility and mildness, so that they ought to be ashamed of themselves.[1] I trust that they will keep quiet. I seek, as far as I am able, to persuade our friends to remain unconcerned. Servetus lately wrote to me, and coupled with his letter a long volume of his delirious fancies, with the Thrasonic boast, that I should see something astonishing and unheard of. He takes it upon him to come hither, if it be agreeable to me. But I am unwilling to pledge my word for his safety, for if he shall come, I shall never permit him to depart alive, provided my authority be of any avail.[2]

More than fifteen days have now elapsed since Cartelier[3] was imprisoned, for having, at supper in his own house, raged against me with such insolence as to make it clear that he was not then in his right senses. I concealed what I felt, but I

[1] See letter of the 26th January, p. 14, note 2.
[2] See the preceding letter. It appears that relations between Calvin and Servetus continued in a state of interruption, as is proved by the following passage of a letter of Calvin to Viret, dated 1st September 1548:—" I think I once read to you my answer to Servetus. I was at length disinclined from striving longer with the incurable obstinacy of a heretic; and, indeed, I ought to have followed the advice of Paul. He now attacks you. You will see how long you ought to persist in rebutting his follies. He will twist nothing out of me henceforward."— *Library of Geneva*, Vol. 106.
[3] One of the most violent members of the party that combated the influence and institutions of the reformer at Geneva.

testified to the judge that it would be agreeable to me were he proceeded against with the utmost rigour of the law. I wished to go to see him. Access was prohibited by decree of the Senate; and yet some good men accuse me of cruelty, forsooth, because I so pertinaciously revenge my injuries.[1] I have been requested by his friends to undertake the part of intercessor. I refused to do so, except on these two conditions, viz., that no suspicion should attach to me, and that the honour of Christ should remain intact. I have now done. I abide the judgment of the Council.—Adieu, brother, and most sincere friend. We all salute you and your sisters. You will convey to the brethren the best salutations in my name, and that of my brethren in the ministry. May God ever bless you and prosper your labours.—Yours,

JOHN CALVIN.

[*Lat. orig. autogr.—Imp. Library Dupuy.* Vol. 102.]

## CLV.—To FAREL.

Pacification of the Church at Neuchatel—Report of the speedy arrival of the Emperor in Savoy—Dangers at Geneva—Withering mention of Francis I.

GENEVA, 20*th February* 1546.

I specially congratulate you and all your friends, yea, ourselves also, and the whole Church of Christ, that the Lord has in His authority stilled all tumults, by restraining the ungodly. Viret had already requested me to be prepared at all points in case there should be need of my presence, and assuredly I should not have been behind; but God is twice to be praised, who by his own counsel has adjusted matters that were in so great confusion. We acknowledge that he was present with you when he opened up to you that plan of admonishing the heads of the citizens. We again acknowledge a memorable work of His, in having given to you those who of their own

---

[1] Calvin shewed himself, on more than one occasion, disposed to forgive personal injuries, as the Registers of Council testify:—"A woman having abused M. Calvin, it is directed that she be consigned to prison. Liberated at the request of the said M. Calvin, and discharged with a reproof."—12th December 1545.

accord were disposed to act well towards you. I feel confident that the matter has been brought to a conclusion in harmony with the desire of all good men. If our service be desired, you know that we are all yours. I now hourly expect your brothers. May the Lord restore them to us safe and with good fortune.[1] A confident report is spread abroad here of the arrival of the Emperor. I hold it for certain that a passage across will by no means be opened up to him without a bloody conflict. It cannot be doubted, that even though our neighbours were willing that we should be left exposed to the danger of becoming the prey of the conqueror, they would nevertheless find it necessary to guard their own territories; although I do not know why our party have so soon become careless, unless they wished to subject themselves to their sway, and thus save themselves from other masters. It is a hard condition that you must give up your liberty in order to secure allies as defenders.[2] Our party erred in one particular, that they made too violent a reply. But what could I do? On me, nevertheless, the odium redounds, though I strove with great vehemence to prevent the ground of it; but I have bid adieu to the perverted judgments of men. I pass on to another subject. Matters will go more severely with Cartelier, because he mixed up with myself part of the Senate. After that I have respectably enough discharged the duty of clemency, I have resolved to halt. The malevolent will heap obloquy upon me, but if there be an opportunity of replying, I have the means of stopping their mouths. No one certainly will allege that any word less than fair fell from me, for among good and bad I have endeavoured to extenuate his offence. The Parliament of Paris, as I hear, now wages war with fire and faggot against Christ.[3] It is indeed certain that a great

---

[1] See p. 8, note 2.

[2] Allusion to the Bernese and to their pretensions of ruling Geneva under cover of the Alliance.—See p. 14, note 2.

[3] The year 1546 was especially remarkable for the great persecutions that arose within the bounds of the jurisdiction of the Parliament of Paris. Meaux, Seulis, Orleans, reckoned numerous martyrs. One named Jean Chapot of Dauphiné, colporteur of Geneva, arrested at Paris, was condemned to death, after having undergone the most cruel tortures. He had his tongue cut out before he was cast into the flames. "The dispersion," says Beza, "was widespread, but it led to

multitude of the godly are everywhere held in bonds. Sardanapalus,[1] meanwhile, in the midst of his courtezans, feeds his fancy with victories. May the Lord have respect to His Church!

Adieu, most upright brother in the Lord, together with all your fellow-ministers, whom you will respectfully salute in my name, and in that of the brethren. May Christ ever direct you all by right counsel, and bless your auspicious endeavours.—Yours,

JOHN CALVIN.

To the four Presidents of the citizens, special compliments in my name. May the Lord bless them exceedingly.

[*Lat. orig. autogr.*—*Library of Geneva.* Vol. 106.]

## LVI.—TO VIRET.

Election of a minister at Neuchatel—Sickness of Viret's wife.

GENEVA, 22*d February* 1546.

I learned from Farel's last letter, that the commotions at Neuchatel were allayed. And I now feel assured that the matter of the choice of a pastor is concluded; for it had at length been agreed that the ministers should promise on oath to nominate in good faith the person whom they deemed most suitable. It was already considered as almost certain, that Christopher would be the man, provided the Bernese would part with him;[2] and there is hope that they will offer no objection. Farel wrote that the good cause had been not a little aided by the Consul Wateville.

Had they invited us as brethren, I should have been ready at any hour. But I rejoice especially, that you were of more ser-

the great advancement of many churches which were built up of the stones of that ruin."—*Hist. Eccl.* tom. i. p. 82. *Histoire des Martyrs*, pp. 170, 177.

[1] Francis I., King of France.

[2] On the death of the minister Chaponneau, the people of Neuchatel wished to have in his room Christopher Fabri, minister of Thonon; they accordingly asked him from the Seigneury of Berne, who with a good grace conceded him to them. —Ruchat, vol. v. p. 299.

vice than you thought you would be ; for all loudly assert that your arrival was highly advantageous.

I see that Textor does not hold out much further hope of your wife. You need no more words to admonish you to hold yourself ready to bear with moderation the issue, whatever that may be. Would that I also could fly thither, that I might alleviate your sorrow, or at least bear a part of it ![1] But so long a ride would cause me pain. I rather advise, should matters happen otherwise than as we wish, that you come hither for a few days.—Adieu, most sound-hearted brother, along with your wife and family. The Lord comfort and strengthen you all. Amen.—Yours,

JOHN CALVIN.

[*Lat. orig. autogr.—Library of Geneva.* Vol. 106.]

## CLVII.—To VIRET.[2]

Calvin invites his friend to repair to Geneva after the death of his wife.

GENEVA, 8*th March* 1546.

Come, on this condition, that you disengage your mind not only from grief, but also from every annoyance. Do not fear that I will impose any burden upon you, for through my means you will be allowed to take whatever rest is agreeable to you. If any

[1] We again find marks of the same solicitude in a letter of Calvin to Viret of the preceding month. " Adieu, with your wife, whose health we will commend to the Lord. Be assured that we are not less solicitous about her than if she were the wife or daughter of each of us. The Lord keep you and sustain you with the consolation of his Spirit."—(January 1546,) Vol. 106, from Geneva.

[2] Viret was at that time plunged into the deepest affliction. He had just lost, after a long illness, his wife, Elizabeth Turtaz, of Orbe, with whom he had lived for many years in a godly union. The grief which he felt on that occasion is expressed, in a very touching manner, in a letter written many years afterwards to Calvin :—" I was so completely dispirited and prostrated by that arrow of affliction, that the whole world appeared to me nothing but a burden. There was nothing pleasant, nothing that could mitigate my grief of mind."—*Calv. Epist. et Resp.*, p. 53. The friends of Viret, and especially Farel and Calvin, lavished upon him, during that trial, marks of the tenderest and most brotherly affection. The familiar correspondence of Calvin furnishes us with precious revelations in this respect.

one prove troublesome to you, I will interpose. The brethren, also, make the same promise to you as I do. I will also be surety that the citizens do not interfere with your wishes.

I know not what I ought to imprecate on the wretches who had spread a report of your death. Never did a letter from you arrive more opportunely. Although your death was announced, yet as mention was made of poison, Textor was already in the midst of preparations for the journey, that he might speed to Orbe on fleet horses. A great part of the brethren were present, all overwhelmed with deep affliction. Shortly afterward your letter made its appearance, and such exultation instantly broke forth, that we were hardly masters of our senses. It was fortunate that we did not pass a night of sorrow, else I should not have borne it without danger. But why do I detain you, and not rather incite you to hasten hither as quickly as possible? Adieu, brother and most agreeable friend. Salute respectfully the brethren James, Ribitti, Hubert, Cordier, Celio, Francis, Merlin. The Lord protect you and the remainder of your family.—Yours,

JOHN CALVIN.

[*Lat. copy—Library of Geneva.* Vol. 111.]


## CLVIII.—To VIRET.

Renewed and more pressing invitation to come to Geneva.

*15th March* 1546.

I have hitherto delayed writing to you, because I daily expected you to come hither, as you had promised; nor should I have written even now, as I remain in the same state of expectation, were it not that I might incite you to hasten your journey; for I wonder why it is that you thus put off from day to day. I remember that John de Tournay[1] told me that you had a horse; but why not rather come by boat? Unless David has sold his [horses,] that difficulty could be easily got over, although I believe that one may now be more easily procured than it could have been eight days ago, for fewer

[1] Nephew of Viret, and minister in the Pays de Vaud.

couriers have passed this way during these days. Make haste, therefore, that you may recruit a little, and gather heart again with us; for people from your quarter say that you are half dead. Since I can draw you out by no other inducement, I make the announcement, that you shall have no letter from me until you come. Quick, then.—Adieu. Salute all friends. May the Lord shortly bring you in safety to us.— Yours,

JOHN CALVIN.

[*Lat. orig. autogr.—Library of Geneva.* Vol. 106.]


## CLIX.—To THEODORE VITUS.[1]

Indication of the various documents wherein are set forth the opinions of Calvin regarding the Lord's Supper—earnest desires for union and peace among the Churches—condition of Geneva.

GENEVA, 17*th March* 1546.

Your letter gave me the greater pleasure, as I had not ventured to look for it, for it was my part to draw a letter from you by being the first to write. But that you, without being called upon, should of your own accord have anticipated me, I take as a proof of your greater friendship towards me. If, however, you would know the reason of my not writing, I refrained more from modesty than negligence. And generally the testimony of Philip [Melanchthon] is with me sufficient; but when no great familiarity intervenes, the crooked policy of the times sometimes makes me apprehensive. Wherefore, I am the more grateful to you for having removed every scruple. I greatly

---

[1] To the most honourable Doctor Theodore Vitus, most faithful Minister of Christ at Nuremberg.

Theodore Vitus, (Dieterich de Weit,) a distinguished theologian, friend of Luther and Melanchthon, preached the Gospel with great success in the city of Nuremberg, his native place, and was worthy of the esteem and affection of Calvin, not more on account of his learning than his moderation. He died in 1549. Melanchthon wrote, at the foot of his portrait, the following verses :—

Ingenii monumenta sui, sed plura Lutheri
Edidit; his poterunt secla futura frui.
—[Melch. Adam, *Vitæ Theol. Germ.*, pp. 199, 200.]

rejoice, also, to find that my pamphlet, *De Coenâ*, has met with your approbation.¹ It was written in French ten years before. When, without my knowledge, it had been already translated into Latin by two individuals, I at length consented to its publication, being afraid, in fact, that some worse version might forestall it. A style of instruction, simple and popular, and adapted to the unlearned, shews what my purpose was from the first ; for I usually write more carefully for those acquainted with Latin. I laboured, however, not only faithfully to express my views, and reduce them within a brief compass, but also to unfold them lucidly, and without technicalities. Since then the *Institution*, having been revised, was again given to the public, in which, unless I am mistaken, I expound and more fully confirm the same doctrine, under a different form of expression, and with somewhat greater development. I at length also published a *Catechism*, which is trustworthy and pertinent evidence of the kind of doctrine with which the common people are imbued by me. Would that the people of Zurich, as you say, were willing to give their assent to that confession !² I do not think Luther is so unyielding but that there might easily be an agreement, and they do not, withal, venture to disapprove of my views. The chief obstacle to their giving a public assent to my doctrine is, that being pre-occupied by a meaning, once and now for a length of time prescribed to them, they so stick to their customary forms as to admit nothing new. But if you consider the tyranny manifested by certain of the adverse party in the attempt to force the world, not only into their peculiar views, but also into a prescribed form of words, the furious insolence they shew, what commotions they excite,—the moderation as well as rectitude by which you are characterized, will

---

¹ The following is the passage of the letter of Vitus to Calvin to which he here refers :—" I have read your short address to the people on the Sacrament of the Supper, and I approve of your calling the bread and wine signs in such a sense that the things signified are in reality present. Would that they who leave only the naked signs, might be led by you to adopt that view !"—*Calv. Epist. et Resp.*, Amst., p. 37.

² This desire was happily realized some years afterwards, by the adoption of a common symbol on the Supper, approved alike by the theologians of Zurich and Geneva.

lead you to condemn in the matter the absurd conduct of those parties, not less than the people of Zurich. May the Lord by His Spirit dispose us all to true moderation. You know that I am not in the habit of complaining when there is no ground for it; nor do I doubt but that you yourself, as might be expected from your eminent piety, sigh in secret over the same evils, while it is not in your power to remedy them. With respect to the assurances you give me regarding yourself, I wish you in turn to believe, that I am and always will be your sincere friend and brother. I now, with many others, request you to go on strenuously, and make no halt in your progress, until you have handed over to us Genesis completed.[1] For as Luther has just grounds for congratulating himself in having found such an artist to polish his works, so others experience how advantageous the labour is to the public. I may have wished, however, that you had been more sparing in your mention of the Sacramentaries, because I see that the minds of some are thereby exasperated, of whom there was a hope that they would be brought to moderate views. It will be for you to consider what may be more conducive to that end. I will be satisfied if you take my warning in good part, whether or not you act upon it. The Ratisbon Assembly will indeed bring forth smoke for us, which the Lord will soon dispel.[2]

Here we are tranquil unless the Emperor molest us. Some suspect him of having an eye on Burgundy, with the view of threatening the kingdom of France from that quarter, while he would harass Provence by means of the young Duke of Savoy, and send in the English from the other side. I hold myself under the protection of God alone when I see that we are not far from certain danger. Adieu, most honoured Sir, and most sincere friend. May the Lord Jesus ever guide and direct you by His Holy Spirit, and bless your labours. All my colleagues

[1] Vitus lent useful aid to Luther in the revision of his different writings, and rendered a real service to the Church by collecting and offering to the public the Commentaries of Luther on the Prophet Micah, and the first eleven chapters of Genesis.—Melch. Adam, *Vitæ Theol. Germ.*

[2] The Conference opened by the Emperor at Ratisbon, and to which Bucer had been summoned, was a mere feint to divert men's minds, and to transfer the decision of the points at issue to the Council of Trent.

respectfully salute you. To yours also you will convey the highest respects in my name, and in that of my colleagues.—Yours,

JOHN CALVIN.

[*Lat. Copy, Library of Zurich, Coll. Simler.* Vol. 59.]


CLX.—TO VIRET.[1]

Instructions to Viret about a journey to Geneva.

GENEVA, 26*th March, before supper.*

The person who delivered yours to me did not know whence it came. I thus received it somewhat later than I wished. I attended to the wish you expressed, that a suitable horse, and one without show, should be sent to you. It would, however, have been sent off sooner, had I not told our people beforehand that you could not leave your place of residence before the morning discourse. I certainly could have wished, if your letter had arrived in time, that you had been sent for sooner. But I supposed that you had set out with Christopher: for that was the reason why I gave you no letter by the messenger belonging to my household. If, after preaching, you can come as far as Nyon, you will be here on Monday before supper; but take care lest you fatigue yourself. You had better come to Nyon on Monday. We shall have you with us in good time, if we get you well. Salute all the brethren.

May the Lord bring you to us safe and in good spirits.—Yours,

JOHN CALVIN.

[*Lat. orig. autogr.—Library of Geneva.* Vol. 106.]

---

[1] Viret, yielding to the entreaties of Calvin, went to Geneva towards the end of March, and there received the most honourable marks of public affection. We read in the Registers of Council, of date the 2d April 1546,—"Grand reception given to Farel and Viret, who had just arrived at Geneva."

## CLXI.—To Monsieur de Falais.

Calvin's labours—the diet at Ratisbon—the Church of Metz—the reformation at Heidelberg—*apology* for M. de Falais—opinion regarding the sermons of Ochino.

[*April* 1546.[1]]

Monseigneur,—I thank you for the care which you have of my health, anxious that I would not overburthen myself, in straining a point to write to you, when I am not in a fit state to do so. But had I only to write to you, it would be to me a very easy labour, if that can be called toil wherein one only finds pleasure. The difficulty arises from the annoyances and interruptions of the train of thought which intervene, to break off a letter in the midst twenty times over, or even more, beyond all bounds. As regards health, I was much more feeble when I wrote to you a while ago than I am at present. But being in a good state of general bodily condition, I am unceasingly tormented with a heaviness, which, as it were, suffers me not to do anything. For, besides the sermons and lectures, there is a month already gone in which I have scarce done anything, in such wise that I am almost ashamed to live thus useless. But if it please God, of His goodness, to make use of me, He will release me and allay this ill, which holds me so fast that I cannot set about any labour of importance, to employ the leisure which He gives me. Nevertheless, He does not cease to exercise me by some means or other, in order that I may not grow rusty through laziness. If, however, He does not graciously restore me to a better condition, I am not likely ever to get on horseback. Even more than that, were I ever to be sent for, I could not stir out of the house in such a state. But, as you observe, they let me alone, from fear of setting astir the frantic blockheads; and on my side, I willingly give up the diets to those who have a liking for them, as for any good they do.[2] I am

---

[1] *On the back*, in the handwriting of M. de Falais,—Received the 16th of April 1546.

[2] A new diet had been assembled at Ratisbon, for the pacification of the religious troubles of Germany. That assembly opened in the month of June 1546,

glad that our Lord has put you out of pain as regards Norberg. As for what remains to be done, you will have an opportunity of considering what it ought to be, having been informed by Jéhan de Rochefort, and after having established your case, as it can be done, in coming forth out of Egypt and out of Babylon. It is like what is said by Moses and by Ezekiel,—*in much stir and with haste.* I hope, should it so please God, that all is over by this time. I would not have you to be too much astonished at the length of time you have been in receiving letters from him, considering the length of the journey. But if God has been so gracious to him, and to you also, as to make a way of escape out of danger, he will not have tarried so long on the way as not to be, by this time, on his return. Thus, being at rest in regard to that matter, you will take counsel for the future.

As to Constance, I had not spoken to you, but that your present abode did not please you. When the crisis comes, however, Strasbourg is more suitable, and I like it better, were it not for the reason which you allege.

In Metz,[1] I see a great evil, the want of guidance and of cordial interest, albeit that these are rather two evils. But God will find the remedy. We must try every method which He presents to us, and even stir up ourselves, where the means appear to be wanting. And whereas I know that you have no need to be exhorted not to spare yourself, I forbear to do so.

I am not at all amazed, if Master Peter Alexander is bold, having his chin thus held above water, and that besides he is quite accustomed at Heidelberg to hear that doctrine already for a long time past.[2] He is even well aware that he has no

in presence of the Emperor, and like those which had preceded, concluded without any result whatsoever.

[1] See the notes, pp. 80, 91. The Protestants of this town, feebly supported by the league of Smalkald, and intimidated by the presence of the imperial legate, devoted to the Roman Catholic clergy, had already lost the rights which had been guaranteed to them by the accord of 1543, and so found themselves deprived of the exercise of public worship and of the pastorate.—(See a letter of Myconius to Calvin, 13th November 1543. *Calv. Epist. et Responsa*, Amst., p. 26.)

[2] In the year 1546, the Palatinate witnessed the accomplishment of a great religious revolution. The Elector, Frederic II., yielding to the wish of his subjects,

other means for advancing himself. Thus it is no wonder if he takes advantage of it where there is no danger at all. But I see quite well that he is not an over-confident man, were it only by his conclusions. What is worse, he makes a stupid blunder in this, that he says, the swearing an oath is forbidden by God ; and that with a blasphemy, inasmuch as he attributes authority to Saint Paul to permit what has been prohibited by his Master ; but these are matters for the civil magistrate to decide.

*The Apology* would be much better drawn up where you are than at a distance. This I say not to exempt myself, but inasmuch as I think that such is the case ; for I am quite ready to undertake the employment. So also would Master Peter Viret, but his style of writing would not be altogether suited to such an argument, owing to his want of conciseness. And for myself I would have to bite my nails in more than a hundred passages, if we could not confer together so as to resolve by common accord what might be fit to say or to omit. Nevertheless, we shall take care to meet your wish whenever you shall have come to a determination upon the whole case and the state of your affairs. Howbeit, I have retained no memorandum of the particulars beside me. What I have told you about the Emperor, was not so much to find fault with what has been done, as to set forth the reason why it ought not to be inserted so as to be seen. I praise our Lord that the present of my Commentary is agreeable to you. In conformity with your answer, our brother sent his translation to Vendelin, addressing the preface to you, in order that having seen it beforehand, you may judge what course shall appear to you to be expedient.

The request which I made to you so affectionately, not to separate your household from the French Church,[1] was not founded upon any report, but solely upon a passage of your letter

proclaimed the establishment of the Reformation, and the abolition of the old worship in his states. The chief instrument of that revolution was the minister Paul Fagius, the disciple of Capito.—Sleidan, *Comment.* lib. xvi. p. 266. De Thou, lib. ii. c. 3.

[1] The French Church of Strasbourg, of which Calvin had been pastor during his exile from Geneva.

where you signify that you were in course of doing so, not perceiving any amendment in that quarter. It suffices, that I am aware of your intention, so as not to be further troublesome to you on that score. I see indeed the reasons you may have, but I take into view the scandal which would thence arise. All is well, since you have condescended to my request.

I would desire, Monseigneur, that the hundred crowns [escus] might be sent to the lady, and they would be returned to you forthwith, sending to the Ladies de Tilly what is resting due to them, since the father shews himself such a one as he is. I would earnestly wish, that in disposing ourselves willingly and patiently to bear the cross, we were framing our shoulders to such a charge. But these are matters about which we shall better talk together than we can write.

I pray you to hold me excused, if I do not as yet signify my opinion of the translation of the Sermons of Messire Bernardino.[1] I may, however, speak a word in your ear, that they are more useful in Italian than in other languages, were it not that the name of the man is of use ; and then there is such a variety of minds, that it is not amiss to endeavour to draw some of them by that means. Of the translator, I shall let you know my opinion, please God, in a few words shortly.

As touching the *apology* of the ladies,[2] I think, Monseigneur, you have my opinion of it signified already in brief, at least I would here declare it, that the author has not observed what the Latins call *decorum*. For the course of procedure is un-

[1] Introduced by Calvin to Myconius, Ochino made but a very short stay at Bâle, where those writings made their appearance which have been such a blot upon his memory. In 1545 he went to Augsbourg, where he became minister to the congregation of Italian refugees until the epoch of the *Interim*, which was the cause of his betaking himself to England. His leanings toward heterodoxy were veiled from the eyes of every one, except perhaps the clear-sighted discernment of Calvin, who valued his abilities, without having an entire confidence in the solidity of his doctrines. The ever-recurring changes of his unsettled life led him, at a later period, to class himself with the sect of the anti-Trinitarians. His discourses, so much admired by Cardinal Bembo, and the Emperor Charles V. himself, are less remarkable for their purity of doctrine than for the warmth of feeling and the poetical flash of the style. They have been printed under the following title : *Prediche di Messer Bernardino Ochino*, 1543, and reprinted on several occasions ; but we are not aware of any translation, whether Latin or French. See Schelhorn, *Ergötzlichkeiten*, tom. iii. pp. 2022, 2161, 2166, and pp. 2174-2179.

[2] The sisters of M. de Falais.

befitting the individuals. Everybody will not perceive this, only those who have their wits about them. This is the reason why I have retained it beside me.

The letters of Diaz[1] were not needed to shew me on what authority you had opened those which he might write to me. For you have sufficient authority without any one else giving it to you. I humbly thank you for the offer which you have so kindly made for the baptism of our child.[2] And now, Monsieur, to conclude, after having humbly, and with all possible kindly affection, commended me to your good favour and that of Madame, and having also presented the humble salutations of my wife, I pray our good Lord to guide you always as He has done, shewing Himself the true protector both of you and of all that concerns you.

Your humble brother, servant, and ever your entire friend,
JOHN CALVIN.

[*Fr. orig. autogr.—Library of Geneva.* Vol. 195.]


## CLXII.—To MONSIEUR DE FALAIS.

Advice regarding the editing of the *Apology*—details of a loan contracted for M. de Falais—news from Germany and Italy—Farel and Viret at Geneva—death of Juan Diaz.

*16th April* 1546.

MONSEIGNEUR,—You see here what I have done desiring to comply with your wish.[3] That it shall altogether satisfy you

[1] Juan Diaz, originally of Cuença, in Spain, studied letters at the University of Paris, and was distinguished, amid the scholars of his nation, "by superior learning, adorned with pure morals, great mildness, prudence and benignity." Initiated in the knowledge of the Gospel, he left Paris and visited Geneva, Bâle, Strasbourg, where he acquired the friendship of Bucer, whom he accompanied into Germany. The Jesuit, Malvenda, a stout defender of Popish idolatry, having made vain efforts to lead him back to the Romish Church, the adversaries of Juan Diaz planned a most detestable conspiracy against his life, and, on the 27th of March, he was assassinated by order of Alphonso Diaz, his own brother, who had come from Rome in order to the accomplishment of this execrable outrage, the instigator of which remained unpunished.—See the record of this odious fratricide in Sleidan, and *Histoire des Martyrs*, pp. 162, 168; and Letter CLXIII.

[2] Calvin had this year a child by his wife, Idelette de Bure, which died in the birth.

[3] At the request of M. de Falais, Calvin had prepared an apology for his Lord-

I shall not venture to promise myself. It will be quite enough for me if you have the persuasion that I have not failed from lack of good-will. Indeed, I fear you may not find that which you had looked for. But it is not reasonable that I bear the blame of the too great credit which I may have with you. If I had been in a right frame, and had I had leisure, possible it is that I might have done better. But since these two things have been wanting to me, I pray you that you may please hold me as excused. It would not have cost me very much to fill up a much larger extent of paper; but I have studied brevity, thinking that nothing could be better, considering the personage to whom the writing is addressed. It did not occur to Saint André that it wanted anything, except that, on having come to the passage about your retirement, you might insist upon deducting separately in detail the travelling expenses which you had incurred up to that time. I had, indeed, thought of another conclusion to be urged, but because I did not well know how to keep within bounds, I have let it alone. You will exercise your own discretion as to adding an article to that effect, if you think fit, namely, with regard to the property, which you did not venture to make any other request to him about, fearing that it would be trouble thrown away, to speak to him about the property before being reinstated in his good graces, and also because that is the thing you most of all desire and prefer to anything else. In any event, let it please him to have regard to such a family, and not allow himself to be led by those who only seek its destruction. I know not whether it would be of advantage to your brothers[1] to make

---

ship, which was to be presented to the Emperor at the Diet of Ratisbon. This memorial, drawn up at first in French, then translated into Latin, and along with a profession of faith, containing valuable details for the history of M. de Falais, has the following title:—*Apology of the very Illustrious Lord James of Burgundy, of Falaise, and of Breda, wherein he has wiped away the accusations wherewith he has been branded in the sight of the Imperial Majesty, and sets forth the Confession of his Faith.* This morceau has been published by the Amsterdam editor at the end of the letters of Calvin to M. de Falais.

[1] M. de Falais had five brothers. Those alone of whom mention is made in the letters of Calvin, are John, Seigneur de Fromont, and Peter, Pronotary apostolic, who had embraced the Reformation.

mention of them. You will consider about that. Towards the end, it would be needful to add an express clause, to remove the suspicion that you had too great regret, declaring that for the honour of God you bear the loss patiently, beseeching God that He would always make you sensibly aware of the work of Jesus Christ, and of the benefits bestowed on you by Him, so as to reckon all things but loss and dung in comparison of Him. If you determine to enter upon the subject of the property, it appears to me that it would be advisable to mention it thus briefly; I have explained the reason why I have not done so.

But to proceed, Monseigneur, I have detained the man who has brought me your last, hoping that he would be the messenger to carry you this answer. But, at the end of six days, there has occurred a sudden piece of business to Sire Nicolas the present bearer. I have thereupon sent away the other, delivering to his care the two young children, because he could not have arrived so soon. He has been sufficiently admonished, not so much by me as by the others, to settle and choose some manner of livelihood; but I see clearly that he is not yet tired of running about. That arises in part from his too great simplicity,—for he has no great head-piece. Some clodpole, scarcely wiser than himself, had whispered in his ear in passing, that I would be quite able to recommend him to Berne, and put him in the way of his becoming a preacher. I have done everything to repress such an expectation: but he does not leave off his roving about; and although he seems to approve an advice when offered to him, immediately afterwards he begins to do the same thing again. I am sorry for it, for, in other respects, I find him well disposed, and without malice.

As for the business of Sire Nicolas, the case is thus:—He had no means of squaring his accounts, but in taking the place which had been adjudged in hypothec to another preferable creditor, having struck off some pieces for law expenses. Thus he would have been excluded, had he not undertaken to reimburse the other party. What is worse, he who held the security was himself under hypothec elsewhere, in danger that his property might be sold, and needed to re-assure his interest therein. The subject is well worth what the said Nicolas has bargained for. The hardship was for him, that he would have had to pay seven hundred crowns before next Easter, and also that it is too large for him. But the necessity made him forget all that. It is true that he has to receive from Sire Antony Sieglessen a sum in satisfaction thereof, but he fears that it may not be ready at so short a term, seeing that he will have to transact with people who have no pity. In that perplexity, he has thought that if, peradventure, Antony de Sieglessen might not so readily be forthcoming with that which he has to receive from him, that you would afford him some assistance for a month, or six weeks' delay, on his giving you the security of Sire Antony and the place, on good and equitable terms. When he asked advice of me, I requested him to try all means before having recourse to you, which he had already indeed determined, as he told me, but that it was his last remedy. In any event, however, he would bring you letters of assurance over the place. To this I have not agreed, fearing lest it might appear to you that it would have the effect of protracting a settlement, promising to him to assure you that the responsibility lies not with himself but with me.

I have wished much to make this statement to you, Monseigneur, on purpose that you should be informed, that he did not rashly go beyond his authority, but that he had been constrained thereto; in order also, that when he could nowise do without your help, you might the more be induced to aid him. I can indeed assure you, that there will be no risk, for the assignation is quite valid. And if money were to be had here, he would not need to stir out of the house. But the country is stripped so bare of money, that it is lamentable, the more so that there is more due to him at Strasbourg than he has need for. I do not take upon me to ask it of you, for that is not my business. In so far as I have endeavoured to remove the doubts which might prevent you, I hope you will take it in good part, and that you will not ascribe it to importunity. Besides that, it is my duty, for I have been the cause, along with Monsieur David, of involving him in this anxiety. For we made the first purchase in his absence, because the said Monsieur David was fully resolved from that time forward to complete the transaction.

I believe that you have been otherwise informed of the death of the Marquis of Guasto.[1] We are not aware what the Emperor intends to do, except that people are coming from Naples toward Genoa. One can scarce think that he would go so far for pastime as to Argiers. And, indeed, I believe, that considering himself secure upon the side of France, and leaving the English to occupy the King's attention, having fully ordered everything to his own advantage in Germany, that he would not make a mere feint of going to Argiers.[2]

Master William Farel and Master Peter Viret, in passing from hence, have requested me to present you their humble commendations. They have been here eight days to my great comfort, except in so far as they have made me put off my excusing myself to you. I am glad of your well-disposedness, and principally for your cheerfulness, and also because I hope that it will prove a means of our seeing you. We shall, in the meanwhile, however, pray God, that He would restore you from better to better, albeit that we must not look, neither you nor myself, to be ever of much worth in this world.

We have made Saint-André preacher, at which possibly you will be amazed. He did not look for it ; and I believe also, that at the first move his courage would not have inclined him that way. But we have made conscience of it, seeing his zeal and readiness, not to leave him always idle. I hope that God will make use of him for the profit and upbuilding of his Church. He has not been brought to it without a struggle, but perceiving that the call was from on high, he has not resisted it.

To conclude, Monseigneur, after having presented the humble commendations as well of myself as of my wife to your kind favour and to that of Madame, I shall supplicate our good Lord to have you always in His protection, guiding you with a view to His honour, as He has done hitherto, and shewing

---

[1] Alphonso d'Avalos, Marquis of Guasto, governor of the Milanese, and one of the ablest generals of Charles the Fifth. He died in 1546.

[2] The Emperor, in 1544, had undertaken a disastrous expedition against the town of Algiers. The military movements which were then going forward in Italy, were intended to cover his real projects of attack against the Protestant princes of Germany.

Himself so powerful in you, that we may always acknowledge the fruit of that great victory with which Jesus Christ consoles us.

Your humble servant and brother in our Lord Jesus,

JOHN CALVIN.

When I had finished these presents, I received the sad news of the death of good Diaz.[1] But it so happens, that the unhappy Papists shew more and more that they are led by the spirit of their father, who has been a murderer from the beginning.

[*Fr. orig. autogr.—Library of Geneva.* Vol. 194.]

## CLXIII.—To FAREL.[2]

Troubles at Geneva—imprisonment of the several members of the family of Favre—account of the assassination of John Diaz at Neubourg.

[*April* 1546.]

After your departure the dances caused us more trouble than I had supposed. All those who were present being summoned to the Consistory, with the two exceptions of Corna and Perrin, shamelessly lied to God and us. I was incensed, as the vile-

---

[1] See the following letter.

[2] The Ecclesiastical Ordinances, digested by Calvin and adopted by the councils of the republic, daily encountered the keenest opposition in the heart of a party which reckoned at its head men belonging to the most distinguished families among the Genevese. The Consistory and Councils together took care that the laws were rigidly enforced, and checked improprieties without respect of persons. The Captain-General, Amy Perrin, the Syndic Corna, and several other persons, having, contrary to the prohibitions, danced in a private house, "It is ordained," as is contained in the Registers of 12th April 1546, "that they all be imprisoned;" and with regard to the wife of Amy Perrin, who spoke insolently to the Consistory, that she also be imprisoned, and be required to find security. Perrin, to avoid undergoing the punishment pronounced against him, had recourse to the pretext of a journey to Lyons; but he was incarcerated on his return. The Syndic Corna acknowledged his fault, and, after a deposition of some days, he was reinstated in his office. The minister, Henry de la Mare, was deposed, for having been present at the ball, and taken the side of the dance and dancers against the Consistory. See *Registers of Council*, April 1546.

ness of the thing demanded, and I strongly inveighed against the contempt of God, in that they thought nothing of making a mockery of the sacred obtestations we had used. They persisted in their contumacy. When I was fully informed of the state of the case, I could do nothing but call God to witness that they would pay the penalty of such perfidy; I, at the same time, however, announced my resolution of unbaring the truth, even though it should be at the cost of my own life, lest they should imagine that any profit was to come of lying. Francisca also, the wife of Perrin, grossly abused us, because we were so opposed to the Favres.[1] I replied as seemed proper, and as she deserved. I inquired whether their house was inviolably sacred, whether it owed no subjection to the laws? We already detained her father in prison, being convicted of one act of adultery,[2] the proof of a second was close at hand; there was a strong report of a third; her brother had openly contemned and derided the Senate and us. Finally, I added, that a new city must be built for them, in which they might live apart, unless they were willing to be restrained by us here under the yoke of Christ; that so long as they were in Geneva, they would strive in vain to cast off obedience to the laws; for were there as many diadems in the house of the Favres as frenzied heads, that that would be no barrier to the Lord being superior. Her husband had meanwhile gone to Lyons, hoping that the matter would be silently buried. I thought that they should be forced to a confession of the truth by an oath. Corna warned them that he would by no means suffer them to perjure themselves. They not only confessed what we wished, but that

---

[1] At the head of the opposition to the ministers were observed the different members of the family of Francis Favre, a dissolute old man, and father-in-law of Amy Perrin. Francisca, his daughter, wife of the latter, made herself remarkable by the violence of her invectives against the Consistory. "They remonstrated with her, and made no more account of herself and her father than of the lowest in the city. Being again interrogated whether she would name the dancers, twice replied, that she would rather submit to punishment, and be dragged before all the justices, than appear before the Consistory."—Notes Extracted from the *Registers of the Consistory of Geneva*, by M. the late Syndic Cramere, 4to, 1853.

[2] "That the father-in-law of Amy Perrin, who has committed adultery, be also imprisoned, and put upon his trial."—*Registers of Council*. Ibid.

they, on that day, danced at the house of the widow of Balthazar. They were all cast into prison. The Syndic was an illustrious example of moderation; for he publicly spoke against himself and the whole herd so severely, that it was unnecessary to say much to him. He was, however, severely admonished in the Consistory, being deposed from his office until he gave proof of repentance. They say that Perrin has returned from Lyons; whatever he may do, he will not escape punishment. Henry was stripped of his office with our consent. With him there fell out a ludicrous enough altercation. He had admitted that what had been taken down from the witnesses was true. Meanwhile he had recourse to the defence, 'against an elder admit no accusation unless before two or three witnesses.' I inquired whose saying this was,—'Out of thine own mouth I judge thee, worthless servant;' for that now the case did not lie in the trustworthiness of the witnesses, but in his confession. Besides, when he repudiated the witnesses, that he was pressed by the dilemma, either his confession was true or it was false; if true, there was no further ground for hesitation; but if he had said what was false, he was to be held as answerable for perjury, because he had sworn to something different from the reality. It therefore came to this, that he might say that he had spoken falsely and without regard to principle. When he said that it was unfair that he should be pressed by one who ought to have been his defender, I inquired by what obligation I was bound to him to defend a bad cause, for that I had taken no oath to the Franciscan faction. Much was said to the man, backwards and forwards, but the result was, that he departed loaded with the reproach and odium of all. Being deprived of his ministry, he was, at the same time, thrust into prison, whence, however, he was liberated in three days. There he was a strenuous patron of the dances, that he might embitter, as far as was in his power, the hatred towards me of those who were already more than sufficiently alienated from me. But whatever Satan may essay by the like of him, he will afford a striking example. For two things are already matter of public talk, that there is no hope of impunity since even the first people of the city are not spared, and that I show no more favour to friends than to those opposed to me. Perrin with his wife rages in prison; the widow is absolutely furious; the others are silent from confusion and shame.

Diaz, the Spaniard, whom you saw here, Viret, at the house of Des Gallars, and who, setting out from Neuchatel for Germany, had passed through with the two Senarclens, was most cruelly put to death. When the Emperor was said to be approaching, he had repaired to Neubourg, a town under the rule of Duke Otho Henry. From that place he wrote to me on the 13th of March. He had a brother at Rome of the name of Alphonso, who came thither with the express design of making away with this godly man. They conferred together for some days. When Juan observed that he was of no service, he left Alphonso. The latter, pretending that he had forgotten something, sends a servant to recall his brother, and put him to death in the house. He followed him to the house, nor did he believe the domestic that the slaughter had been perpetrated until he himself had viewed the corpse. Then he hurried off on fleet horses to the county of Tyrol.[1] Duke Otho sent the prefect of the palace to demand that he should be given up to punishment. Unless Ferdinand be willing to throw into confusion all things, both human and divine, he must of necessity avenge so base and abominable an outrage. For the prefect has at the same time surrendered himself a prisoner.

Adieu, dearest brethren; may God ever protect you. Salute all friends. You, Farel, will convey to the heads of the citizens my best greeting. I wish that I could one day creep your length, in whatever way it might be possible.—All ours salute you.

[Calvin's *Lat. Corresp.* Opera, tom. ix. p. 38.]

---

[1] See the whole of this narrative in the *Histoire des Martyrs*, from the tract of Claude de Senarclens· *Vera Historia de Morte Joannis Diazii Hispani.* 1546.

## CLXIV.—To Amy Perrin.[1]

*Complaints regarding the conduct of Perrin—firm and courageous declaration by the Reformer of his resolution to persevere in his duty unto death.*

[*April* 1546.]

I should willingly have met you, Lord Captain, had it not appeared to me that a different course was expedient. You will have an opportunity of hearing the reason from me at a proper place and time. I could have wished, however, that you had appeared at the Consistory, by way of example to others. As in that respect you did not do your duty, because you had perhaps not been warned, I desired you at least to be present at the close of the meeting to-day, that the Syndic Corna and I might there discuss the matter with you. What there was to prevent you I do not see. But this I wish you to consider, that we cannot enjoy weight for weight with an unequal balance; and if impartiality must be observed in the administration of human law, any departure from it cannot be tolerated in the Church of God. You

---

[1] Letter without date, of which the original French is lost. It is here reproduced from the Latin translation inserted in the collection of the published Latin letters of Calvin, with restoration of date, April 1546.

Amy Perrin, one of the earliest hearers of Farel and Froment at Geneva, contributed powerfully to the disenthralment and reformation of his native country. At one with the Reformers in the abolition of the ancient worship and in the proclamation of the new, which he regarded as the security for the independence of Geneva, he broke with them the moment they undertook to correct manners, after having reformed beliefs. He then became the head of that party of undisciplined children of Geneva, " who wished to live according to their own inclination, without suffering themselves to be restrained by the words of the preachers," and whose triumph led to the banishment of the ministers, (1538.) Commissioned, two years afterwards, to negotiate their recall, he appeared to be reconciled to Calvin, and to submit to the institutions of the Calvinistic discipline; but the submission could not be lasting, and we again find him, in 1545, along with Pierre Vandel and the two Bertheliers, at the head of the party that must needs continue to strive with the ministers, until their total defeat, (May 1555.) Of an irascible temperament, of easy and frivolous manners, Amy took pleasure in fêtes, and in appearing in public magnificently dressed. Being accused (see the preceding letter) of having taken part in unlawful dances, he refused to compear before the Consistory, incurred, with his wife, the just rigours of the Seigneury, and became the implacable enemy of Calvin, who, in a letter at once moderate and powerful, essayed in vain to bring him back to the path of obedience and duty.

yourself either know, or at least ought to know, what I am; that, at all events, I am one to whom the law of my Heavenly Master is so dear, that the cause of no man on earth will induce me to flinch from maintaining it with a pure conscience. I cannot believe that you yourself have any other end in view, but I observe that no one has his eyes wide enough open when the case is his own. As far as I am concerned, I desire, in this very matter, to consult not only the edification of the Church and your salvation, but also your convenience, name, and leisure; for how odious would be the imputation which is likely to fall upon you, that you were apparently free from and unrestrained by the common law, to which every one is subject? It is certainly better, and in accordance with my zeal for your welfare, to anticipate the danger than that you should be so branded. I have heard, indeed, what has proceeded from your house, viz., that I should take care lest I stir up a slumbering fire, lest what occurred before should again take place, in the course of the seventh year. But these speeches have no weight with me; for I did not return to Geneva either for the sake of leisure or of gain, nor will it again grieve me to be constrained to leave it. The convenience and safety of Church and State made me willing to return; and if measures are now being taken against me alone, I should wish it to be said, once for all, to all who think me troublesome, "What you do, do quickly." But yet, the unworthy treatment and ingratitude of some parties will not cause me to fail in my duty, and I will lay aside that devoted attachment to this place only with my last breath, of which I take God as my voucher. Nor will I ever so far yield to the humours of any other individual, as hereafter to dispense with his personal attendance. These observations do not refer to you, but to that member of your family that is nearest to you. Nor do I write them with the view of spreading quarrels, but that it may be manifest with what firmness I am about to proceed, whatever may happen. I am especially desirous to impress upon you the necessity of earnestly seeking to acquire the primary virtue of obedience to God, and respect for the common order and polity of the Church. May the Lord protect you by His own defence, and discover to you how greatly even the stripes of a sincere friend are to be preferred to the treacherous blandishments of others!—Adieu.

Your attached and sincere brother,

JOHN CALVIN.

[*Calv. Lat. Corresp.* Opera, tom. ix. p. 80.]

## CLXV.—To FAREL AND VIRET.[1]

Requests in favour of the faithful in France.

GENEVA, 1*st May* 1546.

This pious brother is a citizen of Uzés,[2] a place where many have been utterly ruined by the severity of the ungodly. They have all agreed to try whether any succour is to be found among the Germans. I replied, that I had somewhat greater hope to-day, in that our princes have shewn, by clear indications, their aversion from imprisoning. I had, besides, been reminded that there was a certain person at Worms, sent by the Dauphin, who makes many promises. I am, indeed, aware of the hollowness of courts, but there will be no harm in making trial. I should not have refused what they strenuously insisted upon, viz., that I should undertake this journey, were I not still a prisoner, so slow is the process of my convalescence. I hardly know what progress I have hitherto made towards recovery, unless that my sufferings are allayed.[3] I have, therefore, left

---

[1] Menaced by a common peril, and having equally to resist the pretensions of Charles V. to universal rule, the King of France and the Protestant Princes of Germany had resumed negotiations, that must seemingly issue in a lasting treaty. This treaty of alliance was for long the object of the prayers and the hopes of Calvin, who reckoned upon extracting from it advantageous results to the French Protestants, and an implicit toleration for churches until then subjected to the most violent persecutions. He pressed Farel and Viret, one or other, to repair to Germany, to hasten the progress of negotiations and determine the conditions of the alliance.

[2] Is this Uzés a small town of Languedoc, now comprised in the department of Gard? Beza and the historian of the martyrs furnish us with no information on this point.

[3] Desirous of rendering assistance to Calvin during his illness and recovery, the Seigneurs of Geneva decided upon allowing him an attendant at the public expense.—*Registers of Council,* 4th March 1546.

this duty to one of you. Whoever of you finds it convenient will provide the expenses. As you, Viret,[1] are on the eve of setting out for Berne, it is right that our friend Farel be relieved by you of this burden, if the Senate give its permission. But if you shall not be free to go, Farel himself, I know, will spare neither himself nor his age; certainly otherwise he will be absolutely indispensable. Wherefore, if leave of absence be denied to Viret, take care you do not fail, Farel, for I have almost given a pledge in your name to the brethren. It remains with you, therefore, to fulfil the pledge, even though it were given rashly. Moreover, because, from the present state of the kingdom, it would be in vain to ask of the King what he ought to do of his own accord, we have judged that he must at least be required to undertake the commission of inquiry. This, again, will be equivalent to interdicting the Parliaments from engaging in it. In the next place, he must be asked to nominate extraordinary impartial judges. If this is obtained, a great step will be made. To aim at anything beyond this would, as I said, be superfluous. If the Chancellor is disposed to favour us, all will be well.[2] But as he is timid and tardy, we must see to it that he is vigorously urged on. Accordingly, not less pains must be taken in these secondary matters than in those of prime importance. But abjuration is always to be expressly excluded; for we do the work of Satan, if we open up a path to the godly whereby they may be permitted to abjure Christ. I diligently commend the whole matter, first to Master James Sturm, whose authority in the conventions is of the highest order; in the next place to Bucer, that he may stimulate those whom he can; again to Sturm and Dr. Ulrich, that they may also interpose the weight of their personal influence. The affair itself will give you counsel. You are not, however, tyros. May the Lord

---

[1] Viret was on the point of repairing to Berne, in order to discuss certain matters relative to the ordinances of the Reformation in the Pays de Vaud.—Ruchat, vol. v. p. 298.

[2] After the disgrace of the Chancellor Poyet, this high office was filled by François Olivier, Seigneur of Louville, President of the Parliament of Paris. He resigned in 1550, and again became Chancellor in 1559, in order to give his sanction to the lamentable executions of Amboise, which he survived only for a short time.

prosper his journey who shall undertake this sacred cause.—
Yours,
JOHN CALVIN.

[*Lat. orig. autogr.—Library of Geneva.* Vol. 106.]


CLXVII.—To MADAME DE FALAIS.

Expression of Christian sympathy and condolence on occasion of the illness of M. de Falais.

FROM GENEVA, *this* 21*st of June* [1546.[1]]

MADAME,—Notwithstanding that the addition which you have made to your letter has marvellously saddened me, yet nevertheless it was kind to have informed me of it, for that will serve to bestir us, so that we may pray to God with so much the better heart, as danger is to be feared.[2] And, indeed, I had already heard somewhat thereof by Monsieur Dallein, and Master Peter Viret has confirmed it to me. Beside that in praying to God to look down with pity upon us in this strait, we must look patiently for an outlet such as He shall please to send; and whichsoever way He disposes thereof, that we may be prepared to bear with it in suchwise that it must effectually appear how obedient we are to Him. Bethink yourself, also, how by that wearisome sickness and so many relapses, our Lord admonishes you, before the blow, so to strengthen you, that you may not be taken by surprise, whatever may happen. However the event may be, I do well believe that for all that, although he may get the better of it, we must not count, neither he nor myself, upon a long sojourning here below. And possibly you also may very soon after follow us. But, after all, I do not give up hope of more gladsome news.

To conclude, Madame, after having humbly commended me to your good graces, I pray our good Lord to have ever His eye

[1] On the back, in the handwriting of M. de Falais: "Received the 22d July." This note, taken in connexion with the beginning of the next letter to M. de Falais, settles the date of the present one.

[2] M. de Falais was at the time dangerously ill.

upon you, and to make you know it by experience for your consolation, increasing in you all those graces with which His children ought to be enriched.

Your humble brother, servant, and old friend,

JOHN CALVIN.

My wife presents you her humble commendations.

[*Orig. autogr.—Library of Geneva.* Vol. 194.]

## CLXVIII.—To Farel.[1]

Excitement caused at Geneva by the Representation of a Play.

GENEVA, *4th July* 1546.

Our plays narrowly escaped being converted into tragedy. When the senate had asked my opinion, I said that I would make no reply unless concerning the common resolution of the brethren. The brethren having been heard, I replied, that for many reasons it did not seem to us expedient that the games should be proceeded with, and at the same time I explained the grounds of our opinion. I said, however, that we did not wish to oppose them, if the senate held out for them. When the day was coming on, Michael, (who had done so once before,) instead of preaching, inveighed against the actors; but so vehement was this second invective, that a concourse of

---

[1] Certain persons having obtained from the magistrate permission to act in public a *Morality*, entitled, *The Acts of the Apostles*, which had received the approbation of the ministers; one of them, named Michael Cop, less conciliatory than his colleagues, preached a very violent discourse in the church of St. Peter, and said that the women who should mount the theatre to act that farce, would be *shameless creatures.* These words stirred up a great tumult in the city, and Calvin required to put forth all his influence to quiet the agitation, and to preserve the life of his imprudent colleague.

The plays were celebrated in presence of Viret. "It is ordained," say the Registers of Council, " that booths be erected for our seigneurs, that they may comfortably witness the representation of the *Acts of the Apostles.*"—1st July 1546. It does not appear, however, that these representations were frequently repeated. "Upon the remonstrances of the ministers," we read in the Registers, "resolved to delay the representations of the theatre to a less calamitous time."—July 1546. Ruchat, vol. v. p. 313. The minister inculpated was not Abel Poupin, as Ruchat relates, but Michael Cop, as the Registers attest.

people straightway made towards me with loud shouts, threats, and what not. And had I not by a strong effort restrained the fury of some of them, they would have come to blows. I endeavoured in the second discourse to appease their exasperation, observing moderation, for I judged that he had acted imprudently in having at an unseasonable time chosen such a theme for declamation. But his extravagance was the more displeasing, since I could by no means approve of what he had said. He maintained it to be true; I firmly denied it. There were some of the brethren who encouraged the man in his obstinacy. About nine in the evening I was told that a hundred or thereabouts would meet on the following day in the council-room. I immediately called the brethren together: we came to the resolution that we ought to accompany Michael. He was hardly suffered to go out along with me. I bring him to the place of meeting; meanwhile I order the others to be sent for. His accusers indicate their refusal to speak while we are present; for they said they had no concern with me, beyond that they regarded me with reverence, and were therefore unwilling to enter into any dispute with me. I strenuously insist that the cause is common, until it appear that Michael has erred in his duty. We are ordered to withdraw to separate sides of the house; from the opposite party arise seditious shouts; they threateningly assert that they would have killed Michael were it not that they revered me. To restrain the tumult, he was detained in the council-room, but in a respectful manner. On the following day, by the favour of the Lord, we quieted all disturbance; for Abel,[1] by the esteem in which he is held, and I by my authority, prevailed with the actors. The senate, however, was on our side. I was so far displeased with it, that it was not more courageous and spirited, for as usual it behaved too timidly; the result is, that the games are now going on. Viret is present as a spectator, who has again returned, according to arrangement, with a view to restore our furious friend to sanity.[2]

[1] The minister, Abel Poupin, exerted his interest with the actors to appease the tumult excited by his colleague.

[2] It is seen by this instance, that Calvin was not so stern as to proscribe public

Of your brothers I hear absolutely nothing. There is with you one Elie Limousin by name, a native of Rochelle, who has now in a third letter asked me to certify to you what I have known of his former life. Pious people who come from that district declare that he was an upright man, and of honourable life, and also that he was unmarried when he removed thence to us. There is no reason therefore, why any suspicion of this nature should be a hindrance to his marriage. You will apologize for my not having replied to him, and also for having so cursorily gone over to you what perhaps demanded a longer discourse. Adieu, dearest brother in the Lord, and most sincere friend. Salute respectfully all the brethren; there is no salutation from any one here to you or them, as no one knew I was going to write except Nicolas, the father-in-law of a brother, who came in. May the Lord be ever present with you, and bless your sacred labours.

[*Calvin's Lat. Corresp.* Opera, tom. ix. p. 43.]

## CLXVIII.—To Monsieur de Falais.

Proposals of matrimony on behalf of Viret.

Geneva, 4*th July* 1546.

Monseigneur,—You see, by the date of the other letters, what a length of time they have lain by me since they were written, forasmuch as the bearer could not find means to fill his letter-case; whereof I wished to inform you, fearing that you might suppose that he had kept them up for such a length of time in his own hands. We are in great anxiety for news concerning you, on account of the rumour which is abroad. The Lord graciously vouchsafe that you may have matter wherewith to gladden us. Now, however, since the bearer has been tarrying for a while, I have taken upon me, Monsieur, to make a

---

games and amusements that harmonized with decency. "He himself made no scruple in engaging in play with the seigneurs of Geneva; but that was the innocent game of the *key*, which consists in being able to push the keys the nearest possible to the edge of a table."—Morus, quoted *Hist. de la Suisse*, vol. xi. p. 356.

request of you. You know that our brother Viret is about to marry. I am in as great anxiety about it as himself. We have plenty of wives here, both at Lausanne and at Orbe; but yet there has not hitherto appeared a single one with whom I should feel at all satisfied. While we have this matter in hand, I would beseech you earnestly, if you have remarked any one in your quarter who appears to you likely to suit him, that you would please let me know of it. I have not thought fit to apply to any other than yourself, seeing that every one has not the prudence which is herein required. You may reply to me, that I am at least acquainted with some one in your neighbourhood; but I shall not venture to breathe a word before having your opinion, which you can tell me in one word, for I shall hold your silence for a *non placet*.[1] I have not felt the least difficulty in addressing you privately in regard to this, although the subject may be rather delicate, for the necessity of the case would excuse me, were I even somewhat importunate, because there was no one else in whom it appeared safe to confide; and I am well aware that, for your part, knowing of how much consequence the marriage of such a man is for the Church of God, you would not spare yourself any pains therein. Indeed, I would not hinder your acting directly for him, supposing that a suitable party can be found there; but in regard to asking advice, I have taken for granted that you will allow me that liberty.

In conclusion, Monseigneur, after having commended me to your kind favour with such affection as that wherewith I love you, I pray our good Lord to have always a care of you, guiding you in suchwise that you may be more and more serviceable for the advancement of His glory.

Your servant, humble brother, and entire friend,

JOHN CALVIN.

[*Fr. copy—Library of Geneva.* Vol. 194.]

[1] Allusion to a sister of M. de Falais.

### CLXIX.—To Viret.

*Account of the steps taken relative to his marriage.*

*13th July* 1546.

Think of what you are going to do, and then write to me again what resolution you have come to. The more we inquire, the more numerous and the better are the testimonies with which the young lady is honoured. Accordingly, I am now seeking to discover the mind of her father. As soon as we have reached any certainty, I will let you know. Meanwhile, do you make yourself ready. This match does not please Perrin, because he wishes to force upon you the daughter of Rameau. That makes me the more solicitous about pre-occupying the ground in good time, lest we be obstructed by having to make excuses. To-day, as far as I gather, he will enter upon the subject with me, for we are both invited by Corna to supper. I will gain time by a civil excuse. It would tend to promote the matter if I, with your permission, should ask her. I have seen her twice; she is very modest, with an exceedingly becoming countenance and person. Of her manners, all speak so highly that John Parvi lately told me, he had been captivated by her. Adieu; may the Lord govern you by His counsel, and bless us in an undertaking of such moment.—Yours,

JOHN CALVIN.

[*Lat. orig. autogr.—Library of Geneva.* Vol. 106.]

### CLXX.—To Viret.

*Fresh details regarding the projects for his marriage.*

GENEVA, 15*th July* 1546.

Three days ago, towards the conclusion of supper, mention was made of your marriage, which I had foretold you would be the case. But Dominic Arlot, whose assistance I had employed, presently interrupted the conversation; for he said that the matter was completed. On hearing this our friend instantly sprung up from table, and, in his usual way, gave reins to his indignation; for, says he, his whole body shaking, "Will he then marry that girl of low connexions? Could there not be found for him in the city one of better family? Whoever have been the originators or abettors of this business, I regard them as vile and infamous. Of a brother and sister I am thus unwillingly compelled to speak." I, in reply, say, "I could not be the originator of it, inasmuch as the young lady was unknown to me. I acknowledge that I was a promoter of it, and, indeed, the principal one; but that the matter is finally settled, as Dominic has asserted, is not true, beyond this, that I have gone so far in it that to draw back would be dishonourable. In that there is nothing for me to be ashamed of." His fury was thus turned into laughter. But he again began to grow hot, because the matter had been concealed from him by you. He was especially inflamed with a foolish jealousy, because Corna confessed that you and he, while riding, had talked over the thing together. "Is it even so?" he proceeded to say to Corna, "Was it for this I attended him along with you, that he might in the most insulting manner shut out from his counsels the most attached friend he has in the world? [for] I would cheerfully prefer him to myself."

I objected that he himself drew a false conclusion, since you had not disclosed your mind even to Farel. He was, therefore, again pacified, though he talked of the daughter of Rameau, whom he extolled in an extraordinary manner. I nodded assent to all the encomiums, that I might remain firm in regard to the other party.

Consider, now, whether it be expedient for you to come into the city disengaged. For there will be a hateful apologizing, if they proceed to obtrude her upon you. I know how dangerous even it may be to give a promise before the natural disposition of the girl has been ascertained. I am full of anxiety, nor can I easily clear a way for myself. I think, however, that this course would not be ridiculous. Suppose you consent to my asking the young lady in your name, the condition being added, that before the betrothal takes place, you are to meet her, that we may give some certain promise. They will thus not dare to press you. Write in return, therefore, by the earliest possible messenger what your views are, although, at the same time, I give it as my advice that you should not delay long, but come on an early day. Of the lady, I hear nothing that is not highly pleasing. In her father and mother, also, there is nothing blameable. I am the more confirmed, when I see that our opponents have nothing to carp at beyond this, that it was impossible for them to frighten us from our purpose. There are some things about the daughter of Rameau which I fear; nevertheless, as it is your own affair you will be free to choose. I will never, however, allow that there is any man on earth who has greater concern about his own matters than I have about the present.

This youth came to us from Italy, with the view of giving his attention to sacred literature, if a situation had been found such as he had hoped for. But as he has been disappointed, he wished, before he returned home, to pay you a visit. I have observed in him a truly good disposition. You will say a few words to confirm him in the fear of the Lord, and in reverence for His teaching.—Adieu. May the Lord direct you by His counsel, and bless you in a recommendation of so much moment. Salute respectfully all the brethren.—Yours,

JOHN CALVIN.

Forgive me for not having, some time ago, sent to you this letter by our treasurer—I mean Bucer's, for, as the messenger brought it open, I thought that it had been already read by you and Farel. Afterwards, he reminded me that not even Toussain had read it. You will therefore send it to Farel, as soon as you shall have an opportunity. I am surprised that Bucer was not aroused by the murderous outrage so greatly to be execrated, which the Emperor perpetrated when he struck off the heads of the principal senators at Ratisbon. I am also surprised that he has made no mention of the incendiaries, but I set it down partly to his engagements. The other matter he has perhaps passed over on purpose, because he did not dare to commit everything to writing in these dubious times.

[*Lat. orig. autogr.—Library of Geneva.* Vol. 106.]

## CLXXI.—To Viret.

Same subject as the preceding.

[*July* 1546.]

Only say the word, the thing is settled. I should never have been in such haste, had I not been stimulated by so many remarkable testimonies. But nothing gave me a greater impulse than the desire to be freed from those embarrassments of which you are aware.

Adieu, again.—Yours,

JOHN CALVIN.

[*Lat. orig. autogr.—Library of Geneva.* Vol. 106.]

## CLXXII.—To Viret.[1]

Breaking off of the match treated of in the preceding letters.

GENEVA, 25*th July* 1546.

What I wrote to you, by the treasurer, regarding the settlement of the matter, was told to me by Peter Ursier, whom I was then employing as negotiator; because I was unwilling to say anything myself, until I had received a more definite commission. But after reading your letter, I waited on the father and daughter, that I might be absolutely certain of success. As soon, however, as reference was made to a change of residence, the father took exception to it, on the ground that something different had been promised him. I said that no promise to that effect had been made with our knowledge; and, moreover, that I had carefully enjoined Peter Ursier not to cajole them by

---

[1] The project of marriage, developed in the two preceding letters, not having been realized, Viret turned his attention in another direction; and a passage in his will, preserved in the Archives of Geneva, informs us that he espoused, in his second marriage, Elizabeth Laharpe, daughter of a French refugee of Lausanne. This marriage was celebrated in October or November 1546, and the nuptial benediction was pronounced by Calvin himself, who, in a subsequent letter, (of the 3d December,) makes allusion to the journey which he had accomplished, in order to be present at the nuptials of his friend.

such promises. I pointed out how absurd it would be if we were to leave our churches to follow whither our wives called us; that a marriage consummated under such a condition would be an unhappy, because an unholy, alliance, that would not pass without punishment falling on both you and the girl; finally, that you would never be prevailed upon to afford the first example of so disgraceful a practice, and, therefore, that it was in vain to make the request. I added, that Lausanne was not so far distant from this as to prevent his daughter from being with him as often as might be necessary; that it would, likewise, be more satisfactory to have daily to congratulate his absent daughter than constantly to see and hear her weeping and bewailing the cruelties of her husband, which he observed was the case with so many. He requested space for deliberation, and, at the end of three days, he replied, that he was unwilling to send his only daughter from home. I felt greatly indignant at being so deluded by the folly of those in whom I trusted. I restrained myself, however, and dissembled my anger. But I do not need to offer any more lengthened excuse to you, as I am free from all blame. We may accordingly turn to some other quarter. Christopher spoke to me of a certain widow, who, he asserts, pleases him admirably. If such is the case, I am at rest, and leave it. But if not, indicate your mind. We shall very shortly, also, have a messenger from Strasbourg.—Adieu, brother, and most sincere friend. Salute all the co-presbyters very affectionately. May the Lord preserve you all safe, and direct you by His Holy Spirit even to the end.—Yours,

JOHN CALVIN.

Excuse me for not writing by the female servant of Petronilla, for I was not then fully aware of the state of the case; in other words, there was still a gleam of hope.

[*Lat. orig. autogr.—Library of Geneva.* Vol. 106.]

## CLXXIII.—To Farel.

Violence of the family of Amy Perrin—declamations of the wife of Froment against the ministers of Geneva.

GENEVA, [1st *September* 1546.]

Although the letter was not in every respect to my mind, for I was afraid that its undue harshness might hurt so delicate a stomach, I took care to have it forwarded, but in such a way that he should not know that I had seen it.[1] For this person conveyed it to his house as if it had been intrusted by you to himself. Should he thunder after his peculiar fashion, his bolts will die away in mere clatter. I not only appear before him, but almost obtrude myself upon him; only, I observe a mean, that I may keep in mind the place I hold; nor is this done on my own account, but because the man, being accustomed to adulation, would abuse my modesty, to the derision of Christ. I therefore despair of him, unless God apply a remedy. His wife is an unnatural fury. The widow N. is so shamelessly wanton, that you would say she is quite youthful. Then, having an evil conscience, she is excited by every word that is spoken before the congregation, and discharges upon us at home the venom she harbours. She has manifested towards you, however, marvellous good-will; for she took to her house your two nephews, when they were dangerously ill, and treats them as her own sons. This kind office deserves a liberal meed of thanks, which you will not omit to convey to her, whenever a messenger shall present himself. She is so opposed to all of us, that I believe Cæsar[2] himself is not more of an enemy; and yet, I confess I do not know what cause is to be assigned for this, unless that she shamelessly undertakes the defence of all her crimes.

[1] At the request of Calvin, Farel had written a letter to Amy Perrin, in order to calm his resentment, and lead him back to the good path. The message of Farel, like that of Calvin himself, was without effect, and the quarrel between the Reformer and his old friend, now his adversary, became daily more confirmed and violent.

[2] A term frequently employed by Calvin to designate Perrin, with the adjunct of a derisive epithet,—*Cæsar our comedian*.

I am now going to give you a humorous story. The wife of Froment[1] lately came to this place. She declaimed through all the shops, and at almost all the cross-roads, against long garments. When she knew that I was aware of it, she excused herself by alleging that she had said with a smile, that we were either unbecomingly clothed, to the great detriment of the Church, or that you taught what was erroneous, when you said that false prophets could be distinguished by their long vestments. When I was rebutting so stale a calumny, she began to ascribe even to the Holy Spirit what she had directed against us. What is the meaning, said she, of that passage of the Gospel, " They will come to you in long garments ?" I replied, that I did not know where that sentence was to be found, unless, perhaps, it might occur in the gospel of the Manichæans; for the passage of Luke, xx. 45, is as follows : " Beware of the Scribes, who desire to walk in long robes," but not, " They will come to you," &c., which she had interpolated from Matthew vii. [15.] Feeling that she was closely pressed, she complained of our tyranny, because there was not a general license of prating about everything. I dealt with the woman as I should have done. She immediately proceeded to the widow of Michael, who gave her a hospitable reception, sharing with her not only her table, but her bed, because she maligned the ministers. I leave these wounds untouched, because they appear to me incurable until the Lord apply His hand. We are to celebrate the Supper on the next Lord's-day. You may thus form a judgment of the straits by which I am encompassed. Would that it could be celebrated without me, even on condition that I should creep to you on my hands ! I wish that the verse of Terence would occur to your brothers, " To lose in time is to make gain." I have admonished them, but they do not make the haste I wished. They may bear, however, for a short time the delay that has taken place, although it is disagreeable to us.—Adieu, brother and most sincere friend. Salute respectfully, in my name, all the brethren, your family, and the godly citizens. May the

---

[1] See note 1, vol. i. p. 319. It appears, from this passage, that Froment was not at that time settled in Geneva. He was called thither a short time afterwards to assist François Bonivard in digesting the Chronicles of the city.

Lord preserve you, and always direct you by His Spirit! Amen.

[Calvin's *Lat. Corresp.* Opera, vol. ix. p. 38.]


## CLXXIV.—To Farel.

*Calvin's indisposition—literary labours—apparent reconciliation with Perrin and his family.*

GENEVA, 2d *October* 1546.

Not to beguile you by a vain hope, I may say that I do not think I shall come to your place before winter; for having once experienced the inconvenience of a voyage, I shall not venture again to commit myself to the waters. A good part of the journey would thus fall to be accomplished on foot, for the jolting of a horse is not only hurtful to me, but the rubbing also is dangerous. I am not acquainted with the physician of whom you speak, nor do I rightly understand what druggist you blame, unless, as I conjecture, you hint at Francis. What Textor may now think I do not know, except that he was too stringent in his prescriptions. For by involving himself in the lawsuits of his father, he has woven, in his native place, a Penelope's web that will have no end. Meanwhile, you see him complaining that he was deprived of my advice. But this peevishness of the good man must somehow or other be tolerated by us. As you exhort me to write, I wish I had more leisure occasionally, and more robust health. I have now, however, set myself in earnest to the Epistle to the Galatians.[1] I am not free in the matter of publication, as far at least as the Epistles of Paul are concerned. You once heard from me when I was at Strasbourg, that Wendelin laid me under obligations by services of such a nature, that I should be constrained to charge myself with ingratitude unless

---

[1] The Commentary on the four Epistles of St. Paul to the Galatians, the Ephesians, the Philippians, and the Colossians, were not published until 1548, by the bookseller Girard, of Geneva. Is there a previous edition of the Commentary on the Galatians? We are not aware of any.

I offered this work to him. For at the time of my greatest straits, he expended on my behalf above forty golden pieces; and he was not less prompt in his assistance in taking charge of my domestic affairs, than if I had hired him for the express purpose of superintending them. I am, therefore, now not at liberty to refuse him the Epistles. If I should write anything else, it will rather be published here, and yet Des Gallars could find no one to undertake to bring out two short treatises he had composed. Before, however, I subject my writings to any risk, I shall retain a copy. I left off for a time a short treatise, *De Scandalis*,[1] that I had begun, because the style did not flow so freely as I wished, nor have I a mind to resume it, until I shall have completed the Commentary on the Epistle to the Galatians. I had lately some conversation with our friend Perrin. If he perform what he promised, matters will not be at the very worst.[2] Penthesilæa, while in her outward deportment she affects a wonderful friendship, rages within doors in a terrible manner. I observe that you have written to her. I shall call for her on the earliest opportunity. I shall then discover what effect your letter has had.—Adieu, brother and most sincere friend. May the Lord be ever present with you, always protect you, and render your labours prosperous! I wrote to the ministers of Berne. If you desire to know the contents of the letter, Viret, I think, retained a copy. My wife reverently salutes you, as also Des Gallars, Feron, my brother, (for since I received yours I have not seen the others.) The best greeting to the brethren and friends, and to your whole family.—Yours,

JOHN CALVIN.

I had no talk with Perrin about your letter. I was unwilling to touch that sore, until it should have been somewhat molli-

---

[1] This, one of the most remarkable of the works of Calvin, appeared only in 1550.

[2] This apparent reconciliation was without satisfactory result. Perrin could not tolerate, nor Calvin sacrifice, the right of censure vested in the Consistory, and which the excesses of the *Libertins* daily rendered more necessary. " Complaints to the Council by M. Calvin regarding the dissoluteness of the youth, there being nothing more common in the city than acts of debauchery and licentiousness."—*Registers of Council*, 11th October 1546.

fied by the lapse of time. If there is any news, provided it be certain, let us immediately know, I pray you.

[*Lat. orig. autogr.—Library of Geneva.* Vol. 106.]

## CLXXV.—To Monsieur de Falais.

*Recurrence to the matrimonial projects of Viret—explanations on various subjects.*

From Geneva, *this* 4*th of October* 1546.

Monseigneur,—While hour after hour I was on the outlook for James on his return from Lyons, to reply to you by him, I was amazed the other day when my brother told me that he had passed through without speaking with me. And now it happens that I must write you very much in haste, because of the sudden departure of the bearer. It is very true I was told of it yesterday, but it was at eight o'clock at night, when my megrim troubled me so severely, that it was with great pain I could open my mouth. This morning I thought that he would be gone away, until, at the end of the sermon, he told me that he would wait a quarter of an hour to oblige me; wherefore, I must beg of you to excuse the brevity.

As to the affair of the individual for whose sake I have made the request, he has replied to me, thanking you very humbly for the kind affection you have shewn him; that he would desire above all things to have communication with the party, fearing lest, from the want of a mutual understanding, they might not assort so well together in future. Besides, while these troubles last, it appeared to him that the journey could not be well undertaken, and I am much of that opinion; for thereby there would be some danger of a long protraction of the affair, and this is by no means your intention, which I find very reasonable. As for the rest, there is no sort of hindrance arising from health; but I find this to be an annoyance, that a matter, uncertain at any rate, should be kept for so long in suspense, although I do not find fault with his request, considering the reasons which he has alleged to me for it, that it is necessary that the wife he shall take may be informed beforehand of some domestic charges which he is obliged to bear. Besides, love requires previous acquaintance, and the household affairs never go on well without a private mutual understanding, and a settlement of the conditions required on both sides. The mischief is, the waiting for that length of time ; and besides, I do not see any great object to be gained by it. I pray God that, in any event, He would well order it.

About the book,[1] it strikes me that I have told you enough already of what occurred to me, and therefore I do not comprehend wherefore you ask my opinion anew, unless it might be to shew it to him. Besides, he will take it better, methinks, if it may please you, to shew him the passage of my letter on that point, the more that I speak therein more freely, not knowing the author. Nevertheless, if it appears to you that there is somewhat more to be said, when you shall please to inform me of it, I will follow your advice.

Furthermore, Antony Maillet has written to me, that he had spoken to Peter Telsen, and tells me that the twelve crowns which Master Valerand has disbursed, are to be refunded to you, although I need not be in very much haste about it, but suit my own convenience. I know not whether he has done so by mistake, but if he has still twelve crowns to pay, Peter Telsen must have laid out twice as much as he ought ; for I have sent you twelve crowns by my brother, the which you have told me you had received. Notwithstanding, if Peter Telsen have failed to do so, I would not that you should be the loser, albeit I know not for what purpose he can have employed the money ; but as to that, it will be my business to settle with him. Before saying a word about it, I was desirous to know the truth. I pray you, then, that you may please let me know whether, besides the twelve crowns which my brother returned to you, there has a still further sum of like amount gone out of your purse. Seeing that they have roused so much indignation down there, I see not what hinders you to publish your *Apology*, and it seems to me very fit that you do so. Nevertheless, I say

---

[1] M. de Falais had sent Calvin a theological work by a certain Denis de la Roche, requesting his opinion of it.

what I think about it without prejudice. The rest remains still in the pen, for the bearer has not given me a long enough time. And thus, Monseigneur, after commending me humbly to your kind favour and that of Madame, I pray our good Lord to have you always in His keeping, vouchsafing you grace in suchwise ever to walk, that He may be ever more and more glorified in you. I render thanks to Him for that He hath set you up again, but I beseech of Him to increase you in strength daily, until you are completely restored. My wife presents her humble commendations.

Your servant, humble brother, and entire friend,
JOHN CALVIN.

[*Fr. Copy—Library of Geneva.* Vol. 194.]

## CLXXVI.—To MADAME DE FALAIS.

Sad communication to be made to M. de Falais—promise to send several discourses.

FROM GENEVA, *this* 19*th of October* [1546.]

MADAME,—Forasmuch as you informed me by your last, that you sent me therewith the letter of Monsieur de Fresne, I feared that the bearer had not done his duty in taking proper care of what had been committed to him. But he has assured me that he had received nothing else but what he has delivered to me. Wherefore, I guess that it has been left behind by neglect. I believe that your intention in sending it to me, was in order to have my advice how to inform Monsieur of it.[1] Now, as he must be made aware of the news, I could have no hesitation in opening up somewhat of the business, whenever he shall be in a good humour, and then telling him all about it. Except when he is ailing, he is not a man that lets himself be overcome by sadness, and who does not know how to make a profitable improvement of the grace which God vouchsafes him for his consolation.

[1] Allusion to the death of one of the sisters of M. de Falais, which they had not ventured to communicate to him.

He has put me in mind that you were complaining lately of Monsieur enjoying himself all alone in the reading of my Commentary.[1] You request me also to have some thought of those who only understand French, that they also may partake, and you ask for my sermons. Well, if there had been a demand for putting them forth, I would indeed have set about it in good earnest; but that will not be this year. However, if God bestow grace to finish the Epistle to the Galatians, which ought to be summary, I have the framework of something of a treatise which shall speak French as well as Latin, that may prove somewhat useful, as I hope.

After having affectionately commended me to your kind favour, and presented the humble salutations of my wife, I beseech our good Lord to have you in His safeguard, making you more and more serviceable for the advancement of His kingdom.

Your servant and humble brother,

JOHN CALVIN.

[*Fr. orig. autogr.—Library of Geneva.* Vol. 194.]


## CLXXVII.—To MONSIEUR DE FALAIS.

Congratulations on his convalescence—uncertainty of prospects in Germany—confidence in the all-powerful protection of God.

FROM GENEVA, *this* 19*th of October* 1546.

MONSEIGNEUR,—I believe that you have received my last letter, by which you will have understood that yours had been delivered by Alexander, but somewhat tardily. I give thanks to our good Lord affectionately for the news which Madame has communicated to me of the recovery of your health. I hope that it may please Him, who has begun so well, that in the spring you will feel yourself so nimble that you will not know how to restrain your merriment, so as to make up for past time. We shall look for that, and for all else, as it shall please Him of His infinite goodness to allot, having good ex-

---

[1] The Commentary on the First Epistle of Saint Paul to the Corinthians, dedicated to M. de Falais.

pectance that the rage which the Court of *Malines* has vented upon you will pass off in smoke.[1]

I believe that it will soon be time to sound a retreat for both camps.[2] I pray God so to direct the whole that the upshot may prove for the advancement of His own honour. I am better pleased that He makes war upon that unhappy tyrant with His own hand, than otherwise. For if we were to attempt anything of importance, I should always fear the fatal consequences of the presumption. We have never yet heard what has become of that harebrained fellow, the Count de Buren,[3] whether he has passed on with his army, or whether he has been driven back. Howsoever it may be, *it is not the multitude nor the arm of flesh that can prevail.*

Master Valerand is returning; you shall know better from him the whole state of your affairs. Howbeit, I see no other means, unless you yield somewhat on your side, until God opens up a better. You will know who this bearer is, and his purpose in going to you. Because I believed his determination to be right, I have not desired to turn him back from it.

To conclude, Monseigneur, after my humble commendation to your kind favour, I shall pray our good Lord to have ever His hand stretched out to guide you by His grace.

Your servant, humble brother, and entire friend,

JOHN CALVIN.

My wife also entreats to be always humbly commended to your kind favour.

[*Fr. orig. autogr.—Library of Geneva.* Vol. 194.]

---

[1] The confiscation of the property of M. de Falais had been pronounced by the Court of Malines. That decree had been submitted to the confirmation of the Emperor.

[2] The sentence which put the Elector of Saxony and the Landgrave of Hesse to the ban of the empire, 20th July 1546, was the signal for war in Germany. The Imperial army, and that of the Protestant Princes, observed one another for several months, on the banks of the Danube, without the one being able to obtain any decisive advantage over the other. But the troops of Charles the Fifth were decimated by want and sickness, while there was an overabundance in the camp of the confederates.

[3] Maximilian d'Egmont, Count de Buren, a valiant and adventurous captain. He brought a powerful reinforcement to Charles the Fifth from the Netherlands, and he executed that difficult operation with the most happy success.

## CLXXVIII.—To Monsieur de Falais.

Excuses for Viret—uses of Sickness—various rumours concerning the War in Germany—explanations on the subject of the Supper.

*From Geneva, this* 16*th of November* 1546.

Monseigneur,—Although I was expecting a letter from you from day to day, I could not let this messenger go away without writing, to make some reply to your last. I shall begin upon the subject of the little book which you sent me. Having read my answer, and the opinion I had of it, you have mentioned to me the name of the author; and because he is somewhat opinionative, you request me to let you know my mind about it, in order that you may tell him on his return the opinion you have formed. Your words are these, " The author is Denis de la Roche, who has requested of me that I would send it you privately. In consequence of this I feel puzzled how to set about finding fault, for I fear he will suspect that the criticism comes from you, and he is a little proud, and withal tenacious of his own views. Inasmuch as you have known him longer than I, write me your advice, so that upon his return I may be able to tell him the judgment which I have come to, when he shall ask me for it."

You must hold me excused in this matter. I know not how to proceed therein, since I have already shortly stated to you my opinion in regard to it. If you ask me for a lengthened discussion, I could not do it so well as when it was fresh in my recollection; and indeed I have doubtless forgotten part of what I formerly wrote. What made me doubtful as to your drift, was that it seemed to me you were asking me to do over again what I had already done. And even now I do not comprehend wherefore you would have a new declaration of my opinion, unless you were dissatisfied with the first. It would be very difficult for me to discuss in detail the things which have escaped me. For I have retained but a confused idea of the general argument, and of some points here and there.

As concerns the marriage in reference to which I have put you in requisition,[1] I beseech you, Monseigneur, to believe what I shall tell you, for I shall recount the pure truth without any dissimulation whatever. The reason which induced me to write you about it was, that a party had been proposed here who was nowise suitable for him. But on account of the forwardness of some of those who had meddled in the affair, we had very great difficulty in getting the proposal set aside. And so, to break the blow, it was my earnest desire to have found some one in another quarter; for there would have been less envy and jealousy had he taken one from a distance, as we have already had ample experience in the murmurs which some have made when we would not follow their leading-string. I assure you, however, that he has not been making indirect application elsewhere. But without reference either to her whom you kindly named in your reply, nor yet to any other, I have thought it advisable, under the circumstances of the case, to recommend the man to you. Then you know the first letter loitered long upon the way, before we had any news from you, which was the occasion of my writing again, and that at his own instance, although I did not comprehend very clearly why. For in the meantime, from what I have since learnt, he had a proposition from another quarter. Nevertheless, after receiving tidings from you, I communicated with himself, and the result was such as I have told you, without feigned civility or double-dealing. Since then, I have understood that the proposal about a widow was still under consideration, although to this hour I know not how it stands. And so far was I from meddling, that knowing in this town of a widow as well endowed as I could have wished for myself if God had so far afflicted me as to have deprived me of my helpmate,[2] and that there was a necessity for my marrying again; on considering the other proposals which were under consideration, I have not felt inclined to bring forward her name. And notwithstanding, I have no doubt whatever that it would prove an admirable match for him.

[1] For Peter Viret. See preceding letters to M. de Falais, pp. 49 and 60.

[2] Calvin lost his wife, Idelette de Bure, in the beginning of April 1549, and never married again. His Latin correspondence contains two beautiful and touching letters to Viret and to Farel (7th and 11th April) on that sad event. They will be found reprinted in this collection.

But all the more that I refrained from active friendly interference, it was sufficient for me to commit him to God, and to let the stream find its own channel. You see how I have thanked you without hypocrisy, now that I have set before you the difficulties that I have had here. And I do not think that there was any want of honesty in the man for whom I spoke; indeed I might venture to assure you of it. But purposes change in a few hours. Seeing the present position of matters, I did not like to communicate to him anything of what was contained in your letter. I shall not trouble you with long excuses; and besides, it is well that the thing has not taken wind. Wherefore, if you think fit, consider the whole matter as if it had never been mooted. Meanwhile, your goodwill toward me must not be buried out of mind, nor toward the man who is principally concerned in the affair. For I assure you that he was truly grateful for your interference, and I know that he has it imprinted on his heart, although it was attended with no result.

With regard to the money which has been laid out on account of our child, that you may not be further troubled about it, Antony Maillet will settle the amount. And now, please God, I shall do my duty, thanking you most affectionately that you have been pleased to have patience until the settlement could be made.

Since the *Apology* has not yet gone forth, it is very desirable to have the news which Master Valeran[1] may bring along with him. And, indeed, over and above the circumstance which has befallen in your particular case, the general declaration which the man has made against the whole cause, well deserves that the style should be altered, and that some additions be interwoven. And seeing that God has allowed you to wait so long, He will so end all as to instruct you the more certainly.

Although I have indeed heard of a man having been seized at Berne for poisoning and fire-raising, nevertheless, I have so little correspondence in that quarter, that I have heard nothing of it but upon common report. On which account I did not care to say much to you about it. If it be really so as has been re-

---

[1] Valeran Poulain, of Lille, who was at a later period minister of the French Church at Frankfort.

lated to you, I must acknowledge that it is a good thing that God is more concerned about my life than are my neighbours.

Although your weakness may be protracted, it is much that you go on steadily, though by slow degrees, in the way of amendment. And when I consider the complaint, I feel that there is still greater reason to be well content. Notwithstanding, we shall not give over praying to God that it would please Him to confirm you entirely, with thanksgiving that He has brought you back from the brink of the grave. Besides, I hope, from present appearances, that He is minded yet to make use of you in health, since He has employed you in sickness. For although laid powerless upon a bed, we are by no means useless to Him, if we testify our obedience by resigning ourselves to His good pleasure,—if we give proof of our faith by resisting temptation,—if we take advantage of the consolation which He gives us in order to overcome the troubles of the flesh. It is in sickness, especially when prolonged, that patience is most needful; but most of all in death. Nevertheless, as I have said, I confide in this good God, that after having exercised you by sickness He will still employ your health to some good purpose. Meanwhile, we must beseech Him that He would uphold us in steadfast courage, never permitting us to fall away because of lengthened on-waiting.

Howsoever doubtful the retreat of Renard[1] may be, it is nevertheless no small matter, that instead of reaching the point aimed at, which would have been his great advantage, he has made a crablike movement backwards. And from what we have heard, he has left behind the marks of the persecution of God's hand. I am much better pleased that God should cut off his finger than we his arm. Not that that is not still God's work, which He performs by us, but I always fear so much the effect of glory, that I rejoice the more when it is plainly the doing of the Lord. And the unhappy man has likewise still greater occasion to feel uneasiness at heart. Whatever may come of it, I think that I have only spoken the truth, after the news of his departure, in writing what follows :—Whither is he going? Whither is he gone? What will become of that

[1] The Emperor Charles V. See note 2, p. 64.

wicked man?—By thus driving him away God has at least lowered his pride.

A report is afloat, which troubles and plagues more than it astonishes me. It is that Maurice has entered into an understanding with him to ruin his own cousin and his father-in-law, and in the end to ruin himself;[1] for Satan must assuredly have got entire possession of him. We shall await, however, whatsoever shall please God, prepared to accept all that shall please Him.

Concerning the advice which you require of me, whether it were expedient to refresh the memory of the ambassadors: before I had an opportunity of writing to you, the time to do so had gone by; I therefore rather held my peace, not so much from forgetfulness as from this consideration: *Ne pluvia post messem.*

There is one point, however, that I think I have forgotten, namely, the complaint they make, that it appears I would shut up the body in the bread alone. I know not where they have dreamed that dream. In several treatises I speak of that matter, but chiefly in the *Institution*, in the *Catechism*, in the *Commentary on Corinthians*, and in the manner of administration of the Lord's Supper. In the *Supplication* I have only touched upon it very lightly. Besides that, I have written a little book upon the subject, in which I believe a reader of sound judgment will meet with nothing to find fault with. But here is their mistake: many think that we make no distinction between the sign and the truth signified, unless we separate them entirely, to make God like a mountebank, who exhibits delusive representations by sleight of hand. It is our duty, however, to proclaim, that this comes by the craft of Satan, who only seeks to bewilder the understanding, that he may render our labours of no avail. Let us therefore pray to God that He would bestow increase by His grace, so that our labour may not be in vain. Such examples ought to incite us thereto, and likewise to admonish us, not to think that we have done some great thing by merely having written.

---

[1] Maurice of Saxony, cousin of the Elector John Frederic, and son-in-law of the Landgrave of Hesse, unworthily betraying the cause of the Confederates, concluded a secret treaty with the Emperor, to whom he took the oath of fidelity, and who guaranteed to him in return the spoils of his father-in-law.

Monsieur, having presented the humble commendations of myself, as well as of my wife, to your kind favour, and also that of Madame, I pray our good Lord, that it would please Him ever to preserve you in His holy protection, strengthening you in all might by His Spirit, making His glory to shine forth in you ever more and more.

I beg to be excused for faults, for I have not been able to revise the present letter, being engrossed by headache with which I have been seized. Our friend and brother, Des Gallars,[1] also humbly commends himself to you, and sends you a distich which he has composed upon Renard. We greatly desire to have some news. If the war did not give holiday to the printing-presses, I would have sent Vendelin the *Galatians;* but since the *Corinthians* lie quiet in his desk, there is no need for my being in any hurry.

[*Fr. orig. autogr.—Library of Geneva.* Vol. 194.]

## CLXXIX.—To Monsieur de Falais.

### Consolations on the death of his sister.

FROM GENEVA, *this 20th of November* 1546.

MONSEIGNEUR,—The day before Camus arrived, I had written to you, as well as to others, by a young tailor of Picardy; but because I was not certain whether they had as yet informed you of the death of Madame your sister,[2] I did not venture to mention it. Now I have rejoiced, and have thanked God with my whole heart, perceiving by the letter of Madame that you had at once taken your stand upon the point whereon I would have founded my principal argument, if I had wished to console you. And, indeed, you have much occasion for gratitude on account of the grace which God has vouchsafed to her, and to you also. For seeing that her husband had waxed so

---

[1] Nicolas des Gallars, of Paris, (M. de Saules,) the friend and secretary of Calvin, and one of the most distinguished ministers of Geneva. He was sent as pastor to the Church at Paris in 1557, reappointed in 1560 to the French Church of London, assisted the following year at the conference at Poissy, was named minister of the Church of Orleans, and became, in 1571, preacher to the Queen of Navarre. We have several of his works mentioned by Senebier, *Hist. Litt.*, tom. i. p. 341.

[2] Hélène de Falais. She had married Adrien de L'Isle, Seigneur de Trénoy.

cold, the good lady would have been in an unhappy captivity had she remained longer in the world, and would only have languished her life away. On your part, you would not have had it in your power to lend her a helping hand, nor to solace her sorrows; and so you never could have thought of her without regret and vexation. God, therefore, has had pity upon you and her, in thus providing, and above all, in preventing the dangers into which she might have fallen in a long career, by reason of the frailty which is in us. And we have yet a better ground of further consolation, that it will not be long ere we find ourselves together again. Meanwhile, let us think of preparing ourselves to follow her, for the time will soon come. But I like much better to congratulate you, seeing that our Lord has already put these things in your heart, than to labour in recalling them to your memory. The other news which Camus has told me about you, has also cheered me to await the time when God will bring to pass what He has put into so good a train.

Monseigneur, after humble commendations to your kind favour, and having presented the humble remembrances of my wife, I pray our good Lord to have you ever in his safeguard, to strengthen you in body and in spirit, so as always to make you more abound in His service.

Your humble servant and bounden friend,
JOHN CALVIN.

I assure you that you make me desire the arrival of the spring-time more than I would otherwise have done. Our brother Des Gallars commends himself also very humbly to your kind favour.

[*Fr. orig. autogr.—Library of Geneva.* Vol. 194.]

### CLXXX.—TO MADAME DE FALAIS.

Assurances of affection for herself and her husband.

FROM GENEVA, *this 20th of November* 1546.

MADAME,—Having been made aware that Monseigneur had been informed of the death of his sister, I have only given him one word on the subject, knowing beforehand from yourself that he has no need of long consolation, seeing that God, without human means, has put into his heart that which cannot fail to alleviate his sadness.

As for my promise, to which you hold me bound, I shall discharge myself of it, when God shall have vouchsafed me the means wherewith to do so. But I am astonished that you should even hint at the reward which my said Lord intends for me, as if I were looking to that, and had not other considerations in the discharge of my duty to him. The love and reverence which I may well bear toward him in our Lord are so strong, that I am very sorry that I cannot devote myself more to his and your service, to shew what is in my heart. Howbeit, I beseech you not to take amiss what I have now said, for I have had no other feeling than the fear that you may not place such reliance upon me as I desire. Besides, I do not mean to make any complaint which deserves a reply; for it is quite enough for me that you have neither entertained a doubt nor a suspicion which has induced you to mention it.

Now therefore I shall make an end, after having humbly commended me to your kind favour. I pray our good Lord to have you always in His holy protection, guiding and governing you after His own good will, so as to glorify His holy name in you.

Your humble servant and good brother for ever,

JOHN CALVIN.

[*Fr. orig. autogr.—Library of Geneva.* Vol. 194.]

## CLXXXI.—To VIRET.

Statement of the expense of a visit to Lausanne, on the occasion of Viret's marriage—ecclesiastical difficulties at Berne.

GENEVA, 3d *Dec.* 1546.

Two letters of Bucer were delivered to me after a short interval. I send both of them to you, although they may contain almost nothing which you have not learned from other sources. With regard to the King of France, I think that he will shortly be brought to give some assistance with money to our party—the only thing that is sought from him. It is, moreover, in the highest degree, his interest to distract the attention of Charles by another war.[1] I have enjoined Peter Textor to pay to you sixteen crowns; for although I had ten with me when I came to the marriage, it escaped my memory. But here is a greater lapse of memory; when I had found them laid aside in my desk, I stood still for some time, not knowing whether I had ever seen them before. Raymond came upon me, who reminded me of the fact, that he had given them to me by order of Antony Maillet. You will therefore add this sum to the former. In the other six [crowns], I am afraid that I have made a mistake; for they may possibly belong to my brother. For as a teacher of Orleans was in his debt, he arranged that payment should be made by the son of Bruno. He had lately received five [crowns.] You will therefore retain these until I shall have learned with certainty from Saint André, whether they ought to be given to you or to my brother.

Sulzer lately wrote to me that matters had reached an extremity.[2] He implores our aid. I consulted with the brethren. As we could discover no plan of procedure in circumstances so perplexed, and almost desperate, I repaired to Nyon. I became aware that they had committed much more grievous errors than the letters contain any mention of. They are not, in my opinion, fighting for a cause that is good in every respect. All see that their proceedings are preposterous; and yet when we also see that everything is going to ruin, with what conscience shall we be silent? I asked Nicolas,[3] whether he thought that a letter from us would be of any service? He gave a

---

[1] This diversion, dictated to the King of France by sound politics, was not effected, and Francis I. remained a peaceable spectator of events, whose necessary tendency was to secure, by the defeat of the Protestant party in Germany, the ascendency of Charles V. in Europe.

[2] The ministers of Berne were divided by incessant disputes on the subject of the Supper. Sulzer and certain of his colleagues inclined to the Lutheran view, which Erasme Ritter combated; and by an abuse of power, that was not uncommon at that period, the Seigneury of Berne claimed to determine by itself the sense of the controverted dogma, the settlement of which ought to have been remitted to a Synod.—Ruchat, tom. v. pp. 225, 226.

[3] The senator, Nicolas de Zerkinden, friend of Calvin and prefect of Nyon.

trembling and hesitating consent to our writing. Should a messenger present himself in good time, I wish that you also would intimate your opinion ; thereafter consider whether it be not time to press for obtaining a Synod.

Adieu, brother, and most sincere friend, along with your wife, whom you will respectfully salute in the name of all ours, as well as James and the rest.—Yours,

JOHN CALVIN.

[*Lat. orig. autogr.—Library of Geneva.* Vol. 106.]

## CLXXXII.—To Monsieur de Falais.

*Military movements in Switzerland—policy of the Cantons in reference to the Emperor.*

FROM GENEVA, *this 8th of December* 1546.

MONSEIGNEUR,—I have nothing to write you at present, except that we are waiting to see what will be done by the Swiss.[1] All is in readiness at Berne as if to start at any moment,—the captain, his council, officers, soldiers, chosen and commissioned ; a second order sent, to be ready to march, with artillery and baggage. Their army consists of ten thousand men. I believe they would not have delayed so long, if there had not been an impediment which holds them as it were tied by the leg. For it is now about a year since all the Cantons agreed that none should leave the country to engage in war, without the consent of the rest. Now there is fear that the Papists may be urged to invade the country while it is depopulated, under colour of breach of treaty ; which, if the King of France had only thrown in a word, would have happened a long time ago,—namely, had he called the Papists to enter his

[1] The Roman Catholic and Reformed Cantons, solicited, the former by the emperor, the latter by the Protestant princes, to take part in the struggle of which Germany was the theatre, had both observed a strict neutrality. But the Seigneury of Berne having received information that military movements were taking place in Franche-Comté, then under the rule of the Spaniards, summoned ten thousand men to arms, and occupied the passes of the Jura. That measure, which arose out of the pressure of circumstances, would perhaps have brought about a division among the confederates, and serious complications from without, if the treachery of the Elector Maurice had not hastened on the course of events in Germany.—John de Müller, *Hist. de la Confédération Suisse*, continuation of M. Vulliemin, tom. xi. p. 292.

service, which ours would have readily agreed to do. Thus would the one side have spoken German to Charles, the others Italian or Picard.

I fear indeed that there must be a want of good management as well in that as in other things. Thereby are we so much the more admonished to pray God that He by His infinite goodness would be pleased to supply so many shortcomings. True it is, that the ignorant are apt to judge foolishly. But however that may be, every one is amazed that they are so long          ,[1] without putting forth an effort. For it looks as if God were holding out the hand to us, as much as to say—enter in. And in letting the time slip by, we only invigorate *him* who is already almost desperate. Let us pray, therefore, and seeing that it pleases God to make trial of our patience for our good, let us be content with what He sends us, never growing weary of serving Him, on any account whatsoever.

There has been murmuring of late on account of some appointment. They would indeed need wondrous masons to complete the building. But I fear that our people, or some of them at least, may let themselves be so far led away as to entertain the proposals, which would be to replace the enemy, not only in the exercise of his former tyrannous sway, but even of that to which he has always aspired. Yet, inasmuch as I feel assured that it will not so happen unless God shall be altogether exasperated against us, I trust that He will avert so great a danger. For I have no doubt that He looks rather upon His own work in us, than upon our sins and shortcomings, that He may have pity on us.

And now, Monseigneur, having humbly commended me to your good favour, and that of Madame ; having also presented the commendations of my wife, and of our neighbours, I pray God of His goodness to keep you always in His protection, and to make you feel more and more the joy of His help.

Your servant and humble brother, and ever bounden friend,
JOHN CALVIN.

[*Fr. orig. autogr.—Library of Geneva.* Vol. 194.]

[1] A word effaced in the original.

## CLXXXIII.—To Madame de Budé.[1]

Calvin exhorts this lady to leave France, and retire with her family to Geneva.

*This* 20*th* . . . . 1546.[2]

MADAME,—Howbeit that I have occasion to praise God for the great zeal and constancy He has vouchasfed to you, as I have heard from the bearer, yet, believing that my exhortation might not be superfluous to you, in the midst of such diversified trials and conflicts, I was unwilling to forego writing you some words by him, and, above all, to help you to come to a determination upon the point on which you are still somewhat doubtful; that is, as to your retiring hitherward that you may serve God in peace of conscience. Were it possible for you to discharge your duty where you are, I would by no means advise you to stir. But I am well aware in what captivity you are held. If God had given you strength and constancy to prepare for death, and not to flinch for any fear of the danger wherein you are, there would be nothing better than to keep that grace in exercise. But if you feel that the weakness of the flesh gets the mastery, and hinders you from doing your duty, seeing that

---

[1] The original letter is without address. But it is generally believed that it was addressed by Calvin to the widow of the celebrated William Budé, great-grandson of the secretary to King Charles V., and one of the most learned personages of the period of the revival of letters. William Budé having declared in his will that he wished to be buried without ceremony, this circumstance led to the supposition that he had died in the faith of the reformed. His widow not being able to make free profession of her faith at Paris, was about to settle at Geneva, on the solicitation of Calvin, (June 1549.) She was accompanied by her daughter and three of her sons, Louis, Francis, and John de Budé, who held a distinguished rank in the republic. The best known of the three brothers is John de Budé, Sieur de Vérace, the particular friend of Calvin and of Théodore de Bèze. He was received an inhabitant of Geneva the 27th June 1549, burgess the 2d May 1555, member of both Councils in 1559, fulfilled several important missions to the Protestant princes of Germany, and died in 1589, after having rendered distinguished services to his new country, and thereby added fresh lustre to his family, whose descendants still live at Geneva.—Galiffe, *Notices Généalogiques des Familles Genèvoises*, tom. iii. p. 83, *et seq.*

[2] *On the back*, in another handwriting,—" Of 46. I think that this letter must be to Madame Budé."

your conscience must needs be troubled and in continual torment, the only way is to seek a suitable remedy. For it is no slight perplexity, yea, even agony, to feel ourselves blameable in a matter of so great moment ; yea, and that the evil continues to such an extent, that we can make no end of offending God. Although many deceive themselves in this matter, making themselves believe that it is but a trifling fault to defile themselves with superstitions which are repugnant to the Word of God, and derogate from His honour, I reckon that His honour, to whom we owe everything, is so precious to you, that it is felt to be a subject of intolerable regret to you to offend against it daily, as you are constrained to do at present. I do not doubt, therefore, but that you have a special desire to escape out of such wretchedness, and that until you do, you cannot but be in very great anxiety and sadness. Consider, now, whether this is not an unhappy condition, thus to linger for ever. I know, indeed, that there are many who reply to us, that we here are no more angels than themselves, and that we offend God even as they do ; which is true. But as the proverb says, " Sickness upon sickness is not health." If, then, we come far short in other respects, what need is there to increase our condemnation by adding to the rest this sin which is so grievous ; to wit, that of not giving glory to the Son of God, who became as nothing for our salvation ?

Besides, after you have done your best by dissimulation, to keep clear of the perils which surround you, you are not a whit better ; for the wicked are very sharp-sighted, and you will never content them but by an entire renunciation of God ; wherefore, you have no rest for the body any more than for the soul. And after declension from God, in order to comply with the world, you have derived no benefit from it, except that you languish as in a trance. You will ask me if, being come hither, you shall always have assured repose. I confess that you will not ; for while we are in this world, it is fitting that we should be like birds upon the branch. So it has pleased God, and it is good for us. But since this little corner is vouchsafed to you, where you may finish the remainder of your life in His service, if He so please, or profit more and more, and be confirmed in His word, in order that you may be more ready to endure persecutions, if it shall so please Him, it is not right that you refuse it. We have always to take care lest we be the cause of our own misfortune, and draw it down upon ourselves by not accepting the means of escape which God presents to us. I know that it is a hard thing to leave the country of our birth, most of all to a woman like yourself, of rank, and advanced in life. But you ought to overcome such difficulties by higher considerations; such as, that we should prefer to our own country every region where God is purely worshipped; that we should not desire any better repose for our old age than to abide in His Church, His dwelling-place and the place of His rest; that we should prefer to be contemptible in the place where His name may be glorified by us, to being honourable in the sight of men, while we defraud Him of the honour which belongs to Him.

Concerning the doubts which may come into your mind, it would be too tedious to reply to them all. But you have always this as a settled point, that we must refer our many anxieties to the Providence of God, trusting that He will provide an outlet in cases where we see none. And in fact it is undoubted, that if we seek Him we shall find Him. That is to say, He will be with us to guide our steps, and to have a care of our affairs, to order them well for us. True it is, that we shall not cease to be subject to many troubles and annoyances; but let us pray Him that, having been strengthened by His Word, we may have wherewithal to overcome them. And assuredly you possess many helps, which deprive you of the excuse which many others have. If it shall please God to lead you hither, you will not come so bereft of property as to have nothing to live upon, while there are many poor people who have only burdens without temporal provision. How many Christian women are there who are held captive by their children! while our Lord has given you this advantage, that you have children who not only are ready to aid in your deliverance from captivity, but also exhort you thereto. You have the liberty which many wish for, of which you ought to avail yourself, that you may all the more freely engage in the service of God. Among the other hindrances that it appears you have, your daughter may be one, inasmuch as she is still unmarried. But instead of reckoning that to be a hindrance, it ought rather to serve as a spur the more readily to decide you. I understand that you love her not merely with the common love of mothers, but with a peculiar affection. I beseech you, then, to consider well whether it would be better for her to be there tied down in marriage, to live in perpetual bondage, or to be brought by you to a place where she may be free to live as a Christian with her husband; for you must trust that God will find out for her a worthy person, who will be a comfort to you as well as to herself.[1] There is one thing of which it is right that you should be made aware, in order that nothing may alarm you as new and unforeseen. It is this, that Satan will stir up many troubles in order to upset or to delay your pious purpose; but when you shall have taken your fixed resolve, it will not be difficult for you to rise above all. Meanwhile, profit by the opportunity, now when it is offered to you; for as, in matters of conscience, it behoves us to resolve speedily, without seeking advice or long dalliance, it is also necessary to perform soon what we have decided on, fearing, because of the frailty which is in us, to grow cold upon our good intention.

To conclude, knowing that all my exhortations must be vain and useless, unless God make them effectual by gaining an entrance to your heart, I shall beseech Him to instruct you with true prudence to decide upon what shall be most fitting for you to do; to bestow steadfast constancy upon you in obeying His will; to stretch out the hand, and be Himself your guide; to grant you such grace, that in leaning upon Him, you may perceive His assistance in everything, and all throughout.

Your servant and humble brother,

CHARLES D'ESPEVILLE.

[*Fr. orig. autogr.—Library of Geneva.* Vol. 107.]

[1] Catherine de Budé married, in 1550, William de Tric, Seigneur de Varennes, a gentleman of the Lyonnais, a refugee at Geneva on account of religion.

## CLXXXIV.—To the Avoyer Nœguely.[1]

Complaints of the misconduct of several ministers in the Pays de Vaud.

FROM LAUSANNE, *this* 12*th January* 1547.

MONSEIGNEUR,—Seeing that this present bearer[2] has brought me so good a testimony regarding Lion, and also that I myself have known him to be both well qualified and zealous, insomuch that I have no doubt of his fitness to serve the Church of God, I am constrained to recommend him to you, assured also that the letter of introduction which I give him to you will be of service to him, considering the kind affection which you bear to me. I pray you then humbly that it may please you to hold him as recommended, to the intent that by your means he may hereafter find an opening for the service of our Lord Jesus, in which you may have occasion to rejoice; for were not such my expectation, I would be very sorry to breathe a word about it.

Moreover, Monsieur, if God granted me an opportunity of speaking to you, I would willingly disburden my heart of the scandals which lie heavy upon us here, on account of the misconduct of some who are ministers of the Word of God in your demesne, and in their whole life give constant occasion to blaspheme the name of God.[3] I am well persuaded that you, on being made aware of the wretchedness in which every one thereabouts is sunk, will be as well disposed to provide for it, as I have great regret and sorrow even to hear it spoken of. I believe, indeed, that you will have spoken about it in council, seeing that a poor brother who goes to your quarter, named

---

[1] John Francis Nœguely, one of the most illustrious magistrates, and one of the most able captains of the republic of Berne, in the sixteenth century. In 1536 he commanded the Bernese army, which conquered the Pays de Vaud from the Duke of Savoy; discharged the functions of Avoyer from 1540 to 1568, and died at a very advanced age.

[2] In a note, by an unknown hand, "Philippe Buissonnier de Bresse."

[3] Several ministers of the Pays de Vaud, and particularly Zebedee, later pastor of Nyon, Lange, pastor of Bursins, delivered from the pulpit the most virulent declamations against the doctrines of the Reformer.

Master Francis Maurice, will give you occasion to think thereupon. I do not touch further on the maladies, except that I earnestly desire that it would please God to put it in your heart to apply an effectual remedy. And because I know that individually you are well inclined, as becomes you, I do beseech you, inasmuch as I ought to have the interest of the Church of God at heart, that it would please you to hold out a hand to those who are in trouble for having borne themselves faithfully in God's service and yours : Wherefore, Monsieur, after having humbly commended me to your kind favour, I pray our good Lord to uphold you in his safe keeping, guiding you always by His Spirit in obedience to His will.—Your humble servant,

JOHN CALVIN.

[*Fr. orig. autogr.*—*Library of Geneva.* Vol. 106.]

## CLXXXV.—To FAREL.[1]

Mission of Calvin in Switzerland—dispositions of the various Cantons.

GENEVA, 20*th* *February* 1547.

Textor will have returned to us before my letter reaches you. The reason why I did not proceed by way of [Neuchatel] in returning from the Swiss, was, that I had engaged to be present with the brethren on a day that must have elapsed had I not made very great haste. With regard to the present disturbances, I have to remark, that the people of Bâle are either in a state of marvellous insensibility, or they possess a wonderful power of concealing their real feelings. They did, however, make some exertion, but coldly, and their zeal was not to my

---

[1] On the news of the dangers that menaced the churches of Germany, an important mission had been confided to the Reformer. " Calvin is despatched by the Seigneury to Zurich, to obtain certain information of the condition of the war between the Emperor and the Protestant princes."—*Registers of Council*, 23d January 1547. " Calvin having returned, reports that the war between the Emperor and the Protestants is more enkindled than ever, and that the Swiss, apprehensive of that prince turning his arms against them, are putting themselves in a state of defence."—Ibid., 23d January 1547.

In a letter to Farel, he gave with greater detail the impressions he had received during his hasty journey.

mind. I observed great fervour at Zurich. The inhabitants of that place were as much concerned about the people of Constance[1] as about themselves. They made over to them all their resources, and yet the wretched state continued still to vacillate, just as if it had been without any help whatever. If it had stood to this hour, I think there would have been no danger for the future. If you are in possession of any information, make us aware of it. Some people were furious, because of a report that the ambassadors of the people of Strasbourg were seen in the court of Charles. To me it does not appear probable. The people of Zurich were soon persuaded. I was, however, greatly pleased to find that they forgot all causes of dissension, and thought only of the common weal, being prepared to spend their strength not less in behalf of Strasbourg than of Constance. You can hardly credit how offensive are the terms accepted by the cities that have surrendered; but the most disgraceful of all is Wurtemberg.[2] This, to be sure, is the reward of tyrants. I observed that the Bernese were occupied in defending their own bounds, that they might be the less conscious of the neighbouring conflagration. But there are very many more private matters regarding the churches that cannot be committed to writing. It would therefore repay the trouble if you came hither speedily, because I have now in hand certain materials which I must send back in a short time. I am desirous that their contents be communicated to you, and you will infer that I am not desirous of that without good grounds.—Adieu, my brother, along with your whole family, to the members of which you will convey the best greeting in my name and that of my wife. Salute also respectfully all the brethren.—Yours,

JOHN CALVIN.

[*Lat. orig. autogr.—Library of Geneva.* Vol. 106.]

[1] Situated at the extremity of the Confederation, without forming part of it, and sharing the faith of the Reformed Cantons, Constance, the first city open to the attacks of the Emperor upon the banks of the Rhine, invoked the aid of the Cantons, whose rigorous neutrality left it exposed without defence to its adversaries.—*Histoire de la Confédération Suisse,* tom. xi. p. 296.

[2] Ulrich, Duke of Wurtemberg, although among the first to submit to the Emperor, was compelled to sue for pardon on his knees, and to pay a ransom of 300,000 crowns.—Robertson, *Hist. of Charles V.,* book viii.

### CLXXXVI.—To Monsieur de Falais.

Search for a house for that gentleman in Geneva—Various details—
Mention of Charles V. and Francis I.

From Geneva, *this* 25*th Feburary* 1547.

Monseigneur,—Having received your letter by the Sieur de la Rivière, I feared that the other, of which you made mention, must have been lost. It has since been brought to me. In reply, I thank God for having increased your joy and contentment. I have written briefly a joint letter to the three companions, to congratulate them on their welfare. I know not whether God will one day so bless us, that they shall have no more need of my letters. If not, I shall another time be a little more liberal on paper.

As for yourself, in obedience to the commission which you gave me, I have looked about since my return for a convenient lodging. As for that of Clébergue,[1] you would be too far away from the neighbours you desire;[2] although I have long had a wish for it myself, for the sake of retirement, when I seek to have leisure: And they promised to let me have an answer; but none has come. If I had it at my disposal, as they had given me to hope, you know that it would be very much at your service. Near us, I have not been able to find one having a garden, which would be more suitable for you than the one which I have taken. Not that I am quite content with the lodging, but I took it for want of a better. You will have in front a small garden, and a tolerably spacious court. Behind there is another garden. A great saloon, with as beautiful a view as you could well desire for the summer. The other rooms have not so pleasant an aspect as I would like. But when you have arrived, possibly we may devise some satisfactory arrangement. With the exception of the saloon, one might find houses

---

[1] The present *Quai des Bergues*.
[2] Calvin at that time inhabited the house of the Sieur de Fréneville, situated in the *Rue des Chanoines*, near St. Peter's Church, and corresponding to the house in the same street which is now No. 122.—See the *Mémoires de la Société d'Histoire de Genève*, vol. ix. p. 391.

better furnished and more conveniently laid out; but there would have been no garden, and I see that is a feature which you desire above all. However that may be, it is hired for twelve crowns. When you see it, if you say that this is too much, I shall have my excuse ready, that I am not such a manager as to be very sparing of my purse, any more than of that of others. I have hurried on the bargain solely on account of the garden. If time hangs heavy with you where you are, it appears to me the season will be as suitable in a month as at a later period, provided that the weather be as favourable as it usually is at that time. As for escort, although my brother is not here at this moment, I can safely venture to undertake for him that he will willingly serve you; and he has gone that road so often, that he ought to know it well. Moreover, he has already had to do with the boatmen: and I believe you will recollect my advice, that you should come part of the way by water, to refresh you. Awaiting your full resolve, we shall sow without making any stir about it, and prune the vines.

As for your causes of complaint, I beseech you, Monseigneur, to overlook many things, to avoid that vexation which does not alleviate the ill, and cannot mend it; above all, to please to bear with what may have been done from inconsiderate zeal, for that is a fault which happens with the best. But I believe the matter has been already settled in some way or other. I hope the consequences have been modified by your prudence.

With regard to Sieur de Paré,[1] if peradventure he should come straight to you without passing this way, and that besides he makes fresh overtures in regard to the proposal, you have there Monsieur D'Albiac, who being very intimate with him, will be able to inform you of everything better than Maldonado can have done. And it will be right to make diligent inquiry; for I would fear that by the follies of his youth he may have had some disease, such as many persons have now-a-days. I openly avow to you my fear, choosing to exceed in that respect, rather than to conceal anything until it be too late. You will ask me wherefore then I have put off so much time already? But my conjectures on this point have arisen since. It would indeed

[1] He sought in marriage a relation of M. de Falais.

have been the shortest way to communicate by word of mouth, if I had conceived in my mind all that I do now. I set the matter before you, that you may think of it. For I would not have that reproach,—I mean not only in the sight of the world, but also before God,—that the girl should have been in any way wronged by my concealment. I am aware, that by reason of its being a malady so common and prevalent, many make scarcely any difficulty about it. But I suspect that you, like myself, will have your scruples.

To make an end, Monsieur, after having humbly commended me to your kind favour, and that of Madame, I entreat our good Lord to have you in His keeping, which is the one thing needful of our whole life, as well for this present time as that which is to come ; I mean that He may always make you to feel, as He does now, that you are under His guidance. All those who do not write, humbly commend them to your good graces, and to those of Madame.

Your servant and humble brother,

JOHN CALVIN.

Monsieur, he who will present you this letter, is the ambassador from this town. There are two who proceed to your quarter, I know not wherefore, that is to say, on account of their private affairs, which they have to settle together. I have thought it well to inform you of this, for no other reason, save that I presume you would have been sorry not to have been told of it. For if your affairs admit of your deciding to come, you may avail yourself of this means of communication ; not that there is need of great ceremony, as we have already spoken of it, but only in order that they may not fancy themselves slighted, especially if you should come hither. I speak the language of the country. If there are any good tidings, I hope that they will bring them to us. But there is need for God humbling us, from whichever side it may come. I hope, however, that our Antiochus,[1] who presses us at present, will be so

---

[1] The Emperor Charles the Fifth,—conqueror without a combat, of the army of the confederate princes: thanks to the treason of Maurice of Saxony, this prince, although suffering severely from the gout, was at this very time receiving

hard pressed, that he shall be regardless of the gout in his hands and in his feet ; for he will have it over his whole body. As regards his companion, Sardanapalus,[1] may God have a like care of him ! for they are both well worthy to have the same measure meted to them.

[*Fr. orig. autogr.—Library of Geneva.* Vol. 194.]

## CLXXXVII.—To Monsieur de Falais.[2]

Instructions regarding the *Apology*—alarming rumours current at Geneva—Calvin's confidence.

From Geneva, *this 7th of March* 1547.

Monseigneur,—I forgot in my last letter to mention the subject of the *Apology,* and I know not how it had escaped me. Saint André had the copy ; and in so far I was not deceived in my opinion. But as matters stand at present, if you should think of printing it, I do not see anything there will be to change. To soften it down, that is not possible ; and the times will not warrant its being kindled into greater vehemence, at least with any effect. And if you determine to have it printed at Strasbourg, I am not very sure that they will venture to admit it as it is. "*For what can he dare to do who hath once involved himself with a tyrant?*"[3] Here there would be more liberty. I recollect that you spoke to me, immediately after having seen it, about correcting some points, but without signifying to me what these were, nor how to be corrected. Will you therefore please to let me know your wish by the first opportunity, and what you desire that I should do. As for some one

---

the submission of the confederate towns of Suabia and of the Palatinate, from which he exacted enormous penalties.

[1] The King, Francis I. He died the following month, the 31st March 1547.

[2] *On the back*—To Monseigneur, Monsieur de Fallez, at Basle, near to the Cauf-Houff.—M. de Falais was in fact about to quit Strasbourg, then threatened by the imperial army, to fix his residence in Switzerland.

[3] " Quid enim audeat, qui tyranno se implicuit?" The town of Strasbourg had submitted itself to the emperor. The terms of that submission bore, that it shall renounce the League of Smalkalde, and shall contribute with the other states, to the execution of the sentence pronounced against the Landgrave and the Elector.

to translate it into Latin, you have one at hand sufficiently elegant, should you think proper to make use of him.[1] Here, also, we might doubtless find one; for want of a better, I shall undertake it myself,—and that I hope I may do, without boasting; for provided that it is perspicuous, that will be sufficient; and besides, the barbarism of *Majestas vestra,* which one must employ, forbids a too exquisitely ornate style. In any event, however, we shall have need of your advice, in case we undertake it here. Moreover, our people are in some alarm. But I do not think they have any cause. You know very well that frontier towns are very apt to take fright; and forasmuch as we have Granvelle for a neighbour,[2] and we hear talk of a levy of men, one is somewhat in doubt. As for me, I think differently, for it is not the proper season for attempting anything here. But we must let many rumours glide past, even as we cannot hinder water from going downwards. However matters turn out, I am very glad that our Lord arouses us, in order to make us turn to Himself; and that is the greatest mercy that can happen to us, that we may be led to commit ourselves in real earnest to His protection.

Making an end for the present, Monsieur, after having humbly commended myself to the kind favour both of yourself and Madame, and having presented the respects of our neighbours, I pray our good Lord to have you in His holy keeping, to guide you in all your paths, to show you what is right and fit for you to do, and to give eventually a good and prosperous result.

You will perceive by the letter of Sire Nicolas how it goes with your money. He has also informed me of the choice which he sets before you; you will make your election as opportunity presents itself.

Your servant and humble brother for ever,

JOHN CALVIN.

[*Fr. orig. autogr.—Library of Geneva.* Vol. 194.]

---

[1] Sebastian Castellio, who had then retired to Bâle.

[2] Antoine Perrenot, Bishop of Arras, Cardinal de Granvelle, the celebrated minister of Charles V. and of Philip II. He was born at Ornans, near Besançon, in 1517, and died in 1586 at Madrid.

## CLXXXVIII.—To Monsieur de Falais.

*Disputes of M. de Falais with Valeran Poulain—Reports of the expected arrival of the former in Geneva.*

From Geneva, *this 15th March* 1547.

Monseigneur,—I am glad that you have our brother, Master Peter Viret, to cheer you in the midst of the annoyances which must have been very hard upon you, seeing that I have been tormented more than I can express through mere sympathy. But I hope that God has applied a remedy as regards the actual issue; and assuredly He has cared for you by sending you him from whom you may receive as effectual consolation as from any man in the world, so that I am in nowise sorry that I did not undertake the journey; for I do not fear that you will have any need of me. For this reason, also, I shall make my letters to you shorter.

Concerning the person you allude to,[1] I am not aware of having given him any reason to think that I deemed your complaints excessive; but, fearing lest some illness might attack you, and also thinking it unbecoming that you should enter into contention with a man of his disposition; considering on the other hand his audacity, and what a venomous animal is apt to emit when pressed, I entreated you to take the whole with moderation, so far as might be possible. Besides, I know him well, and do not so much fear his ill-will, as to wish that the Church of God should suffer from my dissimulation. But I do not see now what I can do in the matter, and indeed there is no present need. For where he is known, his reputation is already lower than we need. Where he is unknown, nothing would be gained by speaking of him, unless he endeavours to insinuate himself. But yet God may make him wise, after having suitably chastised him on account of his foolishness.

---

[1] Allusion to Valeran Poulain. It appears from the next letter in this Series, pp. 90-92, that Valeran sought, in spite of the opposition of M. de Falais, the hand of Mademoiselle de Willergy, a relation of this Seigneur, likewise sought by M. de Paré.—See Note 1, p. 84.

I now come to your journey. Although I see no danger in the way, either of ambush, or of other proceedings of a like kind, nor yet of open violence,—nevertheless, as for the first, I have given no assurance to any one to that effect, but on the contrary rather have my suspicion. In the second place, as regards the time of your coming, I have spoken as one who knew nothing at all about it. It is true that when I am asked if you have an intention of coming to see us, I am not very obstinate in the denial thereof to my friends, fearing lest they might think me a double dealer. And even when I have hired the house, not only he who spoke to you, but some others also, have at once conjectured that it was for yourself. I have answered them, Yea, that it was possible, but that there were others whom it might be; that I took it thus at a venture, not doubting, however, to find a tenant to put into it. I cannot, however, hinder many from guessing about it, and persuading themselves, without my breathing a word on the subject, that you are coming. However, if it please God, you shall have no prejudice thereby so far as I am concerned. I hope, if the Lord will, that next week Master Peter Viret will bring us your news. If after having heard our brother Saint André, you have anything new to tell me, you will find a suitable messenger in him.

Whereupon, Monsieur, having affectionately commended me to your kind favour, and to that of Madame, and having presented to both of you the remembrance of my wife and friends, I beseech our good Lord to have you always in his keeping, to comfort you, to strengthen and perfect you in every work for His glory, and your salvation. Amen.

Your very humble servant and brother,

JOHN CALVIN.

[*Fr. orig. autogr.—Library of Geneva.* Vol. 194.]

## CLXXXIX.—To Valeran Poulain.[1]

Severe reprobation of his behaviour towards M. de Falais—reply to a calumny directed against the Reformer.

[GENEVA, *March* 1547.]

Greeting,—I only received your letter this day, which was later than was proper. Meanwhile, however, I think that the conversation of our friend Viret has done something towards changing your mind on the point. When I heard Saint André's account of the matter, I briefly replied that I was not a little grieved to find that you had thus sullied by your last act whatever praise you had earned, in the discharge of a mission so illustrious. And I am not indeed so light-minded, as to pronounce a judgment after hearing merely the one side of a question. Nor is my vision blinded by the splendour of rank; but while I hear men indifferent, and giving expression to no accusing word, I am constrained to think that you acted neither with prudence nor propriety in soliciting the girl in marriage. But I am still more displeased, seeing she complains that you circumvented her by means of numerous baseless accusations, and indirect arts. You mention to me Bucer and Bernardino. If you had done nothing but with their advice, you would, assuredly, never have set about what you did. Do you suppose that your cause will meet with their approval? I mentioned in a former letter, regarding the younger [lady] to whom you aspired, what I thought was cen-

---

[1] Enclosed in a letter to M. de Falais, with the words,—Copy of a letter written to Valeran.

There has been already repeated mention of Valeran Poulain in the correspondence of Calvin with M. de Falais, and we shall again find his name in the subsequent letters of the Reformer, when a refugee at Strasbourg on the ground of religion. He aspired at that time to the functions of the ministry, which he exercised at a later period at London and Frankfort; and if, by his indiscretion, he at first drew down upon himself the severe censures of Calvin, he afterwards succeeded in regaining his esteem and meriting his affection. See the correspondence of the Reformer, (years 1555, 1556.)

surable in her. In seeking after this one, you seem to have forgotten what you wrote to the other on your departure. Even although nothing else had stood in the way, you ought to have absolutely abstained from the mention of marriage until she had reached her destination. But if what she herself testifies be true, the engagement was brought about through the influence of the worst inducements. Accordingly I shall not believe that the marriage is, as you say, from the Lord, until you prove that she says what is untrue, when she affirms that you had beforehand engrossed her mind with numerous calumnies. Albeit, she strongly asserts that she gave you no credence, and that no engagement was formed between you, but that she always expressly stipulated to be allowed to do everything in accordance with the advice of Monsieur de Falais. She says, however, that you affirmed that his will was quite well known to you, that the only difficulty would be with his wife, as she still regarded with admiration the fumes of nobility. These were not the tokens of God; but you prohibit me from believing them. I can do nothing less, however, than hear both sides. When I reflect on the whole circumstances, certain particulars appear with which, I confess, I am displeased. You remind me that illustrious men are sometimes guilty of grave offences. It is on other grounds, however, that I love and reverence M. de Falais, than on account of the mock greatness on which alone most of the nobility pride themselves. In the next place, I have, as yet, heard nothing from him but reasonable complaints. Moreover, I have looked more to the matter itself than to the persons. I wish that you had never involved yourself in those troubles; but since it has so happened, it remains for me to desire to see you relieved from them in a short space, which I trust is now accomplished.

With regard to the estate which I am said to have purchased, with so many thousands, I should indeed be silly if I spent many words in rebutting falsehoods so gross. There is no one here, or in the whole vicinity, who is not aware that I do not possess a foot of land. Moreover, my acquaintances well know that I never had money sufficient to purchase an acre, unless when I am paid what enables me to meet the expenditure of the quarter. I have surely not reached the point alleged, as I am still using in my house another's furniture; for neither the table at which we eat, nor the bed on which we sleep, is my own. Whence, then, those reports? I know not, unless it be that godless men so malign me, in order to fix a brand on the Gospel. They will never, however, prevent me from being truly rich, because I am abundantly satisfied with my slender means; and while my poverty is a burden to no one, it is nevertheless an alleviation to some.

Adieu, and believe that I am friendly disposed towards you. I wish there may sometimes occur occasion for correspondence, &c.

[*Lat. Copy.—Library of Geneva.* Vol. 196.]

## CXC.—To VIRET.[1]

Weakness of the Genevese magistracy—Expectation of Viret's arrival in Geneva.

GENEVA, 27*th March* 1547.

I AM in doubt with regard to your coming to us.[2] Roset, as far as I hear, exceeded due bounds in explaining to you the necessity for it, although he is not the only one who errs in this respect; for the whole council is in a state of groundless agitation. I see no one of the whole number in whom I can put confidence. I certainly observe no one here who can be said to be judicious. They show no boldness in a good and praiseworthy cause. So childish are they all, that they are frightened by the silly shake of a head, while a man of no consequence displays his insanity. I do not defend my cause

---

[1] Invested with the right of censure and ecclesiastical excommunication, the Consistory daily beheld its authority assailed and disowned by numerous adversaries, who accused it of encroaching upon the power of the magistrates. "The ministers complain that they are accused of exceeding the authority accorded them by the edicts, and request permission to put into force the right of excommunication, in order to bring offenders to their duty. Resolved to hand over to the Consistory rebellious and obstinate offenders, and to leave the others unmolested."—*Registers of Council,* 21st and 29th May 1547.

[2] "Arrival at Geneva of the minister Viret, a very excellent man."—*Registers,* April 1547.

under the form of a public one, carried on in my absence. If I desist from prosecuting it, the whole consistory will of necessity go to ruin. Moreover, they so conduct themselves, as to extort daily clamours in the course of their sermons; otherwise, the entreaties of Roset would not have particularly influenced me. Just now, our brother has made known to me from Saint André, that our comic actor Cæsar, and certain of his faction, have been making diligent inquiry as to whether you were coming hither immediately. I observe, therefore, that there is a strong desire for you on the part of some, that others expect you because they are aware that you have been summoned. With no one belonging to the council have I any communication that can be relied on, Michel[1] alone excepted; but he is neither very sharp-sighted, nor is he even admitted to the more private deliberations. John Parvi makes a magnificent offer of his services, but he is not the thing. Besides these, no one has come near me. Certain guesses, not lightly formed, have made me suspicious of Corna. I indeed love the man, but he does not permit me to confide in him. In the first place, he is timid; in the next, he is distrustful; and, finally, he adores that shadow, or ghost if you will.[2] Those who are desirous that the matter should be arranged without disturbance, hope that you would prove a suitable pacificator. The party composing the faction itself is anxious for you, with the view of being somewhat relieved from its difficulties by your mediation. We desire and solicit you, I myself in particular, that you may see, judge, and do whatever in your opinion shall be for the interest of the Church. But observe its wretched condition. Farel lately learned that he had been unfortunate in turning to me for assistance, because nothing could be done unless he were separated from me. Nothing assuredly would be more agreeable to me, than if all matters here were brought to a happy issue by your interference, even though I were banished to the Garamantes. But this mode of procedure will be as little satisfactory to you as to myself. I mention this plan as that prescribed by the most moderate, as they

[1] Doubtless Michel Morel.
[2] Is this an allusion to the gradually declining influence of Amy Perrin?

wish to be thought. But if you could be here by Tuesday next, and remain until Monday, you might have my opinion of this complicated matter; you would, in that case, I presume, conduct public worship. Should it be necessary for you to return sooner, I do not advise you to subject yourself to so much trouble for no purpose. If the arrangements of your church do not permit you to come in such good time, I have nothing to say; but if I were in your place, I know what I would do; I do not, however, wish you to be guided by my judgment. Adieu, therefore, brother and dearest friend, along with your wife and brothers, all of whom you will greet in my name. Des Gallars sends his warm thanks to you through me, and he expresses the same to me, on the ground that I am the cause of your undertaking the journey.—Yours,

JOHN CALVIN.

[*Lat. orig. autogr.—Library of Geneva.* Vol. 106.]

## CXCI.—To WOLFGANG MUSCULUS.[1]

Anxiety regarding the Churches of Germany—advice to Musculus.

GENEVA, 21*st April* 1547.

If I were to follow out the subject in this letter, as time and the present condition of things demand, I see that there would be no end to it. There are, besides, other reasons that prevent me from entering on this forest so full of thorns. I was un-

[1] To the excellent servant of Christ our Lord, Doctor Wolfgang Musculus, most reverend pastor of the Church of Augsbourg, brother, and fellow-minister.

Wolfgang Musculus, born in a small town of Lorraine and of an obscure family, raised himself by his talents, and the varied range of his accomplishments, to a place among the most distinguished men of his time. He cultivated with success music, poetry, and theology; was converted to the Gospel in a convent by the perusal of the writings of Luther; gained the friendship of Capito and Bucer, and quitted Strasbourg in 1531, with a view to the discharge of the functions of the ministry in the church of Augsbourg. Driven from that city in 1548, by the proclamation of the *Interim,* he withdrew at first to Zurich, and afterwards to Berne, where he died in 1563. His numerous manuscripts, as well as those of Abraham Musculus his son, are preserved in the Library of Zoffingue.—Melch. Adam, *Vitæ Theol. Germ.,* p. 367.

willing, however, to send away this youth wholly empty, who had come in my way, without at least testifying to you, in the present calamitous state of your church, and as becomes the friendly relations subsisting between us, that I ever bear you in mind. Indeed, when the earliest rumours reached this, you were among the first, of those whose danger caused me agony, to occur to my mind; and when the ungovernable violence of my grief had hurried me to Zurich, as soon as I fell in with Bernardino,[1] who had arrived about half an hour before I met him, I began at once, forgetful alike of salutation and everything else, to make inquiries after you. I confess, however, that I was solicitous about your safety, in proportion to the strength of the fear I had, lest you should abandon the Church in such a time of need, as usually happens when matters are desperate and past recovery, or rather lest, being as it were deserted by your flock, you should betake yourself elsewhere;[2] for it is difficult, amid so great darkness, to discern what is most expedient. Now, howsoever severe the trial may have been, I yet rejoice that the Lord has caused the spirit of prudence and counsel to spring up in you and your fellow-ministers, and has sustained your minds with the spirit of fortitude, as far as might be in circumstances not the best. I also give God thanks, that in whatsoever way matters have been improved, a short breathing time is granted you, until at length tranquil serenity may clearly dawn upon you. Meanwhile, it is proper we should learn, that it has been usual with God in all ages to preserve His own Church in a wonderful way, and without human protection. Relying therefore on this ground of confidence, let us strive to break through whatever difficulty there may be, and let us never lose heart, even although we should be destitute of all things.

Adieu, most upright brother, and one dear to me from the

[1] Named pastor of the Italian church at Augsbourg in October 1545, Ochino fled from that city on the approach of the imperial army, in the early part of the year 1547.—Schelhorn *Ergoetzlichkeiten*, vol. iii. pp. 1141, 1142.

[2] Wolfgang Musculus did not cease to proclaim the Gospel in Augsbourg until the church in which he preached had been closed by order of the emperor, and his congregation dispersed. He was himself obliged to take his departure the year following, (26th June 1548.)—Melch. Ad., p. 381.

bottom of my heart, as also your fellow-ministers, all of whom you will very affectionately salute in my name. May the Lord Jesus be present with you, guide you by His Spirit, and bless your holy labours. You will also convey to your family my best greeting.—Yours,

JOHN CALVIN.

My colleagues also reverently salute you all. If any opportunity be afforded you, you will make me aware of the state of your affairs.

[*Lat. orig. autogr.*—*Library of Zoffingue.* Vol. i. p. 10.]


### CXCII.—To Monsieur de Falais.

Steps taken at Basle to retract a promise of marriage made to Valeran Poulain.

FROM GENEVA, *this first of May* [1547.]

MONSEIGNEUR,—I wrote to Myconius,[1] as you will see by the copy which I send you. I was of opinion that it was enough, because the judges will better comprehend my meaning from his mouth. It will have more weight, because the prosecution of the suit will not thus be so vehement on my part, as if I should take upon me to write to them, thus making myself too much a party in the matter. I believe that our brother, Master Peter Viret, will do the same in regard to the Sieur Bernard Mayer, in consequence of what I have told him. Should there be any need for it, he condemns himself of treachery in the letters which he has written to me. For after having requested me, in the month of January, to intercede for him in regard to the marriage of Merne, he has told me that Wilergy was in love with him *many months before :* so much so, as to ask him in marriage, rather than wait to be asked. How is that to be reconciled, unless he wanted to have both of them? But he

---

[1] See *ante*, vol. i., pp. 288, 289, *note*. Calvin called on him for his aid with the magistrates of that town for having a promise of marriage cancelled between Mademoiselle de Wilergy and Valeran.—*Bibl. de Genève*, vol. 106.

must be cut short in the whole of his troublesome nonsense; seeing that it is quite unworthy of a hearing. I have no doubt that the judges will very soon put an end to that.

Monsieur, having heartily commended me to your kind favour and that of Madame, without forgetting the three Demoiselles, I pray our good Lord to have you in His keeping, to confirm you always in patience, to deliver you from the annoyance of this importunate suitor, and to bring you into assured prosperity.

Your servant and humble brother,
JOHN CALVIN.

[*Fr. orig. autogr.—Library of Geneva.* Vol. 194.]

## CXCIII.—To FRANCIS DRYANDER.[1]

### Confused state of the Church—Hopes and fears for the future.

GENEVA, 18*th May* 1547.

Greeting :—It would not require a letter of very great length, were I to comply with your request to write to you at full length my opinion of the present state of general disorder; because when matters are in so great confusion, I not only abstain from passing any judgment, but I do not even venture to inquire into what may be the issue of them. For as often as I have begun the attempt, I have been immediately involved in darkness so intense, that I thought it better to close my eyes upon the world, and fix them intently upon God alone. I only speak of myself, as I am here situated. Had I been placed in the situation which some others occupy, my mode of procedure

---

[1] To the most erudite Doctor Francis Dryander, and very dear friend.

François Ensinas, better known under the name of Dryander, born at Burgos in Spain, was the disciple of Melanchthon, and embraced the Reformation with ardour. Imprisoned for having published a translation of the New Testament in Spanish, he recovered his liberty in 1542, and visited Calvin at Geneva. He afterwards withdrew to Strasbourg, whence he passed over to England, after the adoption of the *Interim*, and occupied a chair in the University of Oxford. There are several letters of Dryander to Bullinger (1549-1552,) in the fine collection of *Zurich Letters*, published by the *Parker Society*, 1st series, Vol. i. p. 348, and following.

might then have required to be changed. Besides, I cannot from this retreat as from a watch-tower observe the circumstances that go to the formation of a judgment. And if anything reaches me, it comes late. Further, nothing can with certainty be determined, until the whole particulars are gathered together. But at present the more private counsels, from which an opinion is chiefly to be formed, are unknown to me. What folly then would it be for me to fatigue myself to no purpose or profit, by occupying my attention with what is obscure! "What," therefore, you will say, "do you alone wish to enjoy undisturbed quiet amid the ruins of the Church?" On the contrary, I sigh anxiously night and day, but I repel as much as I can all needless reflections that from time to time steal upon me. I do not, nevertheless, succeed in this so far as I could wish; it is, however, something, that I do not indulge a prurient disposition. I occupy myself in considering what is already done; and I connect matters that occur from day to day, with what preceded them. Reflection on these things furnishes me, I confess, with various grounds both of hope and fear. But because, as I have said, there are so many opposing reasons, I restrain myself in good time, lest I say anything rashly and beyond what is proper. The prediction, indeed, which you gave in your letter, will never deceive us, even although heaven and earth were mingled in confusion together, viz., that God will take so peculiar a care of His own Church, as to preserve it even amid the annihilation of the whole world. Excuse the brevity of this epistle, as I was warned a little before supper of the departure of the messenger. [My] brother had told me before mid-day, that he was ready for the journey: I would not have written, if he had gone so soon. He returned after three o'clock: I had thus less time than I should have had. Adieu: may the Lord direct you by His Spirit, and preserve you safe.—Yours,

JOHN CALVIN.

[*Lat. orig. autogr.—Protestant Seminary of Strasbourg.*]

## CXCIV.—To Monsieur de Falais.

*The sending of a minister—perplexities regarding anticipated events in Germany.*

From Geneva, *this* 18*th of May* 1547.

Monseigneur,—Since your convenience has not permitted your coming hither as we had hoped, it is enough if God graciously grants you health where you are. For albeit I might desire to be near you, nevertheless I prefer what is best for you. Concerning the man of whom Maldonado spoke to you, besides the knowledge which I have had of him while he has been here, I have made inquiry about him at his old master, Gallars, who tells me that he found him very leal and serviceable. It is true, that he would not reckon him qualified to manage great affairs, unless one should instruct and set him his lesson. But that in the carrying out of whatsoever he shall be commanded to do, there will be nothing wanting, nay, that he will even be vigilant. And even as regards the former quality, I do not undervalue him. For a staid and modest man is far better, than one who is overbold and venturesome. You will decide according to the turn of your affairs, in order that the Sieur d'Albiac may send him; and thus you may not remain long unprovided. Moreover, I hope that God has rid you of the annoyances wherewith that marplot[1] has been so long teasing you. That done, you may be altogether at ease about your house.

We are still on the outlook for news about the general state of the Church. If God intends so sorely to afflict us, as to let loose that tyrant upon us,[2] who only seeks to ruin everything, we must be quite prepared to suffer. Considering that He who has us in charge, rules in the midst of His enemies, it becomes us to have patience, consoling ourselves in the assured hope, that in the end He will confound them. But yet I hope

---

[1] Valeran Poulain. See pp. 90, 96.

[2] The Emperor Charles the Fifth had just gained a decisive victory at Mühlberg (24th April 1547) over the Protestant princes.

that He will provide against these great troubles, supporting our weakness; and that He will check the boldness of those who triumph before the time, and that against Himself.

Monsieur, having humbly commended me to your kind favour, and that of Madame, and having presented to both of you the remembrances of my wife, I pray our good Lord to guide you continually, to watch over you and to enlarge you in all His mercies. I abstain from entering upon the proposal which the Sieur Maldonado has brought me, about settling a church in that quarter;[1]—for I know not what to say about it, except that I would desire that all may be well done.

Your servant and humble brother,

JOHN CALVIN.

[*Fr. orig. autogr.- Library of Geneva.* Vol. 194.]

## CXCV.—To Monsieur de Falais.

*Information in regard to a house—advice on the subject of a marriage proposed for a relative of Monsieur de Falais.*

FROM GENEVA, *this 26th of May* 1547.

MONSEIGNEUR,—I hope that the bearer of these presents will be the captain of our town,[2] from whom I have hired the house. He has a mind to betake himself to your quarter, in order to confer with you. He has offered me an alternative condition. In the first place; should it please you to lend him money for a certain term, that the house shall remain pledged to you in security for the repayment, without paying any rent; and that of the repairs which you may make for your convenience, he shall bear a part: secondly, that he should sell it to you. It is

---

[1] That is to say, at Bâle. The French church of that town was founded after the massacre of *Saint Bartholomew*, at the request of a great number of refugees, among whom we find the children of the Admiral de Coligny.—MSS. of the archives of the French Church of Bâle.

[2] The bearer of this letter was the captain-general, Amy Perrin, then on his way to Bâle. He had been charged with a secret mission to the new king of France, Henry II., and was imprisoned after his return to Geneva, because of unfaithfulness in the fulfilment of his commission.

true that he is not the feudal superior, but he engages at all risks to maintain and warrant you in the sale of it out and out. In this case, he must have three hundred crowns for it. If your intention is to purchase, you will discuss the price with himself, making the best bargain you can. It is very certain, that assuming the responsibility of keeping it in repair, he will not readily give it for two hundred crowns. You will have to choose between these two conditions, and to arrange with himself, if you see it to be for your advantage. If so be that you do not enter into agreement with him, I have told you already that the house could not be secured to you, consequently you would need to look about elsewhere. For you will not prevail on him to put it into a proper state for your accommodation, unless you go about it in this way. And in good earnest, if you purpose to come here about the end of summer, I advise you to endeavour that the repairs may be made before your arrival, to avoid having your heads broken, and many other inconveniences. I believe that the plan I have laid down would please you very well, so that your absence need be no hindrance, and it will be quite easy to have the thing done. He does not think much repair is needed, but I suspect it will not amount to less than forty crowns. Wherefore, the purchase would seem to me more expedient, especially if you could agree at two hundred crowns, and that he would take upon himself to warrant in perpetuity. I desire that you may do something in this matter, provided it be to your advantage.

The Sieur de Parey[1] arrived last evening, and came to call for me about nine o'clock. As it was rather late, we had scarcely leisure to speak together, so that I do not yet know the position of his affairs. After having spoken to Sieur Maldonado, I would advise that you only inform the girl of the nature of the objection, without mentioning to her any mishap which may have occurred to him ; for all that would be told over again afterwards. Therefore, I would merely let her understand : " He sleeps little, there is somewhat of levity about him, wherefore some danger might be apprehended from his peculiar constitution. Consider, then, whether you would be

---

[1] A pretender to the hand of Mademoiselle de Wilergy.

patient if God were to visit you with such a trial." That, in my opinion, would be sufficient. And according as you shall see her disposed, you will do what you think right in the matter. We have had some report of the decision, and he,[1] complaining of the sentence of the judges, glories in his shame. May God give him a better mind.

Monsieur, having humbly commended me to the kind favour of yourself and of Madame; and having presented to you the remembrances of Des Gallars and of my wife, I pray our good Lord to have you always in His keeping, to rule and guide you, and bestow grace upon you to glorify Him always.

It is enough that you be informed who the bearer is. I do not know if he will have other company along with him, for he went away in such haste, that without having spoken of it to me, he came this morning all booted and spurred, to bid me adieu. You see what has been the cause of my not having been able to communicate with Maldonado, for he went away yesterday evening to sleep at Tourné. That is also the reason wherefore I have not sent you any compliments from him.

Your servant and humble brother,

JOHN CALVIN.

[*Fr. orig. autogr.—Library of Geneva.* Vol. 194.]


## CXCVI.—To Viret.

Interview of Calvin with a senator of Berne—advantage secured over the party of the Libertins.

GENEVA, 28*th May* 1847.

Zerkinden[2] was here. I laid bare the ailments, and at the same time suggested the remedy of which we had spoken together.[3] He approved of it, but he thinks it will be difficult to obtain it. If, however, he come to Berne in time, he will make trial; for he admits that, in such an emergency, there is

---

[1] Valeran Poulain. See note 1, p. 99.
[2] Nicolas Zerkinden, senator of Berne, prefect of the town of Nyon.
[3] The establishment of discipline in the churches of the Pays de Vaud.

nothing that should not be attempted. I am, however, afraid that others may be sent thither before him, who, as is usual with them, after making a great display, will perform nothing. Thus, what has been for long desired will be granted too late. But may God look to this, as to all other matters!

We had here lately some little trouble about slashed breeches.[1] This was the pretext, but they had already begun to break out into the greatest license. When the *Two Hundred* had been summoned at their request, we were all present. I made a speech, which in a moment extorted from them what with firm expectation they had eagerly swallowed; for I discoursed about sources of corruption in general, premising that I was not speaking against these trumperies. They fall into a rage, and gnash with their teeth, as they do not dare openly to shout. By this one experiment, however, they learned, what they had not supposed to be the case, that the people are on our side. The tragic Cæsar hastily set off on a journey the following day, to avoid being present at the public procession, which that meeting rendered hazardous and puerile, whereas he was hoping that it would be the token of a certain supreme authority. He had returned to terms of friendship with Romanel, with a view to concuss the whole city, with no one to interpose. We, however, have unexpectedly shattered all his plans. Thus does God make sport of those Thrasoes!

Adieu, brother and most sincere friend. May the Lord be continually present with you, and bless and prosper your labours. You will hear the rest from Rebitti. Salute your wife in the name of me and mine.—Yours,

JOHN CALVIN.

[*Lat. orig. autogr.—Library of Geneva.* Vol. 106.]

[1] An ordinance had recently interdicted the use of slashed breeches at Geneva. The reasons which Calvin gives for this prohibition may be seen in a subsequent letter to the faithful of France, (24th July 1547.)

## CXCVII.—To Monsieur de Falais.

Recommendation of John de Budé—Uncertainty of the news from Germany.

*From Geneva, the 4th of June* 1547.

MONSEIGNEUR,—I have nothing to write you at present, except that the bearer is one of the sons of the late Mr. Budé.[1] When you shall have made his acquaintance, you will find him so excellent, that you will esteem him worthy of being loved by all those who love God, even if the memory of his father had not of itself recommended him. He is none of those who make a great show and parade. And all the more on that account is he valued by me, and I know that so it will be with you. His intention is to go to see Bâle and Strasbourg, then to return without making any long sojourn in those parts. Notwithstanding, I have advised him to make full inquiry whether the roads will be safe before going farther, and he has promised me to do so; for where there is no necessity, it would answer no purpose to put himself in danger. I believe that before he arrives there, you will be no longer in deliberation with regard to Sieur de Parey. For the prolonged delay which he asks for, is by no means with a view to strengthen his resolution; and indeed I conjecture, that it has been cautiously suggested by his relations, thinking that between this time and that he might alter his mind, seeing that they must be acquainted with his humour.

We are quite amazed to have no news that can be depended upon. One may perceive the disorder which prevails in Germany, and the wretched management. If there had been a grain of salt among them, they would have looked well to their affairs, before they came to the knowledge of that which was to be known far and wide three days afterwards. But what do I say? *Non est consilium, non est fortitudo absque domino.* Therefore they are taken unawares.

---

[1] John de Budé, Sieur de Vérace. See note 1, p. 76.

I hope to know by the first what decision you have come to with our captain.[1]

To make an end, Monsieur : having humbly commended me to your good grace and of Madame, and having presented the like remembrances to you on the part of my wife and others, I supplicate our good Lord always to have a care of you, to rule you by his Spirit, to strengthen you against all stumblingblocks and annoyances, as well as the whole of your household. Although I have not leisure to write to the young ladies, I desire to be very affectionately remembered to all three.

Your servant and humble brother,

JOHN CALVIN.

[*Fr. orig. autogr.—Library of Geneva.* Vol. 194.]


CXCVIII.—TO MONSIEUR DE BUDÉ.[2]

He exhorts him to follow the example of the rest of his family, and retire to Geneva.

*This* 19*th June* 1547.

MONSIEUR,—Although I am personally unknown to you, I do not hesitate on that account to write you privately, hoping that my letter will be welcome, as well for the sake of the Master whom I serve, as for the matter of which it treats ; and

---

[1] Amy Perrin.
[2] See the notice concerning the family of Budé, p. 76. We believe, contrary to the opinion of M. Galiffe, *Notices Généalogiques*, tom. iii. p. 83, that this letter is addressed to Louis or to Francis Budé, and not to John de Budé, Sieur de Vérace, their brother. This latter had already made a journey to Geneva, and he was known to the Reformer, who had introduced him in very kind terms to M de Falais.—Letter of 4th June 1547, p. 202. It is not then to the Sieur de Vérace, that the first words of Calvin's letter can apply, but to one of his brothers : " Although I am personally unknown to you, I do not on that account hesitate to write you privately, in the hope that my letter will be welcome," &c. The family of Budé were then preparing to leave France. Two years afterwards, they settled at Geneva, as appears from their registration in the list of the inhabitants. 27th June 1549, and the following passage of a letter from Viret to Calvin, 12th June of the same year : " *I rejoice that the Budé have arrived, along with their mother.*"—MSS. of the Library of Geneva.

also that those who have induced me to do so, have credit enough with you, as I believe they have, to secure me access. I have heard of the upright spirit which our Lord has given you, wherefore let us all praise Him. For although you may have many temptations of a worldly kind where you are, to impede and distract you, you nevertheless do not cease to groan under the unhappy captivity in which you are held, desiring to escape from it. And indeed your honest zeal has been already partially manifested, when, in place of hindering the party who were about to shift their quarters, you confirmed them in their good purpose, and instead of delaying, have endeavoured to forward their departure, only regretting that you could not follow them immediately. Now, then, seeing that Satan has many means to damp our zeal in well-doing, and that our nature is very apt to side with him, you must stir up the fire which God by his Spirit has already lighted in your heart, until the good desire be realized. You must abandon everything as hurtful which separates you from him, in whom lies all our happiness, and with whom if we are not united, we forfeit life and salvation. We do not mean, however, to condemn all those who live elsewhere, as if the kingdom of God were shut up within our mountains, while we know it is extended over all. But it is right, wheresoever we are, that God should be honoured by us, and we are nowise to be excused if we pollute the earth which He has sanctified to our use. If we are in a place where we are not permitted to acquit ourselves of our duty, and where the fear of death leads us to do what is evil, we ought, knowing our grievous infirmity, to seek the remedy: which is, to withdraw from such bondage. Since our Lord has opened your eyes to let you see what an evil it is to defile yourself with superstition, it only remains for you to come forth of it. Besides, you have less excuse than another, considering the position which you hold, for the reckoning will be twofold, if instead of shewing the way, as you are bound to do, you give occasion to those who see you, to step aside out of it.

As for the other difficulties which are peculiar to your present circumstances, I refer myself to your own experience. More than all that, you have to consider that if the good lady

with just reason dreaded to finish the remainder of her life there, you may well fear a longer period of languishing, according to the ordinary course of nature. There is assuredly no to-morrow that we can make ourselves sure of. Therefore, on the other hand, you ought to make the greater haste, for fear you should be taken unawares. You see, therefore, that God is urging you in every way. Howsoever the matter may be settled, I pray you, Monsieur, not to allow the grace which God has given you to be quenched. If He has given you worldly riches, have a care lest in place of rendering them in homage to Him, you may be hindered by them from serving him. I need not tell you, that He has given you a help which every one has not. This is, that you have a Sarah who will be ready to follow you, whithersoever that kind Father shall call you; so that it depends upon yourself alone whether or not you shall follow the example of our father Abraham. It is quite true that you will find no spot on earth where you can be beyond the reach of trial, as indeed it is not reasonable to expect our faith to be exempt from these anxieties. But since the present is a time of conflict, there is nothing better for us than to fall back upon our standard, where we may receive courage to do battle stedfastly even unto death. It is an advantage not to be despised, when God gives us leisure to confirm our faith, that the preparation may be of service to us in due time and place. For this ought to be quite enough for us, when He arms us with His strength for victory, before putting us to the proof. But seeing that the very beginnings are difficult, and perseverance still more so, the best resource is to pray God that he would stretch out His hand to you, and give you courage to surmount all obstacles. To which end we also would beseech Him along with you, and that He would please to shew Himself your protector even unto the end, upholding you not only against the wicked, but also against Satan their chief. Having humbly commended me to your good favour, and to that of Madame your wife . .
. . . .

JOHN CALVIN.

[*Fr. copy.—Library of Geneva.* Vol. 111.]

## CXCIX.—To Viret.

Citation before the Consistory of the wife of Amy Perrin—case of Gruet—news from Germany.

*2d July* 1547.

We must now fight in earnest. The wife of the comedian Cæsar was again summoned to the Consistory, on account of her frowardness.[1] While there, though she received no provocation, in the form even of too harsh a word, she vomited forth more venom than on any previous occasion. First of all, she denied the right of our court to take cognizance of her, even supposing she had been guilty of a delinquency. In the next place, she complained that she was deeply branded with ignominy, by being compelled to appear in a place to which the depraved and criminal could alone of right be summoned. When one of the assessors sought to restrain her intemperate behaviour, she turned her fury upon him. Abel then interposed, and expressed his surprise that she had at first professed that she was too modest, or too little given to speaking, to be able to answer at greater length, whereas she was a match in abuse for as many as there might be. At this her fury boiled all over. "No, indeed," she says, "but you are a reviler, who unscrupulously slandered my father. Begone, coarse swine-herd, you are a malicious liar!" She would have almost overwhelmed us by her thunders, had she not been forcibly extruded. The Senate desired that she should be more closely imprisoned. She escaped by means of that matron who is wont to take under her patronage all bad causes. One of her sons accompanied her in her flight. Accidentally meeting Abel not far from the city gate, she insulted him afresh, and even more shamelessly than before. Abel said nothing, but conducted himself with the greatest moderation, just as he had done in the Consistory. Next day a paper is found in the pulpit, threatening us with death, unless we remain silent. I

[1] "Complaint of Calvin against the wife of Amy Perrin, who insulted the minister Abel in full Consistory."—*Registers of Council*, 24th June.

send a copy of it to you.[1] The Senate, startled by such audacity, orders a rigid inquiry to be made into the conspiracy. The investigation is committed to a few. As many suspected Gruet, he was immediately arrested.[2] It was, however, a different hand; but while they were turning over his papers, much was discovered that was not less capital. There was a humble petition which he had designed to present to the people in the Assemblies, in which he contended that no offence should be punished by the laws but what was injurious to the state ; for that such was the practice of the Venetians, who were the highest authority in the matter of government ; and that in truth there was danger while this city submitted to be ruled by the brain of one man of melancholy temperament, of a thousand citizens being destroyed in the event of any outbreak. Letters were also found, chiefly written to André Philippe, and to others. In some he named me ; at other times, he had enveloped me in figures of speech, so clumsily contrived, however, that one could lay his finger on what he meant to conceal. There were, besides, two pages in Latin, in which the whole of Scripture is laughed at, Christ aspersed, the immortality of the soul called a dream and a fable, and finally the whole of religion torn in pieces. I do not think he is the author of it ; but as it is in his handwriting, he will be compelled to appear in his defence, although, it may be, that he himself has thrown into the form of a memorandum, according to the turn of his own genius, what he heard from others ; for there are mutilated sentences, crammed with sole-

---

[1] The import of this note, written in the Savoyard language, and affixed to the pulpit of the ministers, was, " that people did not wish to have so many masters ; that they (the ministers) had now gone far enough in their course of censure ; that the renegade monks like them had done nothing more than afflict all the world in this way ; that if they persisted in their course, people would be reduced to such a condition that they would curse the hour in which they emerged from the rule of monachism ; and that they (the ministers) should take care lest as much should be done to them as was done to the Canon Vernly of Fribourg." The last passage was equivalent to a threat of death.

[2] The former canon, Jacques Gruet, of dissolute manners, of licentious and perverse doctrine, constantly opposed to the ministers, and intolerant of all rule in the Church as in the State, had lain under the imputation of having been the instigator of the attempt at poisoning Viret in 1535.—*Histoire de la Suisse*, vol. xi. p. 364.

cisms and barbarisms. I know not whether Jacoba, whose sister is the wife of Des Gallars, has been apprehended. There is, indeed, a decree of the Senate [for that purpose.] What Vandel's sentence will be is still doubtful; but he is in considerable danger.[1] Such was the state of things when I wrote. You know that our Syndics have little enough judgment, otherwise the Senate is exceedingly well disposed to the cause.

The brethren have replied to me regarding Sonnier, that they mean to make no change in their former resolution; for I relaxed, as I had abstained from writing, with a view to spare him. He eagerly made reference to the minister De Coppet, who also wished to change his place. I advise you to examine whether there is any truth in this.

The statements contained in Bucer's letter regarding those two victories are quite certain; for a friend of mine[2] passed through this, who had ascertained the truth of the whole matter. He also informed me that tidings of a third victory had been brought away within two hours before he left Strasbourg; but he did not venture to assert this for certain. He further mentioned to me, that when the Landgrave had come to Leipsic on the strength of the promise made to him, he returned without accomplishing the matter, and in despair, and that he was collecting a new army. The name of Henry[3] was erroneously given in Bucer's letter; for the Landgrave still keeps him in fetters, or at least closely imprisoned. But Bucer was speaking of Erich,[4] who professes the same doctrine with ourselves, and yet hires himself to the tyrant in disturbing the Church. I wish that your Senate could be induced to take the initiative in the stipulated treaty; for Pharaoh wishes to be asked, and thinks it unbecoming his dignity to solicit the

---

[1] Pierre Vandel, one of the chief of the reprobate children of Geneva. Handsome and brilliant, he loved to exhibit himself surrounded by valets and courtezans, with rings on his fingers, and his breast covered with gold chains. He had been imprisoned on account of his debaucheries, and his insolent behaviour before the Consistory.

[2] Doctor Chelius, in the handwriting of Calvin.

[3] Henry of Brunswick.

[4] The personage here designated is doubtless Erich, hereditary prince of Sweden, who ascended the throne in 1560, and was deposed in 1568.

weaker parties.¹ But let them look to these and other matters, that are now in course of arrangement. I desire nothing to be done, unless what I judge to be fitting and useful to you.

Adieu, brother and most sincere friend, along with your wife and your whole family. May the Lord always direct you and be present with you. You will salute the brethren respectfully in my name. I and my wife salute thee and thine in the Lord. —Yours,

JOHN CALVIN.

[*Lat. orig. autogr.—Library of Geneva.* Vol. 106.]


CC.—TO MONSIEUR DE FALAIS.

Solemn lessons afforded by the sad occurrences in Germany—troubles in Geneva—energetic attitude of Calvin.

*This* 14*th of July* 1547.

MONSEIGNEUR,—From what you have written me, I am certainly of opinion that our brother, Master Francis de la Rivière,² should withdraw at least for a season. For should it so be that it suited him to return hither, he would not have to make a long journey: and bringing with him some recommendation from Bâle, he might make application at Berne to be sent to Lausanne, with some provision in the meantime. I should not however have come to this resolution, unless your letter had helped me to it. I have merely told him that you would be glad of his coming, in order that your family might receive instruction from him several times in the week. For I desired to avoid any more definite engagement, that you might remain at perfect liberty in that matter.

¹ A common interest at that time conciliated the King of France and the Swiss. The ambassadors of Henry II., Brissac and Marillac, assured Geneva of the friendship of the King, and took in charge letters of Calvin to the Helvetic Churches.—*Histoire de la Suisse,* vol. xi. p. 358.
² The minister Francis Perucel, called La Rivière.

With regard to the house, I beg you will inform me what you wish me to do about it. But let me have your letter by the middle of August. For according to the use and wont of the town, I have leave to renounce the bargain for the following half year, giving intimation to that effect six weeks before the term. By doing this, you will not be burdened with needless expense; while I fear that by holding it for a longer period, you may incur outlay without return.

I believe Saint André has told you what we have done with *the Apology*. The printing shall not be delayed for want of copy. As for the money, I am not of opinion that you ought to withdraw any of it merely to avoid the murmurs which might thence arise, but rather, that enjoining those who have the charge thereof, to apply it as they ought—correcting abuses, if there be any, you should depute some one to act for you in the matter. However, you will determine that according to your own discretion. But I did not like to withhold what occurred to me, seeing that you have been pleased to consult me on the subject.

We have had no news from Germany since the capture of the Landgrave,[1] who has been suitably rewarded for his baseness. In the present position of affairs, I recognise our God's intention utterly to deprive us of a triumphant Gospel, that He may constrain us to fight under the cross of our Lord Jesus. But let us be content that He return to the early method of His dealings, in the miraculous preservation of His Church by His own power, without the help of an arm of flesh. The trial is hard, I confess; but our fathers have had the like, quite as depressing, and have never been shaken in their stability. Now is the time to put in practice the proverb, "Let us hope and we shall see." Besides, we need not be astonished that God has corrected us thus roughly, considering the life we have led. But as you say, may those who have not hitherto been touched, take note of such examples, that they may humble

---

[1] Intimidated by the defeat of the Elector of Saxony, the Landgrave of Hesse had submitted himself to the Emperor, and only obtained his pardon by imploring it upon his knees, and surrendering his person and states into the power of this prince.

themselves, and by that means prevent the hand of the Judge.

There has been some want of consideration on the part of the commissioners from this town, in not informing me of their departure. However, I do not give up the expectation of tidings from you by them. I do not know whether any report of our troubles has yet reached you, but they talk of them so loudly throughout the neighbouring country, that it would appear all is over with us. More than that, they have often had me dead, or at least sorely wounded. Be that as it may, I feel nothing of it myself. And in the town we are not aware of the hundredth part of what is said. There have, indeed, been some murmuring and threats on the part of loose-living persons, who cannot endure discipline. Even the wife of him who was to go to see you,[1] and who wrote to you from Berne, rebelled very proudly. But it has been necessary that she should betake herself to the country, feeling herself but ill at ease in town. The others, indeed, lower the head, in place of lifting up the horn; and there is one of them who is in danger of paying a very heavy reckoning; I know not even whether it may not cost him his life.[2] The young people think that I press them too hard. But if the bridle were not held with a firm hand, that would be the pity. Yea, we must look to their wellbeing, however distasteful to them it may be.

Monsieur, having humbly commended me to your kind favour and that of Madame, I pray our good Lord that He may have you always in His keeping, strengthening you by His Holy Spirit to resist all temptations, and making you abound in all well-doing to His honour. And seeing that the time of

---

[1] Amy Perrin. His wife, daughter of a rich burgess, François Favre d'Echallens, and reprimanded incessantly by the Consistory, was the implacable enemy of the ministers and of Calvin.

[2] Jacques Gruet, formerly a Canon, and a man of licentious and irregular morals, impatient of all restraint either of Church or State. Severely censured by the ministers on account of his debaucheries, he had uttered threats of death against them, which he even ventured to affix to the pulpit of St. Peter's Church. His trial, conducted with all the rigour of that period, terminated by a sentence of capital punishment. Condemned for sedition, blasphemy, and atheism, he perished on the scaffold the 26th July 1547.

the trial of Madame draws near, we shall remember her in prayer for her happy delivery. My wife also presents her humble remembrance to both of you.

Your servant and humble brother,

JOHN CALVIN.

[*Fr. orig. autogr.—Library of Geneva.* Vol. 194.]

## CCI.—To VIRET.[1]

Indecision of the Seigneurs of Geneva—inflexibility of Calvin.

GENEVA, 24*th July* 1547.

There is nothing new in our affairs. The Syndics protract the case of Gruet against the will of the Senate, which does not, however, as would be proper, utter any protest against the delay. For you know that few of them are judicious. I exercise my severity in dislodging common vices, and principally the sources of corruption among the youth. I conceal all sense of the dangers which good men from several quarters allege to exist, lest I should appear over solicitous about myself. The Lord will give the issue in the way that may please himself. Adieu, brother, and most sincere friend, as also your wife and family. May the Lord Jesus continually direct you, and be present with you. You will convey best greetings to the brethren, and to your wife in my name. My wife salutes you and your family.—Yours,

CALVIN.

[*Lat. orig. autogr.—Library of Geneva.* Vol. 106.]

[1] Subjected to torture, Gruet admitted his guilt, and as well on the ground of his impious and blasphemous productions, as of a letter written to a private individual, in which he exhorted the Duke of Savoy to turn his arms against Geneva, he was condemned to death. It appeared, according to the letter of Calvin to Viret, of which a fragment is here reproduced, that this sentence was not unanimous, and that Gruet reckoned up to this time, in the councils of the republic, friends or accomplices who were desirous of saving him. This did not prevent his execution on the 26th July 1547, and the example threw terror into the ranks of the party of the Libertins. On the trial of Gruet, see the various historians of Geneva,—Spon, Picot, and the *Histoire de la Suisse*, vol. xi. pp. 364, 365.

## CCII.—To the Faithful of France.[1]

State of Germany—details regarding the struggles of the Reformer in the cause of the truth at Geneva.

*This 24th of July* 1547.

The electing love of God our Father, and the grace of our Lord Jesus Christ, rest always upon you by the communion of the Holy Spirit.

Very dear lords and brethren, I doubt not that you have daily much news, as well from hence as from Germany, which might prove a stumblingblock to those who are not overmuch confirmed in our Lord Jesus Christ. But I trust in God He has so strengthened you, that you shall not be shaken, either thereby or by any still greater marvel which may yet arise. And verily, if we are indeed built upon that solid stone which has been ordained for the foundation of the Church, we may well sustain more boisterous storms and tempests without being foundered. It is even expedient for us that such things should happen, that the firmness and constancy of our faith may be approved.

As for the state of Germany, our Lord has so abased the worldly pride of our people, and given all power and authority to him from whom we can look for nought but ill, as that it indeed appears that He means Himself to maintain His spiritual kingdom wheresoever He had already set it up. It is very true, that according to the carnal mind it is in danger; yet in commending to Himself the care of His poor Church and the Kingdom of His Son, let us hope that He will provide for all, beyond what we can think. The danger hitherto has been,

---

[1] *Entitled:* To our very dear lords and brethren who desire the advancement of the Kingdom of our Lord Jesus Christ.

During the period that the Reformation was for a while overcome in Germany, and that it had to sustain the rudest conflicts in order to its establishment at Geneva, the most alarming reports were spread among the French Protestants, and carried discouragement and dismay into their ranks. Calvin, addressing his brethren from the midst of the struggle in which he was engaged against the party of the Libertins, reassured and comforted them by his letters, and exhorted them to place their entire confidence in God.

lest human means might have dazzled our eyes. Now, however, since there is nothing to prevent our looking to His hand, and recalling to mind how He has preserved His Church in time past, let us not doubt but He will glorify Himself in such sort that we shall be amazed. Meanwhile, we must never grow weary of fighting under the ensign of the Cross of our Lord Jesus Christ, for that is worth more than all the triumphs of the world.

As regards the rumours of our troubles which have flown abroad, they seem, the greater part of them, in the first place, to have been improvised; because, were you upon the spot, you would not see a tenth part of what is told at a distance. True it is, that we have many hard-headed and stiff-necked rebels, who on all occasions seek only to raise themselves, and by riotous courses to dissipate and abolish all order in the Church, and these, indeed, as well young as old. And the state of our young people, especially, is very corrupt; so that, when we will not allow them every license, they go from bad to worse.[1] Of late, they were sorely enraged under cover of a small matter. It was because they were not allowed to wear slashed breeches, which has been prohibited in the town for these twelve years past. Not that we would make overmuch of this, but because we see that, by the loop-holes of the breeches, they wish to bring in all manner of disorders. We have protested, however, in the meantime, that the slashing of their breeches was but a mere piece of foppery, which was not worth speaking about, but that we had quite another end in view, which was to curb and to repress their follies. During this little conflict, the devil has interjected others, so that there has been great murmuring. And because they perceived in us more courage than they could have wished, and more determination to resist them, the venom which some of them had concealed within their heart burst forth. But this is nought but smoke; for their threats are nothing else but a splutter of the pride of Moab, who is powerless to execute what he thus presumes to threaten.

Howsoever that may be, you need not be astonished. There have been greater commotions stirred against Moses and against

[1] Ils font des mauvais chevaulx à mordre et à regimber.

the prophets, although they had to govern the people of God; and such exercises are needful for us. Only beseech our Lord, that He would vouchsafe us grace not to flinch, but that we may prefer His obedience to our life if need be, and that we may be more afraid of offending Him than of stirring up all the fury of the wicked against ourselves, and that at length it may please Him to allay all the tumults which might otherwise break the courage of the unsettled, for it is that which downweighs me more than all the rest. This grace our Lord has vouchsafed us, that we have a right good will to remedy the evil, and all our brethren are well agreed to go forward earnestly in that which is our duty, so that there is the same constancy in all. Nothing is needful, except that this good Lord continue to conduct His own work.

I entreat of you, my dear brethren, continue steadfast on your part also; and let no fear alarm you, even although the dangers were more apparent than you have seen them hitherto. May the reliance which God commands us to have in His grace and in His strength always be to you an impregnable fortress; and for the holding fast the assurance of His help, may you be careful to walk in His fear, although, when we have made it our whole study to serve Him, we must always come back to this conclusion, of asking pardon for our shortcomings. And inasmuch as you know well from experience how frail we are, be ever diligent to continue in the practice which you have established, of prayer and hearing of the holy word, to exercise you, and to sharpen and confirm you more and more. Let nothing turn you aside, as sometimes there are many colourable pretexts adduced to justify the remission of such duties. I am convinced that it would be much better that all those who desire to honour God should assemble together, and that every one should call the others thither as by sound of trumpet. But yet, it is much better to have what you have, though it be but a part, than nothing at all. And so, watching well against declension, seek rather to advance in the way of proficiency, and make use of what God gives you,—edifying one another, and in general all poor and ignorant ones, by your good life, that so, by the same means, the wicked may be put to confusion. In so doing, you will perceive the hand of God upon you, to whom I pray that He would increase in you the graces which He has put within you; that He would strengthen you in true consistency; that, in the midst of dogs and of wolves, He would preserve you, and every way glorify Himself in you; after having commended me affectionately to your kind prayers.

Your humble brother and entire friend,

CHARLES D'ESPEVILLE.

[*Fr. copy—Library of Geneva.* Vol. 107.]

## CCIII.—To Monsieur de Falais.

Thanksgivings for the happy deliverance of Madame de Falais—false reports concerning the state of Geneva—details regarding the publication of the *Apology*—indisposition of Calvin, and his regret at being separated from Monsieur de Falais.

FROM GENEVA, *this 16th of August* 1547.

MONSEIGNEUR,—Two days after the arrival of M. Budé, I received your letter, which you had delivered to James Dallichant; so that all of them have been delivered. Thinking to find a messenger, I have twice since then been disappointed; and I was also in doubt whether to undertake the journey. For notwithstanding the hindrances which might detain me, I was afraid that I had no sufficient excuse. But the tidings which have since reached us, have removed that doubt. I return thanks to our Lord, and all our friends along with me, for the happy delivery which he has granted to Madame, praying that he would so bless the offspring which he has given you, that you may have a twofold comfort in them in the time to come, as I do also hope. We shall look for a letter from you shortly. It is enough in the meanwhile to know that all is well as to the main point.

In reply to all that you have sent to me, I had requested Gallars to translate the *Apology*, promising to revise it finally myself. But he has been so negligent, that Master Francis

Baulduin[1] came just in time to begin it. I send you, therefore, his translation, which we have revised together, not to polish it very highly, but merely to see whether the meaning had been truly rendered, at the same time with the French copy in the handwriting of Saint André.

In the Latin epistle of Dryander,[2] I have corrected what appeared to me to be right; you can follow that which shall seem best to yourself. I hope that you will understand who has induced me to write many things, which I did not object to, but which appeared to me to be superfluous, or at least that they would be of no weight with the individual to whom they were addressed.

You will see the answers which I have made in the name of Mademoiselle de Wilergy, and may give effect to, if you think they are the right thing. I speak drily enough to the Abbess, because of the suspicion, which is very strong.

If it please God to settle a church there, it will be a great comfort to your family. But the blessing will extend much further, and will have the effect of removing many stumbling-blocks. It is a great pity the scattering of the handful who met at Vezel.[3] Our Lord, I fear, must have been disposed to punish that excessive moroseness which could only arise from a despising of His blessing. However, I hope that, after having

---

[1] François Baudouin of Arras, a distinguished lawyer, fled to Geneva on account of religion. He became the friend and the secretary of Calvin, whose opinions at a later period he attacked, and betrayed his confidence by robbing him of his most precious papers.—(See Drelincourt, Defence of Calvin, pp. 251, 252.) Called successively as Professor of Law to Bourges, to Strasbourg, and to Heidelberg, Baudouin died in 1573, leaving the reputation of one of the most learned men of his time, and of a most versatile spirit in matters of religion. It has been justly said of him, that he was Roman Catholic in France, Lutheran at Strasbourg, and Calvinist at Geneva.

[2] See note 1, p. 97. Dryander seems at this period to have filled the office of secretary to M. de Falais. He carried on at the same time a correspondence with Calvin, expressing the highest esteem for his character and talents.—*Library of Geneva*, Vol. 110. One of his brothers, John Ensinas, had been burnt at Rome in 1545, a martyr to the Protestant faith.

[3] Some Flemish and French refugees had already formed a community at Vezel, which was enlarged in 1553 by the dispersion of the foreign congregation of London, and which was constituted as a church by the minister Francis Pérucel, called La Rivière.

punished the fanatics and crack-brained persons who have been the cause of all the mischief, He will yet set up again His little flock which remains, and will hold out a hand to them, to lead them always in the right way.

What moved me to urge you about the house, was my fear of the shame I should feel if perhaps you did arrive here and should not find a lodging ready. Besides, the repairs which the landlord thought of making thereon, would not make it fit for your occupation. Thus the rent you are paying for it, would be so much money lost, unless we should fall upon some remedy for it. Although I have taken it for three years, it was at my option to be quit of the bargain at the end of the half-year, on giving intimation three weeks before the term. At this time we shall be foreclosed of that liberty. If you could have decided upon coming, I would have desired the whole to be put in proper repair, that you might be exempt from annoyance. But seeing the matter stands as it does, it is very unadvisable indeed to charge yourself with a house here; only I could have wished to cause you no needless expense. But since you have allowed this half year to pass away, we shall need to take care between this and the end of January, so as not to enter upon the second year.

I perceive that the troubles which we have had here are also exaggerated with you as well as elsewhere. At Lyons they have had me dead in more than twenty ways. Everywhere throughout the country they tell of wonders, of which, God be thanked, we perceive nothing. It is very true Satan has here very many firebrands; but the flame passes off with a blaze like that of flax. The capital punishment which has been inflicted upon one of their companions,[1] has laid their horns in the dust. As for your landlord,[2] I know not what face he will wear towards us when he returns. He appeared to go away on friendly terms, at least manifesting more compunction and respect towards me than formerly. Meanwhile, however, his wife has played the she-devil to such a degree, that she has found it necessary to gain the open country. It is already about three months that he has been absent. He must needs walk softly

---

[1] Jacques Gruet. See p. 114.     [2] Amédée Perrin.

upon his return. Up to the present time, we have got on very well, considering the condition of the servants of God. Had we not been so depressed, we should have been too much at our ease. I believe, indeed, that he may have opened the letter, and that that may have given boldness to Valeran, and to that worthy man with whom he was lodged, to take a second look into them. However that may be, in complaining about it as he does, he must at once avow himself to be a breaker-open of letters, which is certainly the act of a lawless man. As for his wrongs, they weigh no more with me than his person in the scale of importance, which is a little less than a feather. Moreover, it is evident that he was drunk, or at least seeing double, when he thus wrote. Provided he does not go the length of throwing stones, our patience, yours and mine, will not find it very hard to bear with his abuse. We are not better than David, were we even called to bear further injury, and he is at least quite as worthy as Shimei. In that and in greater things, let us pray God that he may vouchsafe us grace to call us to His light, despising the calumnies of those who judge in darkness. I am more sorry than for aught else to see him gone so far astray.

If there is no pressing hurry, or if there might be more hope of reasonable despatch in the absence of the protonotary, I think that it would only be right to await his return, as well that nothing may be done by halves as to avoid the suspicion he might take up that you had watched the opportunity, or anticipated the complaint he meant to make, in terms of his letter, which was not a little dissatisfied. But should there be any *damnum aut periculum in mora*, this consideration ought not to hamper you, so at least methinks. Otherwise the better way will be, to wait for an opportunity to get rid of the whole at once.

As for the book-mark—your own arms, as well as the motto, everything will be liable to be blazoned abroad by those who, without good ground, are, nevertheless, always open-mouthed in speaking evil of us. Howbeit, I find nothing amiss, neither in the one nor in the other. Even had there been no diminishing of the expense, there could be no harm in putting the arms at the beginning, and the motto at the end. But I am much puzzled which of the two methods to choose, unless you were to put your armorial bearings with the saying underneath,— *Qui recedit a malo prædæ est expositus,* with the citation of the chapter.[1]

As regards the marriage,[2] for my part, I would by no means consent to it. You see how confidentially I reply to you. 'The family is very poor indeed. The noblesse of Savoy is very different from that of your country; the man himself is well enough, but not so steady as to withstand evil counsels; subject to illnesses, arising chiefly from a sanguine temperament,—(you fear one reproach; I am afraid of a quite different one, which I would only mention if I desired to be put out of the way, &c.) You had been rash in entertaining his proposal.' Pardon me if I am too forward. I would like better to take the other whom I know, if it fell to me to decide. But it is full time for me to pull up, having certainly exceeded due bounds.

Before I have concluded, a cough has seized me, and hits me so hard upon the shoulder that I cannot draw a stroke of the pen without acute pain.[3] There is a letter to Wendelin, to which I would much desire to have a reply, because there is some inquiry regarding the Commentaries on St. Paul, of which several persons urge the printing. I hope that it shall be profitable, otherwise I would not have composed them. Seeing that the present bearers are not quite certain of going so far as Strasbourg, and that even if they do go, I could not be sure to have an answer by them, I beg you kindly to charge some one of your servants to convey the letter in good time, and to procure the answer.

Monsieur, having heartily commended me to your kind favour, and that of Madame, and also presented to you remembrances from my wife, I pray our Lord that it would please Him to have you in His holy keeping, to preserve to you the blessing He has bestowed, that you may even see the fruit of it, so as to derive more full consolation and joy; and, in the

---

[1] Isaiah lix. 15.  [2] Of Mademoiselle de Wilergy.
[3] The conclusion of the letter is in the handwriting of Francis Baudouin.

meanwhile, to help you in everything, and that continually. I am sorry that I cannot be with you for at least a half of a day, to laugh with you, while we wait for a smile from the little infant, under the penalty of bearing with his cries and tears. For that is the first note, sounded as the key-note, at the beginning of this life—the earnest of a better, that we may smile from the heart when we shall be about to depart from it.

I entreat of you to bear with my indisposition, commending me to the goodly company.

Your servant and humble brother,

JOHN CALVIN.[1]

[*Fr. orig. autogr.—Library of Geneva.* Vol. 194.]


## CCIV.—To FAREL.

False report of Calvin's death—proposition (query) by the wife of Amy Perrin—calumnious accusation against Idelette de Bure—journey of Farel to Geneva.

GENEVA, 21*st August* 1547.

I am more grateful to you than words can readily express, for having spontaneously transferred to us your credit and service, when you thought that we were pressed by great difficulties. In this, however, you did nothing that was novel or unexpected. The reason why I did not avail myself of your offer, was that various rumours were everywhere flying about which I thought had been extinguished, but which would have been the more increased had I summoned hither you and Viret. You know with what sort of men we have to deal, and how eager they are for an opportunity of speaking against us. Letters were daily arriving, especially from Lyons, from which I learned that I had been more than ten times killed.[2] It was therefore proper that the ungodly should be deprived of the

---

[1] The signature of the letter is autograph.

[2] "M. Calvin has represented that letters have been written to him, as well from Bourgoyne as from Lyons, to the effect that the children of Geneva were willing to give five hundred crowns to have him put to death; he does not know who these are."—*Registers of the Consistory,* 1st September 1547.

occasion of talking. The senate is now quieted, and is favourably disposed to the good cause. Amy, our friend, is still in France.[1] His wife is with her father, where she carries on her revels in her usual fashion, and yet we requested the Senate that all past offences might be forgiven her, if she shewed anything to warrant a hope of repentance. That petition has not been granted, for she has gone so far as to have cut off all hope of pardon for herself. As the day of the [Lord's] Supper draws near, I may meet with Penthesilæa. Froment lately made a movement about a reconciliation, but he wished the matter to be settled according to his own arbitration. I replied that our church was not so destitute but that there were brethren competent to undertake that duty. We shall make every effort. And yet she has cruelly wounded me. For when at the baptism of our child James, I had admitted the truth about the fault of my wife and her former husband,[2] she calumniously asserted among her own friends, that my wife was therefore a harlot; such is her bold impudence. I shall treat her not according to what she deserves, but according to what my office demands. Add that N. had invented a most calumnious fable,—to the effect, that I had received a severe reprimand from you and Viret, on the ground that, having been placed here by you in your room, and by way of deputy, I abused my precarious authority. You will now, however, come at a much more opportune time than you would have done before. You would hear everything that cannot be committed to writing. You might apply your hand to wounds that are not yet well healed. We might con-

---

[1] Charged with an important mission to the court of King Henry II., Perrin, on his return, was subjected to the accusation of treason in the carrying out of his commission. The King of France had said that he would give two millions to be master of Geneva. Perrin was accused of having replied, that two hundred horse would be sufficient to conquer the city.—*Hist. de la Suisse,* vol. xi. p. 361. It could not however be proved, that he had contracted secret engagements with France. He was nevertheless imprisoned, afterwards released at the request of the Seigneury of Berne, and stripped of his offices.—*Registers of Council,* September and November 1548.

[2] Idelette de Bure is known to have espoused in her first nuptials an Anabaptist, Jean Storder. According to the doctrines of that sect, which denied the authority of the civil power, the marriage to be legitimate had no need of the sanction of the magistrate.

sult together about the remedying of occult diseases. You will therefore see whether you will have any leisure. I have commenced work upon the Fathers of Trent;[1] but the beginnings proceed slowly. The reason is, I have not an hour that is free from incessant interruptions. Adieu, most sound-hearted brother, and matchless friend; salute respectfully fellow-ministers and your family in my name. May the Lord be always present with you, direct you, and bless your labours. Amen.—Yours,

JOHN CALVIN.

[*Calvin's Lat. Corresp.* Opera, tom. ix. p. 240.]


## CCV.—TO VIRET.

Mention of a letter from M. de Falais—Emmanuel Tremellius—a book by Viret—journey of Budé and Nicolas des Gallars to Paris.

GENEVA, 29*th August* 1547.

Before bringing to a conclusion the matter of Beat, it seems proper to wait the return of Textor, who I know will be here in a short time, unless some new obstacle intervene. For he had been compelled to remove from Macon, when Claude the dyer lately returned from that quarter. The letter from Bâle contained absolutely nothing of interest to you or me. There was but one letter of Falais to me, in which he mentioned the birth of a daughter,[2] of whose death he spoke in a second letter to Maldonado. He had besides sent a copy of the letter of recommendation which the Landgrave had obtained from the Emperor; but I had read a translation of it by Pagnet fifteen days before. I send it you, in case you should not have seen it. I had forgot the epistle of Valeran, in which that wretch so unblushingly insults a perfect nobleman, that I am ashamed to read it. Budé strongly solicited me to exert

---

[1] Allusion to the work which Calvin was at that time preparing against the Council of Trent, and which appeared at the end of the year.—See the Letter to Farel of the 28th December 1547.

[2] See the letter to M. de Falais of the 16th August, p. 118.

myself to bring Emmanuel[1] hither, if it could be accomplished on any ground. His services could be of no avail to us, unless in the professorship of Hebrew; and this office is filled by Imbert. I wish you would excuse me to him, if you have no objection, that he may at least understand that I am not guilty of neglect. Girard has not yet brought the preface, although I reminded him that he should do so to-day. Send the book on the Church and Sacraments.[2] I would read it with pleasure, even although you did not impose that task upon me. Only I request your permission to consult my own convenience; for I never had less leisure than at present. The long nights, however, will presently afford me somewhat more. Des Gallars has left for Paris, along with Budé, as he could not otherwise satisfy his mother; and he could not have had a better opportunity than now, in the absence of his father-in-law. Besides, he has it in view to bring his sister along with him; a modest girl, I hear, and who is harshly treated by her step-father. I wished you to know that. Adieu, most sound-hearted brother and friend, with your wife and brothers, all of whom you will salute in our name. May Christ be ever present with you.

But I had forgot about Veron. Sulzer obtained from the Senate a supplement for him, so long as he should be sick, to meet the unusual expenditure; and also half stipend for Maigret.[3] Lest that arrangement should displease me, Sulzer charged him to return to terms of friendship with me. After asking me to come to him, he made a long enough petition for forgiveness. I replied as I was disposed, and as I was bound to do. The result was that he promised amendment, and I fraternal affection, if he changed his course of life for the better. —Yours,

JOHN CALVIN.

[*Lat. orig. autogr.—Library of Geneva.* Vol. 106.]

[1] Emmanuel Tremelli, a learned Hebraist of Ferrara, disciple of Peter Martyr, at that time in retirement at Strasbourg.

[2] The book,—*De la Vertu et Usage du Saint Ministère et des Sacremens*, Genève, 1548. Senebier, *Hist. Litt.*, vol. i. p. 156, *Art.* Viret.

[3] The minister Antoine Maigret, who was shortly afterwards deposed from his charge.

## CCVI.—To Monsieur de Falais.

*Dedication of the* Apology—*mention of M. de Montmor—Sickness of Maldonado.*

From Geneva, *this* 10*th of September* 1547.

Monseigneur,—By your last, I perceive that I have not yet satisfied you concerning the *Apology*. Although the three points which you have noted need not retard the publication, the excuse may be made in three sentences; because should we enter somewhat further on explanation, we must touch upon rather ticklish matters, which it would be better to let sleep. I do not know to whom it would be well to address it at present, considering the temper of the times. She has already played a principal part: I cannot think of any of the other persons who would be suitable. To dedicate it to the noblesse of the Netherlands, would be a hateful proceeding. In Germany, what States would you choose? I would therefore prefer that no change be made in the beginning. Touching the conclusion, although there is plenty of material, and that very pertinent, that might be added, even as it stands it is not incomplete. Hereafter, should occasion call for it, you will consider whether you should add thereto, or make some other distinct publication. However, I refer the whole to your discretion, and merely express to you my opinion.

Concerning the party you inquire about, I fear that you suppose I build marriages in the air very much at random. But why so? for indeed I believe that I have some foundation of reason and sound confidence. Eight months ago, the son of M. de Montmor, with whom I was brought up in my childhood,[1] informed me that he would desire above all else to retire hither, and he continues of that mind; for it is not

---

[1] We read in the Life of Calvin by Theodore Beza, "From his youth he was all the better, and liberally brought up,—at the expense of his father, however,—in the society of the children of the house of Montmor, whom he also accompanied as the companion of their studies at Paris." It is to one of the members of that noble family, Claude de Hangest, Abbot of Saint Eloy, that Calvin dedicated, in 1532, his Commentary on Seneca's Treatise *De Clementia.*

merely on one occasion that he has so written. He is a young man, at least he is of the age of thirty-four years, good-natured, very gentle, and docile. Though he has drunk deep of youthful follies in earlier life, now that God has given him a knowledge of himself, I believe he will be quite to your mind. I have made diligent inquiry of Nicolas Loser, and Nicolas Picot his son-in-law, who have spoken to him, whether there was any taint of disease about him, such as young men acquire in their dissolute courses. They have replied to me in the negative. My desire has thereupon led me to build an expectation. Should he come, as I expect, I would send him at once to yourself; and then you can consider whether he would be a suitable person. If he does not come within a month, I know not whether I ought to expect him. But I think he will come, to communicate to me, and forthwith return to expedite his departure.

We have been like to lose the good Maldonado, for he has been at the point of death: and the fever even now confines him to bed, but not with imminent danger, so far as we can discern, by the favour of God. I have prepared some verjuice, enough for a year's provision, which awaits you, if perchance you come. It is the produce which you have got from your garden for the bygone year.

In conclusion, Monsieur, having humbly commended me to your kind favour, and that of Madame, I pray our good Lord to have both of you in His holy protection, to lead and direct you, to send you whatsoever He perceives to be needful for you.

Your servant and humble brother,

JOHN CALVIN.

[*Fr. orig. autogr.—Library of Geneva.* Vol. 194.]

The title would appear to me to read well thus: *Excuse composed by M. Jacques de Bourgoigne, &c., to clear himself towards his Imperial Majesty from the calumnies laid upon him on account of his faith, whereof he makes confession.* For the word *Apology* is not used in French.

## CCVII.—To Henry Bullinger.

Comments by Calvin on a work by Bullinger—state of Germany and Italy—policy of the Cantons.

[GENEVA, 19*th September* 1547.]

It is now six months since I returned your book, with annotations, such as you had requested me to make.[1] I am surprised that I have received no reply from you since that time. When I was in your quarter, you reminded me that there was to be frequent interchange of letters between us. In the meantime, I have heard of some of your townsmen having at different times passed through this place; I have had no one going to you, so far as I remember. Should an opportunity of writing be at any time afforded you, I earnestly request you will not allow it to pass without availing yourself of it.

I am compelled to hear more about the disaster of Germany than I could wish; and yet nothing is said of the condition of Constance, which remains deeply fixed in my mind. There was great trepidation at Strasbourg when it was supposed that the Emperor would winter there. Moreover, even to this day, they assert that the gates will not be opened to him, if they receive support from any other quarter. I do not know what the Helvetic cities may think. For a short time, indeed, all rumours of a war to be waged against them have ceased, on

---

[1] Bullinger had submitted his book on the Sacraments to Calvin, (*Absoluta de Christi et ejus Ecclesiæ Sacramentis Tractatio,*) in which he departed slightly from the doctrine of Zwingle, with the view of approximating to that of the French reformer. Still, however, the mystery of the spiritual presence of Christ, under external and material symbols, was not expressed in it with sufficient clearness. Calvin had fully criticised this book in a letter, or rather in an extended memoir, the original of which is preserved at Zurich, under the title, *Censura Libri Bullingeri de Sacramentis,* Geneva, 27th February 1547. This memoir, written with a brotherly freedom, concludes with these words:—" You thus have what in your book I desire to see corrected, that it may meet with absolute approval. I make no note of the parts that merit commendation. I have discharged the office of a friend, by complying with your wishes, and freely admonishing you; it now remains for you to take my liberty in good part. This I am confident you will do."
—*Library of Zurich. Coll. Hottinger,* M. F. 80, p. 338.

account of the Italian commotions. But what if all these cities, struck with terror of him, do not venture upon any movement? He already occupies Placentia and Parma,—Peter Farnese[1] having been put to death as some suppose, or at least, quite prostrated; and so great a success may possibly be the means of bringing Italy into a state of peaceful subjugation in the course of this year. Were he to enter Strasbourg, he would, you perceive, occupy an encampment whence he could invade us. Would there then be time, my Bullinger, for you to deliberate? For by keeping silence, do you not, as it were, present your throat to be cut? On this point, however, I have no good reason for making an appeal to you, for I know that your fellow-citizens will be so wise as to desire to apply a remedy. The neighbours [Bernese] are manifestly acting the part of fools, in withstanding the adoption of any measures for curbing this wild beast.[2] Nevertheless, as they are of their own accord bent on destruction, may the Lord direct His own elect by the spirit of wisdom, to make a seasonable stand against the dangers. There are many things which ought to deter you from the French alliance. But just as, on the one hand, it is by no means expedient that you should be wholly bound up with him [the French king], so, on the other, I do not see that you are to shun all connexion with him.

As to the rest, the boy who has delivered my letter to you, is the son of a senator with whom I am on terms of the greatest intimacy. He has, in virtue of our friendship, requested me to give his son a letter of introduction to you. He lives with your treasurer, as far as I understand. But it is his father's design that he should prosecute the study of letters, of which

---

[1] Peter Farnese, son of Pope Paul III., had in truth been recently assassinated at Placentia, and that city had opened its gates to Charles V. But Parma remained under the power of the Pope, who in vain sued for justice from the Emperor on account of the murder of Farnese, and the dispossession of his children.—Robertson, *History of Charles V.*, B. ix.

[2] The Catholic cantons having engaged to take no step that should have the effect of connecting them with the Emperor, the reformed cantons, with Berne at their head, bound themselves to the strictest neutrality, and informed the German princes, that they could give them no aid without throwing the half of the confederate states into the hands of their enemy.—*Hist. de la Suisse*, Tom. xi. p. 291.

he has acquired the rudiments. He is of a teachable disposition, and fond of study. I therefore beg of you to recommend him to the masters of your school, in your own as well as my name, not simply in the ordinary fashion, that greater attention may be paid to him than if he were unknown. This service will be highly gratifying to me.

Adieu, illustrious sir, and highly revered friend in the Lord, along with your fellow-ministers and brethren, all of whom you will salute in my name and in that of my brethren. May the Lord be continually present with you, and bless your labours. I also wish well to your wife and children.—Yours,

JOHN CALVIN.

[*Lat. orig. autogr.—Archives of Zurich, Gallicana Scripta,* p. 4.]


CCVIII.—To MONSIEUR DE FALAIS.

Return of Nicolas des Gallars—stay of Farel and Viret at Geneva.

FROM GENEVA, *this* 29*th of September* 1547.

MONSEIGNEUR,—Since my last letter nothing new has occurred, except that our brother Des Gallars has returned, and has also brought with him the present bearer for your service, seeing that M. Budé did not find the person ready of whom he had spoken to you. I think and feel assured, that this man will quite suit you; he is so loyal and serviceable, and knows well what is good breeding, so as to demean himself becomingly. I have advised that he should come hither along with you as soon as possible, and chiefly because I do not know whether you have resolved to undertake the journey. I have had no tidings of the individual about whom I wrote to you,[1] only I have heard that some disturbance had broken out at Noyon, which may possibly have delayed him, because he was to have been accompanied by a steward of his own, who must have been detained along with the others.

Master William Farel and Master Peter Viret have been here for a week: your presence alone was wanting to complete

[1] M. de Montmor. See note, p. 127.

the festival. Everything goes on as usual. May God of His grace correct whatever is defective, and increase whatever little good there may be. The good Maldonado cannot raise himself up; so that there is no hope of his being of service to you for the present. But when you have work for my brother to do he will make up for the former failure.

Monsieur, having presented our affectionate remembrances, all, as well to yourself as to Madame, I pray our good Lord to have you always in His holy keeping, to govern you by His Holy Spirit, to bless and to help you in every way.

Your humble brother and servant,

JOHN CALVIN.

In the above remembrances, Master William, Master Peter, my wife, all the friends are included, more than a dozen. I pray also to our Lord, that He may please to rule your whole household, to which I desire to be heartily commended.

[*Fr. orig. autogr.—Library of Geneva.* Vol. 194.]


CCIX.—TO MONSIEUR DE FALAIS.

Re-assuring intelligence on the state of Geneva—restoration of Maldonado.

*The 26th of October* [1547.]

MONSEIGNEUR,—In turning over my papers the other day for another purpose, I found a few words of a preface[1] which I had written on the return of Master Peter Viret. I now send it you, not so much in order that it may be made use of, as to let you know that I had carefully attended to what you had requested of me, although from forgetfulness it had been left there.

I have no doubt but that many reports are flying about at present concerning the affairs of this town. Whatever you may hear of them, let it not prevent your sleeping quite at your ease; for there is a vast number of people who take a

[1] For *The Apology* of M. de Falais.

pleasure in lying, not merely among our neighbours, but also of those within the town.

The good Maldonado is raised up again by the favour of God, but not without great difficulty.

Monsieur, having humbly commended me to your good grace and that of Madame, I pray our good Lord to have you always in His holy keeping. I look for tidings of you about the end of this week.

Your humble brother and servant,

JOHN CALVIN.

[*Fr. orig. autogr.—Library of Geneva.* Vol. 194.]

## CCX.—To FAREL.

*Sad state of the Republic—discouragement of the Reformer.*

GENEVA, 14*th December* 1547.

I am not surprised, and I am thankful that you feel impatient because so few letters from me reach you at this time; for I see from this that we are the objects of solicitude on your part. You are, moreover, daily hearing many reports, some of which may cause you bitter sorrow, and others inspire you with various fears on our account. The rumours that are spread abroad are almost all groundless; but we are oppressed by intestine evils that are so little public as hardly to be known, unless to a few in the city. The wild beast that lately, by the treachery of his keepers, escaped from his den, breathes nothing but threats.[1] Macrin being cast out, there is nothing they do not promise themselves, because they are confident that matters are now entirely in their own hands. For they count upon this [ejection] as constituting the proof of oppressed liberty. Affairs are certainly in such a state of con-

---

[1] According to the testimony of the Registers of Council, Amy Perrin had been restored to liberty, on bail, at the instance of the Seigneury of Berne and his family, and on condition of begging the forgiveness of God and men, and paying the expenses of justice.—*Register*, 23d November 1547. Had this legal liberation been preceded by the escape of the prisoner? We are not aware.

fusion that I despair of being able longer to retain this church, at least by my own endeavours. May the Lord hear your incessant prayers in our behalf. [My] brother will give you a better account of all the circumstances [than I can do by letter.]

Adieu, most upright brother. Salute respectfully all the brethren.—Yours,

JOHN CALVIN.

[*Lat. orig. autogr.—Library of Geneva.* Vol. 106.]

## CCXI.—To VIRET.[1]

Rising at the Hôtel de Ville—heroic bearing of Calvin—trust in God alone.

[GENEVA,] 14*th December* 1547.

[The enemy] are so blinded that they pay no regard to propriety. Yesterday not a little confirmed a suspicion previously entertained by us, that they were shamelessly striving to excite some commotion. The *Two Hundred* had been summoned. I had publicly announced to my colleagues that I would go to the senate-house. We were there a little, indeed, before the hour of meeting. As many people were still walking about in the public street, we went out by the gate that is contiguous to the senate-house. Numerous confused shouts were heard from that quarter. These, meanwhile, increased to such a degree as to afford a sure sign of an insurrection. I immediately ran up to the place. The appearance of matters was terrible. I cast myself into the thickest of the crowds, to the amazement

---

[1] The scene of tumult and sedition described in this letter left so lively an impression on the mind of Calvin, that he recalled it seventeen years afterwards, on his deathbed, in his farewell to the ministers of Geneva, subjoining these memorable words:—" Although I am nothing, yet I know that I prevented three thousand disturbances from taking place in Geneva; but take courage, you will become strong, for God will make use of that city, and will maintain it; and I assure you He will keep it."—*Collection de M. Tronchin, à Genève. Adieux de Calvin, recueillis par Pinaut.*

The Registers of Council are silent on this scene, the date of which has been given, by a frequently repeated mistake, as the 17th September; but the circumstances tally with the 13th December 1547.

of almost every one. The whole people, however, made a rush towards me; they seized and dragged me hither and thither, lest I should suffer any injury. I called God and men to witness that I had come for the purpose of presenting my body to their swords. I exhorted them, if they designed to shed blood, to begin with me. The worthless, but especially the respectable portion of the crowd, at once greatly relaxed in their fervour. I was at length dragged through the midst to the Senate. There fresh fights arose, into the midst of which I threw myself. All are of opinion that a great and disgraceful carnage was prevented from taking place by my interposition. My colleagues, meanwhile, were mixed up with the crowd. I succeeded in getting them all to sit down quietly. They say that all were exceedingly affected by a long and vehement speech, suitable to the occasion, which I delivered. The exceptions were at least few, and even they, not less than the respectable part of the people, praised my conduct in the circumstances.

God, indeed, protects myself and colleagues to the extent of the privilege implied in the declaration of even the most abandoned, that they abhor the least injury done to us not less than they detest parricide. Their wickedness has, however, reached such a pitch, that I hardly hope to be able any longer to retain any kind of position for the Church, especially under my ministry. My influence is gone, believe me, unless God stretch forth His hand.

I can make no certain reply regarding the daughter of our neighbour, because having once already found the father difficult to manage in this matter, I do not venture to raise any expectation. Nothing, however, would be more expedient, in my judgment, than for the man himself to come hither; for the father will strenuously demand that at the very first. Nevertheless, if you so order it, we shall make every endeavour even in his absence. I have not yet spoken to the brother of Du-Plessis. About their quarrel, more at another time.

Adieu, brother and most sincere friend. Salute your colleague and all the brethren. My wife and I wish yours every greeting. May the Lord be perpetually present with you.—Amen.

[*Lat. orig. autogr.—Library of Geneva.* Vol. 106.]

### CCXII.—To Monsieur de Falais.

Printing of *The Apology*—troubles at Geneva.

*The* 19*th December* 1547.

MONSEIGNEUR,—I shall not at present write a very long letter to you, because I was not informed that the messenger would go away so soon. He is an engraver, who had left about two hours before I could speak to our printer. Seeing, therefore, that your armorial bearings would not have been very well suited to the form of the book, I immediately sent after him, and have had them done in lead, as you will see by the proof. I feel quite confident that you will not be sorry that a crown was expended to make the thing quite complete. The printing of the book is not yet begun, because it has been necessary to recast some letters of the fount, which is the same with which the supplication was printed, very readable and handsome. We shall begin it this week, if the Lord will; but we shall not touch the Latin at all, until we hear from yourself. As I have no spare time at present, I shall put off all other matters, and send you an answer in regard to them by Robert, my wife's cousin.

We are somewhat annoyed here by those who ought to bring us peace. I hope, however, that good shall result from it, and that shortly, to the rejoicing of those who desire that God may be honoured. But while our brethren are persecuted by open enemies, we ourselves must needs be troubled by those of our own household. There is one mercy, however, that all is for our profit, provided that we are so well advised as thus to take it. As I have formerly told you, do not be disturbed by anything that is said, setting down the whole as falsehood, until you hear from us how matters go.

Monsieur, having humbly commended me to your kind favour, and to that of Madame, and the whole of your worthy family, I beseech our good Lord to have you in His keeping, to guide you by His Spirit, to send you what to Him may seem meet as best for you.

Your servant and humble brother,
JOHN CALVIN.

I have sent by a trusty man the letter of M. de Varan.
[*Fr. orig. autogr.—Library of Geneva.* Vol. 194.]


## CCXIII.—To Viret.[1]

Invitation to come to Geneva.

GENEVA, 26*th December* 1547.

Amid the great swellings of our commotions, I ought not, nevertheless, to have gone so far as to ask you to come hither, because I knew that you were detained in your own locality by necessary occupations ; and another obstacle stood in the way of it, as it was possible some rumour of your coming might thereupon reach the Arctei. Now, as I hope you have more leisure, you would do a valuable service were you to make yourself ready for the journey on the earliest possible day. I have not yet made up my mind as to what I am finally to do, beyond this, that I can no longer tolerate the manners of this people, even although they should bear with mine : and withal I do not understand why they object to my severity. I should not, however, take it so ill, did I give them offence without even any fault on my part, were I not becomingly impressed with a sense of their wretchedness. For how little of life remains to me, that I should be solicitous about myself ? But I am foolish in handling these matters in a letter, when I am

[1] Disarmed for a moment by the heroic attitude of Calvin in the rising of the 13th December, the parties that divided Geneva were not slow to renew their lamentable strife. The voice of the Reformer was disregarded, and he wrote with deep sadness on the 23d December,—" Our affairs are in no better condition. I do not cease to press upon them, but I cause them to make little or no advancement. I am now returning from the Senate ; I said a great deal, but it is like telling a story to the deaf. May the Lord restore them to their right mind."—Calvin to Viret, MSS. of Geneva, Vol. 106.

confident you will be here presently. Adieu, brother, and dearest friend. May the Lord Jesus protect you along with your wife and whole family. You will salute in my name, and in that of the brethren, your fellow-ministers.—Yours,

JOHN CALVIN.

[*Lat. orig. autogr.—Library of Geneva.* Vol. 106.]

## CCXIV.—To FAREL.

Publication of *The Antidote*—statement regarding the condition of Geneva.

GENEVA, 28*th December* 1547.

My *Antidote*[1] now begins to please me, since it is so greatly approved of by you, for before, I was not satisfied with it. But you who know my daily labours, and still more the contests with which I am not so much occupied as quite wasted, are perhaps ready to excuse me when there is anything not quite perfect. I certainly marvel that any composition worthy of perusal can emanate from me. With regard to your exhortation, that my colleagues and I should persist with unbroken resolution, I may say that neither dangers nor troubles weaken my determination. But as I am sometimes destitute of counsel in matters where confusion so greatly prevails, I desire that God would grant me my discharge,—a foolish wish you will say; I admit that it is so; but what did Moses, that illustrious example of patience? Does he not complain of too heavy a burden being laid on his shoulders? I also am in truth, simply tempted by these thoughts; I do not, however, give way to them. We have inspired some fear in our men, and nevertheless there is as yet no appearance of amendment. Such is their shameless-

---

[1] Calvin had just published his celebrated treatise of the *Antidote*, (*Acta Synodi Tridentinæ cum Antidoto*, 1547,) which he translated into French the year following, with changes fitted to bring it within the comprehension of the people.—*Opuscules*, p. 881. In this work the Reformer passes in review the decrees of the Council of Trent, and refutes them with a merciless logic and a marvellous eloquence. The Catholic theologian Cochlæus replied to him by personal attacks, which Des Gallars and Beza undertook to refute.

ness, that they devour with open and regardless ears all our clamours; finally, the diseases of many are incurable. For thus far we have essayed almost all methods with no success. The last act remains, at which I wish you to be present. You will, I suppose, have learned from my letter to Viret, how God stilled the tragical tumult; for I had given him an injunction to that effect.[1] The *Two Hundred* ordered us, and the other ten peace-makers, to make away with all dissensions.[2] I wished that the initiative should be taken by me. Our Cæsar yesterday denied that he had any quarrel with me; I immediately pressed out the matter from the sore. In a grave and calm speech, I made certain sharp strictures, but such as were calculated to wound very slightly. Although he promised reformation hand in hand, I am afraid that I have preached but to the deaf. I wish you would again gladden me by your arrival. I am aware that some people have complained to Viret of my immoderate severity. I know not what his belief is. I scented out the fact, however, that he was afraid lest I should too greatly indulge my ardour. I have requested him to come hither. One in Terence says: If you were here, you would feel differently. I might say the same. If you were in my place, I know not what you would do. But amid a multitude of sorrows, this likewise must be patiently borne. I do not say these things in reply to you or Viret, but to others who idly censure us. I seem, moreover, to see your *sympathy* for me, so far am I from thinking that you have any hostility towards me. Adieu, best and most upright brother, along with your whole family, whom you will affectionately salute in my name and in that of my wife, as well as all fellow-ministers, and all the godly.—Yours,

JOHN CALVIN.

[*Calvin's Lat. Corresp.* Opera, tom. ix. p. 49.]

[1] See Letter, p. 134.

[2] In testimony of regard for Calvin, the Council adopted the following decree: "Resolved to present to Calvin all the furniture that is in his house belonging to the city, 29th December 1547." The preceding year he had been offered ten crowns as a present, but he refused them, praying the Council to distribute them among the other ministers who were poor compared with him, "and even to diminish his stipend in order to benefit them."

## CCXV.—To the Family of Budé.[1]

Consolations on occasion of the Death of one of its Members.

[1547.[2]]

MESSIEURS AND WELL-BELOVED BRETHREN,—Although the present is addressed particularly to two of you,[3] I nevertheless write in suchwise, that if you think fit it may serve for the whole household. If the account which I have heard of the death of your good brother and mine have been the occasion of joy to me, as, indeed, there was good reason for it, you who have known better the whole matter, have, assuredly, far more ample matter for rejoicing, not for that you have been deprived of so excellent a companion, on which account both you and I have good ground for regret—all the more that the number of those who in the present day walk constantly in the fear of God is so small and rare, but because of the singular grace which God had conferred upon him, of perseverance in the fear of His name, the faith and patience which he has manifested, and other tokens of true Christianity. For all that is as a mirror wherein we may contemplate the strength wherewith our kind heavenly Father assists His children, and most of all, out of their greatest difficulties. Then, also, we may conclude that his death was indeed happy and blessed, in the face of Him and

---

[1] This family had not yet quitted France. See the letters, pp. 76, 105. They received this new letter of Calvin, on the occasion of the death of one of its members, perhaps Mathieu de Budé, who had corresponded with the Reformer in 1546, and of whom, subsequent to this period, all trace is lost. There exists (MSS. of the Library of Geneva, vol. 109) a letter of Mathieu de Budé to Calvin, relative to the assassination of John Diaz at Neubourg. We remark the following passage: —" I have received your letter . . . which was most welcome to me, as well because I recognise in it your disposition of goodwill and love, as on account of the ordinary consolation which I have received from it. . . ."—26th April 1546. The author of that letter is not mentioned by M. Galiffe.—*Notices Généalogiques*, tom. iii. p. 83. He had died, no doubt, before the establishment of his family at Geneva.

[2] Dated, on the back of the letter, in a foreign hand.

[3] Doubtless these were John de Budé, Sieur de Vérace, and Louis, Sieur de la Motte, his brother.

of all His angels. At the same time, you must reflect that it is a fine example for you, lest it be converted into a testimony against you, to make you inexcusable before God, the great Judge. For inasmuch as he, dying as a Christian, has shewn you how you ought to live, it is certain that God would not have such a testimony to be useless. Know, then, that the death of your brother is as God's trumpet, whereby He would call upon you to serve Him alone, and this far more loudly than if your brother had lived ten years longer to exhort you: while, besides, the pious exhortations which he addressed to you are ever sounding in your ears, that his zeal may glow in your hearts, that his earnest and instant prayers may quicken you, to draw you towards Him to whom he has been gathered and restored as one of His own. I do not doubt that his expressed condemnation of the abuses and superstitions which exist in Christendom, may have given occasion of murmuring to many, and that it may have somewhat aroused the rage of the adversaries of the Gospel against the whole family; but it is not fitting that the plots and threatenings of the wicked should have more power to discourage our hearts than so effectual a call from God to uphold us. In short, you must take heed that the blessing become not an occasion of evil to you; wherefore, if hitherto ye have begun well, which, indeed, ought to prove a help to you in going forward, do not slacken, but rather redouble your ardour, so as to run with greater diligence. I am not ignorant of the dangers which environ you, and am not so devoid of fellow-feeling, as not to have that sympathy which I ought. But you are aware, that will not excuse such a degree of timidity as there is among those who mingle in the world, disguising themselves in every way; and so much the more that there are few who are quite exempt from it, our duty is to urge and provoke one another forward; and inasmuch as every one ought to do his utmost to walk according to the measure of knowledge vouchsafed to him, you should examine the more narrowly whereunto ye have attained. For you cannot pretend the common excuse wherewith the most part cover themselves, as with some moistened rag of a palliative, namely, that God has not yet bestowed so much grace upon them. For besides that God has opened your eyes to make you understand with what zeal you ought to glorify Him before men, above all, the profession you have made obliges you to it as well. Nought remains, therefore, except that you disencumber yourself of worldly anxieties, to seek in good earnest the everlasting kingdom of our Lord Jesus Christ. And if it be not possible to confess Him as your Saviour where you are, you should far rather prefer to be removed for a little while from the country of your birth than to be for ever banished from that immortal inheritance to which we are called. Whether willingly or no, we must needs be strangers in this world; shall we then refuse even to stir from the nest? Happy, indeed, are they who declare, not merely by empty profession, but effectually, that they are so, and rather than decline from the faith, are quite ready at once to quit their home, and, in order to dwell in union with Jesus Christ, make no difficulty about parting with their earthly comforts. These are hard sayings to those who have not tasted the worth of Christ; but to you, who have felt His power, all else ought, after the example of Saint Paul, to be counted but as filth and dung. Indeed, it is not enough that you yourselves keep steadfast, but if there be others who are weaker, you ought to strengthen them by your admonitions, and to look well to it that there be no falling away.

I myself am far from the dealings of the present time; whether that will be of long continuance I know not. But I speak of a thing known and experimentally ascertained. It is a great shame that with such a measure of knowledge as God has vouchsafed us, there is so little heart, compared with the ardour of the martyrs who have gone before us, who were ready to go to death so soon as God had enlightened them with a far less amount of understanding. We learn somehow to make shift while we ought rather to be learning to live; but there are others in worse plight than we; for, to speak the truth, there are many who dare not venture to breathe a word, but are content to dream apart, and to feed upon their fancies, instead of rather seeking, as they ought, to be continually exercised, as well by reading together as by conference and godly conversation, the more to confirm and enkindle holy zeal. I have no reason to distrust you ; but you will pardon my anxiety, which proceeds from an upright love, if I am moved to warn you in the name of God, not to let such a blessing be lost, as that which God has sent to your family; and that you may not lessen it, take heed to grow in grace ; that you may not draw back, determine to go forward ; that you may not come short, resolve to go on unto perfection.

Wherefore, Messieurs and beloved brethren, after hearty commendations to all of you who desire the kingdom of our Lord Jesus Christ, and serve God with a good conscience, I beseech this kind Father to have you in His protection, and to make you feel it, so as you may lay hold upon Him with such boldness as should belong to you, that He would guide you by His Spirit in the obedience of His will, and glorify Himself in you, even unto the end.

CHARLES D'ESPEVILLE.

[*Fr. Copy, Library of Geneva.* Vol. 168.]


## CCXVI.—TO MONSIEUR DE FALAIS.

*Cost of printing of* The Apology—*despatch of several copies.*

*The* 24*th of January* 1548.

MONSEIGNEUR,—Until the return of Sire Nicolas, I shall not trouble you with long letters, for I expect more ample news by him. Rest assured, that if I may follow my inclination, please God I shall not fail to keep my promise.[1] But seeing that I am not a free man, I must needs abide the course of events. We have, God be thanked, another sort of tranquillity than during the time of billeting. But there is never any season throughout the year in which I have not my work cut out for me, and

---

[1] He refers to the promise of a visit to M. de Falais. Calvin went in fact to Bâle the 2d of February following. We read under that date, in the Council Registers of the state of Geneva :—" Calvin went to Bâle. The Council offers him things requisite for the voyage. 26th February,—Calvin on his return from Bâle."

more than I could well get through, even although I were a tolerable tailor.

That which detains me at this time would be explained if I could only come to you. And, besides, were I to be prevented by some unlooked for business, Master Peter Viret, who is ready to supply my place, will explain it to you. But before speaking of a substitute, we shall see what the Lord will allow.

Concerning the books,[1] at the price which I have agreed upon with the printer, together with what has been paid to the engraver of the armorial bearings, they will cost you about a crown the hundred. I gave three florins of Savoy, that is to say, testons, to the engraver for his trouble : besides which, he got his victuals. That, with about a teston which it cost him in returning, is over and above the amount for printing. There have been eight hundred copies thrown off. I have allowed the printer to retain a hundred for himself, deducting to that amount proportionally upon the whole. By this means the object has been attained of spreading it throughout France. I have sent away here and there about fifty copies ; among others, one to Madame de Ferrara,[2] which, however, need not prevent you addressing another to her, along with a letter. The seven hundred, all expense included, amount to seven crowns. I believe that René, diligence excepted, will have been faithful.

In conclusion, Monsieur, having commended me affectionately to your kind favour and that of Madame, and having also presented to both of you the recommendations of my wife, I beseech our good Lord to have you always in His keeping, to guide you by His Spirit, and to increase you in every grace.

Your humble brother and servant,

JOHN CALVIN.

I desire particularly to be remembered to the excellent young ladies whom I have not yet seen, and my wife the like.

[*Fr. orig. autogr.—Library of Geneva.* Vol. 194.]

[1] *The Apology* of M. de Falais.
[2] Renée of France, Duchess of Ferrara. See, in this collection, the letters of Calvin to that princess.

## CCXVII.—To Monsieur de Falais.

Particulars regarding his departure, and the purchase of a property near Geneva.

*This last day but one of February* 1548.

Monseigneur,—According to our agreement, the coming of Sire Nicolas Loser will afford you a good opportunity for making the journey, if your health admits of it.[1] He ought to go as far as Strasbourg ; but in order that you may not be delayed, I have somewhat hastened his departure. To those who make inquiry of me, I reply, that already you are wishing to be here ; but that whether you shall come or no, will be seen in due time.

Regarding the payment, which you have hinted to me, I believe that you will be disposed to grant it. We shall speak about that, however, when you are on the spot. The minister of the village[2] is a good sort of a man. But it will be for yourself to decide when you shall have arrived. Meantime we shall look about, here and there, that you may choose what best pleases you. I shall take care of the two receipts until your arrival.

To conclude, Monsieur, having commended me humbly to your kind favour, I beseech our good Lord to uphold you always in his keeping, to lead you by His Spirit, and to aid you in all and throughout. We pray you, my wife and myself, to present also our humble commendations to Madame, not forgetting Mademoiselle de Brédan.

Your servant, humble brother, and sincere friend,

John Calvin.

I thought, indeed, that Sire Nicolas Loser would have left, and that he was to be my messenger, but this will not be for

---

[1] In the journey which he had recently made to Bâle, Calvin had decided M. de Falais to come and fix himself definitively at Geneva.

[2] Veigy, near Geneva. M. de Falais made there the purchase of a domain which he occupied during several years.

five or six days yet; and to avoid delay I have thought it well to send the present by M. Brevassis.

[*Fr. orig. autogr.—Library of Geneva.* Vol. 194.]

## CCXVIII.—To HENRY BULLINGER.[1]

Brotherly explanations regarding the difference on the subject of the Communion.

GENEVA, 1st *March* 1548.

I hardly know what prevented me from replying sooner to you, unless it were that no trustworthy messenger presented himself who roused me to diligence. But when I heard that the ambassador of your city was here, I was unwilling to be guilty of allowing him to depart without a letter from me. I pass over in silence the long reply in which you seek to wash away all those points of difference about which I had carefully admonished you. For of what avail is it for us to enter on a controversy? I made a note of those points in your book that did not satisfy myself, or that might prove unsatisfactory to others, or such as I thought might not meet the approbation of the pious and learned. I did that at your request. I discharged the duty of a friend; if you think differently, you are at liberty to do so, as far as I am concerned. It would certainly not be the last of my wishes that there should be perfect harmony between us. But in whatever way I may hold the firm persuasion of a greater communication of Christ in the Sacraments than you express in words, we will not, on that account, cease to hold the same Christ, and to be one in Him. Some day, perhaps, it will be given us to unite in fuller harmony of opinion. I have always loved ingenuousness, I take no delight in subtleties, and those who charge others with obscurity, allow me the merit of perspicuity. Neither, accordingly, can I be charged with guile, who never artfully affect anything to gain the

[1] See letter to Bullinger of 19th September 1547, p. 129. The observations of Calvin on the treatise on the *Sacraments* being badly received, as it appears, by the minister of the Church of Zurich, had led, on the part of the latter, to a temporary coldness, of which Calvin complained in a letter, characterized alike by the noblest independence and the most Christian affection.

favour of men; and my method of instruction is too simple to admit of any unfavourable suspicion, and too detailed to offend on the ground of obscurity. Wherefore, if I do not give uniform satisfaction, indulgence must be extended to me because I study in good faith, and with perfect candour, openly to declare what I have to say. It was on this account that lately, when at Bâle, I felt surprise at your complaint, as a friend reported to me, that I taught differently in my Commentaries from what I had held out to you. I replied in one sentence, which was the truth, that I used the same language at Zurich as at Geneva. I was, however, disposed to attribute the whole statement, be it what it might, to the mistake of my informant. At a time when it was dangerous for me to declare in language what views I held, I did not turn aside from the straight line by foregoing the free and firm announcement of my opinions in every particular, even so far as to bend the most rigid to some sort of moderation. Why then should I now, without any necessity, change at once my general mode of procedure and my convictions? If, however, I fail in persuading men of the truth of this, I shall be content to have God as the witness of my confession.

Your ambassador will give you a fuller and more perfect account of affairs in France than I can compress in a letter. I wish they were of such a kind as it would give you pleasure to hear; but there is nothing except sad news daily. Although he was ordered to abstain from all the abominations of the Papacy, he could not avoid observing a disgraceful profanation of the sacred ordinance of baptism.

Adieu, illustrious Sir, and highly to be revered brother in the Lord. You will respectfully salute in my name Masters Pellican, Bibliander, Walter, and the other fellow-ministers and masters of the school. May the Lord Jesus guide you by His own Spirit, bless your pious labours, and preserve you safe.

All my colleagues also reverently salute you. To your wife and family the best greeting.—Yours,

JOHN CALVIN.

[*Lat. orig. autogr.*—*Arch. of Zurich. Gallicana Scripta,* p. 8.]

## CCXIX.—To Monsieur de Falais.

*Obstacles to his departure—delay of some months.*

*The 3d of April* (1548.[1])

MONSEIGNEUR,—Your letter has arrived just in time to stop the departure of my brother; for that was a settled matter, if I had not been informed. But in my opinion the reasons which detain you where you are, are not of such importance as you deem them. You see how familiarly I write to you on this point, and I do not fear to do so, being authorized by yourself. I had not thought that you would need expressly to renounce your rights as a burgess,[2] although I foresaw clearly that it would amount to a tacit renunciation when you settled your domicile in another seigneury. Seeing that there is an advantage in it, you are right to go thither, unless we could effect some such arrangement as the following: that even were you to be longer absent, they should allow you to remain upon the roll, on condition of your providing a substitute who should discharge during your absence your duties as a burgess; or even if there was no hope of that, might you not present a new request, notwithstanding the reply which they have given you, to beg of them, that in the event of its suiting your convenience to remain here, or that after you were come here, it might not suit you to return, they should be satisfied with your renunciation by a procurator. But I would state the two conditions thus: that notwithstanding the reply they have made to you, inasmuch as you are uncertain when you shall have come hither, whether you shall think fit to fix your residence here, you would therefore beg of them, that on condition of your engaging, as indeed you ought, to supply any deficiency that may arise owing to your absence, it would please them still to retain you for some time on the roll of burgesses—in fact, to grant

---

[1] On the back, in the handwriting of M. de Falais:—Received the 12th April 1548.
[2] M. de Falais could not establish himself at Geneva, without losing the right of a burgess, which he had acquired at Bâle.

an extension of your leave. Or, at the least, fearing to be troublesome by your importunity, that you pray them to accept a renunciation by letter, on account of your bodily weakness, as they are aware that it is not very easy for you to move from place to place. By so doing, you will remove the suspicion they may have conceived, that you mean to abandon them entirely. However it may turn out, I think they will have good reason to be satisfied. In any case, I never expected that the rights of a burgess would be long continued to you.

Touching the rumour which your clowns have spread abroad in order to calumniate you, it scarcely astonishes me. I had quite laid my account with it, that you would not get away without many of them letting loose their tongues. And you must be prepared for that, as well for the other year as for this one. You have this comfort, however, that it all very soon goes off in smoke. I am still less alarmed at the threat whispered in the ear, for it would need great courage to venture on such a step; and I know not who would dare to be the leader in an affair of so great difficulty and hazard. In short, I can perceive no danger for you, according to our arrangement of each day's journey. But seeing that you think it better to put it off for some months, and that the advice of some friends is to that purport, I have no mind to press it further, and would rather agree to this delay, than by urging you to a contrary course lead you to incur the risk of mischief or of annoyance.

I know not whether this summer will disclose the councils of those who may set the world in confusion.[1] For my part, I do not think so, unless some new accident turn up. However, I do not so much place reliance upon my own conjectures, as I await the course of events in submission to the will of God.

Although your coming hither may be stayed for a season, it will be of no consequence as regards the house, for I had concluded no agreement about it. Only I had purchased a good cask of wine, such as it would be difficult to get again. But I have got rid of it without any difficulty, and even as a favour

---

[1] The Emperor, and the new king of France, Henry II. Faithful to the policy of Francis I., a persecutor of the Reformation in his own States, the latter was about to conclude a secret treaty with the Protestant princes of Germany.

to the purchaser. Therefore it will be for you to consider how matters go yonder, and thereupon to decide. And do not annoy yourself lest any one should be offended by your change of plan, for although all your acquaintances desire much to see you here, still there is not one of them who does not prefer your quiet and convenience.

If I could have found a suitable messenger, I would not have waited so long before sending the complement of the *Apologies*. But I know not by what means to do so, for up to this time, no opportunity either of carrier or bearer has occurred. When I can find one, I shall not fail to do so. About the Latin copies you have never expressed to me your wish, as far as I know. Perhaps you would rather defer doing so until your arrival. Let me know your mind regarding this, if you please, in one word; if you would have them printed, it shall be done.

To conclude, Monseigneur, having humbly commended me to your kind favour, I beseech our good Lord to keep you in his protection, to have such a care of you as that all your steps may be directed by him, and to make you serviceable always more and more for his own glory. My wife also presents her humble commendations, and both of us desire to be remembered to Madame and to Mademoiselle de Brédan.

Your humble brother and servant,

JOHN CALVIN.

[*Fr. orig. autogr.—Library of Geneva.* Vol. 194.]

## CCXX.—To FAREL.[1]

Distressing condition of the Swiss churches.

GENEVA, 30*th April* 1548.

My grief prevents me from saying anything of the dreadful calamity that hangs over so many churches. Michael will

[1] While persecution decimated the Reformed Churches of France, and the proclamation of the *Interim* dispersed those of Germany, the Swiss Churches were a prey to the most grievous dissensions, and appeared further removed than ever from that era of unity and peace which Calvin never ceased to invoke for them.

inform you of what I wrote to Viret. The cause is of such a nature that no one is to be reckoned among the servants of Christ who does not come forward boldly in His defence. But there is need of counsel and some moderation. Should Viret agree to it, I shall presently hasten to your quarter, that we three may thence proceed together to Zurich. As to the rest, Viret and I marvelled as to what decision by arbitration you referred to; for neither of us has hitherto heard anything of the matter. I, indeed, assert for certain, that no hint of any kind was ever given to me. See, therefore, who has undertaken this business. You will hear the other matters from the messengers.

Adieu, brother and most sincere friend, along with your family and fellow-ministers, whom I desire respectfully to salute. May the Lord preserve you all and govern you by His own Spirit.—Amen. Yours,

JOHN CALVIN.

[*Lat. orig. autogr.—Library of Geneva.* Vol. 106.]

## CCXXI.—TO FAREL AND VIRET.[1]

Disputes among the ministers of Berne—and Calvin's journey thither.

GENEVA, 9*th May* 1548.

After receiving your last letter, I had set out on my journey; but meeting the father-in-law of my brother Coppet, who told me that you had left Berne three days before, I returned home for several reasons, which, if it shall be deemed necessary, I will detail to you when I see you. Make me now aware of what you intend to do; for I will straightway execute whatever you shall demand, without the slightest deliberation. I have not yet been able to understand the result of your pro-

---

[1] " Calvin informs the Council of certain disputes between the Seigneury and the ministers of Berne, which have gone so far that three of the ministers of said city have been deposed, besides Peter Viret of Lausanne; requests that leave may be given him to go to Berne to defend Viret, which was granted him; the Seigneury, besides, undertaking to defray the expenses of the journey."—*Registers of Council,* May 7, 1548.

ceedings. Giron and Zerkinden requested greetings to me. When Nicolas asked whether they had anything to say besides, he got the answer that there was nothing good. I hence suspect that the matter is worse than they were willing to express. Adieu, brethren most dear to me. Both of you salute the brethren. May God preserve you all, guide you by His own Spirit, and establish you amid these stormy troubles.

When you, Viret, have read Bucer's letter, you will give it to the bearer of this that it may be carried to Farel. I have understood, besides, that Duke Christopher of Wurtemberg, with his father, has set out for the court of the Emperor. We thus see that all is in the hand of one. Nevertheless the Lord will either close it, or wither it, or cut it off, as seems good to Him.

[*Lat. orig. autogr.—Library of Geneva.* Vol. 106.]

## CCXXII.—To Viret.

Communications regarding affairs at Berne.

[Geneva, *June* 1548.]

You will say to Farel that I had written to Bucer before his letter reached me. I send you a copy of a letter to Sulzer. I have resolved to write to Bullinger and Haller, should I be permitted and have leisure. This is the reason why I do not return the letter of Gualter. It is necessary that the threats of Ludovic form the matter of judicial inquiry by the brethren. When he shall have been convicted by them, I doubt not but that he will be proceeded against according to law. I shall indicate in my next letter, what form of process I think should be adopted. Adieu, dearest brother in the Lord, and most sincere friend. I sincerely congratulate you on the safe delivery of your wife, and the addition to your family.[1] I wish that I

[1] By his second wife, Sebastienne de la Harpe, Viret had three daughters, designated in his will as Marie, Marthe, and Jeanne.—(*MS. of the Arch. of Geneva.*)

could be present at the baptism. This desire I assuredly cherish in common with yourself. But I shall be present with you in spirit.

May the Lord continue to bless you in all things.—Amen.

[*Lat. orig. autogr.—Library of Geneva.* Vol. 106.]

## CCXXIII.—To Viret.[1]

Ecclesiastical tyranny of the Seigneurs of Berne—sojourn of Idelette de Bure at Lausanne.

[Geneva,] 15*th June* 1548.

I took care to have a copy of the letter which I wrote to Bullinger and Haller transcribed for you, in case its contents should be reported differently from what you may have thought it proper they should have been; for, as far as I am concerned, the letter itself contains my opinion to the best of my judgment. If the reason must be assigned, I not only look to what is becoming in honourable men, but I further fear that we may suffer a heavy penalty if, by servile dissimulation, we strengthen the tyrannical power which barbarous men already openly usurp. We may serve Jodocus,[2] and other such beasts, provided only they form no barrier to our serving Christ; but when the truth of God is trodden down, woe to our cowardice if we permit this to be done without protest. It should not even be tolerated that an innocent man should suffer injury. At this time, both numerous servants of Christ and his doctrine itself are assailed. Is it not full time that all the godly, both collectively and individually, should raise their heads in His cause? But, nevertheless, that you may come to a free decision,

---

[1] See letter of 9th May preceding. The relations between the Vaudois ministers and the Seigneury of Berne, became daily more complicated. A synod assembled at Lausanne, having ventured formally to propound ten propositions contrary to the celebrated disputation of Berne, and to manifest an inclination in favour of ecclesiastical discipline, with the concurrence of two Bernese ministers, Beat Gerung and Simon Sulcer,—these two clergymen were arbitrarily deposed by the Seigneury, under the pretext of "the maintenance of peace and tranquillity in the Church."—Ruchat, tom. v. pp. 343, 344.

[2] Jodocus, minister of the Church of Berne.

making no account of my pre-judgment of the case, you are not only permitted, so far as I am concerned, but I even wish you to give your opinion. Should it seem proper to allow Farel a reading, I will take care that another copy be sent to him, that I may receive back the one I send to you.

It is truly a source of pain to me that my wife should have been so great a burden to you; for she could not have been of much service to your wife when confined, so far as I can divine, since she herself, on account of the state of her health, stood in need of the assiduous attentions of others. It is matter of comfort to me to be persuaded that you would not bear it impatiently.

Adieu, brother and most sincere friend. May the Lord guide you, and protect your whole family.—Amen. Yours,
JOHN CALVIN.

[*Lat. copy—Library of Geneva.* Vol. 111.]

## CCXXIV.—To HENRY BULLINGER.[1]

New explanations regarding the Supper—Violence of some of the Bernese ministers—Calvinism and Buceranism.

GENEVA, 26*th June* 1548.

Your letter at length reached me, eight days after I had arrived at home. Reust was not himself the bearer of it; it was brought by Roset. The former, I suppose, was less solicitous about the delivery of it, as he had found a master without our assistance. We both, however, courteously placed our services at his disposal. With regard to your small treatise to which you refer in your letter, I wish, my Bullinger, as we were lately in your quarter, it had not been troublesome to you and your colleagues to have talked together in a quiet way of

[1] See the letters, pp. 129, 146. In a new message to Bullinger, Calvin strove to dissipate the still lingering prejudices entertained by the Zurich theologians against those of Geneva and of Strasbourg, regarding the Sacraments; and he proposed the basis of that union, long-desired, which was consummated the following year between Zurich and Geneva. The Church of Berne, now deeply imbued with Lutheran views, refused its adhesion.

the whole matter. There would assuredly have been some advantage in this; for I had not come prepared for a stage display, which is not less disagreeable to myself than it is to you, to say nothing of Farel, whose disposition you are also aware is utterly averse from ostentation. But we were anxious to discuss with you in a familiar way, and with not the least desire to engage in formal debate, those points with regard to which we are most nearly at one. And this indeed were the best method of procedure among brethren, and one we should have found profitable, unless I am greatly deceived. For with regard to the Sacraments in general, we neither bind up the grace of God with them, nor transfer to them the work or power of the Holy Spirit, nor constitute them the ground of the assurance of salvation. We expressly declare that it is God alone, who acts by means of the Sacraments; and we maintain that their whole efficacy is due to the Holy Spirit, and testify that this action appears only in the elect. Nor do we teach that the sacrament is of profit, otherwise than as it leads us by the hand to Christ, that we may seek in Him whatever blessings there are. I do not in truth see what you can properly desire as wanting in this doctrine, which teaches that salvation is to be sought from Christ alone, makes God its sole author, and asserts that it is accepted only through the secret working of the Spirit. We teach, however, that the sacraments are instruments of the grace of God; for as they were instituted in view of a certain end, we refuse to allow that they have no proper use. We therefore say, that what is represented in them, is exhibited to the elect, lest it should be supposed that God deludes the eyes by a fallacious representation. Thus we say, that he who receives baptism with true faith, further receives by it the pardon of his sins. But lest any one should ascribe his salvation to baptism as the cause, we at the same time subjoin the explanation, that the remission flows from the blood of Christ, and that it is accordingly conferred by baptism only in so far as this is a testimony of the cleansing which the Son of God by his own blood shed on the cross procured for us, and which He offers for your enjoyment by faith in His gospel, and brings to perfection in our hearts by His Spirit. Our opinion regarding regeneration is precisely similar to that about baptism. When the signs of the flesh and blood of Christ are spread before us in the Supper, we say that they are not spread before us in vain, but that the thing itself is also manifested to us. Whence it follows, that we eat the body and drink the blood of Christ. By so speaking, we neither make the sign the thing, nor confound both in one, nor enclose the body of Christ in the bread, nor, on the other hand, imagine it to be infinite, nor dream of a carnal transfusion of Christ into us, nor lay down any other fiction of that sort. You maintain that Christ, as to his human nature, is in heaven. We also profess the same doctrine. The word *heaven* implies, in your view, distance of place; we also readily adopt the opinion, that Christ is undoubtedly distant from us by an interval of place. You deny that the body of Christ is infinite, but hold that it is contained within its circumference. We candidly give an unhesitating assent to that view, and raise a public testimony in behalf of it. You refuse to allow the sign to be confounded with the thing; we are sedulous in admonishing that the one should be distinguished from the other. You strongly condemn impanation; we subscribe to your decision. What then is the sum of our doctrine? It is this, that when we discern here on earth the bread and wine, our minds must be raised to heaven in order to enjoy Christ, and that Christ is there present with us, while we seek Him above the elements of this world. For it is not permitted us to charge Christ with imposition; and that would be the case, unless we held that the reality is exhibited together with the sign. And you also concede that the sign is by no means empty. It only remains that we define what it contains within it. When we briefly reply, that we are made partakers of the flesh and blood of Christ that He may dwell in us and we in Him, and in this way enjoy all His benefits, what is there, I ask, in these words either absurd or obscure, especially as we, in express terms, exclude whatever delirious fancies might occur to the mind? And yet we are censured, as if we departed from the pure and simple doctrine of the Gospel. I should wish, however, to learn what that simplicity is to which we are to be recalled. When

I was lately with you, I pressed this very point. But you remember, as I think, that I received no answer. I do not make this allegation so much by way of complaint, as that I may publicly testify to the fact that we lie under the suspicion of certain good men without any ground for it. I have long ago observed, moreover, that the intercourse we have with Bucer acts as a dead-weight upon us. But I beseech you, my Bullinger, to consider with what propriety we should alienate ourselves from Bucer, seeing he subscribes this very confession which I have laid down. I shall not at present declare the virtues, both rare and manifold, by which that man is distinguished. I shall only say, that I should do a grievous injury to the Church of God, were I either to hate or despise him. I make no reference to the personal obligations under which I lie to him. And yet my love and reverence for him are such, that I freely admonish him as often as I think fit. How much greater justice will his complaint regarding you be judged to possess! For he sometime ago complained that you interdicted youths of Zurich, who were living at Strasbourg, from partaking of the Supper in that church, although no confession but your own was demanded of them. I indeed see no reason why the churches should be so rent asunder on this point. But what is the reason that godly men are angry with us, when we cultivate the friendship of a man who, by himself, professes nothing that can stand in the way of his being received as a friend and a brother? As the matter hinges on this, shew me, if you can, that by my friendly intercourse with Bucer I am restrained in the free profession of my views. I may perhaps seem to be so, but I make the thing itself the test of the truth. Wherefore, let us not be so suspicious where there is no call for it. As to the other matters, when I had come to Lausanne I counselled the brethren to send as soon as possible to Haller, for I had the hope they would obtain from him all that was just; and in this expectation I was not disappointed. Jodocus, however, and Ebrard,[1] what brother of the giants I know not, who had been sent, were so grossly violent in their invectives, that they were presently compelled to betake themselves [home]. So great a source of

---

[1] Ministers of the Church of Berne.

indignation was my proceeding to Zurich, as if, forsooth, I had no right to be affected by the danger of a church so near us, or to seek a suitable remedy in conjunction with the brethren. Jodocus said, in a threatening way, that he knew what I had done when with you. I boasted, however, that I had been a party to no transaction that was unworthy of my reputation as an honourable man. But why should I recount to you the insolence and scurrilities of both of them? Take this as the sum of the matter, that the two brethren, both eminently learned, grave, and judicious, were so astounded, that they thought it best to make a seasonable departure. Such is brotherly clemency. It is, however, worth while to make a brief statement, that you may form a judgment of the matter from the beginning to the end. Immediately on our first meeting, in place of salutation, it was asked, Who raised these tragical commotions? When it was said, in reply, that they were known to have proceeded from Zebedee, Ebrard exclaimed, ' Yes, that good man is unworthily traduced by you, because he laid bare your stratagems.' On the brethren requesting those stratagems to be explained to them; ' We have,' he says, ' a Bernese disputation from which we form our judgment of you and all your affairs.' I beseech thee, my Bullinger, to say whether such is the case. What have we profited by shaking off the tyranny of the Pope? Observe, also, how suitable was the interrogation of Jodocus, Who had asked me to form one of the assembly at Lausanne? Finally, that the last part of the proceedings might be of a piece with the first, the brethren were ordered to go away, and have done with their Calvinism and Buceranism. And all this with an impetuosity almost like madmen, and outrageous clamours. Could you expect anything more unfeeling or truculent from Papists? Though we may patiently tolerate this intemperate Bacchantism, the Lord, nevertheless, will not suffer it to pass unpunished. At Paris and in many parts of the kingdom, the ferocity of the ungodly is inflamed afresh. The King himself holds on in his fury. Thus is fulfilled the prediction, Without fightings, within fears; although Jodocus excites not only fears within, but open fightings. But may the very fewness of our numbers incite us to an alliance!

Adieu, most excellent and most honoured Sir, along with your colleagues, all of whom I desire you will respectfully salute in my name. To your wife also, and your whole family, I send the best greeting. May the Lord Jesus protect and direct you all. Amen.

Something is said about the state of Constance, not much fitted to inspire gladness. May the Lord regard you, and rescue you from the jaws of the lion.—Yours,

JOHN CALVIN.

It would be better you should suppress this letter, if you thought proper, than that it should lead to the excitement of a greater conflagration at Berne; for the lack of self-restraint on the part of some is marvellous.

[*Lat. orig. autogr.—Archives of Zurich.* Gest. vi. p. 6.]


CCXXV.—TO MONSIEUR DE FALAIS.[1]

Preparations for the marriage of Mademoiselle de Wilergy, his relation.

FROM GENEVA, *this* 17*th of July* [1548.]

MONSEIGNEUR,—I believe that it will be best as it is. If it had been possible to speak together about the contract,[2] I would have much desired to do so; but I do not know whether you will be able to come this week. However, the man offers, in case he should leave his wife a widow without children, that she shall have a thousand crowns. In the event of his leaving children, she shall have the half, but on condition that, if she marry afterwards, and have also children by the second marriage, she must not have the power of preferring them to those of the first. The present assignment will be founded upon the

---

[1] M. de Falais was on the point of leaving Bâle to settle at Geneva. He arrived, doubtless, in that town the end of July 1548. We read, in a letter of Calvin to Viret of the 20th August 1548: "Dominus Falesius uxor et soror vos salutant;— the wife and sister of M. de Falais salute you."—Vol. 106 *of the Library of Geneva.* The correspondence of Calvin with this Seigneur, thenceforward interrupted, was only resumed occasionally, and in 1552, ceased entirely.

[2] The contract of marriage of Mademoiselle Wilergy.

instrument of Paris, to be implemented, when he shall have made good his money and expenses. I am of opinion that his offer is very liberal; for it is quite right that the husband retain some control in his own hand.

The wedding, I hope, will go off well. There must needs be some company, but no great multitude. And besides, we must not be too hard upon you, for it will be necessary to find lodgings for them. I think ten persons will be a reasonable number, including myself. And seeing that my brother is not here at present, I know not whether we could send notice by letter to Dôle and to Basle. Perhaps, indeed, we might, if they should be here for the whole day to-morrow.

I had forgotten to mention the French traveller;[1] that is, to tell you that I do not find him in any hurry; and yet that is not by any means because all is not quite clear about him, but for the purpose of seeking some advantage over and above. I wish very much that it may please God to bring you hither to drink of the wine upon the spot, and that soon. If the bearer had left this earlier in the morning, you might have had a flask of it. If there were any means of sending you the half of it, I should not have failed to do so, but when I inquired, I found that it could not be done.

And so, Monsieur, having commended me to your kind favour, and that of Madame and your whole household, I beseech our Lord to have you in his keeping.

Your humble brother and servant,

JOHN CALVIN, confined to bed.

M. de Ballesan has written to request of me, that I would see whether he could get any help from you. After making excuses more than enough for you, I have at length been constrained to promise him that I would write to you about it, which I had resolved to do yesterday by Monsieur de Parey; but he forgot to come, so great was his hurry to make the journey.

[*Orig. signat. autogr.—Library of Geneva.* Vol. 194.]

---

[1] M de Montmor. See the note, p. 127.

## CCXXVI.—To Farel.

*Uncertainty regarding the disposition of the Cantons—stay of Monsieur and Madame de Falais in Calvin's house.*

[Geneva,] 27*th August* 1548.

I have no doubt, even although you do not expostulate with me, that you silently condemn me for neglect in having suffered so many bearers to depart for you without my letter. If I were to plead that there was nothing to write about, you would at once confute me. Even though matter for correspondence is never wanting, I permit myself to indulge in silence, when there is nothing pressing. We are waiting to find whether the Swiss will suffer themselves to be circumvented by the artifices of Ulysses. May the Lord look to this, on whose Providence it is fitting we should lean;[1] since reason does not guide the helm, and we know that fortune has no dominion. As far as can be divined, [their policy is as follows:] As on the one hand the Emperor will seek to deceive them by fair words, so they in their turn will keep him in suspense until they have seen that they are protected by those defences which they deem necessary. Here we are occupied in the usual way, but the skirmishes are slight. Unless I am wholly deceived in my conjectures, either some disturbances will speedily arise, or this winter cause suffering to the great crowds in many places. Good Toussain[2] is not grieved by the matter. To his other troubles is added the disease of his son. You will therefore use your influence with Peter the surgeon to get him to repair to that quarter, in case some means of alleviation may be discovered. We shall see about William; we have talked among ourselves regarding him. But as Allen and San Privat are present, we have as yet come to no determination. The godly man offers no objection, but I am unwilling

---

[1] Messengers of the Emperor were then scouring the Cantons with a view to detach them from the French alliance, which was nevertheless renewed, 9th June 1549.

[2] The minister Toussain, pastor of the church of Montbeliard, at that time dispersed by the imperial army.

to send him away for no end. He will also return to Lausanne before he undertakes this journey. If you have found a trustworthy messenger, I wish you would send to me what letters of mine you have in your possession. Viret is to do the same. I shall send them back, with certain marks, if there be any which it is not expedient all should read. I shall send each of you his own, when I am at liberty to do so, that you may add similar marks. I will take care that these are subjoined. I have not yet seen Christopher. M. de Falais is now with me, who I trust will pass the winter here.[1] I have caused him to cast away the unfavourable doubt regarding you, which he had conceived from your conversation. The more he loves you and defers to you, the more anxious was he that you should judge aright of his piety. But it is in truth as you say: when you demanded of him what you thought would be for the edification of the Church, he suspected that you desiderated in him the very thing you sought for, as if he had not manifested it hitherto. Both [Monsieur and Madame de Falais] very affectionately salute you, as also my colleagues; and my wife, who is in bed from prolonged illness. I have been struggling these days past with pain in the head, and spasms of the stomach, to such a degree as to cause violent convulsions. Adieu, brother and most sincere friend, along with your family and brothers, especially my guest Fato, to whom I will send back the token of friendship, unless he sometime visit us.—
Yours, JOHN CALVIN.

[*Lat. orig. autogr.—Library of Geneva.* Vol. 106.]

## CCXXVII.—To VIRET.[2]

Embarrassment occasioned to Calvin by the treacherous publication of one of his letters to Viret.

[GENEVA,] 20*th September* 1548.

I was within a little of letting our friend Merlin depart without a letter. When he was already equipped for the journey,

---
[1] See the letter to M. de Falais of 17th July 1548, and the relative note.
[2] We have reproduced (Vol. i. p. 425.) a letter of Calvin to Viret, containing a

he sacrificed for me the time between sermon and supper; the half of which period I spent in conversation with some people. With regard to a successor to Himbert, I have scarcely ground for giving an advice. I see indeed the dangers that are imminent, unless some one be put in his place as soon as possible. I do not observe among you any one who pleases me in every respect. You cannot call from a distance any but unknown men. Our choice is accordingly restricted to those in whom you may have to desiderate something as wanting; only let it not be piety and a moderate acquaintance with the language,—qualifications that are to be regarded as the chief. But if you make choice of any one with this reservation, that he is not to be under obligation to remain in the office, should anything more suitable shortly afterwards present itself, you will take care expressly to state this to the person himself, and to the senate. When I became aware that the letter, obtained surreptitiously and translated into French by Trolliet, was being circulated, and that oil was thus poured on the flame, I came into the council chamber, and pointed out the injustice of those devices, the danger of such procedure to the Church, and the evil precedent it afforded. That person was summoned; he appeared in the midst of the meeting; I acknowledged my hand, and then made such an apology as the circumstances demanded. We were thus suffered to go home. A resolution, however, was come to,

severe judgment of the Reformer upon the magistrates of Geneva. Stolen from Viret by a faithless servant, and given to the Seigneury by Trolliet, this letter excited real commotions, the traces of which are to be found in the Registers of Council.

"Calvin justifies himself in council with regard to a certain letter he had written, in which it was alleged he blamed the Seigneury of this city. He also complains of the calumnies directed against him by Trolliet."—24th September.

On the 15th October following, Farel appears in Council, "and prays them to entertain a constant regard for Calvin; that he observes with grief they do not show to that servant of God the deference that is due to him . . . . praying the Council to take order therein."—28th October. "Farel testifies anew that too little regard is had for the character and merits of Calvin; that he has no equal in learning; that it was not necessary to take such offence at what he might have said, as he had censured with great freedom the greatest men, such as Luther, Melanchthon, and many others.

"Resolved, to thank the said Farel, and to remit to him the original of the foresaid letter, in order that it might be restored to Viret."

that I should be again summoned after the following Monday. This has not been done. What has prevented it I know not, unless, as I suspect, it be the stratagem of the ungodly to afford them a weapon for the purpose of injuring me, as often as it shall be advantageous for them to employ it. For the council was disposed to allow the whole matter to pass into oblivion. Accordingly, if at any time I have stood in need of your help, you now see that I especially require it. For I shall not be able to urge you without a confession of fear. But if you repair hither, and complain of the injury done to you,—if you then add that you do not deserve at the hands of the republic to have a letter that was stolen from you retained,—if finally you demand its restoration, and moreover signify that you need it for the conviction of the thief,—I do not think it will be difficult to obtain it. Do you now consider whether another course is more expedient. The whole council is censured in the letter. For the time is described when Corna resigned the office of treasurer. I next mention those whom the people then created syndics, and who were allured into the council. Then follow finally the best things they wish to be expected of them. I know not what I ought to expect. For under pretext of Christ they mean to reign without Christ; since among them are reckoned Amy Curtet, and Dominic Arlo, who are now in prison, until they shall have discharged the debts due by them to the public treasury. Perrin, with his friends, goes to them, and urges them to become reconciled to me. Others also solicit this. Last of all, they omit no wickedness by which they may overthrow me. I partly dissemble, and partly openly profess that all their efforts are held by me in derision. For they would think they had obtained the victory, if they observed in me any token [of fear.] Nor indeed is there anything that is more fitted to break the force of their impetuosity, and animate good men in sustaining the cause, than my self-reliance. If you are not at liberty to come shortly, consider whether it be not expedient to write. But I should not wish you to do so, unless by a sure messenger, and one who should have a commission requiring an answer. Adieu, brother, and most sincere friend, along with your wife and young daughter. Respectfully salute the brethren. My wife also salutes you.—Yours,

JOHN CALVIN.

If you can find a faithful friend, I should wish him once to read over what I have here written to you.

[*Lat. orig. autogr.—Library of Geneva.* Vol. 106.]


CCXXVIII.—TO A FRENCH SEIGNEUR.[1]

Exhortation to come to Geneva, that he might there serve the Lord faithfully.

*This* 18*th of October* 1548.

MONSIEUR,—I have partly been informed of your intention by the Sieur François de la Rivière, and praise our Lord for the good courage he has given you to serve him fully. As we ought to yield ourselves up to him entirely and without reserve, if we desire to be approved as his, you must now ascertain how you can employ yourself as is your duty in his service. It is true that the earth is the Lord's, and that we are at liberty to dwell in any part of it, provided we take care to keep ourselves unpolluted, to honour him in our body as well as our spirit. When we are told that the whole earth is holy, we are thereby admonished, that we ought in nowise to defile it by leading a sinful life. You must now take good heed, that by concealing as you are doing the light that is in you, you do not make yourself a partaker in the pollutions which you very properly condemn in unbelievers. I fully believe, that your heart is very far from consenting thereto; but in making the outward show of communicating, there can be no doubt that you thereby make a profession of consenting to it. And as before God we ought to manifest our detestation of idolatry, so also before men, we ought to abstain from whatsoever may

[1] Perhaps to Charles de Jonvillers, who became some years afterwards the secretary and friend of the reformer. It was in fact in 1549, and in consequence of the advice of Calvin, that this Seigneur left Chartres, his country, to go to Geneva, which received him as inhabitant in 1550, and as burgess in 1556.

make it appear that we approve thereof. It is surely right that the body be kept quite pure for the service of God, as well as the soul, seeing that it is the temple of the Holy Spirit, and has the promise of the immortal glory which shall be revealed at the last day. But is it possible to employ body and soul with sincerity of heart in the service of God, while we make a semblance of agreement with idolaters, in an act which we know to be dishonouring to God? It is not enough to reply to this, that you make no oral declaration, indeed, that you would be ready to protest the contrary, were you required to do so, for you are well aware that you go thither with no other intention, than that of leading God's enemies to believe that you do not repudiate their doings, for if it was not for the sake of gratifying them, and by such means shrinking from the declaration, that you are utterly opposed to their sacrileges, you never would join them in an act of worship. And that is nothing else than rendering a feigned homage to their idol, albeit without the homage of the heart. If it seems to you that I am too severe in dealing with your faults so narrowly, I ask you to enter upon the work of self-examination, and you will find, that I bring forward nothing against you, whereof your own conscience does not reprove you. Judge, then, whether God does not see there much more to find fault with, for he sees our state far more clearly than we ourselves do. Therefore, I cannot, consistently with the understanding which God has vouchsafed me, advise a Christian man to continue in such a state; and can only say, that to my thinking he is truly happy who is free from such constraint. Whosoever therefore, has the means of withdrawing from it, ought not in my opinion on any account to neglect to do so. True it is, that never shall man have things so entirely to his mind, that he shall be exempted from difficulty, but, on the contrary, must expect many annoyances, even wrong and loss of property. But let us learn to prefer the honour of God to all things else. In your case, I understand that your merciful God has already brought you so far, that you are resolved not to stagnate in a place where you knowingly offend Him. Wherefore, I forbear from any more lengthened exhortations; only, be careful not to quench that zeal which he has vouchsafed you, but rather stir it up as a remembrancer to keep you in mind to carry out your good intention. For I know well, and experience will convince you, how many distractions there are to make you forgetful of it, or so far to delay that you might grow cool about it. Regarding the alternatives which Sire François has set before me, I have told him what to give you as my opinion. However, your departure must be like that out of Egypt, bringing all your effects along with you. For all this, I believe you will need stedfast and very determined courage. But you are able to do all in Him who strengthens you. When He has brought you hither, you shall see how He will guide you farther. For my part, I would gladly help thereunto cheerfully and steadily, as bound I am to do. I am confident, that after leading you by the hand in greater things, He will not fail you on this occasion. But he is sometimes pleased to exercise and try our faith, so that while quitting hold of that which is within our grasp, we know not what we shall receive in place of it. We have an example of this in our father Abraham. After having commanded him to forsake his country, his kindred, and everything else, He shewed him no present reward, but put that off to another time. "Get thee out," said He, "into the land which I shall shew thee." Should it please Him at this time to do the like with us, that we must quit the land of our birth, and betake ourselves into an unknown country, without knowing how it may fare with us there, let us surrender ourselves to Him, that He may direct our way, and let us honour Him, by trusting that He will steer us to a safe harbour. It is needful, at least, that you be informed beforehand that you shall enter here no earthly paradise, where you may rejoice in God without molestation : you will find a people unmannerly enough ; you will meet with some sufficiently annoying trials. In short, do not expect to better your condition, except in so far, that having been delivered from miserable bondage of body and of soul, you will have leave to serve God faithfully. You will have the pure doctrine of the Word, you will call upon His name in the fellowship of faithful men, you will enjoy the true use of the sacraments. But that may well be all in all to us, if we only prize it as we ought. As for other comforts, you will take those which God vouchsafes to you, willingly suffering the want of those which He denies. Make up your mind, then, to follow Jesus Christ, without flying from the cross; and indeed you would gain nothing by trying to avoid it, because it will assuredly find you out. But let us be content with this invaluable blessing, that we are allowed to live not only in peace of conscience, but daily to exercise ourselves in the doctrine of salvation, and in the use of the sacraments, for our confirmation. He who builds on this foundation, shall rear a solid edifice, and in truth you cannot evidence whether you do value Jesus Christ or not, unless by reckoning all the world as filth in comparison of Him.

To conclude, having recommended me affectionately to your kind favour, I beseech our good Lord to fill you with the spirit of counsel and discretion, to discern what will be right and fitting for you to do, and to strengthen you in true constancy, to put in practice whatsoever shall be according to His will; that having done so, it may please Him to lead you by the hand, to bless you in going out and coming in, to turn all into godly prosperity.

Your humble brother and servant in our Lord,

CHARLES D'ESPEVILLE.

[*Fr. copy—Library of Geneva.* Vol. 107.]


CCXXIX.—TO THE PROTECTOR SOMERSET.[1]

Duties imposed on the Protector by the high office which he holds—plan of a complete reformation in England—preaching of the pure Word of God —rooting out of abuses—correction of vices and scandalous offences.

GENEVA, 22*d October* 1548.

MONSEIGNEUR,—Although God has endowed you with singular prudence, largeness of mind, and other virtues required in that

[1] Edward Seymour, Earl of Hertford, Duke of Somerset, Regent of England, under the minority of Edward VI. It was under his administration that the reformation was victoriously established in England. Supported by Parliament, he

station wherein He has set you, and for the affairs which He has put into your hand; nevertheless, inasmuch as you deem me to be a servant of His Son, whom you desire above all else to obey, I feel assured, that for the love of Him you will receive with courtesy, that which I write in His name, as indeed I have no other end in view, save only, that in following out yet more and more what you have begun, you may advance His honour, until you have established His kingdom in as great perfection as is to be looked for in the world. And you will perceive likewise as you read, that without advancing anything of my own, the whole is drawn from His own pure doctrine. Were I to look merely at the dignity and grandeur of your position, there would seem no access whatever for a man of my quality. But since you do not refuse to be taught of the Master whom I serve, but rather prize above all else the grace which He has bestowed in numbering you among His disciples, methinks I have no need to make you any long excuse or preface, because I deem you well disposed to receive whatsoever proceeds from Him.

We have all reason to be thankful to our God and Father, that He has been pleased to employ you in so excellent a work as that of setting up the purity and right order of His worship in England by your means, and establishing the doctrine of salvation, that it may there be faithfully proclaimed to all those who shall consent to hear it; that He has vouchsafed you such firmness and constancy to persevere hitherto, in spite of so many trials and difficulties; that He has helped you with His mighty arm, in blessing all your counsels and your labours,

suppressed the troubles which arose in some parts of the kingdom after the death of Henry VIII., confirmed the king's supremacy, abolished the worship of images, private masses, and restored the communion in both kinds. He held a correspondence with Calvin, who dedicated to him, June 24, 1548, his Commentary on the First Epistle of Paul to Timothy; and by advice of the reformer, he offered an asylum to the exiles, Bucer, Fagi, Ochino, and Peter Martyr,—banished for the sake of their religion from the Continent. Beloved by the people, hated by the nobles, he made himself unpopular by his want of success in the war, which he kept up against the Scots, and in France; was overthrown by a conspiracy of the nobility, imprisoned in the Tower of London, (October 1549,) and only recovered his liberty the year following, to perish in 1552 on the scaffold, victim of the ambition of Warwick, Earl of Northumberland, his relative.

to make them prosper. These are grounds of thankfulness which stir up all true believers to magnify His name. Seeing however, that Satan never ceases to upheave new conflicts, and that it is a thing in itself so difficult, that nothing can be more so, to cause the truth of God to have peaceable dominion among men, who by nature are most prone to falsehood; while on the other hand, there are so many circumstances which prevent its having free course; and most of all, that the superstitions of Antichrist, having taken root for so long time, cannot be easily uprooted from men's hearts,—you have much need, methinks, to be confirmed by holy exhortations. I cannot doubt, indeed, that you have felt this from experience; and shall therefore deal all the more frankly with you, because, as I hope, my deliberate opinion will correspond with your own desire. Were my exhortations even uncalled for, you would bear with the zeal and earnestness which has led me to offer them. I believe, therefore, that the need of them which you feel, will make them all the more welcome. However this may be, Monseigneur, may it please you to grant me audience in some particular reformations which I propose to lay here briefly before you, in the hope, that when you shall have listened to them, you will at least find some savour of consolation therein, and feel the more encouraged to prosecute the holy and noble enterprise in which God has hitherto been pleased to employ you.

I have no doubt that the great troubles which have fallen out for some time past, must have been very severe and annoying to you, and especially as many may have found in them occasion of offence; forasmuch as they were partly excited under cover of the change of religion. Wherefore you must necessarily have felt them very keenly, as well on account of the apprehensions they may have raised in your mind, as of the murmurs of the ignorant or disaffected, and also of the alarm of the well-disposed. Certes, the mere rumour which I heard from afar, caused me heartfelt anxiety, until I was informed that God had begun to apply a remedy thereto. However, since perhaps they are not yet entirely allayed, or seeing that the devil may have kindled them anew, it will be well that you call to mind what the sacred history relates of good King Hezekiah, (2 Chron.

xxxii.,) namely, that after he had abolished the superstitions throughout Judea, reformed the state of the church according to the law of God, he was even then so pressed by his enemies, that it almost seemed as if he was a lost and ruined man. It is not without reason that the Holy Spirit pointedly declares, that such an affliction happened to him immediately after having re-established the true religion in his realm; for it may well have seemed reasonable to himself, that having striven with all his might to set up the reign of God, he should have peace within his own kingdom. Thus, all faithful princes and governors of countries are forewarned by that example, that however earnest they may be in banishing idolatry and in promoting the true worship of God, their faith may yet be tried by diverse temptations. So God permits, and wills it to be thus, to manifest the constancy of his people, and to lead them to look above the world. Meanwhile, the devil also does his work, endeavouring to ruin sound doctrine by indirect means, working as it were underground, forasmuch as he could not openly attain his end. But according to the admonition of St. James, (James v. 11,) who tells us, that in considering the patience of Job, we must look to the end of it, so ought we, Monseigneur, to look to the end which was vouchsafed to this good king. We see there that God was a present help in all his perplexities, and that at length he came off victorious. Wherefore, seeing that His arm is not shortened, and that in the present day, He has the defence of the truth and the salvation of His own as much at heart as ever, never doubt that He will come to your aid, and that not once only, but in all the trials He may send you.

If the majority of the world oppose the Gospel, and even strive with rage and violence to hinder its progress, we ought not to think it strange. It proceeds from the ingratitude of men, which has always shewn itself, and ever will, in drawing back when God comes near, and even in kicking against Him when He would put His yoke upon them. More than that, because by nature they are wholly given to hypocrisy, they cannot bear to be brought to the clear light of the Word of God, which lays bare their baseness and shame, nor to be drawn forth out of their superstitions, which serve them as a hiding-hole and shady covert. It is nothing new, then, if we meet with contradiction when we attempt to lead men back to the pure worship of God. And we have, besides, the clear announcement of our Lord Jesus, who tells us that He has brought a sword along with His Gospel. But let not this daunt us, nor make us shrink and be fearful, for at last, when men shall have rebelled most stoutly, and vomited forth all their rage, they shall be put to confusion in a moment, and shall destroy themselves by the fury of their own onset. That is a true saying, in the second Psalm, That God shall only laugh at their commotion; that is to say, that seeming to connive, He will let them bluster, as if the affair did not at all concern Him. But it always happens, that at length they are driven back by His power, wherewith if we be armed, we have a sure and invincible munition, whatsoever plots the devil may frame against us, and shall know by experience in the end, that even as the Gospel is the message of peace and of reconciliation between God and us, it will also avail us to pacify men; and in this way we shall understand, that it is not in vain that Isaiah has said, (Is. ii. 4,) that when Jesus Christ shall rule in the midst of us by His doctrine, the swords shall be turned into ploughshares, and the spears into pruning-hooks.

Albeit, however, the wickedness and opposition of men may be the cause of the sedition and rebellion which rises up against the Gospel, let us look to ourselves, and acknowledge that God chastises our faults by those who would otherwise serve Satan only. It is an old complaint, that the Gospel is the cause of all the ills and calamities that befall mankind. We see, in fact, from history, that shortly after Christianity had been everywhere spread abroad, there was not, so to speak, a corner of the earth which was not horribly afflicted. The uproar of war, like a universal fire, was kindled in all lands. Land-floods on the one hand, and famine and pestilence on the other, a chaotic confusion of order and civil polity to such a degree, that it seemed as if the world was presently about to be overturned. In like manner we have seen in our times, since the Gospel has begun to be set up, much misery; to such an extent, indeed, that every one complains we are come upon an unhappy period, and there are very few who do not *groan* under this burden. While, then, we feel the blow, we ought to look upward to the hand of Him who strikes, and ought also to consider why the blow is sent. The reason why He makes us thus to feel His rod is neither very obscure nor difficult to be understood. We know that the Word, by which He would guide us to salvation, is an invaluable treasure; with what reverence do we receive it when He presents it to us? Seeing, then, that we make no great account of that which is so precious, God has good reason to avenge Himself of our ingratitude. We hear also what Jesus Christ announces, (Luke xii. 47,) that the servant knowing the will of his Master, and not doing it, deserves double chastisement. Since, therefore, we are so remiss in obeying the will of our God, who has declared it to us more than a hundred times already, let us not think it strange if His anger rage more severely against us, seeing that we are all the more inexcusable. When we do not cultivate the good seed, there is much reason that the thorns and thistles of Satan should spring up to trouble and annoy us. Since we do not render to our Creator the submission which is due to Him, it is no wonder that men rise up against us.

From what I am given to understand, Monseigneur, there are two kinds of rebels who have risen up against the King and the Estates of the Kingdom. The one, a fantastical sort of persons, who, under colour of the Gospel, would put all into confusion. The others are persons who persist in the superstitions of the Roman Antichrist. Both alike deserve to be repressed by the sword which is committed to you, since they not only attack the King, but strive with God, who has placed him upon a royal throne, and has committed to you the protection as well of his person as of his majesty. But the chief point is, to endeavour as much as possible, that those who have some savour of a liking for the doctrine of the Gospel, so as to hold fast, should receive it with such humility and godly fear, as to renounce self in order to serve God; for they ought seriously to consider that God would awaken them all, so that in good earnest they may profit far more from His Word than they have ever yet done. These madmen, who would have the whole world turned back into a chaos of licentiousness, are hired by Satan to defame the Gospel, as if it bred nothing but revolt against princes, and all sorts of disorder in the world. Wherefore, all the faithful ought to be deeply grieved. The Papists, in endeavouring to maintain the corruptions and abominations of their Romish idol, shew themselves to be the open enemies of the grace of Jesus Christ, and of all His ordinances. That ought likewise to occasion great sickness at heart among all those who have a single drop of godly zeal. And therefore they ought every one of them earnestly to consider, that these are the rods of God for their correction. And wherefore ? Just because they do not set a proper value on the doctrine of salvation. Herein lies the chief remedy for the silencing of such calumnies, that those who make profession of the Gospel be indeed renewed after the image of God, so as to make manifest that our Christianity does not occasion any interruption of the humanities of social life, and to give good evidence, by their temperance and moderation, that being governed by the Word of God, we are not unruly people subject to no restraint, and so by an upright holy life shut the mouth of all the evil speakers. For by this means God, being pacified, shall withdraw His hand, and instead of, as at this day, punishing the contempt with which they have treated His Word, He will reward their obedience with all prosperity. It would be well were all the nobility and those who administer justice, to submit themselves, in uprightness and all humility, to this great King, Jesus Christ, paying Him sincere homage, and with faith unfeigned, in body, soul, and spirit, so that He may correct and beat down the arrogance and rashness of those who would rise up against them. Thus ought earthly princes to rule and govern, serving Jesus Christ, and taking order that He may have His own sovereign authority over all, both small and great. Wherefore, Monseigneur, as you hold dear and in regard the estate of your royal nephew, as indeed you shew plainly that you do, I beseech you, in the name of God, to apply your chief care and watchfulness to this end, that the doctrine of God may be proclaimed with efficacy and power, so as to produce its fruit, and never to grow weary, whatsoever may happen, in following out fully, an open and complete reformation of the

Church. The better to explain to you what I mean, I shall arrange the whole under three heads.

The first shall treat of the sound instruction of the people; the second shall regard the rooting out of abuses which have prevailed hitherto; the third, the careful repression and correction of vice, and to take strict heed that scandals and loose conversation may not grow into a fashion, so as to cause the name of God to be blasphemed.

As concerning the first article, I do not mean to pronounce what doctrine ought to have place. Rather do I offer thanks to God for his goodness, that after having enlightened you in the pure knowledge of Himself, He has given you wisdom and discretion to take measures that His pure truth may be preached. Praise be to God, you have not to learn what is the true faith of Christians, and the doctrine which they ought to hold, seeing that by your means the true purity of the faith has been restored. That is, that we hold God alone to be the sole Governor of our souls, that we hold His law to be the only rule and spiritual directory for our consciences, not serving Him according to the foolish inventions of men. Also, that according to His nature He would be worshipped in spirit and in purity of heart. On the other hand, acknowledging that there is nothing but all wretchedness in ourselves, and that we are corrupt in all our feelings and affections, so that our souls are a very abyss of iniquity, utterly despairing of ourselves; and that, having exhausted every presumption of our own wisdom, worth, or power of well-doing, we must have recourse to the fountain of every blessing, which is in Christ Jesus, accepting that which He confers on us, that is to say, the merit of His death and passion, that by this means we may be reconciled to God; that being washed in His blood, we may have no fear lest our spots prevent us from finding grace at the heavenly throne; that being assured that our sins are pardoned freely in virtue of his sacrifice, we may lean, yea rest upon, that for assurance of our salvation; that we may be sanctified by His Spirit, and so consecrate ourselves to the obedience of the righteousness of God; that being strengthened by His grace, we may overcome Satan, the world, and the flesh; finally, that being members of His body, we may never doubt that God reckons us among the number of His children, and that we may confidently call upon Him as *our* Father ; that we may be careful to recognise and bear in mind this purpose in whatsoever is said or done in the Church, namely, that being separated from the world, we should rise to heaven with our Head and Saviour. Seeing then that God has given you grace to re-establish the knowledge of this doctrine, which had been so long buried out of sight by Antichrist, I forbear from entering further on the subject.

What I have thus suggested as to the manner of instruction, is only that the people be so taught as to be touched to the quick, and that they may feel that what the Apostle says is true, (Heb. iv.) that " the Word of God is a two-edged sword, piercing even through the thoughts and affections to the very marrow of the bones." I speak thus, Monseigneur, because it appears to me that there is very little preaching of a lively kind in the kingdom, but that the greater part deliver it by way of reading from a written discourse. I see very well the necessity which constrains you to that ; for in the first place you have not, as I believe, such well-approved and competent pastors as you desire. Wherefore, you need forthwith to supply this want. Secondly, there may very likely be among them many flighty persons who would go beyond all bounds, sowing their own silly fancies, as often happens on occasion of a change. But all these considerations ought not to hinder the ordinance of Jesus Christ from having free course in the preaching of the Gospel. Now, this preaching ought not to be lifeless but lively, to teach, to exhort, to reprove, as Saint Paul says in speaking thereof to Timothy, (2 Tim. iii.) So indeed, that if an unbeliever enter, he may be so effectually arrested and convinced, as to give glory to God, as Paul says in another passage, (1 Cor. xiv.) You are also aware, Monseigneur, how he speaks of the lively power and energy with which they ought to speak, who would approve themselves as good and faithful ministers of God, who must not make a parade of rhetoric only to gain esteem for themselves ; but that the Spirit of God ought to sound forth by their voice, so as to work with mighty energy. Whatever may be the amount of danger to be feared, that ought not to hinder the Spirit of God from having liberty and free course in those to whom He has given grace for the edifying of the Church.

True it is, nevertheless, that it is both right and fitting to oppose the levity of some fantastic minds, who allow themselves in too great license, and also to shut the door against all eccentricities and new doctrines; but the method to be taken, which God hath pointed out to us, for dealing with such occurrences, is well fitted to dispose of them. In the first place, there ought to be an explicit summary of the doctrine which all ought to preach, which all prelates and curates swear to follow, and no one should be received to any ecclesiastic charge who does not promise to preserve such agreement. Next, that they have a common *formula* of instruction for little children and for ignorant persons, serving to make them familiar with sound doctrine, so that they may be able to discern the difference between it and the falsehood and corruptions which may be brought forward in opposition to it. Believe me, Monseigneur, (the Church of God will never preserve itself without a Catechism, for it is like the seed to keep the good grain from dying out, and causing it to multiply from age to age. And therefore, if you desire to build an edifice which shall be of long duration, and which shall not soon fall into decay, make provision for the children being instructed in a good Catechism, which may shew them briefly, and in language level to their tender age, wherein true Christianity consists. This Catechism will serve two purposes, to wit, as an introduction to the whole people, so that every one may profit from what shall be preached, and also to enable them to discern when any presumptuous person puts forward strange doctrine. Indeed, I do not say that it may not be well, and even necessary, to bind down the pastors and curates to a certain written form, as well for the sake of supplementing the ignorance and deficiencies of some, as the better to manifest the conformity and agreement between all the churches; thirdly, to take away all ground of pretence for bringing in any eccentricity or new-fangled doctrine on the part of those who only seek to indulge an idle fancy; as I have already said, the Catechism ought to serve as a check upon such people. There is, besides, the form and manner of administration of the sacraments; also the public prayers. But whatever, in the meantime, be the arrangement in regard to these matters, care must be taken not to quench the efficacy which ought to attend the preaching of the Gospel. And the utmost care should be taken, that so far as possible you have good trumpets, which shall sound into the very depths of the heart. For there is some danger that you may see no great profit from all the reformation which you shall have brought about, however sound and godly it may have been, unless this powerful instrument of preaching be developed more and more. It is not said without a meaning, that *Jesus Christ shall smite the earth with the rod of his mouth, and with the breath of his lips shall he slay the wicked*, (Is. xi. 4.) The way by which He is pleased to subdue us is, by destroying whatsoever is contrary to Himself. And herein you may also perceive why the Gospel is called the Kingdom of God. Even so, albeit the edicts and statutes of princes are good helps for advancing and upholding the state of Christianity, yet God is pleased to declare His sovereign power by this spiritual sword of His Word, when it is made known by the pastors.

Not to tire you, Monseigneur, I shall now come to the second point which I propose to touch upon; that is, the abolition and entire uprooting of the abuses and corruptions which Satan had aforetime mixed up with the ordinances of God. We wot well that under the Pope there is a bastard sort of Christianity, and that God will disavow it at the last day, seeing that He now condemns it by His Word. If we desire to rescue the world from such an abyss, there is no better method than to follow the example of St. Paul, who, wishing to correct what the Corinthians had improperly added to the Supper of our Lord, tells them, (1 Cor. xi.,) *I have received of the Lord that which I have delivered to you.* Thence we are bound to take a general instruction, to return to the strict and natural meaning of the commandment of God, if we would have a sound reformation and by Him approven. For whatsoever mixtures men have brought in of their own devising, have been just so many pollutions which turn us aside from the sanctified use of what God has bestowed for our salvation. Therefore, to lop off such abuses by halves will by no means restore things to a state of purity, for then we shall always have a dressed-up Christianity. I say this, because there are some who, under pretence of moderation, are in favour of sparing many abuses, without meddling with them at all, and to whom it appears enough to have rooted out the principal one. But on the contrary, we see how fertile is the seed of falsehood, and that only a single grain is needed to fill the world with them in three days' time, to such an extent are men inclined and addicted thereto. Our Lord teaches quite another method of procedure, for when David speaks of the idols he says, (Psalm xvi.,) *Their names will I not take up into my lips*, to intimate in what degree of detestation we ought to hold them. Above all, if we consider how we have offended God in the days of our ignorance, we ought to feel doubly bound to flee from the inventions of Satan, which have led us into the commission of evil, as from baits which serve only to seduce souls. On the other hand, we see, even when we remonstrate with men about their faults and errors, though we warn them as earnestly as possible, they are nevertheless so hardened that we can produce no effect. If, therefore, we were to leave them any remnant of abuse, that would only serve to nourish their obstinacy the more, and become a veil to darken all the doctrine which we might set before them. I willingly acknowledge that we must observe moderation, and that overdoing is neither discreet nor useful; indeed, that forms of worship need to be accommodated to the condition and tastes of the people. But the corruptions of Satan and of Antichrist must not be admitted under that pretext. Therefore it is that Holy Scripture, when praising those kings who had cast down the idols and their worshippers, not having swept them entirely away, notes it as a blemish, that nevertheless they had not cast down the chapelries and places of silly devotion. Wherefore,

Monseigneur, seeing that God has brought you so far, take order, I beseech you, that so without any exception He may approve you as a repairer of His temple, so that the times of the king your nephew may be compared to those of Josiah, and that you put things in such condition, that he may only need to maintain the goodly order which God shall have prepared for him by your means. I will mention to you an instance of such corruptions, as, if they were allowed to remain, would become a little leaven, to sour in the end the whole lump. In your country, some prayer is made for the departed on occasion of communicating in the Lord's Supper. I am well aware that it is not done in admission of the purgatory of the Pope. I am also aware that ancient custom can be pleaded for making some mention of the departed, for the sake of uniting together all the members of the one body. But there is a peremptory ground of objection against it, that the Supper of Jesus Christ is an action so sacred, that it ought not to be soiled by any human inventions whatsoever. And besides, in prayer to God, we must not take an unbounded license in our devotions, but observe the rule which St. Paul gives us, (Romans x.,) which is, that we must be founded upon the Word of God; therefore, such commemoration of the dead, as imports a commending of them to His grace, is contrary to the due form and manner of prayer,—it is a hurtful addition to the Supper of our Lord. There are other things which possibly may be less open to reproof, which however are not to be excused: such as the ceremony of chrism and unction. The chrism has been invented out of a frivolous humour by those who, not content with the institution of Jesus Christ, desired to counterfeit the Holy Spirit by a new sign, as if water were not sufficient for the purpose. What they call extreme unction, has been retained by the inconsiderate zeal of those, who have wished to follow the apostles without being gifted as they were. When the apostles used oil in the case of the sick, it was for the healing of them miraculously. Now, when the gift of miracles has ceased, the figure ought no longer to be employed. Wherefore, it would be much better that these things should be pruned away, so that you might have nothing which is not conform to the Word of God, and serviceable for the edification of the Church. It is quite true we ought to bear with the weak; but in order to strengthen them, and to lead them to greater perfection. That does not mean, however, that we are to humour blockheads who wish for this or that, without knowing why. I know the consideration which keeps back many is, that they are afraid too great a change could not be carried through. It is admitted, that when we have to do with neighbours with whom we desire to cherish friendly feeling, one is disposed to gratify them by giving way in many things. In worldly matters, that may be quite bearable, wherein it is allowable to yield one to another, and to forego one's right for the sake of peace; but it is not altogether the same thing in regard to the spiritual governance of the Church, which ought to be according to the ordinance of the Word of God. Herein, we are not at liberty to yield up anything to men, nor to turn aside on either hand in their favour. Indeed there is nought that is more displeasing to God, than when we would, in accordance with our own human wisdom, modify or curtail, advance or retreat, otherwise than He would have us. Wherefore, if we do not wish to displease Him, we must shut our eyes to the opinion of men. As for the dangers which may arise, we ought to avoid them so far as we can, but never by going aside from the straight road. While we walk uprightly, we have His promise that He will help us. Therefore, what remains for us is to do our duty, humbly committing the event unto Himself. And here we may perceive wherefore the wise men of this world are ofttimes disappointed in their expectation, because God is not with them, when, in distrust of Him and His aid, they seek out crooked paths and such as He condemns. Do we then wish to feel that we have the power of God upon our side? Let us simply follow what he tells us. Above all, we must cling to this maxim, that the reformation of His Church is the work of His hand. Wherefore, in such matters, men must leave themselves to be guided by Him. What is more, whether in restoring or in preserving the Church, He thinks fit for the most part, to proceed after a method marvellous, and beyond human conception. And, therefore, it were unseemly to confine that restoration, which must be Divine, to the measure of our understanding, and to bring that which is heavenly into subjection to what is earthly and of this world's fashion. I do not thus exclude the prudence which is so much needed, to take all appropriate and right means, not falling into extremes either on the one side or upon the other, to gain over the whole world to God, if that were possible. But the wisdom of the Spirit, not that of the flesh, must overrule all; and having inquired at the mouth of the Lord, we must ask Him to guide and lead us, rather than follow the bent of our own understanding. When we take this method, it will be easy to cut off much occasion of temptation, which might otherwise stop our progress midway.

Wherefore, Monseigneur, as you have begun to bring back Christianity to the place which belongs to it, throughout the realm of England, not at all in self-confidence, but upheld by the hand of God, as hitherto you have had sensible experience of that powerful arm, you must not doubt that it shall continue with you to the end. If God upholds the kingdoms and the principalities of the infidels who are His enemies, far more certainly will He have in safeguard those who range themselves on His side and seek Him for their superior.

I come now to the last point, which concerns the chastisement of vice and the repression of scandals. I have no doubt that there are laws and statutes of the kingdom both good and laudable, to keep the people within the bounds of decency. But the great and boundless licentiousness which I see everywhere throughout the world, constrains me to beseech you, that you would earnestly turn your attention to keeping men within the restraint of sound and wholesome discipline. That, above all, you would hold yourself charged, for the honour of God, to punish those crimes of which men have been in the habit of making no very great account. I speak of this, because sometimes larcenies, assault, and extortions are more severely punished, because thereby men are wronged, whereas they will tolerate whoredom and adultery, drunkenness, and blaspheming of the name of God, as if these were things quite allowable, or at least of very small importance. Let us hear, however, what God thinks of them. He proclaims aloud, how precious His name is unto Him. Meanwhile, it is as if torn in pieces and trampled under foot. It can never be that He will allow such shameful reproach to remain unpunished. More than this, Scripture clearly points out to us, that by reason of blasphemies a whole country is defiled. As concerning adulteries, we, who call ourselves Christians, ought to take great shame to ourselves that even the heathen have exercised greater rigour in their punishment of such than we do, seeing even that some among us only laugh at them. When holy matrimony, which ought to be a lively image of the sacred union which we have with the Son of God, is polluted, and the covenant, which ought to stand more firm and indissoluble than any in this world, is disloyally rent asunder, if we do not lay to heart that sin against God, it is a token that our zeal for God is very low indeed. As for whoredom, it ought to be quite enough for us that St. Paul compares it to sacrilege, inasmuch as by its means the temples of God, which our bodies are, are profaned. Be it remembered also, that whoremongers and drunkards are banished from the kingdom of God, on such terms that we are forbidden to converse with them, whence it clearly follows, that they ought not to be endured in the Church. We see herein the cause why so many rods of judgment are at this very day lifted up over the earth. For the more easily men pardon themselves in such enormities, the more certainly will God take vengeance on them. Wherefore, to prevent His wrath, I entreat of you, Monseigneur, to hold a tight rein, and to take order, that those who hear the doctrine of the Gospel, approve their Christianity by a life of holiness. For as doctrine is the soul of the Church for quickening, so discipline and the correction of vices are like the nerves to sustain the body in a state of health and vigour. The duty of bishops and curates is to keep watch over that, to the end that the Supper of our Lord may not be polluted by people of scandalous lives. But in the authority where God has set you, the chief responsibility returns upon you, who have a special charge given you to set the others in motion, on purpose that every one discharge himself of duty, and diligently to look to it, that the order which shall have been established may be duly observed.

Now, Monseigneur, agreeably to the protestation which I made above, I shall make no further excuse, neither of the tiresomeness of my letter, nor on account of my having thus freely laid open to you what I had so much at heart. For I feel assured that my affection is well known to you, while in your wisdom, and as you are well versed in the Holy Scriptures, you perceive from what fountain I have drawn all that is herein contained. Wherefore, I do not fear to have been troublesome or importunate to you, in making manifest, according as I could, the hearty desire I have that the name of God may always be more and more glorified by you, which is my daily supplication, beseeching Him that He would please to increase His grace in you, to confirm you by His Spirit in a true unconquerable constancy, upholding you against all enemies, having yourself with your whole household under His holy protection, enabling you successfully to administer the charge which is committed to you, that so the King may have whereof to praise this gracious God for having had such a governor in his childhood, both for his person and for his kingdom.

Whereupon I shall make an end, Monseigneur, very humbly commending me to your kind favour.

[*Fr. Copy—Library of Geneva.* Vol. 107.]

## CCXXX.—To Farel.

Election of new magistrates at Geneva—troubles in France—letter from Bucer.

GENEVA, 27*th November* 1548.

You ought not to impute to my negligence your not having received a letter from me since you set sail from this place; for I have found no one setting out in your direction. It is not quite safe, moreover, in these times, for a letter to be carried about by a variety of hands. In the next place, I hardly know what to write to you, because there is nothing that is not fitted to cause you much more annoyance than satisfaction. The prefect Molard is here, with whom are joined as accessors the eldest son of Balthazar and a certain Rigot of that faction. You see, therefore, that there will be no danger this year to the wicked from the severity of the judges. We wait, however, to see in what channel their licence will break forth. On the same day our comic friend Cæsar again donned the socks.[1] Being now rendered somewhat more ferocious, he boasts among his stage-players after his own Thrasonic fashion. Finally, there appears to be no hope of speedy amendment, whatever we may essay. Nor is it to be doubted that they are labouring to effect a great revolution in the republic at the next assembly of syndics ; but the Lord in heaven is vigilant.

The commotions at Bourdeaux are settled, or they are at least lulled for a season.[2] For examples of extreme cruelty have been exhibited, which may in a short time boil forth in greater tempests. The people of Saintonge keep themselves concealed in the isles. Bucer lately wrote to me that Antiochus was looking forward to a day of purification. As far as I can gather from his letter, the council have no heart for that.[3] I also received a letter from Bullinger yesterday. When I reply you will know all.[1] Should our council by chance permit what has been adduced against the Interim of the sons of Cæsar[4] to be printed here, I shall send you a copy by the first messenger I can find. But as Trolliet maintains among his own friends that there is no need of so many books and sermons, I am afraid lest his authority prove so powerful as to force us to seek a press elsewhere. Adieu, brother and most sincere friend, along with your colleagues Fatin, Michel, Thomas, and the rest of the co-presbyters. May the Lord continue to guide you all by His Holy Spirit. You will salute your whole family in my name and in that of my wife. All my city colleagues salute you. The others conduct themselves piously and uprightly, with the two exceptions of Philip and Ludovic Siliniac. James Bernard had

[1] Deprived, the preceding year, of his office of councillor and captain-general, Amy Perrin had contrived, by the force of intrigue, to recover his former dignities.

[2] The city of Bourdeaux having risen in revolt against the authority of the king, on the ground of fresh taxation, the Constable Montmorency, being commissioned to suppress the disturbances, acted with relentless severity, and signalized his entry into the capital of Guienne by frightful executions.—De Thou, Lib. v.

[3] Bucer wrote to Calvin :—" Earnestly entreat the Lord for this republic that it may learn to put away its own will and obey Him."—Calv. *Opera*, Lib. ix. p. 46. But the magistrates had already resolved to make their submission, which involved the suppression of the Gospel in that unhappy city.

[4] Is the reference to the partisans of the Imperial Alliance ?

lately a quarrel with a grandson of Wendelin, because he allied the latter too closely with us. His brother left this for another place three days ago. In haste, yours,

JOHN CALVIN.

[*Lat. orig. autogr.—Library of Geneva.* Vol. 106.]

CCXXXI.—To JOHN STURM.[1]

Evidences of faith and Christian steadfastness, amid the dangers that threaten the Church.

[GENEVA, *December* 1548.]

If the rumour that has suddenly been spread among us be true, it behoves us to hold ourselves ready for the clash of arms. Would that the world were wise, for in that case it would long ago have been accustomed to cultivate peace under the favour of God. But since a good part of it takes too much pleasure in a war with God, it is but just that all those who refuse peaceably to submit themselves to the Author of Peace, should perish wretchedly in their mutual tumults. We ought at least

---

[1] Without date. This letter appears to have been written at the moment when Strasbourg, menaced by the victorious army of Charles V., was disposed, in spite of the counsel of Bucer, to accept the *Interim,* and avoid by a voluntary submission the punishment inflicted on the leagued cities of Germany.—(December 1548.)

John Sturm, a learned humanist and able politician, born at Sleida in 1507, passed through a brilliant course of study at the University of Louvain. Famous from his youth for learning and eloquence, he was nominated in 1529 Professor of Belles Lettres in the College of France, founded by Francis I., and became in 1537 Rector of the celebrated Academy of Strasbourg. Connected thenceforward with the German and Swiss Reformers, he occupied an important place in the religious negotiations of the age, maintained a correspondence with the principal European sovereigns, and died in 1583.

Calvin and Sturm were known to each other, and associated together during the sojourn of the French Reformer at Strasbourg. From this period date the relations they maintained during many years, numerous precious memorials of which are to be found in the correspondence of Calvin. See on the subject of Sturm the curious and learned work entitled :—*La vie et les travaux de Jean Sturm, Premier Recteur de l'Académie de Strasbourg, par C. Schmidt.* 1 vol. in 8vo, 1855.

to take this consolation in the midst of evils, that those stormy troubles bring some cessation of hostilities to the Church of God. The power of Antiochus will be ruined; our Pharaoh being conquered, will turn his violent assaults elsewhere, and relax perchance somewhat of his severity at home. New friends also will be able to effect some mitigation. I refrain from exhorting you to use your efforts in the particular quarter to which I refer, because I am persuaded that there is already sufficient willingness. As to the rest, whether a final dispersion be imminent, or, what is more pleasing to forecast, whether the Lord has resolved to gather together, by means of earthly commotions, into His heavenly kingdom, all those who are now scattered and wandering wretchedly abroad, we shall have cherished a friendship in good faith, the bond of which is inviolable. . . . . . . . . . . .[1]

[*Lat. orig. autogr.—Library of Geneva.* Vol. 107ª.]

## CCXXXII.—To MADAME DE CANY.[2]

Exhortation to a courageous and honest profession of the truth.

*This 8th January* 1549.

MADAME,—I would not have taken the liberty to write to you, if a man, whom I ought to trust among all others, had not emboldened me to do so, by assuring me that my letter would be agreeable to you. That is, Monsieur de Normandie, who, feeling himself obliged to you for the kindness you had shewn him, had a special desire to do you service, so far as he had the

---

[1] Conclusion wanting in the original manuscript.
[2] Peronne de Pisseleu, wife of Michel de Barbançon, Seigneur de Cany, one of the personages of most importance in Picardy. This lady, instructed in the reformed faith by Laurent de Normandie, lieutenant of the king at Noyon, and the friend of Calvin, had for a long time to endure the severity of her husband, who afterwards came at a later period to be a partaker of like faith.—Bèze, *Hist. Eccl.*, tom. ii. p. 244.; De Thou, lib. xxv. Madame de Cany, sister of the Duchess d'Etampes, favourite of the late king, had possessed an unbounded influence at court, which she always used for generous purposes. Her ordinary residence was the Château de Varannes, situated on the Oise, near to Noyon.

means, and besides, has such a care of your salvation as he ought to have who knows that you have loved him, as partaker of a common Christian faith. On this account he has induced me to write to you, thinking that not only you might take pleasure in my letters, but that they might perhaps be profitable for you, as well for your consolation in present extremity, as to exhort you to perseverance so needful in the midst of such manifold temptations. And would to God I might have more ample opportunity of compliance with his request. But seeing that it is His pleasure that we should be separated by so great a distance, which does not permit more frequent communication between us, I beseech you, Madame, to take what I do write as a testimony of the earnest desire which I have to promote your salvation. If, because of the confession you have made of your Christianity, murmurs and threatenings rise up against you, you must bear in mind to what we are called, which is, that notwithstanding all sorts of contradiction on the part of the world, we must render to the Son of God the homage which belongs to Him. These indeed should be to you as so many warnings to prepare yourself for greater things, for neither great nor small ought to seek exemption from suffering in the cause of our Sovereign King, in which His honour is as much involved as our salvation. Above all, since Himself has begun by shewing us the way, who among us shall dare to refuse to follow Him? Where is the greatness, or the elevation, that can bestow greater privilege upon us than on Himself? And more than that, if we can appreciate the honour he confers upon us in making use of our service to maintain His so precious truth, we shall hold it to be a peculiar advantage, rather than be annoyed on account of it. True it is, that the human understanding cannot apprehend that; but, seeing that the infallible wisdom of God pronounces, that those who are persecuted for the testimony of the Gospel are most happy, at all hazards we must needs acquiesce in that judgment. And indeed, who are we that *we* should maintain the cause of God? Where is our sufficiency for it, seeing that we are altogether inclined to falsehood? How should we be witnesses for His truth, unless by His own special gracious permission? On the

other hand, seeing that we deserve on account of our sins to
suffer all shame of face and ignominy, every sort of misery and
torment, yea were it even a hundred thousand deaths, if that
were possible, have we aught to complain of, ought we not
rather to rejoice, when, forgetting our faults, He wills that we
should suffer for His name ? Therefore, inasmuch as we are
so froward and carnal that we cannot reach such elevation, let
us beg of this gracious God that He would please to imprint in
our hearts that which naturally we find so strange. Furthermore, let us take to ourselves the example of the Apostles, who
counted the reproach of the world as a great honour, and
even gloried in it. In short, let us never think that we have
fully received the truth, if we do not prefer above all worldly
triumphs, to fight under the banner of our Lord Jesus, that
is to say, to bear His cross.

Even so, Madame, consider, I beseech you, if hitherto you
have taken pains to serve and honour so good a master, how
you can strive more earnestly than ever to arm yourself against
opposition, to take courage against all difficulties in order to
surmount them ; for, since the worldly often manifest invincible
constancy in the pursuit of their vanities, patiently enduring so
many labours, troubles and dangers, it would be too shameful
were we to grow weary in the midst of the way of salvation ;
albeit that this is by no means all that is required of us, that
we shew ourselves steadfast in the midst of persecutions ; for,
even if there were no enemies to make open war upon us, we
find enough of aversion and indisposedness in ourselves and
all around, to hinder us in making our calling sure, which all
those who have a true zeal to devote themselves to God, experience more fully than any one could tell them. Inasmuch,
then, as I hold you to be of the number, I entreat you to exercise yourself continually in the doctrine of renouncing the
world yet more and more, in order to come nearer to our Lord
Jesus, who has once for all purchased us to separate us unto
Himself. I mean the world, such as we carry it within ourselves, before we are made again after His likeness. And seeing
that our whole nature, inasmuch as by the corruption of the
plague it has been depraved, is enmity against God, the king-

dom of our Lord Jesus Christ cannot be duly established, until all which is ours has been beaten down ; and not only the open vices which are condemned of men, but also even our own reason and wisdom. I am aware that I do not speak to you of any new thing, and that by the grace of God you have long ago begun to follow in the way of the holy heavenly calling. But the study of holiness is one of which we must avail ourselves even to the end. And as I have ample cause to praise God for the graces He has bestowed on you, and whereby He magnifies Himself in you, by making His own glory to shine forth therein ; in also looking to the frailty which we all feel, I think it no superfluous trouble to exhort you to follow on, as indeed you do. And even as it is becoming in Christians to submit in all humility to receive the admonitions which are addressed to them in the name of God, even that the most learned should gladly submit to be taught, I hope that you will receive the whole with a benign and kindly heart. Believe me, when I hear that God has wrought so powerfully in you, and that He has vouchsafed you such commendable qualities, I am incited all the more to desire that He would increase His work in you, until He has quite finished it ; and this it is that has constrained me more freely to declare to you my desire and affection.

In conclusion, Madame, having humbly commended me to your kind favour, I entreat our good Lord to have you in His holy protection, to guide you by His Holy Spirit in all strength and prudence, to vouchsafe you grace to promote His honour, until He gather us all unto Himself.

Your servant and humble brother,

CHARLES D'ESPEVILLE.

[*Fr. Copy.—Library of Geneva.* Vol. 107.]

CCXXXIII.—To Mademoiselle de . . . .

Exhortations to steadfastness in the faith—acknowledgment of liberality.

*The* 12*th of January* 1549.

Mademoiselle my Sister,—I am very glad that your letter has afforded an occasion for my writing to you, so that without further excuse access and freedom have been given me, were it for nought else than to declare the affection I have for you. Therein, that is in your letter, I can perceive evident and clear signs of spiritual vitality; and I have not a doubt but the heart speaks therein quite as much, or rather more than the mouth. Besides, you shew convincingly that you have no longer mere passing convictions, such as many people have now-a-days, but that you have been touched to the quick, and moved with the desire of dedicating yourself wholly to God and to His will. It is very true, as you say, that while clinging from worldly fear to the superstitions which in the world reign paramount, you are still very far from that perfection whereto our gracious God doth call us. But yet it is to have made some progress even to acknowledge our sins, and to be displeased with them. You must now advance farther, and condemning your own weakness, set yourself in earnest about getting rid of it; and if you cannot succeed all at once in compassing your wish, yet nevertheless you must persevere in seeking the remedy for it, until you have been completely cured. To do this, you will find it to be of advantage to call yourself to account day by day, and while acknowledging your faults, to groan within yourself, and mourn over them before God, so that your displeasure against whatsoever is evil may become more intense, until you are quite confirmed and resolved to renounce it as you ought, even as indeed I feel assured you labour hard to do. And it is not in vain that you beg of me to join my prayers with yours, to seek with importunity to God that He would be pleased to have compassion upon you, and to deliver you from this unhappy captivity. Let us continue then with one accord to put up this request, and He will at length make manifest that you have not altogether lost your time. True, sometimes He lets us grow faint, and before declaring effectually that He has heard our prayers, He seems to keep at a distance, as much to sharpen our desire, as to make trial of our patience; and, therefore, you need not reckon that hitherto your prayers to Him have been in vain, but much rather take encouragement, and strive even more and more, knowing that if perseverance be required throughout our whole life, it is specially desired in prayer. And, besides, you must also take care in real earnest to fan the flame which God has already begun to kindle within you; for all the gracious affections He breathes into us, are just so many sparks which we must not extinguish, or allow to go out by our heedlessness. Since, then, God has already opened your eyes so far, that you admit we ought to be His peculiar ones, and dedicated to Him in righteousness, so as to glorify Him as well in our bodies as in our souls; seeing also that He has touched your heart, so that you have some feeling of our unhappiness in alienation from Him, unquestionably you must not now go to sleep or trifle away at your ease, but even as we stir the fire when it does not burn as it ought to do, it is quite right that you be upstirred yet more and more, until the longing desire to devote yourself wholly to Him and to His righteousness, overcomes all hindrances either from the flesh or from the world. I see, or at least take into view, the very great difficulties you have where you are; but since these considerations do not excuse you in the sight of God, when the question is of obedience to His Word, and also in a thing of so great importance as the rendering unto Him the glory which is due, and the making confession of your Christianity,—if I desire your salvation as I ought, as God is my witness that I do, it is my duty to awaken you, so far as I possibly can, not that I can teach you any new thing, but that on my part I may assist you in making a right use of that knowledge which God has vouchsafed you; to wit, how reasonable it is that His honour be preferred to our life, and also that we endeavour to put away all those subterfuges, which our flesh suggests to us, for turning aside from the path which He points out. That we may do so, we must learn a habit of forgetting ourselves, for the allurements of the world are no less dangerous than open war. The most humble have their share. You, on the other hand, owing to the high condition wherein God has set you, have a larger portion. But you must consider that this is a discipline God sends you, in order that you may all the better manifest the strength and vigour of the savour of our heavenly life, when you shall have surmounted those great obstacles, following out in spite of them your heavenly calling. However, Mademoiselle, when you feel your own infirmity so great, that in the midst of dangers you are unable to give glory to God, do not neglect the remedy, which is to betake yourself to the cross, where you may be joined to the flock, and hear the voice of the Shepherd; whatever may happen, shun to be as a sheep straying in the wilderness. When you are in such a disposition, there is no doubt that God will have compassion upon you, that Himself will provide when you shall see no means of doing so; for it is thus that He withdraws His own not only from the mouths of wolves, but from the very depths of hell.

I have received the ten crowns which you have sent for the support of the poor believers who have need of it.[1] I have intrusted them to a discreet hand, to make distribution according to your intention. May the Lord vouchsafe acceptance of this alms at your hands, as a sacrifice of a sweet savour, and cause you one day to rejoice in the spiritual benefits which He has imparted to those you are thus helping in their earthly poverty.

And now, Mademoiselle, having commended me humbly to your kind favour, with prayer to our good Lord to uphold you in His protection, to govern you always by his Spirit, and to assist you in every way and evermore, I shall conclude for the pre-

---

[1] The donations which a pious liberality daily multiplied at Geneva, gave rise to the foundations known by the name of French, German, and Italian *Bourses*. The names of Margaret de Valois, and of the Duchess of Ferrara, shine in the first rank upon the list of foreign contributors.—Bolsec, *Life of Calvin*, c. xi.

sent. My wife also desires to be humbly commended to your kind favour.

Your servant and humble brother,
CHARLES D'ESPEVILLE.

[*Fr. copy.— Library of Geneva.* Vol. 108.]

## CCXXXIV.—To the Ministers of the Church of Montbeliard.[1]

Exhortations to discharge to the end their ministerial duties.

[GENEVA, *16th January* 1549.]

Grace to you, and peace, from God our Father and from the Lord Jesus Christ.—Very dear brethren, deserving of my hearty reverence, what we so long feared has at length come to pass, for Satan has, by the aid of his ministers, overturned among you also the order of the Church as established by God. Yet your letter was consolatory—so far as there could be any consolation in so very sad a state of things—for we learned from it that you were all faithful to the last in the discharge of your duty. In denouncing, as you say you did, those seducers who were making themselves busy in defiling the purity of sound doctrine, you acted with a decision worthy of the ministers of Christ. You now give a bright example of the sincerity of your faith, in preferring even exile to perfidious dissimulation. For when he who had hitherto given a hospitable reception within his dominions to the Church of Christ, and had granted you full permission to preach Christ, now deprives you

---

[1] To the Faithful Servants of Christ, the Ministers of the Church of Montbeliard, dearest Brethren and Fellow-Ministers.

George of Wurtemberg, Count of Montbeliard, having fallen under the disgrace of the Emperor, at the end of the war of Smalkald, in which he had taken part in the ranks of the Protestant princes, was stript of his Principality in 1548, and withdrew to the Canton of Berne.—Ruchat, vol. v. p. 368. At the termination of that revolution, the Churches of the Pays de Montbeliard were dispersed, and their ministers, among whom was to be remarked Pierre Toussain, were banished, and sought an asylum in the different Reformed Cantons of Switzerland, until the period of the restoration, both political and religious, that replaced them some years afterwards in their native country.

of the office of teachers, there is no use in pushing the matter farther, as we think, especially when there is no hope of making progress, and when the sheep, over which Christ had made you pastors, no longer desire your services. As he is a traitor who voluntarily yields up and deserts his post, so it is our duty, when forced, not to offer resistance, unless perhaps we should be expressly called upon by the Church to undergo the extremity; for it is a hundred times better to die, than for those who were prepared to follow Christ to make vain their vows. But your case is far different; for so long as you were pastors, you were faithful and assiduous in your attention to your flocks. Now when there is no use in desiring to persevere, and when the sheep themselves, to whom your faith was pledged, do not consider it profitable for you to proceed farther, you are certainly free from all further obligation. It remains, therefore, for you to commend to Christ the charges committed to you, that He alone by His Spirit may give guidance when you have no longer any opportunity of carrying on your labours. Henceforward we may imagine what your sorrow must be, seeing that nothing presents itself to you but exile and poverty. But your greatest affliction will be caused by the misery of the Church, for whose interests you have evinced greater regard than for your own. And we indeed are equally affected—as we ought to be—by your public and private misfortunes. Would that we could extend a helping hand to you! For the rest, we exhort you to hold on to the end in this your testimony of Christian sincerity. Your lot, however hard, will be more blessed than if you maintained a name and a place where the Son of God was exiled. Yet we shall soon see Him so reigning in heaven, as to make his power appear also on the earth. Meanwhile, it becomes us to be ready for the warfare, since it is not yet the hour of triumph. Adieu, best and most upright brethren. May the Lord Jesus Christ be with you, may He comfort and support you in your devoted steadfastness.

Your brethren truly in the Lord, the Ministers of the Church of Geneva.—In the name of all,

JOHN CALVIN.

[Calvin's *Lat. Corresp.* Opera, tom. ix. p. 50.]

## CCXXXV.—To Henry Bullinger.[1]

*Hope of union with the theologians of Zurich—dedication of several writings.*

GENEVA, 21*st January* 1549.

I at length received your former letter, which I thought had been destroyed, three days before the latter of the two reached me. For when the person who married the other sister[2] sought Hooper's[3] letter from his companion, observing another small packet, he immediately laid hands on it. His companion, either from modesty, or from some cause I know not what, did not dare to take it from him. I have read your annotations, from which I have discovered what you regard as wanting in my method of treating the subject. I have endeavoured briefly to satisfy you, because the matter itself did not demand a long discourse. I shall know how far I have succeeded in this, when I have received your reply. I may at least on good grounds wish to obtain this of you, viz., that you will not allow yourself to become entangled in baseless suspicions. For I observe that, owing to this cause, you are perplexed in regard to many points which present difficulty, simply because you put upon the majority of my statements a different construction from what you have any ground for doing. A pre-con-

---

[1] The year 1549 is remarkable for the tendencies to union manifested by many of the Swiss Churches, and for their happy issue! Several persons, says Ruchat, zealous for religion, imagined that the clergy of Zurich and Geneva did not hold the same doctrine on the Supper, on the ground of some slight difference in the expressions they made use of; and this divergence caused them pain. Accordingly, as they held Bullinger and Calvin in great esteem, and desired to be able to profit equally by writings published by theologians of both churches, they deemed it necessary to institute conferences with a view to union; and Calvin, ever full of zeal for the interests of the Church, did not hesitate to subscribe to this petition.—*Hospinien*, tom. ii. p. 367; Ruchat, tom. v. p. 369.

[2] Valeran Poulain, brother-in-law of Hooper, whose sister he espoused at Zurich. He became this same year minister of the congregation of Foreign Protestants at Glastonbury, near London. We shall find him afterwards minister of the Church of Frankfort.

[3] John Hooper, formerly chaplain to the Duke of Somerset, withdrew to Zurich during the latter years of the reign of Henry VIII. He was at this time disposed to return to England.

ceived opinion regarding me leads you to imagine and attribute to me what never occurred to my mind. Besides, while you are concerned to maintain your own opinions, whatever they may be, to the very last, you sometimes consider more what is in harmony with them, than what is the truth on the subject. If simplicity pleases you, I certainly take no delight in disguise and circumlocution. If you love a free declaration of the truth, I never had any mind to bend what I wrote, so as to receive its acceptance with men. If there be any who have flattered Luther and others, I am not of that number. Our most excellent Musculus knows, that even when wise men were in fear, I was always free [from apprehension]. But had it not been for the obstacle of an unprofitable distrust, there would by this time have been no controversy between us, or none to speak of. Although, however, I differ from you in opinion, that does not imply the least severance of affection; just as I cultivate the friendship of Bucer, and yet am free to dissent occasionally from his views. You are accordingly too severe in saying in your letter that the matter can only go well, provided you understand that you are not regarded as our enemies. On what grounds you form that surmise, I know not. This indeed I know, that I both think and speak of you in a friendly spirit. This, moreover, is known to very many who have heard me speak. It may indeed be that I have found fault with you in private letters to my friends, or that I have not concealed my conviction, that what they censured was deserving of reprehension. There was always, however, such an admixture of praise, as qualified any bitterness, and afforded proof of good intentions. Others may form what opinion they choose, but I shall never have to repent of lack of integrity on my part. If Master Blaurer[1] shall undertake Provence, which is offered to him, and Musculus accept the Professorship of Theology, I shall not only congratulate the Church of Berne, but hope that this will prove a bond of closer relationship between us. I beg you will inform me of your affairs, whenever an opportunity occurs. You would have had my Commentaries on the Five

---

[1] Ambroise Blaurer, formerly minister of the Reformed Church of Constance, at this time minister of the Church of Bienne.

Epistles of Paul before this time, had I not thought that they were for sale with you. As messengers rarely go and come between this and your quarter, I was afraid that the carriage would cost more than the purchase of them. I now send you the Commentaries on the Second Epistle to the Corinthians, and the four [Epistles] immediately following. I have yet published nothing on the Epistle to Titus, and the two Epistles to the Thessalonians. I also send my reply, which is highly approved of by Brentius, whose opinion I do not mention to you in the way of boasting, but that you may therefrom form a conjecture as to how much more moderate he is in his doctrine of the Sacraments than he formerly was. Adieu, most illustrious Sir, and dearest brother in the Lord. May the Lord Jesus always guide you and your colleagues, all of whom you will salute respectfully in my name. Ours in turn desire best greetings to you, of whom Des Gallars presents for your acceptance a small treatise he has composed. The best greeting to Master Musculus, and other pious brethren.—Yours,

JOHN CALVIN.

[*Lat. orig. autogr.*—*Archives of Zurich.* Gest. VI. 166, p. 19.]


## CCXXXVI.—To Bucer.[1]

*Consolations to be found in the study of divine and everlasting truth.*

[*February* 1549.]

As truth is most precious, so all men confess it to be so. And yet, since God alone is the source of all good, you must not doubt, that whatever truth you anywhere meet with, pro-

---

[1] This undated fragment should, we think, be referred to the month of February 1549; that is, to the period at which Bucer, compelled to leave Strasbourg, by the establishment of the Interim in that town, was making preparations for his departure for England. In one of his letters to Calvin we discover the following passage:—" We are only hindered by the tears and sighs of the pious—of whom there are still a great many here—from leaving this place before we get orders. For, if the Lord will, we wish rather to seal than to break up our ministry. You see how our affairs stand, and how much we need the assistance of your prayers, both in our own behalf and on that of this very unfortunate Church."—*Calv. Opera*, b. ix. p. 233.

Sadly disappointed in the dream of his whole life—the union of the Reformed

ceeds from Him, unless you would be doubly ungrateful to Him; it is in this way you have received the word descended from heaven. For it is sinful to treat God's gifts with contempt; and to ascribe to man what is peculiarly God's is a still greater impiety. Philosophy is, consequently, the noble gift of God, and those learned men who have striven hard after it in all ages have been incited thereto by God himself, that they might enlighten the world in the knowledge of the truth. But there is a wide difference between the writings of these men and those truths which God, of His own pleasure, delivered to guilty men for their sanctification. In the former, you may fall in with a small particle of truth, of which you can get only a taste, sufficient to make you feel how pleasant and sweet it is; but in the latter, you may obtain in rich abundance that which can refresh the soul to the full. In the one, a shadow and an image is placed before the eyes which can only excite in you a love of the object, without admitting you to familiar intercourse with it; in the other, the solid substance stands before you, with which you may not only become intimately acquainted, but may also, in some measure, handle it. In that, the seed is in a manner choked; in this, you may possess the fruit in its very maturity. There, in short, only a few small sparks break forth, which so point out the path that they fail in the middle of the journey,—or rather, which fail in indicating the path at all,—and can only restrain the traveller from going farther astray; but here, the Spirit of God, like a most brilliant torch, or rather like the sun itself, shines in full splendour, not only to guide the course of your life, even to its final goal, but also to conduct you to a blessed immortality. Draw then from this source, wherever you may wander, and as soon as he finds you a settled abode, you ought to make that your place of rest. . . .

[*Calvin's Lat. Corresp.* Opera, tom. ix. p. 50.]

Churches of Germany and Switzerland—forgotten by parties who could not forgive his moderation in an age of hatred and intolerance, Bucer carried with him into exile the respect and affection of Calvin, who in a letter, of which we have here only a mere fragment, addressed to him the highest consolations of Christian philosophy.

## CCXXXVII.—To the Pastors of the Church of Berne.[1]

*Desire of union between the Churches of Berne and Geneva.*

GENEVA, 13*th March* 1549.

Seeing that we have, unsolicited, offered you a reading of our views on the sacraments, it seems desirable to furnish you, briefly, with some reason for our resolution in this matter; although, indeed, no lengthened introduction is needed in dealing with us in so just a cause. When your illustrious senate has publicly called upon you to deliberate, among other matters, regarding the peace of the Church, of which the peculiar bond is harmony in purity of doctrine, it is probable there will be some discussion regarding the sacraments, as that subject has for a long time occupied the attention of the Bernese Church. And while we are not required to make any exposition of our doctrine, we have, nevertheless, thought it our duty, even though unasked, to take part with you in bearing testimony on a matter in which we have all been completely unanimous. For since we both preach the same Christ, both profess the same gospel, are both members of the same church, and have both the same ministry, there ought not to be that diversity of authority among us to which we have been subject, either to break up the unity of our faith, or to hinder from flourishing amongst us so many rights of holy fellowship con-

[1] While Calvin was engaged in active negotiations with the ministers of Zurich for the adoption of a common formula regarding the sacrament of the Lord's Supper, he addressed to the ministers of the Church of Berne a statement of what the Church of Geneva held on that important question, in the hope of leading that Church into the proposed union. But the Bernese clergy, placed in a position of absolute dependence on the seigneury, could not adopt any formula without its authority; and the seigneurs, jealous of their influence, regarded with a distrustful eye any communication with the ministers of Geneva. The approaches of Calvin, also, were not well received, and the noble desire of the reformer for the union of the Helvetian churches, realized at a later period by Bullinger, met with no response.—*Ruchat*, tom. v. pp. 578, 579.

secrated to the service of Christ. That proximity of residence, also, which is so influential among the children of this world, in drawing them into close friendship, ought not, at least, to be less powerful among us. We are, in reality, so commingled, that even the situation of the two places brings us, as it were, within a bond of mutual union. So far is this the case, that there is a federal union between the two cities. Some of our ministers, moreover, supply the churches of the Bernese district, just as certain of your body, again, have some of the churches of Geneva under their charge. It is, consequently, to a great extent, as much your interest as it is ours to become intimately acquainted with those doctrines to which we conform. At all events, in this way—passing by other considerations—many unfavourable suspicions will be counteracted, and malicious men will be deprived of a source of abuse. We confidently trust that our wishes will be agreeable, not only to yourselves, but also to your most illustrious senate. It only remains that you receive this communication calmly and with forbearance. And if you do so, as there is the highest hope you will, it will not be found to contain anything which you may not easily comprehend. Adieu, dearly beloved and estimable brethren and fellow-ministers; may the Lord Jesus long preserve, by His strength, the Bernese republic in a most prosperous condition. May He uphold the illustrious senate, under whose auspices ye have been assembled. May He direct and bless your assembly, and guide you by a spirit of wise zeal and uprightness to promote the advancement and edification of the Church.

Signed in the name of all your brethren and fellow-ministers of the Church of Geneva,

JOHN CALVIN.

Then follows an exposition of the sacraments, corrected by the hand of Calvin.

[*Lat. Copy.—Archives of Zurich*, Gest. VI. 105, p. 390.]

## CCXXXVIII.—To Viret.[1]

Death of Idelette de Bure, the wife of Calvin.

*April* 7, 1549.

Although the death of my wife has been exceedingly painful to me, yet I subdue my grief as well as I can. Friends, also, are earnest in their duty to me. It might be wished, indeed, that they could profit me and themselves more; yet one can scarcely say how much I am supported by their attentions. But you know well enough how tender, or rather soft, my mind is. Had not a powerful self-control, therefore, been vouchsafed to me, I could not have borne up so long. And truly mine is no common source of grief. I have been bereaved of the best companion of my life, of one who, had it been so ordered, would not only have been the willing sharer of my indigence, but even of my death. During her life she was the faithful helper of my ministry. From her I never experienced the slightest hindrance. She was never troublesome to me throughout the entire course of her illness; she was more anxious about her children than about herself.[2] As I feared these private

---

[1] A peculiar interest attaches to this and the following letter, written under a load of great domestic affliction. Early in April 1549, Calvin lost the worthy partner of his life, Idelette de Bure, whose frail and delicate health gave way under the pressure of a protracted illness, and whose last hours are known to us by the touching picture given of them by the Reformer. The consolations of friendship, and the consideration of the important duties he had to discharge, supported Calvin in this affliction, and the self-control which he manifested during the first days of his bereavement, excited the admiration of his friends. Viret wrote him on this occasion as follows:—" Wonderfully and incredibly have I been refreshed, not by empty rumours alone, but especially by numerous messengers who have informed me how you, with a heart so broken and lacerated, have attended to all your duties even better than hitherto . . . and that, above all, at a time when grief so fresh, and on that account all the more severe, might have prostrated your mind. Go on then as you have begun . . . and I pray God most earnestly that you may be enabled to do so, and that you may receive daily greater comfort and be strengthened more and more."—Letter of 10th April 1549. *Calv. Opera*, tom. ix. p. 53.

[2] Idelette de Bure had, by her first marriage with Jean Storder, several children known to us only by the pious solicitude of their mother on her deathbed.

cares might annoy her to no purpose, I took occasion, on the third day before her death, to mention that I would not fail in discharging my duty to her children. Taking up the matter immediately, she said, " I have already committed them to God." When I said that that was not to prevent me from caring for them, she replied, " I know you will not neglect what you know has been committed to God." Lately, also, when a certain woman insisted that she should talk with me regarding these matters, I, for the first time, heard her give the following brief answer : " Assuredly the principal thing is that they live a pious and holy life. My husband is not to be urged to instruct them in religious knowledge and in the fear of God. If they be pious, I am sure he will gladly be a father to them ; but if not, they do not deserve that I should ask for aught in their behalf." This nobleness of mind will weigh more with me than a hundred recommendations. Many thanks for your friendly consolation. Adieu, most excellent and honest brother. May the Lord Jesus watch over and direct yourself and your wife.[1] Present my best wishes to her and to the brethren. —Yours,

JOHN CALVIN.

[*Calvin's Lat. Corresp.* Opera, tom. ix. p. 50.]

## CCXXXIX.—To FAREL.

Further details regarding the death of Idelette de Bure.

GENEVA, 11*th April* 1549.

Intelligence of my wife's death has perhaps reached you before now. I do what I can to keep myself from being overwhelmed with grief. My friends also leave nothing undone that may administer relief to my mental suffering. When your brother left, her life was all but despaired of. When the

[1] We read in Viret's letter to Calvin already referred to,—" My wife salutes you most courteously ; she has been grieved in no ordinary way by the death of her very dear sister, and she and I feel it to be a loss to us all." Idelette de Bure kept up with Viret's wife a pious epistolary correspondence, which has unfortunately not been preserved.

brethren were assembled on Tuesday, they thought it best that we should join together in prayer. This was done. When Abel, in the name of the rest, exhorted her to faith and patience, she briefly (for she was now greatly worn) stated her frame of mind. I afterwards added an exhortation, which seemed to me appropriate to the occasion. And then, as she had made no allusion to her children, I, fearing that, restrained by modesty, she might be feeling an anxiety concerning them, which would cause her greater suffering than the disease itself, declared in the presence of the brethren, that I should henceforth care for them as if they were my own. She replied, " I have already committed them to the Lord." When I replied, that that was not to hinder me from doing my duty, she immediately answered, " If the Lord shall care for them, I know they will be commended to you." Her magnanimity was so great, that she seemed to have already left the world. About the sixth hour of the day, on which she yielded up her soul to the Lord, our brother Bourgouin[1] addressed some pious words to her, and while he was doing so, she spoke aloud, so that all saw that her heart was raised far above the world. For these were her words: " O glorious resurrection ! O God of Abraham, and of all our fathers, in thee have the faithful trusted during so many past ages, and none of them have trusted in vain. I also will hope." These short sentences were rather ejaculated than distinctly spoken. This did not come from the suggestion of others, but from her own reflections, so that she made it obvious in few words what were her own meditations. I had to go out at six o'clock. Having been removed to another apartment after seven, she immediately began to decline. When she felt her voice suddenly failing her she said : " Let us pray : let us pray. All pray for me." I had now returned. She was unable to speak, and her mind seemed to be troubled. I, having spoken a few words about the love of Christ, the hope of eternal life, concerning our married life, and her departure, engaged in prayer. In full possession of her mind, she both heard the prayer, and attended to it. Before eight she expired, so calmly, that those present could scarcely distinguish between

[1] The minister Francis Bourgouin.

her life and her death. I at present control my sorrow so that my duties may not be interfered with. But in the meanwhile the Lord has sent other trials upon me. Adieu, brother, and very excellent friend. May the Lord Jesus strengthen you by His Spirit; and may He support me also under this heavy affliction, which would certainly have overcome me, had not He, who raises up the prostrate, strengthens the weak, and refreshes the weary, stretched forth His hand from heaven to me. Salute all the brethren and your whole family.—Yours,

JOHN CALVIN.

[*Calvin's Lat. Corresp.* Opera, tom. ix. p. 50.]

## CCXL.—To MADAME DE CANY.[1]

Account of the instructive death of Madame Laurent de Normandie.

*This* 29*th of April* 1549.

MADAME,—Although the news which I communicate are sad, and must also sadden the person to whom I beg you to impart them, nevertheless I hope that my letter will not be unwelcome to you. It has pleased my God to withdraw from this world the wife of my kind brother, M. de Normandie.[2] Our consolation is, that He has gathered her unto Himself; for He has guided her even to the last sigh, as if visibly He had held out the hand to her. Now, forasmuch as her father must needs be informed,[3] we have thought there was no way

[1] See the letter and the note at p. 187.
[2] Laurent de Normandie, sprung from a noble family of Picardy, fellow-countryman and friend of Calvin, discharged the functions of master of requests and of lieutenant of the king at Noyon, before retiring to Geneva. Received inhabitant of the town, the 2d May 1547, burgess, the 25th April 1555, he lived there in intimacy with Calvin, who dedicated to him in 1550 his *Traité des Scandales*. He had married for his first wife Anne de la Vacquerie, of a noble family, which has merged in that of the Dukes of Saint Simon, and illustrious under the reign of Louis XI., by the first president Jacques de la Vacquerie. A short time after his arrival at Geneva he lost his wife, whose edifying death is the subject of Calvin's letter to Madame de Cany, and he married a second time (14th September 1550) Anne Colladon Galiffe.—*Notices Généalogiques sur les Familles de Genève*, tom. ii. p. 527.
[3] Eloi de la Vacquerie.

more suitable than to request that you would please take the trouble to request him to call on you, that the painful intelligence may be broken to him by your communication of it. What the gentleman has written to us who lately presented our letter to you, has emboldened us to take this step, viz., that you had introduced the good man in question to the right way of salvation, and that you had given him understanding of the pure and sound doctrine which we must maintain. We do not doubt, therefore, that you are willing to continue your good offices, and that even in this present need. For we cannot employ ourselves better, than in carrying this message in the name of God, to comfort him to whom you have already done so much good, that he may not be beyond measure disconsolate. Therefore, Madame, I leave you to set before him the arguments and reasons which you know to be suitable for exhorting to submission. Only I shall shortly relate to you the history, which will furnish you with ample matter for showing him that he has reason to be thankful. And, according to the grace and wisdom that God has given you, you will draw thence for his comfort as opportunity shall require.

Having heard of the illness of the good woman, we were amazed how she could have been able to bear so well the fatigue of the journey, for she arrived quite fresh, and without showing any sign of weariness. Indeed she acknowledged that God had singularly supported her during that time. Weak as she was, she kept well enough until a little before Christmas. The eager desire which she had to hear the Word of God, upheld her until the month of January. She then began to take to bed, not because the complaint was as yet thought to be mortal, but to prevent the danger which might arise. Although expecting a favourable termination, and hoping to recover her health, she nevertheless prepared for death, saying often, that if this was not the finishing blow, it could not be long delayed. As for remedies, all was done that could be. And if her bodily comfort was provided for, that which she prized most highly was nowise wanting, to wit, pious admonitions to confirm her in the fear of God, in the faith of Jesus Christ, in patience, in the hope of salvation. On her part she always gave clear evidence that the labour was not in vain, for in her discourse you could see that she had the whole deeply imprinted upon her heart. In short, throughout the course of her sickness, she proved herself to be a true sheep of our Lord Jesus, letting herself be quietly led by the Great Shepherd. Two or three days before death, as her heart was more raised to God, she also spoke with more earnest affection than ever. Even the day before, while she was exhorting her people, she said to her attendant, that he must take good heed never to return thither where he had polluted himself with idolatry; and that since God had led him to a Christian Church, he should be careful to live therein a holy life. The night following, she was oppressed with great and continual pain. Yet never did one hear any other cry from her, than the prayer to God that He would have pity upon her, and that He would deliver her out of the world, vouchsafing grace to persevere always in the faith which He had bestowed. Toward five o'clock in the morning I went to her. After she had listened very patiently to the doctrine which I set before her, such as the occasion called for, she said: "The hour draws near, I must needs depart from the world; this flesh asks only to go away into corruption; but I feel certain that my God is withdrawing my soul into His kingdom. I know what a poor sinful woman I am, but my confidence is in His goodness, and in the death and passion of His Son. Therefore, I do not doubt of my salvation, since He has assured me of it. I go to Him as to a Father." While she was thus discoursing, a considerable number of persons came in. I threw in from time to time some words, such as seemed suitable; and we also made supplication to God as the exigency of her need required. After once more declaring the sense she had of her sins, to ask the pardon of them from God, and the certainty which she entertained of her salvation, putting her sole confidence in Jesus, and having her whole trust in Him,—without being invited by any one to do so, she began to pronounce the *Miserere* as we sing it in church, and continued with a loud and strong voice, not without great difficulty, but she entreated that we would allow her to continue. Whereupon, I made her a short recapitulation of the whole argument of the psalm, seeing the pleasure she took in it. Afterwards, taking me by the hand, she said to me, " How happy I am, and how am I beholden to God, for having brought me here to die. Had I been in that wretched prison, I could not have ventured to open my mouth to make confession of my Christianity. Here I have not only liberty to glorify God, but I have so many sound arguments to confirm me in my salvation." Sometimes, indeed, she said, " I am not able for more." When I answered her, " God is able to help you ; He has, indeed, shown you how He is a present aid to His own ;" she said immediately, " I do believe so, and He makes me feel His help." Her husband was there, striving to keep up in such sort that we were all sorry for him, while he made us wonder in amazement at his fortitude. For while possessed with such grief as I know it to have been, and weighed down by extremity of sorrow, he had so far gained the mastery over self, as to exhort his better part as freely as if they were going to make a most joyful journey together. The conversation I have related took place in the midst of the great torment she endured from pains in her stomach. Towards nine or ten o'clock they abated. Availing herself of this relaxation, she never ceased to glorify God, humbly seeking her salvation and all her wellbeing in Jesus Christ. When speech failed her, her countenance told how intently she was interested as well in the prayers as in the exhortations which were made. Otherwise she was so motionless, that sight alone gave indication of life. Towards the end, considering that she was gone, I said, " Now let us pray God that He would give us grace to follow her." As I rose, she turned her eyes upon us, as if charging us to persevere in prayer and consolation ; after that, we perceived no motion, and she passed away so gracefully, that it was as if she had fallen asleep.

I pray you, Madame, to excuse me if I have been too tedious. But I thought that the father would be well pleased to be fully informed of the whole, as if he himself had been upon the spot. And I hope that in so good a work you will find nothing troublesome. St. Paul, in treating of charity, does not forget that we ought to weep with those who weep ; that is to say, that if we are Christians, we ought to have such compassion and sorrow for our neighbours, that we should willingly take part in their tears, and thus comfort them. It cannot otherwise be but the good man must, at the first, be wrung with grief. Howbeit he must already have been long prepared to receive the news, considering that his daughter's sickness had increased so much, that her recovery was despaired of. But the great consolation is, the example which she has afforded to him and to all of us, of bowing to the will of God. And thus, seeing that she has presented herself so peaceably to death, let us herein follow her, willingly complying with the disposal of God ; and if her father loved her, let him show his love in conforming himself to the desire which she exhibited of submitting herself to God. And seeing that her dismissal has been so happy, let him rejoice in the grace of God vouchsafed to her, which far surpasses all the comforts we can possess in this world.

In conclusion, Madame, having humbly commended me to your kind favour, I beseech our good Lord to be always your protector, to increase you with all spiritual blessing, and to cause you to glorify His name even to the end.

Your humble servitor and brother,
CHARLES D'ESPEVILLE.

[*Fr. copy—Library of Geneva.* Vol. 107.]


CCXLI.—To VIRET.

Various particulars—recommendation of Francis Hotman, Jurisconsult.

*7th May* 1549.

When Ferron was deposed he said you would write on his behalf. I have not received anything as yet. He behaved so insolently in our assembly that he very much resembled a man deprived of his reason.[1] The Lord will direct the matter according to His will ; we have resolved on acting so moderately as to show him that he has to do with men and with

[1] Accused of having wished to seduce a servant, Ferron was deposed from the ministry on the 5th September 1548.—*Registers of the Council.*

servants of Christ. Cæsar the comedian annoys us in whatever way he can. Hitherto it has so turned out that he has gained nothing by it but the utmost disgrace. And yet, among his own party he gives himself all the airs of a victor.[1] Haller has at length explained what he would desiderate in our confession. This consists of a great many unimportant and trivial points. I shall reply to him as soon as I find opportunity. I did not send you the letter before it was read to the brethren. It is on this account that Hotman[2] has undertaken this journey to you; he will carry it more safely than otherwise. I do not think it proper, nor have I been disposed, to inquire more minutely into that situation to which he aspires, except that he has resolved to dedicate his work to the Lord and to the Church. I especially approve of this resolution. For he has strong native talent, is of extensive erudition, and is possessed of other valuable qualities. However, I know that you think so highly of him that there is no need of me recommending him. And, as you are of opinion that his work would be useful, I have no doubt that you would be sufficiently disposed of yourself to aid him. I was unwilling, however, to act so, that he might think me wanting in my duty to him. I shall only add, that he should understand there is nothing nearer our hearts than that he should devote his labour to the Church.

Adieu, brother and most sincere friend. May the Lord Jesus preserve yourself, your wife, and your little daughter, and send a blessing upon your sacred labours. Salute all respectfully in my name.—Yours,

JOHN CALVIN.

[*Lat. orig. autogr.—Library of Geneva.* Vol. 107.]

[1] In a letter from Calvin to Farel, written on the same day as that to Viret, we meet with a passage regarding Amy Perrin:—"Cæsar, our comedian, in his last mission, exasperated them [the Bernese] exceedingly, and I fear he has commenced a serious tragedy among us."—*MSS. of Geneva*, vol. 106. Charged with a mission to Berne, he had returned to Geneva more insolent and more intractable than ever.

[2] The learned lawyer, Francis Hotman, recently engaged in the evangelical cause, had quitted France, his native country, at the advice of Calvin, to retire to Geneva. He became, during the same year, Professor of Law at the Academy of Lausanne.—See *La France Protestante*, Art. Hotman.

## CCXLII.—To HENRY BULLINGER.[1]

Pleading in favour of the alliance of the Reformed Cantons with France.

*7th May* 1549.

As time does not permit me to reply to your letter now, I am merely desirous of telling you that I have scarcely ever received anything more pleasant from you, as it served to alleviate a very trying domestic grief, which, occasioned by the death of my wife a little before, was causing me very much sorrow. For I am very glad that hardly anything—or at least very little—hinders us from agreeing now even in words. And, certainly, if you think you can so arrange matters, I make no objection against endeavours being made to come hither, that you may the better become acquainted with all the sentiments of my mind. Nor shall it ever be owing to me that we do not unite in a solid peace, as we all unanimously profess the same Christ. But I have, at present, another reason for writing you.

You partly indicate what has kept you back from joining in the French alliance. I confess the godly have just cause of alarm in the example of Jehoshaphat, who bound himself in an unfortunate alliance with a wicked king, to his own ruin and

[1] The new King of France, Henry II., sought an alliance with the Swiss with extreme eagerness. His envoys, Boisrigault, Liancourt, Lavan, and Menage overran the Cantons, scattering everywhere proofs of his liberality, to obtain a renewal of the ancient treaties. Everywhere, says the Swiss historian, their proposals were welcomed, except at Berne and at Zurich. In the latter town, Bullinger rose with great energy against this negotiating with a man who was converting a loyal and Christian people into a nation of hired murderers. He called to their recollection the persecutions of which France had been the theatre, and adjured his fellow-citizens to avoid all terms with a persecuting monarch, who was covered with the blood of their brethren. Better aware than Bullinger of the dangers which the supremacy of the Emperor was spreading over the various states of Europe, and over the Reformed Churches of Germany and Switzerland, and hoping, perhaps, to obtain by a treaty some relief to the faithful of France, Calvin was in favour of the French alliance, and in this remarkable letter attempted to vindicate its legitimacy by examples borrowed from the Old Testament.—*Histoire de la Suisse*, tom. xi. p. 306, *et suiv.*

that of his kingdom. Yet I do not so understand it, that he was punished because he made a league with the King of Israel, but rather because he espoused a bad and impious cause, in order to gratify that king's desire. Ambition was inciting him to an unprovoked attack upon the Syrians; Jehoshaphat complied with his wishes and rashly took up arms. Add to this, that they went forth to battle, the Lord through Micaiah forbidding them. This example does not, therefore, so weigh with me that I should pronounce all alliance whatever with the wicked to be unlawful. For I reflect that Abraham was not hindered by any religious scruples from making a covenant with Abimelech. Isaac, David, and others did the same, and received neither reproof nor punishment. I can, however, so far conclude, that alliances of this nature are not to be sought after, seeing they must always be attended with very much danger. But if we be at all incited—I should rather say urged—to it by a just motive, I see no reason why we should be altogether averse to it.

Moreover, as regards the alliance in question, I cannot hold that it should be so avoided, from this cause, unless the present aspect of the times should compel me to adopt an opposite conclusion. You have to do with a professed enemy of Christ, and one who is daily venting his rage against our brethren. He is too little deserving of trust that could wish that both we and Christ were annihilated. It is absurd that we should enter into friendly alliance with one who is at war with all the servants of Christ without distinction; that we should seize, as that of an ally, a hand polluted with innocent blood. And, certainly, I should be unwilling to come to any conclusion on the matter, unless it were the express and distinct wish of the pious brethren. For his ferocity is indeed extraordinary. Besides, I am suspicious of the war with England. For I do not think it right to furnish any aid against a kingdom in which Christ is worshipped; and the very injustice of the cause, also, is another obstacle.

But, again, when I consider how our cause has been weakened, how great are the calamities which still impend, threatening almost the ruin of the Church, I fear much that if we neglect those aids which it is not unlawful to employ, we may fall into a state rather of excessive carelessness than of devout trustfulness. Nor, in truth, am I ignorant that God is especially present with us, and powerfully succours us when we are destitute of all human aid. I know, also, that there is nothing harder, when he reveals himself through some Egyptian shade, than to keep the eye from turning aside; for if they be not fixed on the one God, they rove wickedly and perniciously. We must, therefore, endeavour zealously to counteract these dangers. Meanwhile, however, we should be on our guard, lest if, in this our critical condition, we reject what, without offending God, could have aided us, we may afterwards feel, to our loss, that we were too careless. My first fear is, that our Pharaoh, shut out from all hope of contracting friendship with you, may betake himself to Antiochus. How much soever they may have weighty grounds of disagreement, this latter is a wonderful master at contriving pretexts; and those who at present hold sway at our court, would desire nothing more than to incline the mind of a youth, both inexperienced and not sufficiently sagacious, to accept of peace on any terms whatever. Certainly, if he has not already concluded it he will do so in a short time. Nor will there be wanting those who will urge him on. And I would there were none among us who would hold themselves and us as slaves to Antiochus, should an opportunity occur for doing so. He will, in truth, attempt every thing, the other not only approving of it, but also, in the meantime, assisting in it; because he will suppose that in this way he is avenging his repulse. In the meanwhile, cruelty will be kindled everywhere through the kingdom itself, for he will, as women are wont, direct his own rage to another,—a consideration, certainly, not to be accounted last by us of this place. If I wished to regard my own life or private concerns, I should immediately betake myself elsewhere. But when I consider how very important this corner is for the propagation of the kingdom of Christ, I have good reason to be anxious that it should be carefully watched over; and, in this respect, it is for your advantage, and quiet partly depends upon it. What man, imbued with wicked schemes, when he has been estranged from you, will not be moved by despair ? But you think that we are wanting in men of a discontented and revolutionary character, or in those suffering from want, who have, for a long period, extended their hands to him. However, as often as I reflect particularly upon our wretched brethren who lie crushed under that fearful tyranny, my mind becomes soft and more disposed to this [alliance], as it the more unquestionably appears beneficial for the alleviation of their sufferings. Why is the rage of the tyrant to be removed when he has seen that he is despised and scorned ? Is it that thereby the wicked are to have the greater license for tormenting the innocent ? Thus, if any alliance does intervene, not only will Pharaoh himself be, for the present, somewhat softened, and the executioners rendered less daring, but it will, indeed, be possible also to extinguish the flames.

I beseech and solemnly implore you then, my dear Bullinger, to ponder in time all these considerations; and if you come to any agreement, strive earnestly to have your brethren remembered whose condition is so wretched and awful. For although I know you have their welfare sufficiently at heart, and am certain that when the matter is raised, you will, of your own accord, be solicitous about it, yet I did not wish to neglect my duty. Indeed, such is his fierceness, that no fixed law can be laid down for you. I hope it is possible to show, however, that some sort of moderation may be exhibited.

Adieu, excellent man, and much esteemed brother in the Lord. Salute especially Theodore, Pellican, Gualter, Vuerduler, and the rest of the fellow-ministers. Present my respects to your colleagues, and to Des Gallars among the rest. I pray the Lord Jesus that He may continue to guide and sustain you by His Spirit ; may He bless you and your labours. I have to thank you greatly for the volume of discourses which Haller sent in your name.—Yours,

JOHN CALVIN.

[*Lat. orig. autogr.*—*Archives of Zurich.* Gallic. Scripta, p. 11.]

## CCXLIII.—To Madame de la Roche-Posay.[1]

He exhorts her and her companions to live in conformity with the law of God.

*This* 10*th of June* 1549.

MADAME AND WELL-BELOVED SISTER,—As we ought to be glad when the kingdom of the Son of God our Saviour is multiplied, and the good seed of His doctrine is everywhere spread abroad, I have been greatly rejoiced in perceiving from your letter that His grace and bounty has reached to you, to draw you on in the knowledge of His truth, wherein lies our salvation and every blessing. Indeed, it is a kind of miracle when He is pleased to make His glorious light shine in the place of such deep darkness; and this I say, that you and your associates may be the more induced to value the inestimable benefit which he has conferred on you. For if the lies of Satan wherewith he has blinded and bewitched the wretched world reign everywhere at present, they have their chief seat in those unhappy prisons which he has reared up, that he may keep souls in a twofold captivity. Acknowledge then that our good Lord has reached out a hand to you, even to the depths of the abyss, and that in so doing He has expressed an infinite compassion toward you. Wherefore it is your duty, as St. Peter has told us, to employ yourself in magnifying His holy name. For in calling us to Himself, He sets us apart in order that our whole life may be to His honour, which it cannot be without our withdrawing ourselves from the pollutions of this world. And indeed there ought to be a difference between those who are enlightened by Christ Jesus, and the poor blinded ones who know not whither they are going. Therefore take heed that the knowledge which He has bestowed upon you be not unimproved, that you may not be reproached at the great day for

[1] *On the back:* It is thought that this letter has been written to Madame de la Roche-Posay, Abbess of Thouars. A Seigneur of that name played an important part in the religious wars of Poitou, but he figured in the ranks of the Roman Catholic army.—Bèze, *Hist. Eccl.* tom. ii. p. 588. There is a letter from the Reformed Church of de la Roche-Posay of the 27th May 1561, addressed to Calvin. (Library of Geneva, Vol. 107.)

having made void His grace. But because I am confident that you do so as much as lieth in you, I shall not dwell at greater length on that subject. It is quite certain that we cannot be too earnestly importuned on this very point. Besides, I believe that you will receive this exhortation as you ought, not thinking it superfluous, inasmuch as it may be of service to you against many assaults which Satan never ceases to make upon all the children of God. Now, while he has many ways in this world for seducing us out of the straight path, we on our parts are so pitiably frail, that we are immediately overcome. Wherefore we have much need to arm ourselves completely at every point. Moreover, being sensible of our infirmity, which makes us so often come short, we should supplement the exhortations which are made to us in the name of God, with prayer and supplication, that it would please our heavenly Father to strengthen us by His might, and to supply whatsoever is lacking. However it may be, let us never seek out excuses to flatter ourselves in our vices as the most part do, but let us be thoroughly convinced that God's honour deserves to be preferred to everything else, yea verily to life itself. And let us not think it strange, if for His name's sake we be chased from one place to another, and that we must forsake the place of our birth, to transport ourselves to some unknown place, for we must even be ready to depart from this world whensoever He shall call us away. I understand quite well, that in such bondage as you now are, you cannot serve God purely without the rage and cruelty of the wicked rising up immediately against you, and without the fire perhaps being lighted. Such being the case, were it even necessary that you should compass sea and land, never grow weary in seeking the liberty to regulate yourself entirely according to the will of your kind heavenly Father. Howbeit, you must remember, that wherever we may go, the cross of Jesus Christ will follow us, even in the place where you may enjoy your ease and comforts. Lay your account with it, that even in the country where you have liberty, as well to honour God as to be confirmed by His Word, that you will have to endure many annoyances. For this is the very way whereby God would make trial of our faith, and know whether, in seeking after Him, we have been renouncing self. It is right that you be informed of this beforehand, so that it may not be new to you when the experience of it comes, though I doubt not that you and your associates are already prepared for it. But the chief thing is to pray God that he would lead you, as well to guide you as to uphold by His strong arm, in order that as He has begun a work in you, He would continue it until He has brought you on to that perfection, after which we must aspire until we are gone forth out of this world. And to confirm you in this respect, recall to mind continually what an unhappiness it is to be in perpetual disquietude and trouble of conscience. In this condition of mind, you will naturally abhor the wretched state in which you are, and count but dung all those delights and all those comforts which you must purchase at so sad a price as that of daily offending God. When you consider that our life is accursed, and, of course, worse than any kind of death, if our state be not approved of God, no bands of any earthly comforts will be so strong that you will not easily rend them asunder, so as entirely to escape from a kind of life which God condemns, especially to live in a place where not only you may be free to follow a holy and Christian calling, but where you will likewise have the means of exercising yourself daily in sound doctrine, of which we are so clearly enjoined to avail ourselves. Such a recompense of reward may well stifle all regret of the flesh-pots and pleasures of Egypt, and encourage us rather to follow God in the wilderness than to befool ourselves in the practice of those lusts which our flesh desires and longs for.

Meanwhile, Madame and good sister, having affectionately commended me to your kind favour, and that of your companions, I pray our good Lord more and more to increase His spiritual blessings upon you, to keep you wholly in His obedience, and to have you under His protection and defence against all the ambushes of Satan and those who belong to him.

Your humble servant and brother,
CHARLES D'ESPEVILLE.

[*Fr. Copy.—Library of Geneva.* Vol. 107.]

## CCXLIV.—To Bucer.[1]

*Encouragements and consolations—desire for the conclusion of peace between France and England—excesses of the ultra-Lutheran party in Switzerland and Germany—agreement between the Churches of Geneva and Zurich.*

*June* 1549.

Although your letter was mixed with joy and sorrow, yet it was extremely pleasant to me. Would that I were able in some measure to lighten the sufferings of your heart, and those cares by which I see you are tortured. We all beseech you, again and again, not to keep afflicting yourself to no purpose. Yet it is neither proper in itself, nor is it in keeping with your piety, nor should we desire to see it, that amid such various and manifold causes for grief, you should be joyous and cheerful. You should make it your study, however, to serve the Lord and the Church as far as you have opportunity. You have indeed run a long race, but you know not how much may be still before you. It may be that I, who have just commenced the race, am at present nearer to the goal. But the direction and the termination of your course are alike in the hand of the Lord. I am a daily witness to many deaths, in order that I may be made as active as possible amid the dangers which threaten us from many quarters. Just as wars keep you busy where you are, so we here give way to sluggish fears. I trust, however, that the internal tumults are already calmed; and there is a report of a cessation of hostilities between you and the

---

[1] This letter is without a date, but is evidently related to the early period of Bucer's residence in England. Proceeding from Strasbourg on the 5th April 1549 with Paul Fagins, he reached London on the 25th, and met with a very cordial reception at Lambeth, in the house of Cranmer, Archbishop of Canterbury. At the desire of his protector, and amid the sorrows inseparable from his exile, he immediately undertook a new translation of the Bible, which he was not permitted to finish, owing to repeated illness, brought on by the change of climate. He was engaged, at the same time, on a revision of the English Liturgy, from which he removed everything that appeared to be tainted with Popery, without going as far in these corrections as he was desired by Calvin, who was pressing him by letter to remove the accusations of his life, by showing himself more resolute and firm than hitherto.—See *La France Protestante* of M. M. Haag. Art. Bucer.

French.[1] Would that a plan of stable peace could be agreed upon: for we see that trainer of gladiators, who is bringing these two kingdoms into conflict, in the meantime laughing at his ease, and ready to seize any turn of fortune, in order that he may attack the victor with fresh forces, and gather the spoils of the vanquished without sweat and blood, and thus triumph over and carry off the booty from both.[2] But when I reflect on the wicked counsels by which France is ruled, I almost despair of this matter. Indeed, they fear him more than enough; but, by haughtily despising others, they do not guard themselves against his craft. And indeed the Lord is by this blindness justly avenging, as I take it, their atrocious cruelty to his saints, which is daily increasing. Just as their wickedness is gathering strength, and is continually becoming worse, so I pray that the English may, with a contrary emulation, make a stand for the genuine purity of Christianity, until everything in that country is seen to be regulated according to the rule which Christ himself has laid down. As you wished, and as the present state of things urgently demanded, I have attempted to encourage the Lord Protector; and it will be your duty to insist by all means, if you get a hearing—and of that I am persuaded—that those rites which savour of superstition be entirely removed. I particularly commend this to you, that you thereby may free yourself of a charge which many, as you know, falsely bring against you; for they always regard you as either the author or approver of half measures. I know that this suspicion is fixed too deeply in the minds of some to be easily rooted out, even if you do your best. And some have been led to calumniate you spitefully for no error whatever. This is accordingly damaging to you, in some measure fatal, as you can with difficulty escape from it. However, you must be on your guard, lest occasion of suspicion be

---

[1] War prevailed at that time between France and England, with Artois and Scotland for its theatre. Peace was concluded only the year following (May 1550). —De Thou, tom. vi.

[2] In allusion to the Emperor, who saw his power increase by the weakness of the English and French monarchs, who were equally interested in opposing his supremacy on the Continent.

afforded the ignorant: the wicked eagerly snatch at any pretext for abuse. I am exceedingly sorry that N.[1] is annoying you without cause. Would that he would learn humanity sometime! I am the more ready to pardon him, as he seems to me to be so moved by malice, as to be driven by a blind impulse. You cannot credit how bitterly he has wounded us at times; alike the innocent, the absent, and the friendly. When Viret was wellnigh overcome by the very great injustice of some, and by the perfidiousness of others, he was as violently attacked by this individual, as if he had been the most infamous traitor to the Church. He would certainly accustom himself to mildness if he knew what hurt is done by the intemperateness of his too fervid zeal and immoderate severity. You must endure with your accustomed forbearance this and other indignities offered to you. The people of Zurich, certainly, did not approve of his cause. I differ from you somewhat in this matter; in that, you think injury will be done to the opposite party. For while you think that they would never labour under such gross hallucinations as to imagine that Christ was diffused everywhere, you do not hold what Brentius, among others, has written, that when Christ was lying in the manger he was, even as to his body, full of glory in heaven. And to speak more plainly, you know that the Popish doctrine is more moderate and sober than that of Amsdorf,[2] and those resembling him, who have raved as if they were the priestesses of Apollo. You know how cruelly Master Philip has been annoyed, because he observed a certain degree of moderation. In their madness they even drew idolatry after them. For what else is the adorable sacrament of Luther but an idol set up in the temple of God? I desired, however, to see all these things buried. Indeed I have done my utmost among our neighbours to keep them from railing; yet as it afforded them satisfaction, I did not hesitate, the names being suppressed, to condemn

---

[1] Doubtless one of the ministers of the Church of Berne.

[2] Nicolas Amsdorf, a learned German minister, exaggerated the Lutheran doctrine regarding Works and the Supper, and wrote a book, in which he endeavoured to prove that good works are hurtful to salvation,—*Bona opera sunt ad salutem noxia et perniciosa.*—Melchior Adam, pp. 69, 70.

all the errors to which I was expressly opposed. You certainly seem to me to enter with too much subtlety into the discussion about place. Others are more seriously offended by your obscurity, which they think you have studied craftily to employ. I know indeed that in this they are wrong. But I do not see why you should shrink so much from what we teach; that when Christ is said to have ascended into heaven, there is affirmed by this expression a diversity of places. For it is not disputed here whether there is place in celestial glory, but only whether the body of Christ is in the world. As the Scriptures have borne clear testimony on that point, I have no hesitation in embracing it as an article of faith. And yet, as you will find from our document,[1] this was yielded to the fretfulness of some, not without a struggle : for I had framed the words differently. Nothing was comprised in this formula which we employed, except what I perceived it would be scrupulousness not to concede to others. You wish piously and wisely, to explain more clearly and fully the effect of the Sacrament, and what the Lord bestows through it. Nor indeed was it owing to me that they were not fuller on some points. Let us bear therefore with a sigh what we cannot correct. You will find here a copy of the document which they sent me. The two paragraphs which you feared they would not admit, were readily adopted. Had the rest imitated the calmness of Bullinger, I should have obtained all more easily. It is well, however, that we have agreed about the truth, and that we are at one in the most important sense. It would be exceedingly appropriate for you to modify these two theses somewhat, in order to bring out more clearly that you place Christ apart from us who are in the world, by a diversity of place; in the second place, that you might discard the more obviously all those false inventions by which the minds of men have been led to superstition; and above all, that you might vindicate the glory of the Holy Spirit and of Christ, lest aught should be attributed to the ministers or to the elements. At the commencement of our deliberations, agreement seemed really hopeless. Light suddenly broke

[1] The common formulary, doubtless, on the Supper, compiled by Calvin, which the theologians of Zurich and Geneva were led to adopt.

forth. Our forefathers wished to deliberate with other Churches. We agreed without difficulty. N.'s dissension must be borne with equanimity. Farel, as you will see, writes you at great length. Viret dare not, for you cannot believe how unjustly he is treated. He salutes you as dutifully as he can, and wishes you to excuse him. All my colleagues, also, salute you respectfully. There is nothing new here except that Zurich and Berne have cut off all hopes of an alliance with France.[1] Adieu, very illustrious Sir, and father in the Lord, truly worthy of my regard.

JOHN CALVIN.

[*Calvin's Lat. Corresp.* Opera, tom. ix. p. 49.]


## CCXLV.—TO LADY ANNE SEYMOUR.[2]

Thanks to the Duchess of Somerset, the mother of Anne Seymour—exhortation to perseverance in the true faith.

*17th June* 1549.

As your mother, illustrious lady, lately presented me with a ring, as a token of her good-will towards me, which I did not at all deserve, it would be exceedingly unbecoming in me not

---

[1] While Schaffhausen, Basle, and Bienne acceded to the French alliance, Zurich and Berne haughtily refused to be the allies of a monarch who was the persecutor of the churches of France. Moved by the eloquence of Bullinger, the Seigneury of Zurich declared that it would lean upon God alone, and dispense with the alliance of the king.—*Hist. de la Suisse*, tom. xi. p. 308.

[2] "To the Most Noble, Most Gifted, and Most Honourable Lady Ann, Eldest Daughter of the very Illustrious Protector of England."

Anne Seymour, the eldest daughter of the Duke of Somerset, Protector of England, was distinguished alike for her illustrious descent, genius, and piety. She married in 1550 the Earl of Warwick, son of the Duke of Northumberland, and thus apparently sealed the reconciliation of her father with the ambitious head of that illustrious house. We read in a letter, from Martin Micronius to Bullinger, of 4th June 1550 :—" On the third of this month was celebrated a marriage between the daughter of the Duke of Somerset and the son of the Earl of Warwick, at which the King himself was present. This event, I hope, will wonderfully unite and conciliate the friendship of those noblemen."—*Zurich Letters*, 1st series, tom. ii. p. 569.

to show some sign of gratitude, by giving expression, at least, to my regard for her. But not being able to find language, again, in which to discharge this sort of duty, nothing seems fitter than that I should call you to my aid, noble lady, distinguished no less by your worth than by your descent. For as you will be, of all others, the most suitable negotiator with your mother, you will be glad to present this mark of respect to her, in virtue of your very great affection for her ; and, particularly, as the address will not, or I am mistaken, be unpleasant to her. For I learn you have understood from her words that she is agreeably disposed towards me. Now, if my prayers be of any avail with you, I would particularly request of you, not to take amiss the humble salutation offered, with all submission, by me to her, that she may, at least, understand, that that gift of which I was held worthy was not bestowed upon one who knew not to be grateful. Moreover, I made bold to use the more confidence with you, as I learned that you were not only cultivated in liberal knowledge, (a singular thing in a young person of rank of this place,) but that you were also so well informed in the doctrines of Christ, that you grant a willing access to His ministers, among whose number, if I mistake not, you acknowledge me a place. It remains for me to exhort you to pursue your so happy course, even although, as I hear, you are willing enough of yourself ; and I trust that the Lord who gave you this disposition, will also grant you steadfastness to persevere to the end. However, you will take my exhortation in good part, as incitements are never superfluous, since there are so many obstacles and hindrances in the world, and so many infirmities in our flesh. Certainly, among so many excellent gifts with which God has endowed and adorned you, this stands unquestionably first,—that He stretched out His hand to you in tender childhood, to lead you to His own Son, who is the author of eternal salvation, and the fountain of all good. It becomes you to strive, with all the more zeal, to follow eagerly at His call. Especially as He has, at the same time, given you that support of which we see not only the daughters of noblemen, but even noblemen themselves, to be often deprived. Salute your brother—a boy of heroic nature—and your very noble sisters. May the Lord enrich you daily with His blessing, and may He be the constant guide of the whole course of your life.

Adieu, most excellent lady, deserving of my esteem. Truly yours to obey you,

JOHN CALVIN.

[*Lat. orig. autogr.—Library of Geneva.* Vol. 107, *a.*]


CCXLVI.—To FAREL.

Reply by the Protector of England to a letter from Calvin.

*9th July* 1549.

The English messenger[1] has at last returned. He has brought a letter from the Regent, in which he expresses himself thankful for my service. His wife sent me a present of a ring, not of great value, not being worth more than four crown pieces. The members of his family lead me to expect a tolerably liberal present from him, in a short time, which I neither desire nor long for. For what has, as I hear, given a keener stimulus to him, is a sufficiently ample reward for me. Adieu, dearly beloved brother in the Lord. May the Lord Jesus keep you and continue to bless you in your sacred labours. I infer that the quarrel with the prefect is settled, from your not writing me regarding it. Salute respectfully your family and our fellow-ministers. My associates send you their regards: Normandie also, and the rest of your friends.—Yours,

JOHN CALVIN.

[*Lat. orig. autogr.—Library of Geneva.* Vol. 106.]

---

[1] The messenger charged with the letter to the Regent of 22d October 1549.

## CCXLVII.—To Farel.

*Imprisonment of two brothers of M. de Falais—persecution in the Low Countries and in France.*

GENEVA, 19*th July* 1549.

You know of the letter we have received from Bullinger. I was hoping the Bernese were going to give over negotiations. At all events, the inhabitants of Zurich see now with what just reason we in time past complained of our broken heads. Haller lately confessed to me that he would gladly have written, had Schirma not been afraid. I certainly excuse what does not provoke such rage. The people of Zurich might have obtained their wishes from the Senate, had they not stripped themselves of all liberty. For they have so often repeated this old song— that they should abide by things as they were, that nothing further should be done, that something deceptive always lurked under the guise of harmony—that they are now ashamed to say a word on the opposite side. Nothing remains for them now but to suppress everything, or follow that new plan of yours. I was astonished that Viret did not indicate by a single word what was your opinion of them both. Be sure to let me know at your very first opportunity what arrangement you think should be made. I have nothing further to add except that two of M. de Falais' brothers are in prison.[1] After the Emperor had given them a polite reception, he sent them to Granvelle. He received them courteously also. On leaving him, they were bound by the officer, and thrust hastily into prison. They were then removed to the Castle of Villenord, whence no one is brought forth except for punishment. Awful persecution blazes now over that region; let us then assist the godly brethren with our prayers.[2] The Frenchman is as mad as ever. He wished to be present at the burning of two

---

[1] The names and fate of these two brothers of M. de Falais are not known.

[2] See the account of the persecutions in Hainault in *L'Histoire des Martyrs*, p. 184. A woman named Mary was buried alive. A learned Frenchman named M. Nicolas, endured courageously the torment of the stake, crying out in the midst of the flames: "O Charles, Charles, how long will thy courage endure?"

[martyrs] lately.[1] May the Lord by His own power put a check upon his atrocious ferocity. Amen.

We all salute you. Salute also, in turn, all our friends, and especially our fellow-ministers. I infer that you have been deceived about Christopher, because you had supposed he was going to come hither. Respectful regards to him.—Yours,

JOHN CALVIN.

De Falais received that sad intelligence with quite heroic courage.

[*Lat. orig. autogr.*—*Library of Geneva.* Vol. 106.]

## CCXLVIII.—To VIRET.

Negotiations in reference to the publication of the *Consensus*—George Count of Montbeliard.

GENEVA, 20*th July* 1549.

You ought also to add your judgment to the letter of Bullinger. The reason which he prefixes for publishing the agreement, has something or other absurd in it. I fear again that the same over-scrupulousness will appear in this affair. I shall neglect nothing, however, which you and Farel think it useful to attempt.

I have written to Paris concerning the Hebrew professor. If one be procured, he can hardly be present on the day of your assembly, as I had not fixed upon so short a time, seeing that it would have been in vain for me to have done so, as two letters had scarcely reached that place.

[1] One of the martyrs here referred to was a poor tailor, who, led before the King and Diana of Poictiers, made a courageous confession of his faith, addressed stern words to *la favorite*, and was condemned to perish in the flames. The king wished to be a spectator of his sufferings, "and, to command a better view, went to the house of Sieur de la Rochepot, opposite the stake. The martyr remained firm, and having perceived the king, he fastened on him a look so fixed and penetrating, that the affrighted monarch was forced to retire; and he afterwards repeatedly confessed, that the look of that man incessantly pursued him, and that he never again wished to be present at a fine spectacle."—*Histoire des Martyrs*, p. 189, Bèze, tom. i. p. 79.

Count George de Wurtemberg, brother of Duke Ulrich, is here.[1] We dined with him yesterday. We had much pious conversation together. He had said so much to my honour before, that Wendelius was almost making an ado about it. Plessiacus will give you an account of the state of France. It is better to talk over our affairs than to write about them.

Adieu, most honest brother, together with your wife and little daughter. May the Lord Jesus ever watch over you all. Salute the brethren in my name. Excuse me to Renier for not having written him.—Yours,

JOHN CALVIN.

[*Lat. orig. autogr.—Library of Geneva.* Vol. 106.]

CCXLIX.—TO THE PASTORS OF THE CHURCH OF ZURICH.[2]

Urgent recommendation of the adoption of a fixed formulary in the celebration of the Lord's Supper.

GENEVA, 1st *August* 1549.

Although I have repeated occasion to act with you concerning the same matter, yet I do not think I should be afraid of seeming troublesome. Since the same subject is a matter of common interest to us, it cannot be that you will disapprove of what I am engaged in; and as the perpetual importunity of

---

[1] George de Wurtemberg, Count of Montbeliard, dispossessed of his estates by Charles V. He had obtained from the Seigneury of Berne permission to reside at Arau.

[2] See letter p. 194.

After the long conferences, in which Farel and Fabri took part in the name of the Church of Neuchatel, and after a correspondence of many months, the theologians of Zurich and Geneva came to an agreement on the doctrine of the sacrament of the Supper, and drew up a common formula, which may be seen in Hospinien.—*Hist. Sacr.*, tom. ii. pp. 369, 370. It is very likely, says Ruchat, that this definite formula was the work of Calvin. We recognise his genius in it at least, and we find in it the same ideas and expressions met with in his Liturgy on the Holy Supper.—*Hist. de la Réf.*, tom. v. p. 378. The adoption of this formula was the first step towards the union of the Swiss churches, sanctioned two years after the death of Calvin (1566), by the adoption of the famous Helvetic *Confession.*

good men urges me to it a little more zealously than is proper. I have oftentimes already given advice regarding a small matter, although many were offended, not without a show of reason, at my seeming to teach something or other different from you regarding the sacraments. Your Church, adorned with so many distinguished gifts, is deservedly held in honour by those men. They show some [respect] to our Church also, and, perhaps, to myself as an individual. So they are anxious to obtain assistance from our writings in coming to a knowledge of the doctrines of sacred duty, lest any sort of discussion should retard their progress. I have thought, accordingly, that no remedy was better fitted for removing this offence than if, to show our unanimity, we were to enter kindly into a consideration of it by means of friendly conference. For this purpose I have, as you are aware, undertaken a journey to you. And our venerable associate, William Farel—that indefatigable soldier of Christ, and my guide and counsellor—has not been reluctant to join me as a companion, in order to unite with us in bearing truly and faithfully what testimony we can on the one side and on the other. But because, in the present state of the question, I do not carry all along with me, I am greatly pained that those, whose peace of mind I should wish to regard, continue in a troubled, or, at all events, in an uncertain state. And, just as I said at the outset, I think I do nothing unseasonable, when I insist on there being some public testimony made regarding those points on which we are agreed. I have indeed thought it a reward for my trouble to draw up briefly and arrange those paragraphs on which we have conferred, in order that, if my plan be approved of by you, any one may see at a glance, as it were, what we have been engaged in, and what we have completed. I certainly do trust that you will be my witnesses, that I have reported faithfully all that I have brought forward. Pious readers will doubtless observe, that we—I mean Farel and myself—have with equal care sought perspicuity, unmixed with any deceit, and void of all guile. Nevertheless, I should wish them, at the same time, to be reminded, that there is nothing contained here which our fellow-labourers also, be they who they may, whether serving Christ under the rule of the Genevese Republic, or in the Neuchatel district, have not by their signature approved.

Adieu, most excellent men and brethren, deserving of my hearty regard. May the Lord continue to guide you by His Spirit in the edification of His Church, and may He bless our labours.

[*Lat. Copy, Archives of Zurich*, Gest. vi. 105, p. 411.]

## CCL.—To Bullinger.[1]

Revisal of the Formulary—persecutions in France.

Geneva, 13*th August* 1549.

I was reminded, when it was too late, of the departure of the registrar. For it was not convenient for me to write then—on account of the Supper namely—especially as I was not able to do it so satisfactorily as could be wished. Indeed this is almost a customary thing with me. But a letter came into my possession to-day which you had written just before mine was composed. I had delayed writing you a private letter, indeed, until a trustworthy messenger might be at hand to convey it to you. And although I had not actually come under any obligation, I was unwilling to forego the opportunity which presented itself. You will ascertain whether the edition with this new preface will satisfy the Bernese. Of yourself and your associates I have no doubt. For, in my opinion, I have followed your outlines and only spread my colours over them. But you remember what I lately wrote regarding your two paragraphs. I am persuaded there will be no one among you who would not, of his own accord, desire my additions. And

---

[1] See the preceding letter. The negotiations entered into with the Church of Zurich, and already near a close, were prosecuted equally at Berne; but they were encountered there by insurmountable difficulties, arising from the hesitation of the ministers and the policy of the seigneury. Calvin did not shrink from any concessions which, without causing injury to the integrity of the doctrine, might rally their spirits to union and peace.—Hospinien, tom. ii. p. 370.

they are of especial importance, lest some might think we were rather artfully silent, and others justly desire what must necessarily be expressly stated. The third correction will present no difficulty save in one or two words. I know the whole matter must so commend itself to you and to the rest of the brethren, that I shall entirely acquiesce in your decision. What you decide upon, therefore, I shall regard as altogether satisfactory. I think, again, that you will understand what I am aiming at.

I dare hardly venture to give you anything new from this place, there are so many idle rumours daily afloat. This, at least, is certain, that numerous dangers are not very far distant, unless the Lord counteract them. All that I wish is, that Christians may live securely, as they can die securely. The Frenchman is so insane, that, as one may say, he wishes, after the fashion of the giants, to fight against God.[1] In the meanwhile, the firmness of the martyrs is wonderful.[2] It was a new thing for the king, when one of them of his own accord devoted himself as a sacrifice, that he might openly address to him at least three words for Christ, when he was preparing to witness the burning. I do not write to Celio, and perhaps he has not yet gone to you. If he is there, I should wish him, as previously ordered, to speak to the bookseller regarding the money for which I became security. He complains that the decision will be unfair. Our friend, however, says the opposite.

[1] In the month of July 1549 the fury of the persecutions was redoubled at Paris and in the provinces, and places of execution were so multiplied everywhere, as if the King had wished, by additional severity, to remove from memory the Edict which he had restored on account of the Vaudois of Provence.—Bèze, *Hist. Eccl.*, tom. i. p. 70, *et suiv*. Notwithstanding all this violence, says Bèze, the churches increased and gathered strength in many places.

[2] Among the number of professors burnt on occasion of the public entrance of the King into Paris, there is found Florent Venot, of Sedane in Brie,—allowed to stand for six weeks in a pit at Chatelet, called *the Hippocras' Cup*, where it was impossible either to remain lying or standing—and whose firmness overcame the cruelty of the executioners. "You think," he said to them, "by long torment, to weaken the force of the spirit, but you waste your time, and God will enable me to bless His holy name even till my death." Compelled, by a refinement of cruelty, to be a spectator of the torment of his brethren burnt at Paris, he exhorted them by look and gesture before he ascended the pile prepared for him in the *Place Maubert*.—*Hist. des Martyrs*, p. 186.

I remain neutral. But since I have pledged my word, I am called upon to pay it.

Adieu, brother in the Lord, and most honourable and accomplished man, together with all your fellow-ministers, whom you will salute respectfully in our name. May the Lord be ever near you and keep you, and may you be instrumental in advancing the glory of His name! Amen.—Yours,

JOHN CALVIN.

[*Lat. orig. autogr.—Archives of Zurich.* Gest. vi. 105, p. 417.]

### CCLI.—To FAREL AND VIRET.

Letter concerning Vergerio—history of Francis Spira.

15*th August* 1549.

You have here the letter which I sent to Bullinger.[1] I resolved, indeed, not to send it until I should learn that it would be agreeable to you. But the messenger, who has just left me, having unexpectedly presented himself, led me to change this resolution. It might perhaps have been written better by another, yet I hope it will appear tolerably satisfactory to you. Having the utmost confidence in your carefulness, my dear Viret, I have not retained a copy of it. You will see then, that a copy of it be put into the hands of Farel, that I may get back this my autograph. I know that what I have written is nothing but some few trifles or other which I have collected, and which are alike unworthy of me to write and of you to read, especially as they are circulated by public report. A few days ago I received a letter from Paolo Vergerio, with a history of Francis Spira, which he desired to be published here.[2] He

---

[1] The preceding letter.

[2] Francis Spira, a jurisconsult of Padua, having abjured the Protestant faith through fear of the tortures of the Inquisition, died a short while afterwards in a state of fearful mental anxiety. Paolo Vergerio, an aged Bishop of Pola in Istria, who was led to give up his bishopric that he might live in the free profession of the doctrines of the gospel, among the Grisons, visited Spira on his deathbed, and endeavoured in vain to console this unhappy penitent. The history of Spira, written by Vergerio, and translated from the Italian into Latin by Celio Secondo

states that he was compelled to go into exile, chiefly because the Pope, enraged by this publication, was laying insidious stratagems for his life. He is living at present among the Raetians. He says, however, that he is strongly inclined to visit us.[1] The history I have not yet examined thoroughly. So far, however, as I may judge of such a communication, it seems to be written with a little more prudence and sobriety than were those epistles [of his] which Celio translated. When I shall have examined it more carefully, I must consider what preface I should write to it. Adieu, most worthy brethren and friends. May God preserve you and your families, and continue to guide you by His Spirit even to the end!—Yours,

JOHN CALVIN.

[*Lat. orig. autogr.*—*Library of the University of Leyden.*]

## CCLII.—To FAREL.[2]

Criticism on a work by Farel.

GENEVA, *1st September* 1549.

You will learn from your brother that the painful case of Curione, was published in 1550, with a preface by Calvin.—(*Miscellanea Groningana*, tom. iii. p. 109.) We have not met with this edition, which is become extremely rare.

[1] We find Calvin's opinion of Vergerio at greater length, in a letter to Farel of July 1550.

[2] Endowed, according to the testimony of his contemporaries, with a powerful and impetuous eloquence which charmed multitudes, and which, with the strong faith with which he was animated, could alone explain his splendid success as a missionary, Farel was abler with the tongue than with the pen, and his various writings, called forth by circumstances, are in general defective. We find in them a few ideas, cast forth at hazard, without plan, in strange disorder, and with a superabundance of explanation, in a diffuse and obscure style. It is not uninteresting to know the judgment which Calvin pronounced upon the works of his friend, and to find in this judgment even a new testimony to the brotherly candour which presided at all times over the intercourse of the two Reformers.—See on the writings of Farel, Senebier, *Hist. Litt.* tom. i. pp. 148, 149; Sayons, *Etudes sur les Ecrivains de la Réformation*, tom. i., 1st sketch; and Haag, *France Protestante*, Art. Farel.

Ferron has been renewed.¹ Bullinger, as you will observe, writing previous to receiving my letter, had good hopes of publishing a union. I make honourable mention of you in my preface; even if it should give pain to the wicked, they must nevertheless swallow it in silence. I have written nothing regarding your book,² as I laid the whole burden on Viret. I said from the first, what is true, that I mistrusted my own judgment regarding your writings, seeing that our mode of writing is so different. You know with what respect I regard Augustine. Not, however, because I disguise from myself how much his prolixity dissatisfies me. Perhaps my style, in the meantime, is over-concise. But I am not at present discussing which is best. For I have not confidence in myself [to do so], for this reason, that whilst I follow my own inclination, I had rather pardon than condemn others. Normandie—who is so great a friend of mine, that he is a great friend of yours also—will furnish the best testimony as to what I think of your book. I am only afraid that the involved style and tedious discussion will obscure the light which is really in it. I know, and that not without pleasure too, that nothing but what is excellent is expected from you. I speak without flattery. Your book seems to deserve a place among [works of] that class. But because the readers of our time are so fastidious, and not possessed of great acuteness, I should wish the language to be so managed, that one might allure them by the fluency of his expression, and bring forward at the same time, that erudition which lies concealed under those coverings of which I have spoken. This is my candid judgment. Although I prefer acquiescing in the opinion of Viret, yet I could not be altogether silent, seeing that you had already insisted on it for the second time. Your brother will let you know about our affairs.

Adieu, brother and very honest friend, with all your fellow-

---

[1] See Note 1, p. 207.

[2] The only work of Farel's mentioned at this date by Senebier, is the following: *Le Glaive de la Parole Véritable contre le Bouclier de Défense, duquel un Cordelier s'est voulu servir*, in 12mo, Geneva, 1550. It is a vehement reply to a Cordelier who had adopted the sentiments of that spiritual mysticism which leads to a denial of all morality. It presents, besides, the ordinary defects of the works of Farel—confusion and prolixity.

ministers, especially Christopher, and Michael Faton. May the Lord ever guide and watch over you.—Yours,

JOHN CALVIN.

M. Normandie[1] sends kindest greeting to you.
[*Lat. orig. autogr.*—*Library of Geneva.* Vol. 107*a*.]


## CCLIII.—To VIRET.

First mention of Theodore Beza—poverty of Calvin's colleagues.

*5th September* 1549.

I understand that Eustace, on his return, had some conversation with you regarding two professors whom he knew about. While some deference is due to the judgment of a pious and learned man, yet I dare not trust it absolutely. Consider the matter calmly, therefore, along with the brethren. For I have promised that I will write to you in no other way than to give you a faithful advice. The Piedmontese author of the long epistle is no better known to me than to you; so we may wish him well when he asks nothing more from us. I have written to Farel my opinion of his book.[2] But it happened, through the negligence of his brother Claudius, that the letter was not delivered; for after he had breakfasted with us, I retired to my library, and he went away without saluting me. I have a messenger here, however, who will, I hope, set out to-morrow. Normandie can tell you how faithfully I endeavoured to send Beza[3] to you. I do not care for mentioning others. Yea, and

---

[1] Laurent de Normandie, a Picard gentleman, and Procurator-general at Noyon, had retired to Geneva some months previously, at the request of Calvin, his countryman and friend.—*Registers of the Council*, 2d May 1549. "Laurent de Normandie retires to this place for the sake of religion, and presses the Council to receive him as an inhabitant, which is granted him."

[2] See the preceding letter.

[3] This is the first time the name of Beza is found mentioned in the correspondence of Calvin. Born on the 24th of June 1519, at Vezelay, in Burgundy, he had left Paris after a brilliant and dissipated youth, to retire to Geneva.—*Registers of the Council*, 3d May 1549. "Eight French gentlemen, among whom is Theodore Beza, arrive here and obtain permission to remain." Beza was, a short time

the individual in question knows that I have entreated him almost importunately. Should he return I will not cease to urge him. The monks are wrong, however, in asserting that my associates are wealthy. For the only one who may be thought rich is involved in debt with three or four :—I mean Cop. Abel and Des Gallars are rich in books; Bourgouin and Raymond have excellent daughters, but nothing more. But even if they do not speak to him, we will consult the good of the Church rather than our regard for him. I think you know of Renier's wishes; and I know that he is so beloved by you and by the right-minded, that you will be especially anxious to find work for him adapted to his capacity.

Adieu, most upright brother and friend, together with your wife, your little daughter, and your whole family. May the Lord keep you and guide you by His Spirit! Salute the brethren earnestly in my name.—Yours,

JOHN CALVIN.

[*Lat. orig. autogr.—Library of Gotha.* Vol. 404, p. 16.]


## CCLIV.—TO JOHN HALLER.[1]

*A reformer's complaints on the malevolence of the Bernese ministers.*

GENEVA, 26*th November* 1549.

I beg you, my dear Haller, not to take it amiss that I ask

afterwards, made Professor of Greek in the Academy of Lausanne, from which place he wrote to Bullinger :—" The Lord has shewn me this, in the first place, for which may I be able to make my boast in Him continually,—that I must prefer the cross to my country, and to all changes of fortune. In the next place, I have received the friendship of Calvin, Viret, Musculus, and Haller; kind Heaven, the friendship of such men! When I think that these are my friends, so far from feeling any inconvenience from exile, I may adopt the saying of Themistocles,— 'I had been lost had I not become an exile.' "—*MSS. of Archives of Zurich,* Gest. vi. p. 139.

[1] " To John Haller, Pastor of the Bernese Church."

John Haller, of the illustrious family of that name, which reflected so much honour on Switzerland, was born at Zurich in 1523, and became a minister at the age of nineteen, as he informs us himself in his *Chronicle.* He became the col-

you to discharge the present duty for me, as I shall impose a new burden on you, by and by, to provide, viz., for the transmission of my letter to Zurich. Conrad Curio, who is at present schoolmaster at Zurtolphi, got me to become security for him with a certain bookseller. My reminding him of it has been hitherto useless, and I am now pulling his ears a little more smartly, lest I pay the penalty of his negligence. I send a letter to be safely delivered to him at an early period, which may be done without trouble to yourself. Had I not been convinced of your love toward me, I should not have ventured to impose any burden on you. Would that I had the same confidence in all! But I see that Satan has too much influence among those who wish to be regarded as ministers of Christ, when Hotman[1] was lately refused a place among the deacons, for which I can see no other reason than that he was for some time my coadjutor. But although I am his familiar companion, he ought not [on that account] to injure the pious and the learned. Those unscrupulous individuals who go about raging so wildly will never cause me to regret the labour which I incur in behalf of the Church. They will assuredly bring upon themselves equal odium and reproach from all good men. I shall defer the rest for two days or four.

Adieu, distinguished Sir, and very dear brother in Christ, deserving of my regard. May the Lord guide yourself and your family!—Yours,

JOHN CALVIN.

[*Lat. copy—Imperial Library of Dupuy.* Vol. 102.]

---

league of Musculus, at Augsburg, in 1545, was recalled to Zurich three years afterwards, and, yielding to the pressing solicitations of the Seigneury of Berne, undertook the duties of a minister of that church in 1548. His zeal and talents, together with his prudence, which was remarkable in one so very young, raised him to the highest offices; and before he was quite twenty-nine, he was chosen president of the clergy of Berne, an office which he filled for a long period amidst very trying circumstances.—Ruchat, tom. v. p. 329, *et suiv.*

[1] See note 3, p. 207.

## CCLV.—To Wolfgang Musculus.[1]

*Prohibition of the Vaudois Conferences—remonstrances on the intolerance of the Bernese ministers towards those of France.*

Geneva, 28*th* Nov. 1549.

If your senate had reasons for forbidding the ministers to assemble in future, according to their custom, to confer upon the Scriptures, it seems to me that I have formed a correct opinion of them. But I deny that this was a useful remedy. I have heard that there were never any contentions at Lausanne until that madman resolved upon perpetually harassing the Church. Every one will admit that such meetings are an excellent institution; and experience has hitherto shown that they have not been without a tolerable amount of fruit. The negligence of those who attend more to other things than to sacred literature, is there best detected. Such are at least stimulated by shame, and all derive benefit. It is certainly unjust that for one man's fault—for the wantonness of one idler—men are to be deprived of a beneficial exercise. It is wronging the brethren also, to visit upon all the transgression of one individual. Haller once saw an appearance of quarrelsome wrangling. But who fanned the flame? who supplied the fuel? It is well known that as long as Zebedee was allowed to rage there with impunity, the brethren were harassed with perpetual contentions.[2] Why was there not a check put to his fury, as there might quickly have been? Whence arose his

---

[1] The ministers of the Pays de Vaud were accustomed to meet weekly to consult about religious matters, and for mutual exhortation. This custom displeased the Seigneurs of Berne, who abolished it by an edict dated 2d September 1549, under pretext that those assemblies, instead of producing edification, engendered disputes, divisions, and disorders. The College of Lausanne protested in vain, through Viret, against this measure, which obtained the approbation of the leading ministers of Berne, notwithstanding the strong representations addressed by Calvin to Haller and Musculus.—Ruchat, tom. v. p. 382, *et suiv.*

[2] Deposed from the ministry, and appointed Principal of the College of Lausanne, Zebedee ranked among the most violent adversaries of Viret and of Calvin. Numerous testimonies to his animosity against the Reformation will be found in the sequel.

shameless audacity? If you do not know, there are too many among ourselves who have helped thus to puff up his arrogance. What now, if those very men, who long took advantage of his rashness that they might continue to harass the brethren, are the cause of the meetings being prohibited? When you inveigh so bitterly against all the ministers of our country, you seem to me to be forgetful both of your mildness and your modesty. As those grievously err who, with the same chalk, as they say, whiten the innocent and the guilty; so, where is the justice of blackening all with the same coal? I admit the great deficiencies of many, and I would that the proper amount of strictness were exercised. I know that many are wicked, wanton, and virulent; but, believe me, such are now permitted to throw off the reins. In the meantime forgive me, if I am indignant, that the whole French name is thus cruelly condemned. Although I make no distinction of nations here, nor am I one who shows indulgence to the vices of my friends, yet it is natural that I should be better acquainted than you are with their virtues. As to those scripture conferences which have hitherto been customary, grant us at least that old proverb, "Experience teaches fools." We have now for a long time had sufficient proof that the brethren are benefited by the exercise of this style of interpretation. Now the less the interchange of opinion, the greater will be the danger from pernicious dogmatisms. The slothful will sleep undisturbed; many will somehow or other grow godless, or become degenerate. This also has very great weight with me, that all good men are groaning under this edict, and the wicked are rejoicing. And when you see the College of Lausanne (to omit others) suffering so much on this account, it is surely your duty to alleviate their holy anxiety, as far as words can do so. In other respects also, your being very closely united is not more for their interest than for your own, if you wish to benefit the Church of God. For, to be frank with you, I was vexed a little lately by the rejection of Hotman, as I suspected that my connexion with him had done him harm.

From my confidence in your friendship, I expostulate the more freely with you and my friend Haller. For I am persuaded that some things which trouble me are displeasing to you also. But however that may be, I hope you will put a just and friendly interpretation on these complaints. Adieu, most excellent and accomplished man, and my revered brother in the Lord. May God keep you and your family, and be ever present with you and guide you!—Yours,

JOHN CALVIN.

My colleagues heartily salute you.

I thought I had given this letter with others to the messenger, but after he left I discovered my mistake when it was too late. I suppose you have not heard that the marriage of the Duke of Mantua with the daughter of Ferdinand has been celebrated at Papia. It is yet uncertain who is to succeed Paul.[1] War is expected in Italy. God grant that we may seek peace with Himself!

[*Lat. orig. autogr.—Library of Zofingue.* Vol. i. p. 14.]


## CCLVI.—To MONSIEUR DE SAINT LAURENS.[2]

### Statement of leading articles of the Reformed Faith.

FROM GENEVA, .... [1549?]

MONSIEUR,—Although I am personally unknown to you, still I believe you will not think it strange that I make so bold as to write to you, having been requested to do so by two persons who ought to insure me free enough access,—I mean Monsieur de Saint-Martin and your daughter. Wherefore, also, I shall forbear making further excuses, and likewise because I have heard that my letters would not be unwelcome to you, but that you would have the patience to read and think over the contents,

---

[1] Pope Paul III. died on the 20th November 1549, of grief and rage, on hearing of the treachery of his grandson Octave Farnese, who, to obtain the restitution of Parma, joined the cause of the Emperor against his grandfather.—De Thou, b. vi.; Robertson, b. x.

[2] The title:—To the father of Mademoiselle de Saint-Lorrans. *Sans* date. (1549?) This gentleman retired in the following year to Geneva.

which gives me good hope that you have the true seed of God in you, which only needs to be cultivated in order to sprout and produce its fruit. Now, as that is the end I propose to myself, that we may attain it, I beseech you above all chiefly to consider, that it is the duty of every Christian, not to consent to the abuses which reign in the world, but rather to ascertain what is the pure truth of God, with the purpose of adhering to it ; further, that you would listen to me, touching the doctrine which we hold,—not that I would make full and entire declaration of it to you, but I shall merely state in few words the summary of the whole, in suchwise that it will be easy for you to perceive what is our principal object. As to the first, there are very many who settle down in their ignorance and superstition, because they will not take the trouble to open their eyes when the clear light is presented to them. Inasmuch as I do not hold you to be of that number, without further exhortation, it suffices me that I have warned you of the fact. There is much reason that all Christians should take care how they live towards God, so as not wilfully to deceive themselves, above all in a matter of such importance as is the salvation of the soul. It is notorious that Christianity has been much corrupted and depraved, as well by the negligence of prelates, as by that of governors, and that by their stupidity, or avarice and ambition. I do not consider that this corruption is only in manners or morals, but what is worse, doctrine and truth have been turned into a lie. The service of God has been polluted by endless superstitions. The order of Church government has been turned upside down, the signs and symbols of the sacraments so jumbled together, that all is confusion. If everybody does not perceive that, it is because they have not brought back all things to the true standard ; but if we compare the religion and doctrine held under the Papacy, with the pure ordinance of God, we shall therein discover more contradiction than between day and night. Therefore, to form a right notion, we must not pause to lay stress upon either the authority of princes, or on ancient custom, or on one's own understanding, but rather look above all, to what God has commanded or forbidden, for He has not spoken in secret, but has desired that His will should be known both of great and small. When you have once settled this point of submitting yourself to be taught of God, to acquiesce in what His Word contains, desiring to know what is the right way of salvation, that will be already a good step towards arriving at the full knowledge of what it is for our advantage to know.

The second request that I have said I had to make, is that you consider calmly the sum of our doctrine, when I shall have shortly stated it to you; for there are many who at once reject and condemn it, without having heard what it is, because they are prejudiced against us, which warps their judgment. I pass over the imputations and crimes which they lay against us, to make us odious to all the world; but do what they will, they cannot reproach us with having any other end than to gather in the people who have long been going astray, and to bring them back to their standard, which is the pure word of God. We demand, however, that all differences of opinion be determined by an appeal to that, and that every one abide by what we know to be the will of God. Our adversaries make themselves a buckler of the name of the Church, which they falsely assume. And it is the same conflict which in their time the prophets and apostles had with those who usurped pre-eminence in the Church, belying in all things the duties of their office. But we know that the Church is founded on the doctrine of the prophets and apostles, and that she ought to be united to Jesus Christ, her Head, who is without variableness. So therefore it is but a bastard church where God's doctrine does not reign as the rule. Following that rule, we desire that God may be served according to His commandments, and we reject all new-fangled ways invented to suit the appetite of men; for it is not lawful for men to impose law or statute upon conscience, and God moreover has reserved to Himself this privilege, to ordain for us whatsoever seemeth good unto Himself. Therefore it is, that we are accused of having abolished and trampled under foot the ordinances of our mother, holy Church, for example, when we say with Isaiah and Jesus Christ, that it is in vain we think to find out God by means of human traditions. Then, when we say with St. James, that there is but one Lawgiver, who is able to save and to destroy. Well, then, when you had searched to the very utmost, you would find that all which is among them called the worship of God, is nothing but pure invention forged at their own pleasure. In like manner, because the Holy Scripture, treating of our salvation, and wherein rests our whole trust and confidence in regard to it, sends us back to the sole grace of our Lord Jesus Christ, declaring that we are poor wretched sinners, utterly lost and useless for good, we endeavour to bring all the world to partake of this grace; and that it may be acknowledged and magnified as it behoves to be, and which cannot be done without casting down the false belief that we can do aught to merit paradise. They take occasion on this account to accuse us of making no account of good works, whereby they do us wrong; for we are far more careful to recommend holy living, than are any of our adversaries. But in order that men may not deceive themselves by an overweening confidence, we teach that we are able to do nothing whatever in our own strength, unless God guides us by His Holy Spirit, and that even when we had done all, this would afford a far too feeble ground whereon to found our justification; that we must therefore have continual recourse to the mercy of God, and to the merit and passion of Jesus Christ; and that it is there that we must rest our hope, making no account of all the rest. Thence it comes, that we say likewise, that we ought to address God in all our prayers, for He calls us to Himself, and forasmuch as we of ourselves are too vile and unworthy to draw near to Him, He hath given us His Son Jesus Christ for our Advocate. Therefore it is, that they reproach us with our hostility to the saints of both sexes, and that we forbid the honouring of them. But this is absurd, for we render to the saints the honour which God assigns them. Only we cannot bear that they should be made idols of, being set up instead of God, or of His Son our Saviour, which besides they do not ask, but on the contrary take to be a great wrong; for those things which, under shadow of devotion, are done with the view of pleasing them, they seek vengeance before God.

The sacraments, which ought to serve for our confirmation in the truth of God and in His fear, have been strangely perverted. When we set ourselves carefully to restore them to their true use and first original, they would have it believed that we are going to destroy them. But would they only look to the ordinance as it has been instituted by the Master, it would then be quite evident that the manner of observance which we practise, does not derogate in anything from what He has prescribed. True it is, we have not the mass as among them, but we have the Supper such as Jesus Christ has left it to us, and our adversaries can say nothing to the contrary, only they object their custom as a reason for everything, but we have another kind of buckler altogether, which is the commandment that must endure inviolable to the end of the world. *Do this*, saith the text, *until I come*. Whereby it follows, that whosoever attempt to change anything until the coming of our Lord Jesus, prove themselves rebels against Him. I should be over-tedious were I to follow out the other details which I omit mentioning to you, because it shall well suffice me, if it please God to lead you to concur in what I have herein lightly handled, in the hope that by more ample reading you may be yet more confirmed in the same purpose. And now, therefore, Monsieur, having humbly commended me to your kind favour, I beseech our good Lord to guide you by His Spirit, to make you conform in everything to His will, and to send what He knows to be good and wholesome for you.—Your servant,

CHARLES D'ESPEVILLE.

[*Fr. copy.—Library of Geneva.* Vol. 107.]

## CCLVII.—To the Protector Somerset.[1]

Congratulations on the royal favour shown to the Duke of Somerset—use to be made of his influence for spreading the Gospel in England.

*January* 1550.

MONSEIGNEUR,—That I have so long delayed to write to you,

[1] *On the back,* in the handwriting of Calvin : " To Monsieur the Protector of England.—Sent."

This letter was addressed to the Earl of Somerset after his first disgrace.—(See

has been from no want of good-will, but to my great regret I have refrained, fearing lest, during the troubles which have been of late, my letters should be the occasion of annoyance. I thank my God that He has now afforded me the opportunity which hitherto I have been waiting for. It is not I alone who rejoice at the good issue which God has given to your affliction, but all true believers, who desire the advancement of the kingdom of our Lord Jesus Christ, forasmuch as they know the solicitude with which you have laboured for the re-establishing of the Gospel in all its purity in England, and that every kind of superstition might be abolished. And I do not doubt that you are prepared to persevere in the same course, in so far as you shall have the means. On your own part, Monseigneur, not only have you to acknowledge the favour God has shown you in stretching out His hand for your deliverance, but also to bear His dealing with you in remembrance, that you may profit by it.[1] I know the regret which you may well entertain, and how you may be tempted to render the like to those whom you reckon to have meditated greater mischief against you than what has come to pass. But you know the admonition which Saint Paul has given us on that head, that is, that we have not to fight against flesh and blood, but against the hidden wiles of our spiritual enemy. Wherefore let us not waste our energies upon men, but rather let us set ourselves against Satan to resist all his machinations against us, as there is no doubt whatever that he was the author of the evil which impended over you, in order that the course of the Gospel might thereby be hindered, and even that all should

the letter of the 22d October 1548, and the Note, p. 261.) Set at liberty, the 6th February 1550, by the favour of the king his nephew, he resumed his place in the Privy Council, but losing the title and dignity of Protector. The letter of Calvin is without any doubt of February or March 1550.

[1] During his disgrace, which was regarded as a public calamity by the friends of the Reformation in England and throughout Europe, the Duke of Somerset had sought consolation in reading and in pious meditations. He translated into English a work on patience, to which he added a preface containing the expression of the most elevated sentiments. He received also exhortations from Peter Martyr, and shewed himself no less constant in his attachment to the Gospel, than resigned to the loss of fortune and credit.—See Burnet, *History of the Reformation*, vol. ii. p. 184; vol. iii. p. 209, fol. London.

be brought to confusion. Therefore, Monseigneur, forgetting and pardoning the faults of those whom you may conceive to have been your enemies, apply your whole mind to repel his malice who thus engaged them to their own destruction in setting themselves to seek your ruin. This magnanimity will not only be pleasing to God, but it will make you the more loved among men; and I do not doubt that you have such regard to that as you ought. But if your humane disposition itself impels you to this course, so much the more may I be confident that you will receive kindly what I say, knowing that nothing induces me to tender such advice to you, but the love I bear you, and the care which I have for your honour and welfare. And besides, it is so difficult a virtue so to overcome our passions as to render good for evil, that we can never be too much exhorted to do so. Moreover, seeing that the Lord has directed the issue so much better than many expected, keep in mind, Monseigneur, the example of Joseph. It would be difficult to find in our day such a mirror of integrity. For he, seeing that God had turned to good the evil which they had plotted against him, is unwearied in showing himself the minister of the goodness of God towards his brethren who had persecuted him. This victory will be more glorious than that which God has already given you, when He saved and secured your person, and your property, and your honours. However, Monseigneur, you have also to consider that if God has been pleased to humble you for a little while, it has not been without a motive. For although you might be innocent in regard to men, you know that before this great Heavenly Judge there is no one living who is not chargeable. Thus, then, it is that the saints have honoured the rod of God, by yielding their neck, and bowing low their head under His discipline. David had walked very uprightly, but yet he confessed that it had been good for him to be humbled by the hand of God. For which reason, as soon as we feel any chastisement, of whatsoever kind it may be, the first step should be to retire into ourselves, and well to examine our own lives, that we may apprehend those blessings which had been hidden from us: for sometimes too much prosperity so dazzles our eyes, that we cannot perceive wherefore God chastises us. It is but reasonable that we should do Him at least as much honour as we would to a physician, for it is His to heal our inward maladies, which are unknown to ourselves, and to pursue a course of healing, not according to our liking, but as He knows and judges to be fitting. What is more, it must needs happen sometimes that He makes use of preservative remedies, not waiting till we have already fallen into evil, but preventing it before it comes. God, besides your native rank, having assigned you a high dignity, has performed great things by your hand, and which shall possibly be more applauded after your death than they are duly appreciated during your lifetime. Moreover, He has caused His name to be magnified by you. Now, the most virtuous and excellent persons are in greater danger than any others of being tempted to forget themselves. You are aware, Monseigneur, of what is written concerning the good King Hezekiah, that after having performed such memorable actions, as well for religion and the worship of God as for the common weal of the country, his heart was lifted up. If God has been pleased to prevent that in you, it is a special favour He has shown you. Were there no other reason for it, save that He would be glorified in your deliverance, and that He would be recognised by you, as well as by all in your person, as the true protector of His own, that alone ought to be all-sufficient to you.

It remains, Monseigneur, that since He has thus given you the upper hand, you do render homage to Him for this benefit, as is due. If we are recovered out of a dangerous sickness, we ought to be doubly careful, and to honour this merciful God, just as if He had bestowed a new life upon us. You may not do less in your present circumstances. Your zeal to exalt the name of God, and to restore the purity of His Gospel, has been great. But you know, Monseigneur, that in so great and worthy a cause, even when we have put forth all our strength, we come very far short of what is required. However, if God, in thus binding you to Himself anew, has meant, in this way, to induce you to do better than ever, your duty is to strive to the uttermost and with all your energy, so that so holy a work as that which He has begun by you may be carried forward. I doubt not that you do so; but I am also confident, that knowing the affection which induces me to exhort you thereunto, you will receive all my solicitation with your wonted benignity. If the honour of God be thus esteemed by you above all else, He will assuredly watch over you and your whole household, to pour out His grace there more abundantly, and will make you know the value of His blessing. For that promise can never fail,—*Those who honour me, I will render honourable.* True it is, that those who best do their duty are oftentimes troubled the most by many violent onsets. But this is quite enough for them, that God is at hand to succour and relieve them. Now, although it is enough for you to look to God and to feel the assurance that your service is pleasing to Him, nevertheless, Monseigneur, it is a great comfort to you to see the King so well disposed that he prefers the restoration of the Church, and of pure doctrine, to everything else, seeing it is a virtue greatly to be admired in him, and a peculiar blessing for the kingdom,[1] that in a youth of such tender age the vanities of this world do not hinder the fear of God and true religion from ruling in his heart. This also ought to be a great help and confirmation, that you discharge the principal service which he desires and asks, in serving our heavenly King, the Son of God.

Monseigneur, having very humbly commended me to your kind favour, I beseech our good Lord, that, upholding you in His holy keeping, He would increase in you yet more and more the gifts of His Holy Spirit, for the furtherance of His own glory, so that we may all have whereof to rejoice.

Your very humble servant,

JOHN CALVIN.

[*Fr. orig. minute.—Library of Geneva.* Vol. 107, *a.*]

[1] The young King Edward VI. Instructed by the most able masters, this prince gave early proof of a strong mind and of a lively piety. When scarcely fourteen years of age, he set forth in a discourse, of which a fragment has been preserved, the plan of the Reformation in England. He drew up with much care a journal of events which happened during his reign. He composed, besides, a collection of passages of the Old Testament condemning idolatry and image-worship. This collection, written in French, was dedicated by the young King to the Duke of Somerset, his uncle.—Burnet, *History of the Reformation,* vol. ii. pp. 224, 225.

## CCLVIII.—To Farel.

Tidings from Germany and England—recommendation of a domestic.

GENEVA, 1st *February* 1550.

Although you have not had a long letter from me for a considerable time, yet I do not think that even now I have anything new to write to you. All the time that our friend Thomas was here, I was either suffering severely from a cough or annoyed by catarrh. A violent headache is now tormenting me, although it has been easier for the past hour. It is well that I am not prevented from labouring, in a kind of way, to discharge my necessary duties; but I usually make but slow progress. Much of my time is wasted, at present, by ill health, which ought to be devoted to useful labour. We hear nothing from Germany, except that the Lord has punished the Emperor by the destruction of some of his ships. Would that some disease would put a check upon his evil deeds! You know that the tutor of the English king has been set at liberty, and, I suppose, you are aware also of what happened to my letter.[1] The prefect of C—— having got it from the messenger took it into the palace; he afterwards restored it to the messenger, who, before giving it to the king's tutor, presented it to [the Archbishop] of Canterbury, to ask his advice. He returned it to him again after retaining it two days. The messenger, fearing that that was done insidiously, or that he was bringing upon his own head the very danger which others were so anxiously avoiding, presented it to the King's Council, although, as I hear, he was advised to do that by good and wise men. I expect an answer immediately. Whatever may turn up, I shall see to it that you be made acquainted with it.

Whether it is owing to the indolence of John Girard that your book is not yet printed,[2] or from the confused state of his affairs at home, or because he has made deliberate choice of many things before it, I dare not affirm. I have certainly

---
[1] The letter to the Protector, of January 1550.
[2] See Note 3, pp. 226-7.

spoken to him frequently on the matter, and he has made serious protestations about it. Normandie also has repeatedly ordered him to get on with it. So the *Institute*, which should have been completed a month ago, is not finished yet. I wished to make this brief statement to you, to let you know that I had not been neglectful. He is not particularly moved by my reproving him, except that he immediately promises to do it forthwith.

Adieu, brother and very worthy friend. May the Lord by His Spirit continue to guide you, and may He watch over yourself and your family! You will salute your fellow-ministers cordially in my name, especially Faton and your colleague.

The short Treatise on the Sanctification of the Infants of Pious Parents, and on Female Baptism, is being printed, although it did not require more than two days' labour.[1] As to what you fear of the venomous creatures which I have irritated giving forth some poison, I am quite easy on that score. Adieu again.—Yours,

JOHN CALVIN.

I understand that you require a maid-servant,—neither yourself nor your brothers told me so. However, having heard it from others, I wish to tell you that there is a woman here who is pious, upright, and careful, and advanced in years, who would gladly serve you if she could be of use to you.

All your friends salute you kindly, especially M. Normandie, yet this does not detract from the regard of the others—from that of Verron, for instance, the writer of the present letter.

[*Lat. orig.—Library of Gotha.* Vol. 404, fol. 5.]

[1] The Reformer having attacked the *Interim* in one of his writings, he was accused of Pelagianism by a German theologian, perhaps Flacius Illyricus. He replied to this accusation in a publication entitled, *Appendix Libelli de vera Ecclesiæ reformandæ ratione, in qua refutat Censuram quamdam typographi ignoti de parvulorum Sanctificatione et muliebri Baptismo.* Geneva, 1550.

## CCLIX.—To Farel.

*Election of a new Pope.*

*3d March* 1550.

I am glad that worthy man has at length so far listened to rational advice as to yield to you. One must overlook what difficulty he occasioned for some time, only he should try to make up for his slowness by assiduity when he has once arrived. This I expect he will be entirely prepared to do. For I know him to be an upright man and one who is diligent in his business. I know that he will be so commended to you that there is no need of words [from me.] His wife will get accustomed to it by degrees. He brings two boys with him, of whom the one is the son of a very excellent and very upright man, the other is a grandson of Pommier's brother. When they reach you, let them understand that you will attend to them. I shall faithfully discharge my duty to the son of M. Michael Schalter. I have just now received your letter.

The Pope who has been created ought to be an extraordinary monster, seeing that the best of workmen have wrought so long at the forging of him.[1] Nor indeed could a fitter than Julius have been fallen upon, as the moderator of the Council of Trent.

Adieu, brother and very honest friend. May the Lord Jesus sustain you! Salute the brethren earnestly, especially my co-patriot, Christopher Muloti, Faton, and the rest. Adieu again.—Yours,

JOHN CALVIN.

[*Lat. orig. autogr.—Library of Geneva.* Vol. 107, *a.*]

---

[1] The pontifical chair, rendered vacant in the month of November 1549, by the death of Paul III., was occupied in the month of February of the following year by the Cardinal del Monte, who took the name of Julius III. The irregularities of his past life, and the disgraceful accusations which rested on his character, rendered him very unfit to be a reformer of the Church.

## CCLX.—TO FRANCIS DRYANDER.[1]

Counsels and encouragements—collection of commentaries on Isaiah by Des Gallars.

GENEVA, *7th March* 1550.

I am happy that you have returned safely from England. If your affairs here are satisfactory and prosperous, and the Lord is providing you with employment, I am the more delighted, although, as matters now stand everywhere, it becomes us so to walk in the world that we may be willing forthwith to depart. England seems as yet unsettled. Elsewhere, whatever was satisfactorily established appears now to decay. So that, unless we can preserve our patience, we shall nowhere find the aspect of affairs so pleasing as to prevent us from longing for a change. This is every day more and more the experience of myself, whose struggle you suppose is almost concluded. For I am perpetually disturbed by new contentions, and new sources of annoyance and disgust, to such a degree, that, were a free choice allowed me, I would prefer any lot to groaning continually under so grievous a burden. The Lord has adorned you with genius and learning; He has gifted you with a zealous and magnanimous spirit. We must pray that He will not suffer these rich endowments to lie unimproved. I know, indeed, that hitherto you have endeavoured to make your life useful to the Church, and that your attempts have not been without fruit. But I desire that your gifts may be more fully displayed, and I trust that they will. My meditations on Isaiah, which you say are expected, will shortly be published. The composition of the work, however, is Des Gallars', for, as I

---

[1] *On the back:* "To the very Illustrious M. Francis Dryander, a Spaniard, at Basle, with M. Myconius."

Dryander left Strasbourg (for England) in 1548. Melanchthon gave him letters of introduction to King Edward and to Cranmer, by whose patronage he obtained a Chair in the University of Cambridge.—(Zurich Letters, first series, tom. i. p. 349.) At the end of the following year (December 1549) we find Dryander in Strasbourg again. What were his motives for returning to the Continent cannot now be ascertained. See the notice of Dryander, p. 97.

have but little time for writing, he jots down to my dictation and arranges his materials afterwards at home. I then make a revision of it, and wherever he has missed my meaning I restore it. When my letter reaches you, I expect the treasurer of our city will be there also, and will remain for two days. If you have any news he will be glad to convey them. I have nothing to say to MM. Myconius and Sulzer till they answer my last. Remember me, however, to them and to Oporinus. My colleagues desire me to salute you cordially. I pray for all joy and prosperity to your wife wherever she is.

Adieu, illustrious Sir. May the Lord continue to guide you by His Spirit, and be ever present with you!—Yours,

JOHN CALVIN.

[*Lat. orig. autogr.—Archives of the Protestant Seminary of Strasbourg.*]

## CCLXI.—To NICOLAS COLLADON.[1]

Settlement of the Colladon family at Geneva.

*12th May* 1550.

I have at present no other reason for writing you than that I thought it absurd that a messenger, sent with difficulty hither

---

[1] "To Nicolas Colladon, a man distinguished for piety and learning."

Among the numerous French refugees whom persecution led yearly to Geneva, there were none more distinguished than the members of the Colladon family, originally from Berry, where they occupied an eminent position, and are reckoned, even in our own day, among the number of the Genevese aristocracy. Nicolas Colladon, to whom the letter of the Reformer is addressed, was the son of Leon Colladon, the celebrated parliamentary advocate of Bourges, who, with his brother Germain, retired to Geneva in the early part of the year 1551. Long initiated in evangelical doctrine, Nicolas Colladon continued to exercise those pastoral functions in his adopted country, which he had previously performed in Berry. In 1564 he was made Principal of the College of Geneva, and in 1566 succeeded Calvin himself in the chair of theology, without ceasing to discharge his pastoral duties with a zeal which, during the plague of 1570, found a perilous opportunity of signalizing itself. He spent the last years of his life in the Canton de Vaud. The precise date of his death is not known.—Senebier, *Hist. Litt.*, tom. i. p. 398. Galiffe, *Notices Généalogiques*, tom. ii. p. 566; and Haag, *France Protestante*, Art. Colladon.

from so intimate a friend, and on business well known to me, should return without a letter from me. I was afraid, also, at the same time, lest your brother should entertain unpleasant suspicions should he hear that I had been altogether silent. My friend Laurent at present declines the journey to which you urge him; his excuse is brief, but such as we both hope will abundantly satisfy you. I will only add this from him, that he was as far as possible from seeking any excuse for not visiting you. I assure you that his inclination is in no respect altered; but having seriously pondered the whole matter, I dare not advise him to leave his home at present. It is well, however, that those with whom you invited him to confer are disposed to entertain a removal.[1] And, indeed, they can accomplish nothing in this affair without coming to us. For as the girl is engaged in marriage here,[2] it would be too hazardous for them to remain at home. It will be your duty, therefore, to urge them to collect their baggage, and prepare for the journey. This may at first sight appear ridiculous, as if, in a matter so difficult and perplexing, I fancied everything was easily managed. I am not so inexperienced, however, as to be ignorant of the obstacles, embarrassments, and delays with which you must struggle. This only I wish, since the matter admits of no delay, that you would exert yourself vigorously in discharging your duty.

Adieu, beloved brother in the Lord. Salute your relatives kindly in my name, both the father and all the families. May God direct you with the Spirit of wisdom and fortitude; may He be present with you and further all your pious efforts! Amen.—Yours,

CHARLES PASSELIUS.

[*Lat. orig. autogr.—Library of Geneva.* Vol. 107, *a.*]

---

[1] In allusion to the various members of the Colladon family, who were contemplating a removal to Geneva.

[2] Anne Colladon, the sister of Nicolas, was on the point of being married to Laurent de Normandie. See Note, 1, p. 203.

## CCLXII.—To the Seigneury of Geneva.[1]

Notice of a publication attributed to Gruet.

[*May* 1550.]

Seeing that it has pleased Messieurs to ask my opinion regarding the book of Gruet, it appears to me, that in the first place, they ought in regular judicial form to identify the handwriting, not so much for the condemnation of the individual, who is quite enough condemned already, as for the consequences which may ensue; as well in order that it may not be thought that they have been lightly moved on account of an uncertain book, as for the sake of adherents and accomplices.

That being done, I think that the suppression of the book itself ought not to appear to be for the sake of burying it out of sight, but be accompanied by a testimony that they had looked upon it with such detestation as it deserved, and that it was done for the sake of example only.

It is true, that seeing we ought to abstain from all filthy communication, and that nothing of that kind ought to proceed out of our mouth,—such blasphemous and execrable speeches ought not to be repeated, as if we had no horror of them at all; but, in obedience to the rule which our Lord has given in his law, it is for the common weal that faithful magistrates specially define the impieties which they punish. Besides, Messieurs are well aware how necessary it is, for many reasons which I leave for them to consider, although God's ordinance regarding it ought to be all-sufficient for us.

[1] Three years after the death of Gruet, beheaded for the crime of rebellion and of blasphemy, (see the note, p. 212) there was discovered in a garret of his house a writing in his own hand, of twenty-six pages, which was brought to the magistrates of Geneva. These latter submitted the document to Calvin, who drew up his opinion in the Memorial which we here reproduce, as an undeniable evidence of the religious doctrines and the morals professed by some of the chiefs of the Libertin party.

The writing in question was condemned, the 23d May 1550, as being full of the most detestable blasphemies, and was burnt by the hand of the hangman in front of the house of Gruet.

The form, under correction, which we should recommend, is that there should be a preamble or narrative something like what follows:—

That whereas, in such a year, and on such a day, Jacques Gruet, as well on account of hideous blasphemies against God, and mockery of the Christian religion, as because of wicked conspiracy against the public state of this city, mutinies and other crimes and malpractices, had been condemned to such a punishment, it has since come to pass that a book has been found in his own handwriting, as has been ascertained upon sufficient evidence, in which are contained many blasphemies, so execrable, that there is no human creature who ought not to tremble at the hearing of them, and wherein he makes a mock at the whole of Christianity, so far as to say of our Lord Jesus Christ, the Son of God and King of Glory, before whose majesty the devils are constrained to bow down themselves, that He was an idle beggar, a liar, a fool, a seducer, a mischievous wicked person, an unhappy fanatic, a clown full of vain-glorious and wicked presumption, who well deserved to be crucified; that the miracles which he had performed were nought but sorceries and apish tricks, and that He deemed Himself to be the Son of God, in like manner as the Hierarchs weened themselves to be in their Synagogue; that He played the hypocrite, having been hung as He deserved, and died miserably in His folly, a thoughtless coxcomb, great drunkard, detestable traitor, and suspended malafactor, whose coming into the world has brought nothing but all sorts of wickedness, disaster, and confusion, and every sort of reproach and outrage which it is possible to invent:

He has said of the Prophets, that they have been only fools, dreamers, fanatics; of the Apostles, that they were rascals, and knaves, apostates, dull blockheads, brainless fellows; of the Virgin Mary, that it is rather to be presumed that she was a strumpet; of the law of God, that it is worthless, like those who have framed it; of the Gospel, that it is nothing but falsehood; that the whole of Scripture is false and wicked, and that there is less meaning in it than there is in Æsop's fables, and that it is a false and foolish doctrine:

And not only does he thus villanously attack our holy and sacred Christian religion, but also renounces and abolishes all religion and divinity, saying that God is nothing, representing men to be like to the brute beasts, denying eternal life, and disgorging execrations, the like of which ought to make the hair stand up upon the head of every one, and which are of such rank infection as to bring a whole country under the curse, so that all people of every degree, having any sound conscience at all, ought to ask pardon of God that His name has been thus blasphemed among them.

In conclusion, it appears to me that sentence ought to be given in such or similar form as follows :—

That whereas the writer of the said book has been, by judicial sentence, condemned and executed, yet, in order that the vengeance of God may not abide upon us for having suffered or concealed such horrible impiety, and also as an example to all accomplices and adherents of a sect so infectious and worse than diabolical, even to shut the mouth of all those who would excuse or cover such enormities, and to show them what condemnation they deserve, Messieurs have ordained . . &c.
. . . .
The sooner this is done the better, for already this unhappy book has been too much in the hands of these gentlemen. . . .

[*Fr. orig. autogr.—Coll. of M. the Chevalier Eynard at Geneva.*]


## CCLXIII.—To MELANCHTHON.[1]

Controversies excited in Germany by the establishment of *the Interim*—
Brotherly reproofs.

[18*th June* 1550.]

The ancient satirist once said,—
" Si natura negat, facit indignatio versum."

It is at present far otherwise with me. So little does my present

---

[1] The proclamation of the *Interim* plunged Germany into a state of extraordinary confusion. Some towns were so bold as to present remonstrances to the Emperor, and protested against an arbitrary edict, which reprobated alike the partisans of the ancient worship and those of the new. But their voice was not

grief aid me in speaking, that it rather renders me almost entirely speechless. Besides, as I cannot express in words how my mind is affected, being overcome with merely thinking on the subject on which I am about to write, I am almost struck dumb. I would have you suppose me to be groaning rather than speaking. It is too well known, from their mocking and jests, how much the enemies of Christ were rejoicing over your contests with the theologians of Magdeburg.[1] They certainly presented a foul and abominable spectacle, as well to the Lord and the angels, as to the whole Church. If no blame attaches to you in this matter, my dear Philip, it would be but the dictate of prudence and justice, to devise a means of curing the evil, or at least of somewhat mitigating it. Yet, forgive me if I do not consider you altogether free from blame. And from this you may conjecture how severe the judgments of others are concerning you, and how offensive and unpleasant their remarks. In the meanwhile, let it be well understood, that in openly admonishing you, I am discharging the duty of a true friend; and if I employ a little more severity than usual, do not think that it is owing to any diminution of my old affection and esteem for you. Although for me to offend by rude sim-

heard, and the greater number of the towns submitted. There were even theologians compliant enough to legitimize this submission. Of this number was Melanchthon, who, by his virtues and his knowledge, deserved the first rank among the reformed doctors, but who, deprived now of the manly exhortations of Luther, and led away by an excessive love of peace, and by the natural weakness of his character, was making concessions which cannot be justified. Led by his example, and seduced by the artifices of the Elector Maurice, the Assembly of Leipsic declared that in matters purely *indifferent* we ought to obey the orders of our lawful superiors,—a dangerous principle, which applied to ceremonies, and led to the revival of the grossest and most pernicious errors of the Romish Church. Melanchthon himself wrote a great number of the letters of 'Ἀδιάφορος [Indifferent], in support of this doctrine, and his weakness drew down upon him the most violent reproaches from the zealous Lutherans, who accused him of being an accomplice of the enemies of the Gospel.—Sleidan, book xxii.; Robertson, book x. Moved by these sad news, Calvin did not hesitate to blame Melanchthon in a letter addressed to him, in which respect and affection are joined to a just severity.

[1] The town of Magdeburg, then besieged by the army of the Elector Maurice, persisted in rejecting the *Interim*, and the theologians of that Church flooded Germany with pamphlets, in which Melanchthon was not spared. The Burghers of Magdeburg, put under the ban of the empire, sustained a long siege, and did not submit till the following year.—Sleidan, book xxii.

plicity, rather than bespeak by adulation the favour of any man, is nothing uncommon or new to you. I also feel, on the other hand, less anxiety about your taking it amiss to be reproved by me when I have just cause for displeasure, inasmuch as I am well aware that nothing gives you greater pleasure than open candour. I am truly anxious to approve all your actions, both to myself and to others. But I at present accuse you before yourself, that I may not be forced to join those who condemn you in your absence. This is the sum of your defence: that provided purity of doctrine be retained, externals should not be pertinaciously contended for.[1] And if it be true that is confidently asserted everywhere, you extend the distinction of non-essentials too far. You are not ignorant that the Papists have corrupted the worship of God in a thousand ways. We have put up with corruptions which were barely tolerable. The ungodly now order these same things to be restored, that they may triumph over a down-trodden gospel. And if any one does not hesitate to oppose this, will you not ascribe it to pertinacity? Every one knows how this is opposed to your modesty. If you are too facile in making concessions, you need not wonder if that is marked as a fault in you by many. Moreover, several of those things which you consider indifferent, are obviously repugnant to the Word of God. Perhaps there are some who insist too positively on certain points, and, as usually happens in disputes, make offensive attacks upon some things which have little harm in themselves. Truly if I have any understanding in divine things, you ought not to have made such large concessions to the Papists; partly because you have loosed what the Lord has bound in his Word, and partly because you have afforded occasion for bringing insult upon the Gospel. At a time when circumcision was as yet lawful, do

---

[1] In a reply to Flacius Illyricus, who maintained that, rather than tolerate the restoration of the Popish ceremonies, he would plunder and destroy the Churches and stir up the people,—"*vastitatem faciendam in templis, et metu seditionum terrendos principes.*" Melanchthon advocated *immovable steadfastness in doctrine, submission in everything else.*—"*In ceremoniis tolerandam aliquam servitutem, quæ tamen sit sine impietate.*"—Melch. Adam. *Vita Melanchthonis*, p. 344. But was it possible to submit to the Church of Rome without deserting sound doctrine?

you not see that Paul, because crafty and malicious fowlers were laying snares for the liberty of believers, pertinaciously refused to concede to them a ceremony at the first instituted by God ? Accordingly, he boasts that he did not yield to them, no not for a moment, that the truth of the Gospel might remain intact among the Gentiles. In our day, indeed, the enemy has not troubled us about circumcision, but that they may not leave us anything pure, they are tainting both doctrine and every exercise of worship with their putrid leaven. As for the theologians of Magdeburg, you say that they were only raising disputes about a linen vesture. I do not see the force of this. I certainly think the use of the linen vesture, with many other fooleries, have been hitherto retained as much by you as by them. And, indeed, good and pious men everywhere deplore that you should have countenanced those corruptions which manifestly tend to destroy the purity of all doctrine, and to undermine the stability of the Church. Lest you may perhaps have forgotten what I once said to you, I now remind you of it, namely, that we consider our ink too precious if we hesitate to bear testimony in writing to those things which so many of the flock are daily sealing with their blood. I spoke thus, indeed, at a time when we seemed to be farther out of the reach of missiles [than at present]. And seeing that the Lord led us forth into the arena, it became us on that account to strive the more manfully. Your position is different from that of many, as yourself are aware. For the trepidation of a general or leader is more dishonourable than the flight of a whole herd of private soldiers. Accordingly, while the timidity of others may be overlooked, unless you give invariable evidence of unflinching steadfastness, all will say that vacillation in such a man must not be tolerated. You alone, by only giving way a little, will cause more complaints and sighs than would a hundred ordinary individuals by open desertion. And, although I am fully persuaded that the fear of death never compelled you in the very least to swerve from the right path, yet I am apprehensive that it is just possible, that another species of fear may have proved too much for your courage. For I know how much you are horrified at the charge of rude severity. But we must remember, that reputation must not be accounted by the servants of Christ as of more value than life. We are no better than Paul was, who held fearlessly on his way through "evil and good report." It is indeed a hard and disagreeable thing to be reckoned turbulent and inflexible,—men who would rather see the whole world in ruin, than condescend to any measure of moderation. But your ears should have been deaf to such talk long ago. I have not so bad an opinion of you, nor will I do you the injustice, to suppose that you resemble the ambitious, and hang upon the popular breath. Yet I have no doubt but that you are occasionally weakened by those goadings. What? Is it the part of a wise and considerate man to rend the Church for the sake of minute and all but frivolous matters? Must not peace be purchased at any tolerable amount of inconvenience? What madness is it to stand out for everything to the last, to the neglect of the entire substance of the Gospel! When lately these and similar remarks were circulated by designing men, I thought and perceived you to be more influenced by them than you should have been; accordingly, I open my mind candidly to you, lest anything should mar that truly divine magnanimity, which, in other respects, I know you to possess. You know why I am so vehement. I had rather die with you a hundred times, than see you survive the doctrines surrendered by you. Nor do I say this as if there was danger lest the truth of God made known by your ministry should come to nought, or as if I distrusted your steadfastness; but simply because you will never be sufficiently solicitous lest the wicked obtain an occasion of cavilling, which owing to your facileness they eagerly snatch at. Pardon me for loading your breast with these miserable, though ineffectual groans. Adieu, most illustrious Sir, and ever worthy of my hearty regard. May the Lord continue to guide you by His Spirit, and sustain you by His might; may His protection guard you. Amen.[1] Salute, I entreat you, any of my friends that are near you. A

---

[1] This letter is without date. We discover the date however, in a letter of Calvin's to Valentin Pacaeus, a doctor of Leipsic, of 18th June 1550, where we meet with these words:—"I make no mention of M. Philip, as I am writing specially to himself."—Calv. *Opera*, tom. ix. p. 54.

great number here respectfully salute you. Multitudes, to avoid idolatry in France, are making choice of a voluntary exile among us. JOHN CALVIN.

[*Calvin's Lat. Corresp.* Opera, tom. ix. p. 54.]

## CCLXIV.—To VIRET.

Hope of an early visit from Viret—projected excursions in the neighbourhood of Geneva.

GENEVA, 23d *July* 1550.

When some one or other informed me lately that you intended coming here in a short time, I snatched eagerly at the intelligence, just as if you had been bound to come by a previous agreement. If you do think of coming, I beseech you, again and again, to stay a Sabbath with us, for you could not have a better opportunity during the whole year. You will deliver a discourse in the city on the morning of the Lord's day. I shall set out for Jussy; you will follow me after dinner, and we shall proceed thence to M. de Falais'.[1] Leaving him again, we shall make a hasty passage to the opposite side,[2] and rusticate till Thursday with Seigneurs Pommier and De Lisle. On Friday, if you choose to make an excursion to Tournet or Belle Rive, you will have my company also. You need not be afraid of any unpopularity, for matters have calmed down somewhat, as you will hear. See you do not disappoint me. Certainly many here are expecting you.

Adieu, again and again, until you come. Salute the brethren, and your wife and little daughters at home. May the Lord Jesus keep you all and watch over you.—Yours,

JOHN CALVIN.

You will give the letters to M. Vergerio, to be delivered to Zerkinden and Haller.

[*Lat. orig. autogr.—Library of Geneva.* Vol. 107, *a.*]

[1] See note 2, p. 161. M. de Falais lived during the summer in a country-seat, situated at Veigy, a small village of Savoy, a few leagues from Geneva.

[2] On the opposite bank of the lake, where rises the delightful eminence of Chambesy, crowned at the present day with beautiful villas.

## CCLXV.—To Farel.

*Opinion regarding Vergerio—intelligence regarding Bucer—letter to Melanchthon—disputes with Berne—literary publications of Calvin.*

*July* 1550.

Although I have not been able to secure a messenger for a long time, who might convey my letter to you with convenience and safety, yet I must really confess that I am ashamed of my long delay. But you will readily excuse me; and I can with truth declare, that I would gladly have written you on different occasions had I been able sooner to find a messenger. It is not expedient for us, in my opinion, to be anxious about our exculpation with the people of Zurich, lest some groundless suspicion should steal in upon them. We shall see by and by whether they have any faith in those clouds of theirs. Defence will be easy then. Let us, in the meantime, cherish our unanimity. Vergerio, Bishop of Pola,[1] is here at present; he will not return to the Grisons, however. I think Viret wrote you concerning him. He came by Lausanne, and spent a few days in familiar intercourse with the brethren. There is much that is praiseworthy about him; and I hope that he will be steadfast in the right path. As I knew he passed through Zurich, I endeavoured to elicit from him whether he had heard of aught unfavourable there. I could not scent out anything, however. We should therefore keep quiet, unless a better opportunity presents itself. Those who come from England, say that matters get on well there. I have heard nothing of Bucer, except that he seems rather pliant to some.[2]

---

[1] Paolo Vergerio, one of the missionaries of Reform in Swiss Italy. Born of an illustrious family of Istria, he had successively studied law and oratory, was made Bishop of Istria, and discharged the duties of Pope's legate in Germany. He became a convert to the Gospel through conversations with Melanchthon, abandoned his diocese, and retired among the Grisons. He died in 1565.

[2] There is a beautiful letter from Bucer to Calvin, Calvini *Opera*, tom. ix. p. 58,] dated from Cambridge, and containing curious details regarding the religious state of England. We find this passage in it relative to the young King Edward VI.,—" Increase in prayer in behalf of the most serene King, who is making quite wonderful progress in pious and literary studies."

There is a fixed opinion in the minds of many regarding him which is not easily rooted out. It is not unlikely that the good man feels annoyed by this prejudice. And whether he affords any occasion for it or not, I cannot tell. We shall have some word soon. No change has taken place in Saxony as yet. Should you feel disposed to spend a quarter of an hour, perhaps, in reading an epistle in which I discuss [the question] of ceremonies, you will find a copy of it enclosed. I have written to Melanchthon also in almost the very same strain, but, owing to my negligence, it turns out that I do not possess a copy of it.[1] Should you also be inclined to look into those points on which I recently advised the Protector of England, I have sent that [document] also. Would that time had allowed me to seek your advice, rather than show you what I have now done regarding the matter. The Collector of Finance[2] of the French king, who was in prison, has cost us no further trouble. The Bernese ambassadors, lately sent in his behalf, were of some use, though of less than I could have wished. They succeeded, however, in quieting the mind of the king. Five or six days after there comes a most polite letter, in which the king returns us his thanks, and courteously asks us to release the captive. This was done. By the wonderful goodness of God, we are now freed from a source of anxiety which often robbed me of my sleep. That new impost which the Bernese are exacting,[3] annoys us sadly. We are resolved not to pay it. We wish it tried at law; our opponents wish us to bow to their authority. Thereupon one evil rises out of another. Moreover, this awkward circumstance attends it, that I dare not refuse my advice to those soliciting it. I commenced Genesis seven days

---

[1] See the preceding letter.

[2] We find no allusion to this fact in the Registers of the Council of that year. But Ruchat mentions, after Roset, the arrest of one Jean Baptiste Didaco, Receiver-General of Finance at Rouen, who, having been imprisoned at Geneva at the impeachment of one of his domestics, was released at the request of the King of France, and of the Bernese, after three months' imprisonment.—Ruchat, tom. v. pp. 311, 313.

[3] The nature of this tax is not known; it was set on foot in the localities belonging to the ancient territory of the Chapter of Saint Victor, and shared between the jurisdiction of the two republics.

ago; may it be auspicious! In the meantime Isaiah is called to press.[1] The printers are at present busy with Paul, but I fear they have been longer of beginning than they should.[2] If it be not out in nine days hence, it will have other companions, for I hope that the book *De Scandalis* and the *Canonical Epistles* will be printed during the coming winter. Adieu, most upright brother, ever to be revered by me in the Lord. Salute earnestly your family and all the brethren. May the Lord watch over you all and guide you by His Spirit!

JOHN CALVIN.

[*Lat. orig. autogr.—Library of Geneva.* Vol. 107, a.]

## CCLXVI.—To WILLIAM RABOT.[3]

Exhortation to the study of the Scriptures.

*24th July* 1550.

Although we have been unknown to each other by sight, yet since you recognise the Master Christ in my ministry, and submit yourself cheerfully and calmly to His teaching, this is a sufficient reason why I should, on the other hand, esteem you as a brother and fellow-disciple. But, as I understand from your letter, that it is not very long since the Lord shed the light of His gospel on you, I could not give a fitter expression

[1] *Commentarii in Iesaiam Prophetam.* In fol. Geneva, 1550. A work dedicated to the King of England.

[2] *In omnes Pauli Epistolas atque etiam in Epistola ad Hebraeos Commentarii.* In fol. Geneva, 1550. With a preface by Theodore Beza.

[3] The title:—To William Rabot, "Dictus a Salena" of Avignon.

It appears from a letter of Rabot's to Calvin, preserved in the Library of Gotha, that, exiled from his native country from conscientious motives, this young man was then engaged in the study of law at the University of Padua, in company with a number of gentlemen, among others Charles de Jonviliers, François and Louis de Budé, &c. Their studies were intermingled with religious discourses, which contributed to the spread of the Gospel in certain distinguished families, among which we remark that of Contarini, originally of Padua. The increasing rigours of persecution soon scattered this focus of Evangelism, and led some of those youthful missionaries to Geneva, where Charles de Jonvillers, one of their number, gained the friendship of Calvin, and became his secretary.—*Divers MSS. of Gotha and of Geneva.*

of my love towards you, than by exhorting and encouraging you to daily exercises. For we see sparks of piety immediately disappear which had shone forth on many occasions; because, instead of increasing the flame, they rather extinguish what little light the Spirit of God had enkindled in them, by the empty allurements of the world, or the irregular desires of the flesh. That nothing of this kind may happen to you, you must first of all give devoted submission to the will of the Lord, and in the next place, you must fortify yourself by His sacred doctrines. But as this is too extensive a theme to be embraced in a letter, it is better for you to draw from the fountain-head itself. For if you make a constant study of the word of the Lord, you will be quite able to guide your life to the highest excellence. You have faithful commentaries, which will furnish the best assistance. I wish very much you could find it convenient at some time to pay us a visit; for, I flatter myself, you would never regret the journey. Whatever you do, see that you follow the Lord, and at no time turn aside from the chief end.

Adieu, illustrious and very dear Sir.—Yours,

JOHN CALVIN.

[*Lat. Copy.—Archives of the Protestant Seminary of Strasbourg.*]

## CCLXVII.—To FAREL.

Publication of the book on *Scandals*—persecution by the King of France—Bucer's discouragement.

GENEVA, 19*th August* 1550.

How I am to repay you for your letter, I know not, unless that, as soon as the Lord shall have enabled me to complete the first three chapters of my Commentary on *Genesis*, I give you a reading of it. If it please you, it will be worth the trouble of plucking the fruit before the time; and, besides, I shall have the benefit of your judgment on the remainder of the context, if you should think there is anything of which I should be made aware. The pamphlet *De Scandalis*, considering the immense fulness of the proof, will be not only short but even concise.¹ But then the evidence is all traced back to this conclusion,—that there is no reason why ungodly men should bring the Gospel into disrepute, and expose it to popular odium, under the pretext of stumblingblocks; and that the weak should be strengthened, in order that by the firmness of their faith they may overcome whatever stumblingblocks Satan may cast in their way. To put so great a check upon error, that should any one turn aside from the right path, or stumble or be disheartened, he may be without excuse. Yet I show, at the same time, how dreadful a vengeance God will take on the authors of offences. Meanwhile, you will attack that monster when the signs are favourable, which I confidently trust you have already done.

Whatever good hopes of Henry, Viret led you to cherish, they were vain.² Rumours of this sort are daily afloat. We should, therefore, place no more reliance on them than they deserve. It is a sure enough token that the ferocity of the beast is in no degree appeased, when our brethren, so far from experiencing any alleviation of their sufferings, are more closely pursued every day. ANOTHER LION is said to be making certain extraordinary exertions.³ We should, therefore, ask God to subdue their rage, or, at all events, to waste their strength by mutual collision—as he has hitherto done—that they may

---

[1] The Treatise on Scandals, one of the most remarkable of Calvin's writings, appeared this same year, with a beautiful dedication addressed by Calvin to Laurent de Normandie, *his old and constant friend.* It was published at first in Latin, under the following title:—*De Scandalis quibus hodie plerique absterrentur, nonnulli etiam alienantur a pura Evangelii Doctrina.* Geneva, 1550. This work was translated into French by Latern during the following year. It is to be found in tom. viii. of his *Opera,* and in the *Recueil des Opuscules,* p. 1145.

[2] Henry II. of France, to gain the good-will of the cantons, pretended at that time to take a lively interest in the protection of Geneva, menaced by the Duke of Savoy and the Emperor of Germany. He even informed the magistrates of the republic regarding certain plots, real or imaginary, laid for its destruction.—*Registers of the Council,* 1549, 1550, *passim.*

[3] The Emperor Charles V. published, at that time, his bloody edict against the Protestants, Lutherans, Zuinglians, and others, and seemed to be preparing himself for a general crusade against the Reformed Churches.—Sleidan, book xxii.

not be able to do any more damage. I am not ignorant of the danger from which the Lord has extricated us. Nor need we thank that abandoned faction, truly, for not bringing this unfortunate, nay devoted, city into utter ruin. But as I had all along good hopes of a remedy, nothing gave me great alarm.

It is to be feared that I shall gain some ill-will on account of the taxes.[1] For they know that Normandie and I are consulted [on the matter]. I prefer running this risk, however, to allowing those to ruin themselves whom I ought to advise. I was not able to bring them to a friendly agreement. All I could do was, to point out to them the best course.

My dear Christopher,[2] confessing as you do in the beginning of your letter, that you are not standing firm in the faith, I am astonished at your refusing to think about the state into which you have fallen. Are you and Mirabeau to be here, then, at Whitsuntide or not ? I shall write to my godmother concerning her little daughter at my earliest opportunity.[3] The whole of yesterday was spent in some trifling manner, I hardly know how.

I return to you again, my dear Farel. I do not know whether you have sent Bucer's letter to Viret. Anyhow, I have gathered from it that the worthy man is labouring under too much moroseness at present.[4] I shall write him a quiet letter by and by. There will be silence in future concerning the Zurichers ; for I perceive that it only heightens his exasperation. Seeing that he longs greatly for your [letter], I should like him to approve of mine. For that saying of Terence's applies to him,—that the unfortunate abuse everybody. For he makes no secret of thinking, that his old friends neglect him

---

[1] See note 3, p. 263.

[2] This passage in the letter is addressed to Christopher Fabri, or Libertet, a colleague of Farel's at Neuchatel.

[3] Calvin had stood godfather to one of the daughters of Libertet, whose wife he habitually called by the familiar name of *my godmother*.

[4] Saddened by his exile, and tormented by a malady under which he sunk the year following, Bucer complained bitterly of being continually the object of an unjust suspicion to the theologians of Zurich, and of being neglected by his friends in Switzerland.

when they do not write frequently. Nor is he deceived in Sturm, perhaps, who formerly stood so high in his favour that he would have wronged most men before him.

Adieu, brethren, both very dear to me. May the Lord be always present with you, to guide and watch over you.—Amen. I was more tedious than I imagined on Saturday. For I did not wish to give [the letter] to Latern just when I had it ready. But, having striven in vain to reconcile him to his wife, I sent them both away, not without considerable displeasure.—
Yours, JOHN CALVIN.

Normandie especially salutes you. Your other friends do the same. We have some here at present, by no means our friends. Maréchal de la Mark, the Duc de Nemours,[1] and too great a host of that sort. They will decamp a short while before dinner.

[*Lat. orig. autogr.—Library of Gotha.* Vol. 404, p. 10.]

## CCLXVIII.—To FAREL.

State of religion in England—Calvin's literary labours—arrival of Robert Stephens at Geneva.

GENEVA, 15*th November* 1550.

As for the circumstances of the English king, I simply charged Hugo to inform you, that the success of the Gospel in that country was highly gratifying. The French and the Germans are allowed to adopt the plain and simple mode of administering the sacraments, practised by us. So well disposed was the King himself to religious matters, that he showed some kindness even to me. But as you will learn all this better from the letter of Utenhoven, I shall not add more.[2] I had

---

[1] Two of the keenest adversaries of the Reformation in France.

[2] See note 2, p. 269. Having left Strasbourg at the same time as Bucer and Fagius, John Utenhoven went to London, where he resided for many years before going to exercise the ministry in Poland. See his correspondence with Bullinger, (1549-1554,) *Zurich Letters*, first series, toms. i. and ii.

hardly any communication with the other brother, for having gone out of the church with him, I met by accident the syndic Corné, with whom I walked on, and while doing so, the worthy man slipped away, and did not again make his appearance. I am afraid he may have taken it amiss that I neglected him for the syndic. But you can easily excuse the thing, although an excuse is hardly needed. But to return to England. You will gather from the same source certain other things, of one of which, I must truly confess, I can by no means approve ; viz., that John Laski can be so much influenced by the slightest breezes of court favour ; I fear its winds will drive him in all directions.[1] I have not as yet made bold to stir up the King himself. As certain parties have repeatedly urged me,[2] I have at last resolved upon dedicating Isaiah to him ; and as I thought there would be room enough for an overplus, I intend adding to it a second work, viz., the *Canonical Epistles*, which was conjoined with the former, and which will be out at the same time. I shall accordingly inscribe his name on both works.[3]

In truth, that on the Acts and on Genesis, of which you remind me, can scarcely be said to have any existence yet. I am ashamed of my slow progress with the Acts ; and the third part which has been completed will, I expect, make a large volume. I was compelled to lay Genesis aside for some time. The revisal of the New Testament has kept me busy for four months past. I am dragged reluctantly into a considerable part of the Old Testament also. I had reminded our printers, in time, to select persons for themselves who, unlike me, were fit for and would undertake the work. They have

---

[1] John Laski, (Joannes a Lasco,) a Polish nobleman, devoted to the cause of the Reformation, who had preached successively in Poland, in Germany, and in England. In the reign of Edward VI. he rose to great favour in the latter country, and was appointed superintendent of the congregation of foreign Protestants in London.—*Zurich Letters*, first series, tom. i. p. 187.

[2] " I am glad your Commentary on Isaiah, and also the Canonical Epistles, are designed for our king ; and I do not doubt but that, even from your letter to him, very considerable benefit will accrue to the English king."—Utenhoven to Calvin. Paris MSS. *Recueil Historique de France*, tom. xix.

[2] See Calvin's letter to the King of England, of January 1551.

not attended to my hint, and so their neglect is now my punishment. I have got Louis de Budé[1] to undertake David, Solomon, and the history of Job, but as he will assist me only with his own labour, he will not entirely rid me of annoyance. I have rolled over the Apocrypha on Beza. What could I do? Many are wanting Bibles to themselves, and it is long since there was a single copy to be had. There is no one to undertake the burden, so the horse's housings fall to the ox. Some time has been expended also on the French version of the treatise *De Scandalis*. But I am annoying you to no purpose with these trifles; and, in truth, if I had to give you a reason for so doing, I could only deal in absurdities. I can truly affirm this, however, that it was not without shame that I read that part of your letter in which you laud my industry, being abundantly conscious of my own sloth and tardiness. May the Lord enable me, creeping along gradually, to be in some manner useful. . . . .

I have not received a letter from Bucer for a long time. What Vergerio is doing I know not, except that he wrote me from Zurich, with certain reasons for not returning at once to his own church. My only fear is that he will have enough to do, as you know the restless disposition of those people. Robert Stephens[2] is now entirely ours, and we shall soon hear what storms his departure has raised at Paris. The retiring philo-

---

[1] Louis de Budé, Sieur de la Motte, brother of John de Budé, was particularly versed in Oriental languages, of which he was made professor at Geneva, a short time after his arrival in that town. He died in 1552. We have of his a *Psautier traduit de l'Hebreu en Français*. 8vo. Geneva, 1550.

[2] The celebrated printer Robert Stephens, a man of the purest reputation, who lived in an age which failed to recognise his genius, and which rewarded his labours with ingratitude. Having become odious to the clergy by his beautiful editions of the Bible, and by his desire for reform, and but ill protected by the King of France against the vexations of the Sorbonne, he resolved to quit his country and remove his presses to Geneva, whither the printer Crespin had already preceded him. He arrived there towards the end of the year 1550, with his son Henry, who afterwards shed a new lustre on the name of Stephens. He publicly embraced the cause of the Reformation, together with the members of his family, and honoured his adopted country by the publication of various works of antiquity, both sacred and profane. Made a burgess of Geneva in 1556, he lived in constant intimacy with Calvin and Beza, until his death in 1559.—Senebier, *Hist. Litt.*, pp. 355, 356; Haag, *France Protestante*, Art. Estienne.

sophers will doubtless be quite insane.¹ If the Lord will, I shall pay you a visit early in spring, since I did not go during the last vintage season, which I hoped, and particularly desired, to do. My colleagues, Normandie and his sister, one of the Budés, who is here, (for John has gone to France for his father-in-law), Trier, one of the Colladons—all, salute you most lovingly and cordially ; so do very many others. Present my best regards to my countryman Christopher, to Michael Faton, and to your own family ; nor do I wish to forget Mirabeau. Be not surprised that the sea of Scandals is wellnigh drunk up by the draughts I have taken of it. Be it known, also, that I was afraid to attempt exhausting it, lest I should drain it dry. May the Lord preserve you long in safety, and may He ever bless your labours.—Yours,

JOHN CALVIN.

[*Lat. orig. autogr.—Library of Geneva.* Vol. 107, *a.*]


## CCLXIX.—To MONSIEUR DE FALAIS.²

*Misconduct of a servant of M. de Falais.*

*This 24th of December* (1550.)

MONSEIGNEUR,—I thank you in the name of all, for the trouble you have been pleased to take in helping us, if perchance the bad business which has been going on underhand can be set right.³ I find, however, that the examination will not be sufficient to enable us to get to the bottom of it. We have of course forbidden all intercourse for the future between the young man and that unhappy woman. But it will be a

---

¹ In allusion to a tolerably numerous party in France, who, on receiving the Gospel, believed they might remain united in external communion with the Romish Church, and escape persecution by an apparent adhesion to its dogmas.

² After leaving Bâle, and his establishment at Geneva, (July 1548). This seigneur lived in the village of Veigy, situated several leagues from the city, between Hermance and Les Voirons.

³ In allusion to the misconduct of a servant of Monsieur de Falais.

more difficult matter to bring home to their consciences their past misdeeds. Indeed there is but one witness who depones that the brother was incensed at it. Now he denies that he had ever perceived it at all.

Yesterday I was called away from the consistory by some extraordinary business, so that I could not see how they dealt with this gallant. And my brethren are at this moment taken up with the *Visitation*,[1] whither indeed I must also go. However, I hope that what we have got will serve very well to make a beginning. I shall, if it please God, let you know of any shortcoming, by word of mouth, humbly thanking you for your so liberal entertainment, although I feel always assured of your good-will, even had you not said a word to me about it.

Wherefore, Monseigneur, being constrained to conclude, I beseech our good Lord to have you in His holy keeping, and to guide you by His Spirit, as seemeth good to Him, for the glory of His name by you even unto the end. I hope that He will vouchsafe us grace to celebrate the Supper together, although we must be locally separate. And so I commend me to the kind favour of yourself and of Madame.

Your humble brother and servant,

JOHN CALVIN.

[*Fr. orig. autogr.—Library of Geneva.* Vol. 194.]

---

[1] We read in the MS. Chronicle of Michael Roset, lib. v. chap. 27, "By advice of the ministers, April 3, 1550, it was enacted, that an annual visitation be maintained from house to house, for the examination of men and women as to their faith, in order to discern between the ignorant, and hardened sinners, and true Christians, which in time has wrought great benefit."

## CCLXX.—To Haller.[1]

Explanations on the subject of the abolition of the great festivals at Geneva.

GENEVA, *2d January* 1551.

I desire you, my dear Haller, not to measure my affection for you by my not writing to you and to our friend Musculus, of late, to lighten the domestic affliction under which you both laboured.[2] There is no need for my occupying many words in expressing how anxious I was about your danger, from the time that I heard of your houses being visited by the plague. But as this remembrance should not be more pleasing to kind-hearted and considerate men than the duty of writing, I trust that when I inform you that my silence did not by any means arise from neglect, I shall fully satisfy you both. The reason why I did not write you is this: a report lately reached this place regarding your calamity, but I could not accurately ascer-

---

[1] See the notice, p. 235.

In a reaction, perhaps exaggerated, against the practices of the Romish Church, the magistrates of Geneva were led to adopt a measure which made a great noise among the Swiss Protestants. While Berne and Zurich celebrated the four great feasts of the year, according to the ancient Catholic custom, the Genevese abolished the week-day feasts, and kept nothing but the Sabbath. This measure, in which Calvin had no hand whatever, and of which he, in some degree, even disapproved, was made nevertheless the subject of very violent personal declamations against him. Some even accused him of wishing to abolish the Sabbath. In letters to his friends, Haller, Bullinger, and some others, he thought it his duty to represent the true character of the reform effected at Geneva, and his real relation to it. He had little difficulty in obtaining the approbation of Bullinger, who replied to him in these words: "You have just given the answer which I expected, my dear brother. For I know that in matters of that sort, where duty is but little heeded, and much ill-will is engendered, you have never been morose. I am anxious, indeed, in such matters, to see that liberty preserved, which I perceive to have flourished in the churches from the very days of the apostles." . . .—Calvini *Opera,* tom. ix. p. 63.

[2] The plague, which had cut off Hedio, the pious minister at Strasbourg, made great ravages at Berne during the same year. It entered the houses of Wolfgang Musculus, and of John Haller, although they escaped themselves. A great number of the ministers of the Church of Berne sunk under the attacks of this awful scourge.—Ruchat, tom. v. p. 470. The *Chronique* of Haller, cited by Hottinger.

tain the extent of its progress. Accordingly, I did not venture to take any active measures; I preferred having recourse to prayer; this I knew both to be more necessary for you, and to be desired by you. Besides, the abolition of the feast-days here has given grievous offence to some of your people, and it is likely enough that much unpleasant talk has been circulating among you. I am pretty certain, also, that I get the credit of being the author of the whole matter, both among the malevolent and the ignorant. But as I can solemnly testify that it was accomplished without my knowledge, and without my desire, so I resolved from the first rather to weaken malice by silence, than be over-solicitous about my defence. Before I ever entered the city, there were no festivals but the Lord's day. Those celebrated by you were approved of by the same public decree by which Farel and I were expelled ; and it was rather extorted by the tumultuous violence of the ungodly, than decreed according to the order of law. Since my recall, I have pursued the moderate course of keeping Christ's birth-day as you are wont to do. But there were extraordinary occasions of public prayer on other days; the shops were shut in the morning, and every one returned to his several calling after dinner. There were, however, in the meanwhile, certain inflexible individuals who did not comply with the common custom from some perverse malice or other. Diversity would not be tolerated in a rightly constituted church : even for citizens not to live on good terms with one another, would beget mistrust among strangers. I exhorted the Senate to remove this disagreement in future by a proper remedy. And indeed I lauded, at the same time, in express terms, the moderation which they had hitherto exercised. I afterwards heard of the abrogation, just as a perfect stranger would. Would that N.[1] had acted less ambitiously on former occasions! For feast-days might have been abolished in that entire province. In order that those four might return to their old condition and former privileges, he contended as keenly against all the French-speaking pastors

---

[1] Ruchat, who reproduces this letter, (tom. v. p. 441,) considers that the name here suppressed is that of Pierre Kontzen, a minister of Berne, who presided, in 1538, at the Synod of Lausanne.

as if he had been acting for the good of the Church. You would have said that Victor was doing battle with the Orientals in behalf of his Easter. When I once asked him why circumcision had a right to more honour than the death of Christ, he was compelled to be silent. But let us forget the past. I am satisfied with having indicated briefly the cause of so sudden a change among us. Although I have neither been the mover nor instigator to it, yet since it has so happened, I am not sorry for it. And if you knew the state of our Church as well as I do, you would not hesitate to subscribe to my judgment. Let me say this, however, that if I had got my choice, I should not have decided in favour of what has now been agreed upon. Yet there is no reason why men should be so much provoked, if we use our liberty as the edification of the Church demands; just as, on the contrary, it is not fair to take a prejudice against our custom.

Adieu, very excellent Sir and brother, deserving of my hearty regard. Salute your colleagues, I pray you, and Mr. Nicolas Zerkinden, in my name. My brethren salute you and those aforementioned, very heartily. May the Lord by His Spirit rule over you, preserve you, and bless you in all things. Amen.

JOHN CALVIN.

[*Calv. Lat. Corresp.* Opera, tom. ix. p. 62.]


## CCLXXI.—To RICHARD LE FEVRE.[1]

*Explanations regarding various points of doctrine in dispute between the Romish and the Reformed Churches.*

GENEVA, 19*th January* 1551.

MY DEAR BROTHER,—As God has called you to give testimony to His Gospel, never doubt that He will strengthen you

[1] Richard Le Fèvre, a native of Rouen, one of the martyrs of the Reformed Church of Lyons. Seized in that town in 1551, and condemned to death, he appealed thence to the Parliament of Paris, and was delivered *in transitu* by some unknown friends. Surprised, two years afterwards, at Grenoble, he was brought back to the dungeons of Lyons, saw his first sentence confirmed by the Parliament of Paris, and went cheerfully to the stake the 7th July 1554. He

in the might of His Spirit ; and that, as He has already begun, so He must needs perfect His work, manifesting Himself victorious in you against His enemies. It is true that the triumphs of Jesus Christ are despised by the world : for while we are under reproach, the wicked are glorifying themselves in their pride, but yet are they still confounded by the power of that truth which God has put into our mouth, and our hearts are also strengthened to obtain the victory over Satan and all his supporters, while looking for the day when the glory of God shall be fully revealed, to the confusion of the wicked and of the unbelieving. All that you have felt and experienced, up to the present moment, of the abounding goodness of God, ought to confirm you in the assured hope, that He shall not fail you in the future ; meanwhile, however, pray Him that He would make you understand always better and better what a treasure there is in that doctrine for which you contend, so that in comparison thereof you may not esteem even your life to be precious. Have always, besides, your eyes lifted up on high to that kind Lord Jesus, who will be your surety, seeing that you are only persecuted for His name. Think upon that immortal glory which He has purchased for us, to the end that you may be able to endure in patience the afflictions wherein you are. Beseech this kind Lord continually that He would give you such an issue as He has promised to all who are His own, and that according as He has thought fit to try your faith, so He would cause you to experience the strength of His promises. And that as He is the Father of Light, He would enlighten you to such a degree, that all the thick fumes which the wicked raise up before you, may not be able to dim your eyesight, and that all their quirks and cautions may not be able to darken your

wrote on the 3d of May to Calvin,—"The present is to let you know, that I hope to go to keep Whitsuntide in the kingdom of heaven, and to be present at the marriage of the Son of God, . . . . if I am not sooner called away by this good Lord and Master, whose voice I am ready to obey, when He shall say, Come, ye blessed of my Father, possess the kingdom which has been prepared for you before the foundation of the world."—(The original autograph letter, *Library of Geneva*, Vol. 109.) During his first captivity at Lyons, Richard Le Fèvre had consulted Calvin on some points of doctrine, and had received pious exhortations from him regarding them.

understanding, that you should ever lose sight of the true Sun of Righteousness, who is the very Son of God.

When you have to reply to arguments, you do well to answer in all simplicity, speaking according to the measure of your faith, even as it is written: *I have believed, therefore I shall speak.* True it is, that all those subtilties which they conceit themselves to have, are nought else but silly twaddle; but rest you content with what God has imparted to you of the knowledge of Himself, so as to bear clear testimony unfeignedly to the truth. For however they may sneer at it, it will be as a thunderbolt of confusion to them, when they hear nothing but what is founded upon God and His Word. Besides, you know who it is that has promised to give a mouth and wisdom to His own, which His adversaries shall not be able to withstand. Ask of Him that He may guide you, according to what He shall know to be good. They will not cease for all that to hold you convicted of heresy; but it has been ever thus with all the apostles and prophets, and with all the martyrs. The clerk of court will only write what suits his own pleasure, but your confession will not fail to be recorded before God and His angels, and He will make it profitable to His own as is best for them.

I shall mention briefly some points upon which they have endeavoured to trouble you. In order to persuade you that we are not justified by the grace of God alone, they have alleged that Zacharias and several others are called just. Well, you must consider how God has accepted them as such. If on inquiry you find that it is on account of His own free grace in pardoning all that might have been charged against them, and not imputing to them their faults and vices, behold merit entirely excluded; for in saying that faith alone in Christ justifies us, we understand in the first place that we are all of us accursed, and that there is nothing in us but sin; and that we are neither able to think, nor to do any good, except in so far as God governs us by His Holy Spirit, as members of the body of His Son. Furthermore, that even when God vouchsafes us the grace to walk in His fear, we are very far from discharging ourselves of our duty. Now, it is written: Whosoever shall not fulfil all whatsoever is commanded, shall be cursed; and therefore we have no other refuge but to the blood of our Lord Jesus Christ, who cleanses and washes us in the sacrifice of His death, which is our sanctification. Thus God also accepts as well-pleasing the good works which we perform in His strength, although they must always be tainted with some shortcomings. And so in this way, whosoever thinks to rest upon his own merits, will find himself as it were suspended in the air, to be driven about of every wind. In short, those who think to merit anything, would fain make God their debtor, whereas we must hold everything of His pure bounty. We shall be rich and abounding in merits, if in Jesus Christ: while we are strangers to His grace, we need not think to have one drop of good in us. If the enemies bring forward the word wages, let it not trouble you, for God gives wages to His own, although they are in nowise worthy of them; but inasmuch as he accepts the service which HE has enabled them to render, having consecrated them in the blood of His Son Jesus Christ, on purpose that they may derive all their value from thence. Wherefore, the wages which God promises to His faithful ones, presupposes the remission of their sins, and the privilege they have of being supported as His children. And in truth this word, justification, implies that God holds us as just, and therefore loves us, the which we obtain by faith alone: for Jesus Christ is the sole cause of our salvation. It is true that St. James takes another signification, when he says, *that works help faith for our justification;* for he means to prove by the effect that we are justified: neither does he not dispute at all in regard to the foundation of our salvation, and wherein our confidence must be placed, but only how the true faith is known, so that no one may make mistakes in regard to it, glorifying himself in the empty name. Should they return to you with further importunity on this point, I hope God will furnish you wherewithal to overcome them.

Concerning the intercession of the Virgin Mary and departed saints, come back always to this principle, that it is not for us to appoint advocates in paradise, but for God, who has ordained Jesus Christ a single one for all. Also, that our prayers ought to be offered up in faith, and therefore ordered by the Word of God, as saith St. Paul in Romans x. Now, it is certain, that throughout the Word of God there is not a single syllable of what they say ; wherefore all their prayers are profane and displeasing to Him. If they further reply to you, that it is not forbidden to us, the answer is easy : that it is forbidden to us to set about anything according to our own proper fancy, yea, in matters of far less moment ; but above all, that prayer is a most high privilege, and too sacred to be directed according to our fantasy. Nay more, they cannot deny that their having recourse to the saints arises from pure distrust that Jesus Christ alone would be sufficient for them.

As for their continual reply, that the charity of the saints is not diminished, the answer is easy : that charity is regulated and limited by what God requires from each individual. Now, he desires that the living exercise themselves in prayer for one another. Of the departed there is no mention made, and in such important matters we must imagine nothing out of our own brain, but keep to what is told us in Scripture.

In regard to what the adversaries allege, that it is said in Genesis that the name of Abraham and Isaac was to be invoked after their decease, true it is that the text runs thus; but it is pure absurdity to bring it forward for the present purpose. That is written in the forty-eighth chapter of Genesis, where it is said, that Jacob in blessing Ephraim and Manasseh, the sons of Joseph, prayed to God that the names of his fathers Abraham and Isaac, and his own, may be called upon these two lads, as on the heads of the tribes lineally descended from himself. Now, that is as much as if he had said, that they were to be reputed and reckoned as being of the number of the twelve tribes, and that they should form two heads of tribes, as if they had been his children in the first degree ; as also that they were born in Egypt. He binds them together by his prayer to the lineage which God had blessed and sanctified, because at that time they were separate, according to outward appearance. And so that form of expression signifies nothing more than the bearing of the name of Abraham, and being owned as of his lineage, as it is said in chap. iv. of Isaiah, that the name of the husband is called upon the wife, inasmuch as the wife is under the shadow and guidance of her husband.

So far as they bring forward Saint Ignatius, you do not require much of an answer. There is one passage where he says: *That Jesus Christ stands for him instead of all ancestry.* Arm yourself then with that single word, to bring them back to the pure doctrine of the Gospel.

Because I have made use of that expression against the Papists, they take advantage of it to say, that I approve and value the book whence it is taken. Now, that you may not be deceived thereby, I assure you, that it contains such a heap of silly folly, that the monks of the present day could not write greater nonsense. But seeing that you are not acquainted with the Latin tongue, and still less with the Greek in which Saint Ignatius has written, (if indeed we have anything which is truly his,) you need not enter upon this question. Be content to answer them, that you can never go wrong while following Jesus Christ, who is the Light of the world. As for the early doctors, those who are better read in their writings will be able to tell them quite enough to stop their mouths. Let it be enough for you to possess the assurance of true faith in the Word of Jesus Christ alone, which can neither fail you, nor deceive. And it is even thither that all the early doctors send them, protesting that they have no wish to be believed, excepting in so far as what they speak shall be found conformable to what is taught us of God, and which is contained in His Word.

On the subject of the Sacrament of the Supper, when they speak to you about transubstantiation, you have a ready answer: that all those passages which they bring together, even if they could be taken in the sense which they adduce, cannot be applied to the mass. For, when it is said, *This is my body and my blood,* it is also then and there added, *Take, eat ye, and drink ye all of this cup.* Now, among them, there is but one who eats the whole; and even at Easter, he gives but a part of it to the people. But there is even yet a sorer evil, that instead of what Jesus Christ said,—*Take;* they presume to offer a sacrifice, which was to be unique and of perpetual efficacy. And, besides, in order to have some help from these words, they ought to maintain the observance of the Supper, which they do not. Moreover, you can always protest, that you do not deny that Jesus Christ gives us His body, provided that we look for it from heaven. In reply to all the cavils which they may allege, you have only to declare to them that which you have seen and heard, well knowing that it is from God you have it; for our faith would be very slender indeed, if it were founded only upon men. There is nothing better, then, than continually to meditate the doctrine wherein lies the true substance of our Christianity, so that in due time and place, you may be able to manifest that you have not believed in vain. And as I have said from the beginning, if the enemies of the truth are stirred by their ambition to contend, manifest on your part, that it is enough for you that you glorify God in opposing their tricks and sophistries. Content yourself with having for your buckler a simple confession of that which God has imprinted upon your heart. Least of all need you torment yourself, if they deal in impudent calumnies against me or others, seeing that they have leave to speak evil without rhyme or reason. Let us bear patiently all the reproaches and slanders which they cast upon us; for we are not better than Saint Paul, who tells us that we must walk in the midst of false accusing and vituperation. Provided we do what is right, when they speak evil concerning us, we may bear it with unconcern. Besides, when they lay fresh calumnies upon us, we may well render thanksgiving to God, that we have a clear conscience in His sight and before men, and that we are free from all suspicion of evil. And on the other hand, albeit that we are wretched sinners, so full of wretchedness and poverty, that we groan by reason of it continually; still He does not permit the wicked to speak evil of us, unless falsely; yea, to condemn them from their own mouth, of having invented regarding us that which they had not very far to search for, inasmuch as it is in themselves. Let us therefore glory in the grace of God with all humility, when we see that these poor unhappy men, like drunkards, glory in their shame. If you are vexed to hear them speak evil thus deceitfully concerning me, you ought to be far more deeply grieved to hear them blaspheme against our Saviour and Master, to whom belongs all honour, since, making full account of all the innocence which shall ever be in us, we might well be overwhelmed in utter confusion.

Meanwhile, comfort yourself in our Almighty God, who has vouchsafed us the grace to knit us together so entirely with His Son, that all the devils of hell, and all the wicked of the world, can never be able to separate us. Rejoice, therefore, that you uphold His quarrel, with a good conscience, hoping that He will strengthen you to bear whatsoever it shall please Him you should suffer. We have such remembrance of you in our prayers, as we ought to have, in beseeching the God of all grace, that seeing it has pleased Him to employ you in the maintenance of His truth, He would vouchsafe you all that is needful for the discharge of so honourable a service; that He would strengthen you in true perseverance; that He would give you true spiritual truth, so as that you may seek only the advancement of His name, without regard to self; and that He would show Himself your protector in such wise, that you may feel it to your own consolation, and that others also may take knowledge of it for their edification. All the brethren hereabouts salute you in the Lord, rejoicing greatly that He has wrought so powerfully in you, having also compassion on you in your captivity, and desiring that it may please this gracious God to unfold His goodness and mercy upon you.

Your brother in our Lord,

JOHN CALVIN.

[*Fr.*—Printed in *Histoire des Martyrs*, Edit. of 1597, lib. v. p. 265.]

## CCLXXII.—To Viret.

Various particulars—literary labours of Theodore Beza.

Geneva, 24*th* *January* 1551.

I send you a reading of three letters, that I may not be any longer in your debt. For, Toussain commends himself to your prayers, and Farel is desirous of your advice, so I thought that you would be interested in the letters of both. I wished you to know also what answer Haller gave me. I am glad that he received me with such moderation, because of the harsh violence with which many attack me. But more of all this when I shall see you. You cannot believe how much I am displeased with the present state of our republic. Indeed, it would be more proper at present to call it an *oligarchy*. Accordingly, familiar conversation is not necessary for the discussion of those matters. Farel had written me before, that the Synod was to meet on the fifth of March. He seems to be wishing advice at present regarding a new day [of meeting]. I have written to him, however, to abide by the day already agreed upon, if he wishes me to be present.[1] John Laski salutes you all. I perceive now that I have been twice deceived by Florian. For he had false letters of recommendation, which he made use of. Excuse me to our friend Beza for not writing him at present. He may take his own way with the Apocrypha, but I have forewarned him that there will be a greater saving, if he undertakes a new version of it. If he has any of the Psalms done, they need not be waiting for company.[2] Request him, therefore, to send some of them, at least, by the first messenger. I shall write to Vergerio and the Zurichers by and by. In the meantime, if you can find a trustworthy messenger, you will

---

[1] In an assembly which met at Neuchatel on the 14th of March 1551, the number of individuals who should compose the Consistory was fixed, and a collection of regulations regarding marriage were drawn out.

[2] The Translation of the Psalms begun by Clement Marot, was continued by Theodore Beza, who obtained, during this same year, the authority of the Council of Geneva for the publication of a part of his work.

attend to the letter to Bernardin. Adieu, most excellent brother, together with your wife and family. Kind regards to the brethren. May the Lord keep you all, and guide you by His Spirit.—Yours,

JOHN CALVIN.

[*Lat. orig. autogr.—Library of Geneva.* Vol. 107, a.]


## CCLXXIII.—To the King of England.[1]

*He exhorts him to persevere in the work of the Reformation in his kingdom—enumeration of abuses, ceremonies, ecclesiastical elections—universities.*

FROM GENEVA, (*January* 1551.)

SIRE,—If I must excuse myself towards your Majesty for having used the boldness to dedicate these books which I now present to you, I would need to find an advocate to speak a word for me. For so far would my letter be from having credit enough to do that, that it would even stand in need of a fresh excuse. And, indeed, as I never should have taken upon me to address the Commentaries to you which I have published with your name, neither should I have ventured now to write to you, but for the confidence I had already conceived, that both would be well received. For inasmuch as, holding me to be among the number of those who are zealous for the advance-

---

[1] Edward VI., son of Henry VIII. and Jane Seymour, King of England, born in 1537, died, in his sixteenth year, the 8th of July 1553. Gifted with a precocious strength of reason, and a lively sensibility, instructed in the ancient languages and foreign literature, this young prince did not live long enough to realize the hopes to which his accession to the throne had given birth. " His virtues," says the historian Hume, " had made him an object of tender affection to the public. He possessed mildness of disposition, application to study and business, a capacity to learn and judge, and an attachment to equity and justice." Devotional reading had a particular attraction for this prince, who was heartily devoted to the cause of the Reformation. Calvin dedicated two of his commentaries to him : *Joannis Calvini Commentarii in Iesaiam Prophetam, Eduardo VI., Angliæ Regi,* 8 *Cal. Januarii* 1551." " *Joannis Calvini Commentarii in Epistolas Canonicas.*" The dedication of the first of these commentaries (25th December 1550,) furnishes us the date of the letter of Calvin, written in the month of January 1551, and brought to the King by the minister, Nicolas des Gallars.

ment of the kingdom of the Son of God, you have not disdained to read what I did not specially present to your Majesty, I have thought, that if, while serving Jesus Christ my Master, I could likewise testify to the reverence and singular affection which I bear you, I could not fail to find a kind and courteous acceptance.

Moreover, Sire, holding myself assured that my letter will have such a reception from you as I desire, I shall not hesitate to pray and beseech you in the name of Him to whom you ascribe all authority and power, to take courage in following out what you have so well and happily begun, as well in your own person as in the state of your kingdom; namely, the consecration of all to God and to our blessed Saviour, who has so dearly purchased us. For as regards general reformation, it is not yet so well established, as that it should be wise to look on it as achieved. And, in fact, it would be very difficult to purge in a day such an abyss of superstition as there is in the papacy. Its root is too deep, and has expanded itself too widely, to get so soon to the bottom of it. But whatsoever difficulties or delays there may be, the excellency of the work is well worthy of unwearying pursuit.

I have no doubt, Sire, but Satan will put many hindrances in the way before you to slacken your pace, and to make your zeal grow cold. Your subjects, for the most part, do not know the blessing which you procure for them. The great, who are raised to honour, are sometimes too wise in their own conceits to make much account of the world, far less to look to God at all. And new and unexpected conflicts arise daily. Now I hope, indeed, Sire, that God has stored you with such greatness and constancy of mind, that you will neither be weakened nor wearied by all that. But the thing itself is of so great importance, that it well deserves that one should apply to it far more than human strength and energy. And then, after all, when we shall have striven to the very uttermost, there will always remain more waiting to be done.

We see how, in the time of the good king Josiah, who has the special testimony of the Holy Spirit, that he approved himself a prince excellent in faith, in zeal, and in all godliness, nevertheless, the Prophet Zephaniah shows, that there was still some remainder of bygone superstitions, yea, even in the town of Jerusalem. Even so, however you may labour with your Council, Sire, you will find it very difficult completely to uproot all the mischief which would well deserve to be corrected. But this ought to be a great confirmation to animate and spur you on ; and even if you should not accomplish all that could be desired, it is a very sufficient consolation to you when you hear that the pains which this good king took, is a service pleasing to God, insomuch that the Holy Spirit magnifies the reformation effected by him, as if nothing more had been desired. Let me entreat you then, Sire, to reach forward to the mark which is set before you in the example of this godly king, that you may have the honour, not only of having overthrown impieties which are clearly repugnant to the honour and service of God, but also of having abolished and rased to the ground, whatsoever served merely to nourish superstition. For when God would praise as with an open mouth the faithful princes who have restored and again set up the purity of His service, He expressly adds this word, that they have also *taken away the high places*, that the memory of foolish devotions might be utterly obliterated.

True it is, Sire, that there are things indifferent which one may allowably tolerate. But then we must always carefully insist that simplicity and order be observed in the use of ceremonies, so that the clear light of the Gospel be not obscured by them, as if we were still under the shadows of the law ; and then that there may be nothing allowed that is not in agreement and conformity to the order established by the Son of God, and that the whole may serve and be suited to the edification of the Church. For God does not allow His name to be trifled with, —mixing up silly frivolities with His holy and sacred ordinances. Then there are manifest abuses which cannot be endured, such as prayer for the souls of the departed, of putting forward to God the intercession of saints in our prayers, as also of joining them to God in invocation. I do not doubt, Sire, that you are aware that these are so many corruptions of true Christianity. I beseech you, in the name of God, that you may please look to that matter, so that the whole may be restored to a sound and wholesome state.

There is another point, Sire, of which you ought to take a special charge, namely, that the poor flocks may not be destitute of pastors. Ignorance and barbarism have lain so heavy on this accursed popery, that it is not easy to obtain all at once men fit and duly qualified to discharge that office. Notwithstanding, the object is well worth pains, and that your officers, Sire, should have an eye upon it, as they ought. Without that, all the good and holy ordinances which you can make, will scarce avail for the reformation of the heart in good earnest.

Further, inasmuch as the schools contain the seeds of the ministry, there is much need to keep them pure and thoroughly free from all ill weeds. I speak thus, Sire, because in your universities, it is commonly said, there are many young people supported on the college bursaries, who, instead of giving good hope of service in the Church, rather show an inclination to do mischief, and to ruin it, not even concealing that they are opposed to the true religion. Wherefore, Sire, I beseech you anew, in the name of God, that you may please to take order therein, to the effect, that property which ought to be held sacred, be not converted to profane uses, and far less to nourish venomous reptiles, who would desire nought better than to infect everything for the future. For, in this way, the Gospel would always be kept back by these schools, which ought to be the very pillars thereof.

Meanwhile, Sire, all honest hearts praise God, and feel themselves greatly obliged to you, that it hath pleased you of your favour to grant churches to your subjects who use the French and German languages.[1] In so far as regards the use of the

---

[1] The privilege granted by King Edward VI. to the Church of the foreign Protestants instituted at London 1550. The royal patent was thus expressed:—
"Considering that it is the duty of a Christian prince well to administer the affairs of his kingdom, to provide for relig on, and for the unhappy exiles, afflicted and banished by reason thereof, we would have you to know, that having compassion of the condition of those who have for some considerable time past been domiciled in our kingdom, and come there daily, of our special grace . . . will and ordain that henceforward they may have in our city of London a church, to be

Sacraments, and spiritual order, I hope that the permission which you have been pleased to confer upon them will bear fruit. Howbeit, Sire, I cannot help beseeching you once more, feeling so deeply how needful it is, not only that you would secure the rest and contentment of the godly who desire to serve God and to live peaceably in obedience to you, but also that you would restrain vagabond and dissolute people, should such withdraw into your kingdom.

I know well, Sire, that you have people of distinguished learning at hand, who can make known to you these things by word of mouth, far better than myself by writing ; also, that in your council you have men of prudence and zeal to suggest all that is expedient. Among the others, I have no doubt that Monsieur the Duke of Somerset spares no trouble to follow out that wherein he has employed himself so faithfully hitherto. But I believe, Sire, that all that, shall be no hindrance to prevent your kind reception of what you will recognise as proceeding from a like source.

To conclude, Sire, forasmuch as I fear to have already wearied you with my tediousness, I pray you, in respect of that as in everything else, that you would please excuse and pardon me of your kind favour, to which very humbly I beg to be commended, having besought our gracious God and Father to maintain and uphold you in His holy protection, to guide you by His Spirit, and to cause His name to be more and more glorified by you.

JOHN CALVIN.

[*Fr. copy—Library of Geneva.* Vol. 107.]

---

called the Church of the Lord Jesus, where the assembly of the Germans and other strangers can meet and worship, for the purpose of having the Gospel purely interpreted by the ministers of their church, and the Sacraments administered according to the Word of God and the apostolic ordinance."

## CCLXXIV.—To Bullinger.[1]

*He excuses the infrequency of his letters, and urges the publication of the Consensus.*

Geneva, 17*th February* 1551.

Although you readily excuse the fewness of my letters, and even, with your usual courtesy, voluntarily relieve me of that duty, I nevertheless feel ashamed of my exceeding indolence and negligence, in having been less attentive to you than to some of my every-day friends. But indeed the reason of this is, that others, by their violent importunity, shake me free of my listlessness. You, with a more generous indulgence, allow me to be silent; and indeed I am so much exhausted by constant writing, and so greatly broken down by fatigue, that I frequently feel an almost positive aversion to writing a letter. Would that others had as much of your moderation as would enable them to cultivate a sincere friendship at the expense of less writing. Our French friends oppress me in this way beyond all consideration. It so happens, that by continually apologizing, I am getting myself suspected of indolence by my particular friends. Add to this, that unless I have a definite subject before me, I seem to act absurdly enough when I drag in matters known to everybody, as if they were possessed of novelty. But as to what you say you wrote me about some time ago, without receiving any answer, I cannot make out what you refer to, unless as I conjecture, you had sent me some

---

[1] The agreement concluded two years before, between the Churches of Geneva and of Zurich, on the question of the Sacraments, had been a source of joy to all the sober-minded in Switzerland and in Germany, who had deplored the excesses of the sacramental quarrel. But it displeased the intemperate Lutheran party, who accused Calvin of fickleness, and went so far as to charge him with having changed his opinions, and with squaring his doctrine to that of Zuingle, since the defeat of the Protestant party in Germany. This was nothing but a calumny, which is removed by a comparison of the previous writings of Calvin upon the Supper, with the formula drawn up under his care, and which he was desirous should be published at Zurich.—Ruchat, tom. v. p. 379.

communication which did not reach me. If such be the case, I shall not neglect to look after it, now that you have given me the hint. As certain individuals of a malignant, morose, and ill-natured disposition, are making an ado about our union, I should, if agreeable to you, wish it to be published.[1] I have calmly endured, overlooked, and swallowed many things, but, believe me, I have failed to observe that it was greatly displeasing to Satan. If the form of the union is published, I trust it will be useful to the Churches of Saxony. However, you will, with your accustomed sagacity, determine upon what is best. When numbers were asking for copies of it, I would on no account allow it to be printed, until I should obtain your permission. I wrote you about the matter on a previous occasion, but inferred from your silence that you considered it as yet premature. I should wish, however, that you would give me your judgment on it. You did me a favour concerning the Bull. Had I received it two days earlier, it would have been of more use to me. For I had already entered upon the composition of the preface, in which that subject is discussed. I send you a copy of it, if you can find time to read it. I wish, however, that you would send it to Vergerio, together with the letter, at your earliest opportunity. The Bull is possessed of one merit, viz., that the Pope breathes out downright tyranny without any show of deceit. We must, therefore, as you say, find refuge in prayer. It is said that Germany will have rest this year from internal war, as the Turk is annoying Ferdinand. But as it is the Lord who who quiets all tumults of arms, we should pray Him to put a check, in all other respects, upon the savage madness of our enemies.

Adieu, distinguished Sir, and specially revered brother.

---

[1] Some have erroneously fixed on 1549 as the date of this publication. Delayed by the theologians of Zurich, it was only finished in 1551, under the title—*Consensio mutua in re Sacramentaria ministrorum Tigurinæ Ecclesiæ et D. Joannis Calvini Ministri Genevensis Ecclesiæ.* Zurich, 8vo. Caused by Calvin to be translated into French the following year, this important document figures in the *Recueil des Opuscules,* p. 1137, with a preface by Calvin to the Ministers and Doctors of the Church of Zurich.

Salute your family and your colleagues in my name, and in that of my brethren. May the Lord watch over you, be present with you, and continue to guide you.—Yours,

JOHN CALVIN.

[*Lat. orig. autogr—Coll. of M. Tronchin of Geneva.*]

CCLXXV.—TO BULLINGER.

Thanks for a document—dedication of two commentaries to the King of England—captivity of Bishop Hooper—Movements of the Emperor in Germany.

GENEVA, 12*th March* 1551.

I was met by a messenger bearing your letter, when lately on my way to Neuchatel. After my return home, I received another from a certain Italian, together with the fifth *Decade*.[1] You say by way of apology for sending your books, that you do not do so in order that I may learn from you; for my part, as I am desirous to make my labours beneficial to all good men, so on the other hand, I am glad to profit by the writings of others. And indeed intercourse like this is brotherly, when we know that the gifts of the Spirit are so distributed among us, that no one individual is sufficient for himself. Your gift was, therefore, acceptable to me. The publication of our agreement was the occasion of very much joy, not only to myself, but also to Farel and the rest of the brethren. Would that your letter had reached me fifteen days earlier; for it might have been issued during these days of the Frankfort fair. How seasonable will the publication be for our beloved France; exceedingly useful too, I hope. I finished lately my Commentaries on Isaiah and the Canonical Epistles. I thought proper to dedicate both of them to the King of England.[2] You may have a reading of a copy of one of the prefaces which I sent to Vergerio. I have added a private letter also, in which I have endeavoured to kindle the generous nature of the young man.

[1] Under this title, Bullinger had commenced publishing a series of discourses concerning the principal points of the Christian religion.
[2] See the letter to the king, p. 284.

Meanwhile, we have heard the sad news of Hooper's imprisonment.[1] I was somewhat apprehensive of this long ago. I am now afraid that the bishops, as if victorious, will become much more ferociously insolent. While, therefore, I admire his firmness in refusing the anointing, I had rather he had not carried his opposition so far with respect to the cap and the linen vestment, even although I do not approve of these: I recently recommended this. He has many and powerful adversaries, and I doubt not but they will set themselves violently to crush him. But I trust that the Lord will be with him, especially because, as I am informed, some treacherously oppose him, who in other respects pretend to be favourable to the Gospel. I congratulate you on the tranquil condition of your Church. There are very vile wretches here who cause us no small amount of annoyance and disquiet, who will meet, however, I confidently trust, with the end which they have merited. The plans of the Emperor are a source of concern to many. It is justly calculated to excite suspicion that some of his troops are being transported across the Alps.[2] Should he invade this country, my only comfort is the hope that the Lord will take me away from this miserable life. He will not, meanwhile, neglect his own flock, about which I am especially harassed. Adieu, very distinguished Sir, and most esteemed fellow-minister, together with the brethren; all of whom you will affectionately salute in my name. Des Gallars also particularly salutes you. May the Lord continue to guide you by His Spirit, to protect you with His own hand, and to bless your sacred labours. Amen.

[*Calvin's Lat. Corresp.* Opera, tom. ix. p. 59.]

---

[1] Having returned to England the previous year, and having been appointed Bishop of Gloucester through the patronage of Cranmer, Hooper was imprisoned and suffered a few days of captivity for having refused to wear, at the time of his consecration, the sacerdotal dress then in use in the English Church. See his correspondence with Bullinger, *Zurich Letters*, 1537-1558, tom. i. p. 9; Burnet, vol. i.

[2] After having proscribed the reformed worship in the town of Augsburg, the Emperor took up his quarters at Inspruck, among the valleys of the Tyrol, from which he could keep an eye at once upon the Council of Trent, Germany, and Italy.—Robertson, book x.

## CCLXXVI.—To Bullinger.

*Mention of a letter to the Duke of Somerset—Re-opening of the Council of Trent—symptoms of War in Europe.*

GENEVA, 10*th April* 1551.

I have received two letters from you within these few days, both full of remarkable goodwill towards me, and therefore very agreeable. It is well that God has not only bestowed on us the same desire to incite the English King and his advisers to go on, but has also made our plans so fitly to harmonize.[1] This circumstance will surely have some influence in confirming them. I begin now to look every day for the return of the messenger who carried thither my books with the accompanying letter. As soon as he returns, if he report anything worthy of mention, I shall take care to inform you of it. Meanwhile, I have written to the very illustrious the Duke of Somerset, and have shown him that it is impossible but that the Papists will become more insolent, unless the disagreement regarding the ceremonies be speedily adjusted.[2] I have advised him to extend a hand to Hooper. Whatever the Pope may pretend, I do not think that the Council of Trent is being seriously assembled.[3] The reason for my conjecture is, that the King of

---

[1] Bullinger had presented the King of England with his third and fourth *Decade,* (see note 1, p. 291,) with a long letter, in which he reminds the young king of the duties which he had to fulfil towards his subjects. "This epistle and book were presented to the King by the hands of Hooper, Bishop of Gloucester, personally acquainted with Bullinger, to whom the King declared his good acceptance thereof, and the respect and esteem he had for the reverend author."—Strype, *Memoir,* vol. ii. pp. 390, 394.

[2] The letter here referred to has escaped all our investigations, and appears to be entirely lost.

[3] One of the first acts of the new Pope Julius III. was to decree the re-assembly of the Council of Trent, on the 1st of May 1551. This session, termed the eleventh—eight having been held at Trent and two at Bologna—was without result. The fathers resolved upon fixing that there should not be another assembly until the 1st of September.—Fra Paolo, *Hist. du Concile de Trente,* lib. iv. sect. i.

France commanded all his bishops to make a careful survey, each of his own diocese, and to return completed records of each visitation to the metropolitan bishops within six months; and informed them that it was his intention to hold a general council of the whole kingdom. No mention was made on that occasion of Trent and the Pope. I have no doubt, however, but that there was an understanding between them; namely, that the French King should, to gain the favour of the Pope, by the pretence of a national council dissolve that at Trent. Thoughtful men are of opinion that the flames of war have been kindled in Italy. The Turkish ambassador is at present at the French court to stimulate the king to war. An immense fleet threatens Italy or Spain. The Lord will accordingly so overrule them, as that they will not be so dangerous to the Church. It was not kind of you, when you knew that my course would lie in your direction when on my way to Trent, not to offer lodgings to at least one of us. You perhaps expect a new Bull which will admit us.[1] We are not, however, of the number of those who obtain a place, either from right or custom, or the favour of the Apostolic See. We may accordingly remain at home. Yet there is something for us to do even at home. For Christ furnishes material for labour, and Satan does not permit us to be idle. You will pardon my haste. For when those young Germans offered me their services, they gave me only an hour for writing, and it has almost expired. Adieu, most accomplished Sir, and very dear brother, worthy of my hearty regard. My colleagues respectfully salute you. They and I present kindest salutations to Bibliander, Pellican, and Gualter, and the rest of the brethren. May the Lord preserve you all by His power, direct you by His Spirit, and bless your labours. Our agreement was not so carefully expressed in Latin as I could have wished; but it will soon be printed

---

[1] An invitation to the Council was, in point of fact, addressed by the Pope to the Cantons, with all sorts of flattering words, to induce them to comply. The theologians of Zurich, appointed to draw up a reply, had little difficulty in showing that the Council was not for the advantage of the Swiss, or for the good of religion, and the Reformed Cantons adopted unanimously the conclusions of the theologians, and refused to send deputies to the Council.—Ruchat, tom. v. p. 426.

again. Meantime, I have added a French translation to the Latin, in which you will not find any blunders. Yours truly,

JOHN CALVIN.

[*Calvin's Lat. Corresp.* Opera, tom. ix. p. 60.]

## CCLXXVII.—To VIRET.[1]

Death of Bucer and of Joachim Vadian.

GENEVA, 10*th May* 1551.

Although you have received no letters from me for a considerable time, let me tell you, that you have, on that account, been a source of constant and even anxious thought to me. The grief which I have suffered at the death of Bucer increases my anxiety and fear. I have now again experienced a fresh wound from the death of Vadian, whose labour, although of wide influence, and calculated to be felt throughout the entire Church, was nevertheless of especial use in the state, and of great importance among the Swiss and Grisons in particular. I feel my heart almost like to break when I think of the great loss the church of God has sustained in the death of Bucer. The Lord grant that I may leave in life all those whose death I should mourn, that I may the more joyfully leave the world.

---

[1] The year 1551 was marked by two grievous losses to the reformed churches of Europe. Bucer, overcome by the sorrows of exile, died in England on the 28th of February, and the decease of Joachim Vadian, one of the most brilliant minds of that age, occurred at Saint Gall during the same year. The earliest notice of Bucer's death is to be found in the Journal of King Edward VI. of England:—
"*February* 28th.—The learned man Bucerus died at Cambridge, who was two days after buried in St. Mary's Church, all the whole University, with the whole town, bringing him to the grave, to the number of three thousand persons. Also there was an oration of Mr. Haddon made very elegantly at his death. . ." &c.
—*Zurich Letters*, first series, tom. ii. p. 492. Vadian, cut off in the prime of life, breathed his last in the arms of his friend Kessler, the poet, leaving behind him a name held in deep veneration by his friends and countrymen. Above two thousand of the present inhabitants of Saint Gall claim the honour of being descended from the burgomaster Vadian. See the notice of him given in the present collection, vol. i. p. 451.

Adieu, most excellent brother. May the Lord keep you together with your wife and family. Salute all earnestly in my name.

[JOHN CALVIN.]

[*Calvin's Lat. Corresp.* Opera, tom. ix. p. 60.]


## CCLXXVIII.—To FAREL.

Renewed expressions of regret for the death of Vadian and Bucer—controversies excited by Osiander—numerous migrations to Geneva—commencement of hostilities in Italy.

GENEVA, 15*th June* 1551.

Nicolas[1] has at length returned from England, having been detained for eleven days by head winds, and afterwards tossed about by so severe a tempest, that he scarcely escaped shipwreck. He reports that he was so kindly and affectionately received, that I have good reason to congratulate myself that my labour was spent to the best advantage. After having delivered my letter to the Duke of Somerset, and having said that he had another also for the King, the Duke himself undertook the duty of presenting it, and on the following day set out for the Court. If I am not deceived, the work not only greatly pleased the Royal Council, but also filled the King himself with extraordinary delight. The Archbishop of Canterbury informed me that I could do nothing more useful than to write to the King more frequently. This gave me more pleasure than if I had come to the possession of a great sum of money. In the present state of the kingdom, many things are still to be desired. Among other evils that are incurable until the King shall have attained his majority, there is this one: that all the revenues of the Church are devoured by the nobles, and they are meanwhile hiring for a miserable pittance, worthless men to discharge the duties, or at least occupy the position of pastors. I nevertheless will not cease to goad the whole of them. I did not allude to the death of Bucer, lest I should open my

[1] Nicolas des Gallars.

own wound afresh.¹ For when I reflect how great a loss the Church of God has sustained in the death of this one man, I cannot but feel the deepest anguish. He would have been of great advantage to England. I was expecting more from his future writings, than anything he had hitherto performed. In addition to this, the Church is now destitute of faithful teachers. Vadian had very great influence among the Swiss.² The Lord has taken him away. Osiander is absolutely mad.³ Let us take courage, however, until we shall have finished our course and reached the goal. One thing I fear, that while holding a place among the runners, I may set an example of slowness. Yet I am not a little comforted by this, that you, who have outstripped all others, extend to me so much pardon and mild indulgence. It is sufficient, if not led away by the unsettled wanderings of others, we hold on in the right way; even although some get far ahead of us, and others lag a great way behind. As for our old friend with the new face,⁴ I shall for my part be careful to encourage him, as you urgently advise, and shall give my colleagues a hint to do the same. But believe me, he manifests no sincerity. I surmised from the first what he was wishing to be at. I concealed that I had detected it; kept my hand on it, as it were. He patronizes, as he used to do, persons given over to shameless pleasures. He is in like manner given to defend bad causes. His arrogance and ferocity are in no degree abated. His cohort runs riot more at

---

[1] In a letter to Calvin of the 25th May preceding, Farel gave eloquent expression to his sorrow at the death of Bucer:—" I have at length received the last letter of the pious Bucer. What a spirit! How calmly he sunk down! We must mingle joy with our sorrow, inasmuch as our friend has gone up to God."—Library of Paris. *Recueil Historique de France*, tom. xix.

[2] A man of distinguished learning, an accomplished statesman, and an able negotiator, as well as a theologian, and an admirable poet, Joachim Vadian left as wide a blank in the political councils, as he did in the churches of his country. He had been elected eleven times to the office of Burgomaster of Saint Gall.—See Melchior Adam, *Vitæ Medicorum Germanorum*; and the *Theatrum* of Pauli Freheri, tom. ii. pp. 1231, 1232.

[3] An allusion to a recent work of Osiander's *On Justification*, which gave rise to keen controversy in Germany.—See the Correspondence of Calvin with Melanchthon in 1552.

[4] By all appearance Amy Perrin.

will than ever. However, I shall so conduct myself, that he will easily perceive that I am heartily reconciled to him. You have heard, I suppose, what a mournful procession they lately made: and yet so shameful a butchering of a most distinguished citizen has not restrained their wantonness. As to Christopher's asking me to attend their suppers, I have, hitherto, indeed, refused none of them: but when the duties were intrusted to Amblard Corné, he, by his procrastination, broke in upon the established order. I am, in the meantime, much occupied with foreigners, who daily pass through this place in great numbers, or who have come hither to take up their abode.[1] Among others, the Marquis de Vico, a Neapolitan, arrived lately. Another will follow by and by. Should you pay us a visit next autumn, you will find our city considerably increased. A pleasing spectacle to me, if they do not overwhelm me with their visits. Viret was here lately, but he went off sooner than I could have wished. There is already open war between the Pontiff and the French.[2] There is a rumour, that all the Cardinals who sided with the King, have fled from Rome. If the emperor is to be involved in this war, he will be forced to give some relief to Magdeburg, and those places allied with it. Adieu, most upright brother; salute my friends earnestly, both your colleague and the other fellow-ministers. Ours also send kindest regards to you, viz., my colleagues, Normandie, Budé, Trier, Saint Laurent, the two Colladons, and my brother. May the Lord long spare you to us; may He shine on you with His Spirit, bless your holy endeavours, and watch over the Church committed to your care!—Yours,

JOHN CALVIN.

[*Calvin's Lat. Corresp.* Opera, tom. ix. p. 240.]

[1] The number of refugees daily increasing at Geneva, permission was granted them to assemble together for public worship in their own languages. English was preached at the Auditoire, Italian at the College, Spanish at Saint Gervais, and Flemish in Saint Germain. The unity of the Spirit shone through the diversity of languages.—Spon and Picot, *Histoire de Genève*.

[2] The Pope and the King of France were at that time engaged in a struggle about the town of Parma, which the former wished to plunder, and the latter to defend in behalf of Ottavio Farnese. The Emperor was not slow in joining the cause of the Pope, and peace was not concluded till the following year.

## CCLXXIX.—To a French Gentleman.[1]

Sickness of Theodore Beza—Calvin's grief.

*30th June* 1551.

When the messenger presented himself with your letter to Beza, I was seized with fresh alarm, and, at the same time, weighed down with a load of grief. For I was informed, the day before, that he had been seized with the plague. I was therefore not only troubled about the danger he was in, but from my very great affection for him I felt almost overpowered, as if I was already lamenting his death; although, indeed, this grief did not rise so much from private regard, as from my public anxiety for the prosperity of the Church. Indeed, I were destitute of human feeling, did I not return the affection of one who loves me with more than a brother's love, and reveres me like a very father. But the Church's loss afflicted me more deeply, when I pictured a man, of whom I had so very high expectations, suddenly snatched away from us by death, at the very outset of his career—a man whose gentle disposition, polished manners, and native candour, had endeared him to all good men. Should you ever happen to make a secret and hasty journey hither—which I am very anxious you should—you will find him far superior in those respects to anything I have stated. I trust that melancholy foreboding is far distant, of an event which you say would be an irreparable loss to you. Your coming would be the more desirable, as he was very anxious to see you when he left. What should we delight in but Christ? Yet I confidently trust that the life of man will not be denied to our prayers. For although he has not yet escaped danger, yet yesterday's messenger brought us more hopeful accounts of him. To-morrow I hope to hear what will remove all doubt. Adieu, distinguished Sir, and take in good

---

[1] This letter, without an address, was written to a friend, perhaps to one of the members of the family of Beza in France, during an illness which endangered his life, in 1551, and which called forth from the Reformer the most touching testimonies of his affection.

part this voluntary service of mine, seeing I write with so much familiarity to one with whom I am not acquainted. May the Lord guide you by His Spirit, and shield you by His protection!

[JOHN CALVIN.]

[*Calvin's Lat. Corresp.* Opera, tom. ix. p. 60.]


CCLXXX.—To THE DUKE OF SOMERSET.[1]

Protestations of attachment—reforms required in the Church of England—squandering of the revenues of benefices and of the universities.

FROM GENEVA, *this 25th July* 1551.

MONSEIGNEUR,—I know not how to thank you enough for the kind reception which my messenger has met with from you, not merely in that you have been pleased to take the trouble of offering my books to the King, but for all other proofs of the singular friendly affection which you have hitherto graciously shown me. As for the youth whom you have taken into your service, I should not have had the boldness to write to you about him, had I not thought, as was generally expected, that he was likely to turn out remarkably well. But so much the more am I obliged to you, since I find that my recommendation has been of use in this quarter. As however all that I could write would be but very feeble compared with what is in my heart, and what your benefits deserve, I prefer to desist from further comment on them. Only I pray you, Monseigneur, to consider me so wholly yours, that had I any way of doing you service, it would not be my fault if you lacked proof of more goodwill than I know how to express. I would have made these excuses to you sooner, or rather these thanks, if it may please you to hold them such, had it not been for the desire which this gentleman had, himself to present my letter to you. And in this also, I can perceive the friendship you are pleased to

---

[1] See the letter to the King of the month of January, p. 284. The minister, Nicolas des Gallars, charged to present to the King the letter and the Commentaries of Calvin, had met with the most flattering reception at Court.*

* See Calvin's letter to Farel, p. 296, *ante*.

show towards me, since those who well deserve to have access to you, hope to be the more welcome by means of my letters.

Nevertheless, Monseigneur, I shall not cease to commend to your attention that which is of itself dear and precious enough to you. It is, that you provide and take heed that God may be faithfully honoured and served; above all, that better order be established in the Church than heretofore. Albeit it may not be easy to obtain people specially qualified to discharge this office; yet, from what I hear, there are two great hindrances against which it would be essential to provide. The first is, that the revenues of the universities which have been founded for the maintenance of scholars, are ill distributed; many being thus supported who openly profess to resist the Gospel, so far are they from affording any hopes of upholding that which has been there built up with great pains and labour.

The second evil is, that the revenue of the cures is diverted and wasted, so that there is not wherewithal to support worthy men who might be fit to discharge the office of true pastors. And thus ignorant priests are installed, who bring in great confusion. For the character of individuals begets a great contempt of the Word of God; and thus whatever their authority, they cannot exercise it. I pray you, therefore, Monseigneur, to advance and improve the Reformation, and so give it permanence; be pleased to exert all your might in correcting this abuse. I quite believe that it has not been your fault that matters have not been better regulated in the first instance. But since it is very difficult all at once to organize an establishment as well as might be desirable, it only remains that we persevere, so as to perfect in time what has been well begun.

It ought not to be ill taken by those who at the present time derive profit from Church property, that the pastors be adequately supported; seeing that every one ought to strive to support them out of his own private means, were there no public ones. It would even be to their own advantage to discharge themselves of this debt, for they cannot expect to prosper while defrauding the people of God of their spiritual pasturage, by depriving the churches of good pastors. And on your part,

Monseigneur, I have no doubt, when you have faithfully laboured to reduce these matters to order, that God will the more multiply His blessings upon you. But since I feel assured that you are so well inclined of yourself that I need not longer to exhort, I shall conclude, after having besought our good Lord, that it may please Him to guide you always by His Spirit, to increase you in all well-doing, and to cause His name to be more and more glorified by you. Even so, Monseigneur, I do commend me very humbly to your gracious favour.

JOHN CALVIN.

[*Fr. Copy.—Library of Simler, Coll. of Simler.* Vol. 75.]

## CCLXXXI.—To Viret.

*Reply to the attacks of Pighius, and of George de Sicile.*[1]

[GENEVA,] 15th August 1551.

I regret the postponement of the Council, now when it is too late. Send for me, however, when you think fit; although it will be much more convenient, in another respect, for you to come to us. I send you the ravings of George de Sicile, which the Italian brethren wish me to refute.[2] I have declined, however, as there would be no end to replies if every single dog of that sort were to be silenced by a special treatise. It is better, therefore, that many do not deem it worthy of a reply. If I ever find leisure, I should prefer executing what I undertook years ago. By replying to Pighius, I shall put a stop to the barking of others. I have nothing to say regarding Matthaeus at present, except that, if while presenting the brethren with his work, he at the same time warn them of its dangers, I hope they will find it agreeable. We can discuss the rest better

---

[1] *Or,* of Sicily.

[2] Calvin published his treatise, *De Æterna Dei Predestinatione,* during the following year, in reply to certain attacks directed against this doctrine by an Italian Doctor named George de Sicile, and the German theologian, Albert Pighius, whom he had already assailed in 1543.—(See vol. i. p. 350 of the present Col-

when we meet. Adieu, most worthy and upright brother. Salute your wife and little daughters, also your colleague, Ribet, and the rest of the brethren. You may tell Hotman, that I gave a willing audience of two or three hours to a fellow-citizen of his, but I fear I was not of much service to him. He is too much puffed up with stolid self-assurance, for anything to make an impression on him.—Yours,

JOHN CALVIN.

[*Lat. orig. autogr.—Library of Geneva.* Vol. 107, *a.*]

## CCLXXXII.—To the Ministers of Neuchatel.

Arrest of a minister from Neuchatel in France—steps for obtaining his release.

GENEVA, 5*th September* 1551.

When the melancholy tidings reached this place that Hugues,[1] with five other brethren, and a lady of rank, had been seized in the neighbourhood of Mâcon, we at once resolved to inform you of it, that you might at least aid them with your prayers. For there is no use, in my opinion, in troubling ourselves with the French at present. We know they have a judge who is merciful as well as just. Textor is here, and is unremitting in his endeavours among [his] friends. If the matter proceeds farther, I shall inform you of it; only keep your mind at ease for a few days; for another messenger

lection.) Little is known regarding George de Sicile. Suspected by the Catholics on account of his professing certain of the reformed doctrines, and by the Protestants from his holding certain heterodox opinions, he was disclaimed alike by both of those Churches, and ultimately fell a victim to the Inquisition, at Ferrara.—*MSS. of the Library of Ferrara.*

[1] Notwithstanding the interested advances made by the King of France to the Swiss Cantons, and despite his alliance with the Protestants of Germany, the persecutions did not terminate in France. A minister of the district of Neuchatel, originally from the neighbourhood of Mans, named Hugues Gravier, having undertaken a journey to his native country, was arrested at the bridge of Mâcon, and, after a long imprisonment, condemned to the flames, notwithstanding the intervention of the Seigneurs of Berne in his behalf. He submitted to this cruel torture at Bourg-en-Bresse, with wonderful firmness; and his death, says the historian of the *Martyrs*, was the means of forming a nursery of the faithful throughout the entire neighbourhood.—*Hist. des Martyrs*, p. 234, anno 1552. *Hist. Eccl.*, p. 86.

brought word to-day, that when he left they had good hopes of a speedy release. Adieu, most excellent brethren, very dear to me. May the Lord be ever present with you, to guide you all by His Spirit. We are desirous of commending the Church of Lyons to you, which indeed is uncalled for.—Yours,

JOHN CALVIN.

My dear Farel, I do not ask pardon for my slothfulness, as if I had rather abstain from writing you, but that you may the sooner hasten hither that we may have a conversation. Adieu, again and again.

[*Lat. orig. autogr.—Library of Geneva.* Vol. 107, *a.*]


CCLXXXIII.—To BULLINGER.[1]

Edict of Chateaubriand, in France—attacks on Calvin in Geneva.

GENEVA, 15*th* October 1551.

My slowness in writing to you is owing to the want of messengers. For I do not care for sending a letter which may have lost its interest by being so long in reaching you. When Beza undertook to see my letter delivered to you without delay, I was unwilling to neglect a duty in which I must confess I am too remiss. I do not know how matters are moving in England. The matrimonial alliance with France does not, in my opinion, forebode so much good as many seem to think. Would, at least, that it might mitigate somewhat the fury of

[1] The new opinions made every day fresh progress in France, in spite of the rigour of the edicts, and the severity of the judges. Inspired by the evil spirit of Cardinals Tournon and Lorraine, the King resorted to measures of great cruelty. *The Edict of Chateaubriand,* issued on the 27th of June 1551, declared Protestants amenable at once to ecclesiastical and civil tribunals, so that if absolved by the jurisdiction of the one, they were liable to condemation by that of the other! This was a violation of the laws of the most ordinary justice; but at a time when the Emperor, aided by the heretic Maurice of Saxony, was attacking the Pope, the King of France could not give too strong a pledge of his orthodoxy. The blood of the disciples of the Gospel flowed like water, to expiate the alliance of this persecuting monarch with the Lutherans of Germany.—Haag, *France Protestante,* Introduction, p. x.

his father-in-law.[1] For in order to gain new modes of venting his rage against the people of God, he has been issuing atrocious edicts, by which the general prosperity of the kingdom is broken up. A right of appeal to the supreme courts has hitherto been, and still is, granted to persons guilty of poisoning, of forgery, and of robbery; yet this is denied to Christians: they are condemned by the ordinary judges to be dragged straight to the flames, without any liberty of appeal. It has been decreed, that the friends of those whose lives are at stake must not dare to intercede for them, unless they wish to be charged with patronizing heresy. The better to fan the flames, all informers are to receive the third part of the goods of the accused. Should any judge appear too remiss, he is liable to a penalty. The King's chancellor is to guard against admitting such to public offices, or any who may have, on any occasion, been open to the slightest suspicion. No one, besides, can hereafter occupy the place of a judge, unless he be hostile to Christ; and whosoever would aspire to a public office, must furnish abundant evidence of being obsequious sons of the Church of Rome; and should any one [gain office] by deception, a penalty attaches to those who recommended him. A penalty is imposed, besides, on all citizens who may, by their suffrages, have raised to the magistracy, any individual known to hold, or suspected of holding, the Lutheran doctrines. The Supreme Council is bound by law to compel any of their number, who may seem to have a leaning to our doctrines, to clear himself by oath. All are commanded, with more than usual earnestness, to adore the breaden god on bended knee. All parsons of parishes are commanded to read the Sorbonne articles every Sabbath for the benefit of the people, that a solemn abnegation of Christ may thus resound throughout the land. The goods of all who have migrated to us are to be confiscated, even although they should be sold, or in any way disposed of, previous to their departure, unless the authorities have

[1] There were at that time proposals of marriage between the young King Edward, and Elizabeth of France, daughter of Henry II., but the negotiations relative to that match were without result.—Burnet, *History of the Reformation*, vol. ii. p. 282, (Nares' Edition.)

been duly apprised of the sale before their departure was contemplated. Geneva is alluded to more than ten times in the edict, and always with a striking mark of reproach. But indeed every place of dissent from the See of Rome is referred to. This ferocity is necessary, in order that the direst confusion may follow. The flames are already kindled everywhere, and all highways are guarded lest any should seek an asylum here. If any opportunity occurs, we must spare no pains to alleviate the sufferings of our brethren. I would already have been on my way to you, for the purpose of holding a consultation, had I not been excluded access to you, at present, by your entreaties. Nevertheless, I beseech you, in the name of Christ, that you keep an attentive outlook in all directions; but I do not see what assistance is to be expected from those who sit down so securely amid their own dangers. How ominous! The sword is whetted for our throats, and we, who are all brethren, seek to avoid a consultation! With these warnings, it becomes us to accustom ourselves to fix our regards on heaven. How I fear we may, by and by, suffer a heavier punishment for this our inactivity than could be wished! In truth, I am not astonished that they are so slow in checking the insult of the enemy, when they take worthless villains to their bosom, by whom the Church is torn and wounded, and exposed to the ridicule of her enemies. A certain Dominican, a minister of the word in a neighbouring village, has emerged from the mud under evil auspices.[1] He bawled out openly in the assembly that he had a dispute with me and the Church of Geneva; and this without the least provocation. Not content with that, he brought forward a paper filled with foul accusa-

[1] Calvin, referring to the same circumstance in a letter to Viret, (Aug. 1551,) expressed himself thus:—" An ignorant monk, from an obscure village, disparaged me. A ridiculous affair. He was a demagogue, who from the front of the platform, bawled out that we were worse than the Papists, and brought forward a paper before the Consistory, written by himself, in which he accused me, by name, of teaching what was false and contrary to the Word of God; called me an impostor; babbled out that those who agreed with me held impious opinions," &c.— (*Calv. Opera*, vol. ix. p. 61.) From these last traits, we recognise the same obscure individual, who made bold to bring forward such accusations against Calvin, and whose disputes with the Reformer were soon to acquire a sad notoriety over all Switzerland. This man was Jerome Bolsec!—See the following letter.

tions, in which I was bitterly reviled for more than twenty times. On the matter being known, he was sent home. Emboldened by impunity, any satellite of the Council of Trent insults me now with equal ferocity. This is the communion of the Church which we daily profess. I omit other matters equally dishonourable, which I endure, not without sadness ; although I am not so much moved on my own account, as on that of the public ; for I see clearly that such a breaking up of all orderly discipline, so foreign to Christianity, cannot stand for any length of time.

Adieu, very excellent and highly revered brother. May the Lord guide you ever ; may His blessing rest on your pious endeavours, and may He shield you by His protection !

Salute Theodore, Pellican, Gualter, and the rest of the brethren earnestly in my name.—Yours,

JOHN CALVIN.

[*Lat. orig. autogr.—Library of Geneva.* Vol. 107, *a.*]

## CCLXXXIV.—TO THE MINISTERS OF SWITZERLAND.[1]

Statement of the controversy with Bolsec regarding Election.

GENEVA, [*October* 1551.]

There is one Jerome here, who, having thrown off the monk's cowl, is become one of those strolling physicians, who, by habi-

[1] At a general meeting, held October 16, 1551, the minister of Jussy, Jean de Saint André, in preaching from the words of St. John, (viii. 47,) " He that is of God heareth God's words . . . ," took occasion to develop the doctrine of eternal election, declaring that " those who are not regenerated by the Spirit of God, continue in a state of rebellion even to the end, because obedience is a gift accorded only to the elect." He had scarcely finished speaking when one of the hearers rose up, and pronounced this doctrine false and impious, accompanying his discourse with coarse abuse of those who make God the *author of sin,* and exhorted the people to guard against this new doctrine as a detestable piece of folly. This man was the old Carmelite monk, Jerome Bolsec, a physician, preacher, and poet, who, wandering by turns in France and Italy, had retired to Geneva some months previously, where he had already frequently attacked the doctrines of Calvin. Unnoticed in the crowd, the Reformer, whom Bolsec had thought absent, immediately rose up, and by a succession of testimonies borrowed from the writings of Augustine, eloquently refuted his adversary. Arrested on account of the temerity of his language, and interrogated by the magistrate, Jerome refused to retract, and was

tual deception and trickery, acquire a degree of impudence which makes them prompt and ready in venturing upon anything whatever. He made an attempt, eight months ago, in a public assembly of our church, to overthrow the doctrine of God's free election, which, as received from the word of God, we teach in common with you. Then, indeed, the impertinence of the man was regulated by some degree of moderation. He ceased not afterwards to make a noise in all places, with the intention of shaking the faith of the simple in this all-important doctrine. At length he openly disgorged what poison was in him. For when one of our brethren, not long since, was expounding, after our ordinary custom, that passage in John where Christ declares that those who do not hear God's words are not of God; he remarked that as many as have not been born again of the Spirit of God, continue in a state of stubborn resistance to God, even to the end, inasmuch as the gift of obedience is peculiar to the elect of God, on whom it is bestowed. That worthless wretch rose up, and affirmed that the false and impious opinion, that the will of God is the cause of all things, took its rise during the present century from Laurentius Valla; but that in this he acted wrongly, for he charged God with the blame of all evils, and falsely imputed to Him a tyrannical caprice, such as the ancient poets fancifully ascribed to their Jove. He then took up the second head, and affirmed that men are not saved because they have been elected, but that they are elected because they believe; that no one is condemned at the mere pleasure of God; that those only are condemned who deprive themselves of the election common to all. In dealing with this question, he inveighed against us with a great deal of violent abuse. The chief magistrate of the city, on hearing of the matter, imprisoned him, especially as he had

thrown into prison. The case was brought before the Council, where he boldly maintained his opinion, adding, besides, that many of the Swiss ministers shared in his sentiments. Before pronouncing a judgment, which the ministers of Geneva earnestly desired, the magistrates wrote concerning the subject to three reformed towns, namely, Zurich, Berne, and Bâle, furnishing them with a list of the errors of Bolsec, and asking their advice as to how they should treat him. See the *Registers of the Council*, Oct. 1551; Gautier, *Manuscript History of Geneva*, and Ruchat, tom. v. p. 456.

been tumultuously haranguing the common people not to allow themselves to be deceived by us. On being brought before the Senate for trial, he proceeded to defend his error with no less obstinacy than audacity. He, moreover, made it his boast that a considerable number of the ministers of the other churches sided with him ; on which we requested the Senate not to give its final decision until, having heard from your church, it should ascertain how this worthless wretch had wickedly abused your name by making you sanction his error. Overcome by shame, he at first did not decline the decisions of the churches, but began to jest about having good reason to mistrust you from your familiar intimacy with our brother Calvin. The Senate, however, according to our request, resolved upon consulting you. Besides, and in addition to this, he was implicating your church. For while denouncing Zwingle above all others, he said that Bullinger was of precisely the same opinion with himself. He has craftily watched for a handle of discord among the Bernese ministers. We are really anxious to have this plague so removed from our church, that it may not infect our neighbours when we have got rid of it ourselves. Although it is of very great importance to us and to the public tranquillity, that the doctrine which we profess should meet with your approval ; yet we have no reason to entreat your confidence in many words. The *Institutes* of our brother Calvin, against which he is especially directing his attacks, is not unknown among you. With what reverence and sobriety he has therein discussed the secret judgments of God, it is not for us to record : the book is its own bright witness. Nor in truth do we teach anything here but what is contained in God's holy word, and what has been held by your church ever since the light of the Gospel was restored. That we are justified by faith, we all agree ; but the real mercy of God can only be perceived when we learn that faith is the fruit of free adoption, and that, in point of fact, adoption flows from the eternal election of God. But not only does this impostor fancy that election depends upon faith, but that faith itself is originated as much by man himself as by divine inspiration. There can be no doubt, on the other hand, that when men perish, it must be imputed to their own wickedness. But by the case of the reprobate whom God, from His own mysterious council, passes by and neglects as if unworthy, we are taught a striking lesson of humility. Yet such is this Jerome, that he will not admit that God does anything justly unless he has palpable evidence of it. In fine, this much is fixed and conceded by us all, that when man sins, God must not be regarded as having any share in the blame, nor that the word *sin* can in any sense be applied to Him. Yet this does not hinder Him from exercising His power, in a wonderful and incomprehensible way, through Satan and the wicked, as if they were the instruments of His wrath, to teach the faithful patience, or to inflict merited punishment on His enemies. This profane trifler cries out that we bring an impeachment against God when we allege that He governs all things by His providence. Destroying, in short, in this way, all distinction between causes as remote and concealed, on the one hand, and as near and patent on the other; rendering it impossible to regard the sufferings to which holy Job was subjected as the work of God, but that He may be held as equally guilty with the Devil, the Chaldeans, and the Sabæan robbers. Our mutual relationship, therefore, demands that you will not consider it troublesome to uphold and maintain, by your countenance, that doctrine of Christ which has been outraged by the profanity of a wanton and ill-disposed man. As we confidently trust that you will do this gladly and of your own accord, we consider it useless to ply you with anxious and earnest requests; and, on the other hand, should our services be at any time of advantage to you, you will ever find us prepared to discharge every brotherly duty.—Adieu, most beloved and esteemed brethren. May God guide you by His Spirit, bless your labours, and defend your church!

[*Calvin's Lat. Corresp.* Opera, tom. ix. p. 63.]

## CCLXXXV.—To Oswald Myconius.[1]

Recommendations regarding the dispute with Bolsec—request on behalf of the Protestants of France.

Lausanne, *November* 1551.

I am compelled to dictate these few lines, being confined to bed with a severe headache. The person who is to deliver my letter to you is my brother's father-in-law. He will, therefore, communicate to me faithfully anything with which you may intrust him. Although in so just and sacred a cause I trust there will be neither difficulty nor delay, yet, as you have especially to do with the general answer of the brethren, I beseech you particularly, and Sulzer also, to undertake the whole matter.[2] Our Senate, indeed, took a correct enough view of the case, but it is of great importance to have the mind of your church as well as of our own.

There is another thing, also, which I am exceedingly anxious of obtaining from you and the rest of the brethren; but as there is no need for pressing you on the matter, it will be sufficient for me to give you a hint of it. Edicts worse than atrocious have lately been published by the King of France, in which all manner of cruelties are employed for the extinction of whatever spark of manliness there is in the kingdom.[3] Not only has he increased the rage of those judges and officers who previously, in most instances, went farther than they should, but if any are more moderate than the rest, they are compelled by violent threats to shed, like very gladiators, the blood of the innocent. The flames have been kindled already in very many places.

---

[1] This is Calvin's last letter to Myconius. Struck by apoplexy while in the pulpit of the Cathedral of Bâle, a few days before the Easter festivals of 1551, Myconius never rallied, till he was carried off by the plague in October 1552, in the sixty-fourth year of his age. His bereaved widow survived him only a few days. Simon Sulzer succeeded him in the office of *Antistes* which he had filled during more than ten years with moderation and wisdom.—See Melch. Adam, *Vitæ Theol. Germ.*, p. 224; Ruchat, tom. v. p. 468.

[2] Alluding to the reply expected from the ministers of Bâle, concerning the case of Bolsec. See the preceding letter.

[3] See letter, p. 304.

There is one mode, perhaps, by which his fury may be somewhat appeased: Were those of the Swiss who profess the sound and pure doctrine of the Gospel to intercede, perhaps, during those commotions of war, their authority might carry the more weight. As the cause is a just one, and worthy also of your compassion, I shall say no more, convinced as I am that it will be to you an object of the deepest interest. Adieu, brother, worthy of my heartfelt reverence. Salute all your friends and fellow-ministers. May the Lord guide you by His Spirit, and protect you by His power!—Yours,

JOHN CALVIN.

[*Lat. orig.—Library of Geneva.* Vol. 107, *a.*]

## CCLXXXVI.—To CHRISTOPHER FABRI.[1]

Calvin's dissatisfaction with the reply of the ministers of Bâle, and the conduct of Monsieur de Falais regarding the affair with Bolsec.

*November* 1551.

I shall attend to your orders. Would that we could obtain our wishes! The ministers of Bâle have replied. We have found by experience how little advice they can give us. Myconius approaches the matter with a certain coldness. There is no use, as you say, in his taking credit to himself for wisdom from his hesitancy. Yet Sulzer writes just as if it would be satisfactory. The Senate had sent their own messenger a short time before. I fear they will repeat the same old song. But if the men of Berne and Zurich go prudently about the matter, we need not take it to heart; for all depends on this, lest he may have been admitted to the Bernese district. I am so much ashamed at De Falais, that I can scarcely bear to be taunted

[1] "To Mons. Christopher Fabri, minister of the Word of God in the Church of Neufchatel."
The theologians of Bâle were the first to communicate their sentiments regarding the case of Bolsec. In a letter dated 28th November, they openly acknowledged the doctrine which was the occasion of the dispute. They regarded election as "the effect of a secret cause, known to God alone, and which man should not attempt to fathom." So far as Bolsec himself was concerned, they were inclined to treat him with indulgence, deceiving thereby the hopes of the Reformer, who desired a triumphant condemnation of his adversary.

about his fickleness.¹ If your reply reach us in time, it will assist us not a little. Adieu, very worthy and very dear brethren. I could not find a messenger up to the present moment. My dear Fabri, I now at length discharge your orders to me. I have not had an opportunity of writing you since the brethren determined upon what kind of testimony should be given to Heroldus. I have been as moderate as I could. Adieu again. Convey my best regards to your friends.—Entirely yours,

CALVIN.

[*Lat. orig. autogr.—Library of Geneva.* Vol. 107, *a.*]


## CCLXXXVII.—To FAREL.

Recommendation of a schoolmaster—complaints against the ministers of Zurich.

GENEVA, 8*th December* 1551.

There is little need for my commending the bearer to you, as he is, in my judgment, sufficiently known and approved by you. It is no ordinary proof of his piety and modesty when I state, that not only did he come down to this quarter willingly, but came forward even with eagerness, when I was almost prevented, through bashfulness, from asking him to undertake the matter. Nor have I any doubt but that he will discharge any duty imposed upon him, faithfully and with care. But the fact of his being regarded, by competent judges, as a learned and skilful physician, will perhaps go farther with your men. Were he not known among you, I should give ampler testimony in his favour. I only trust that your school may furnish him with pupils worthy of his position as a moderately learned master.

I complained lately of the theologians of Bâle,² who, as compared with those of Zurich, are worthy of very great praise.³

---

[1] In the theological disputes between Calvin and Bolsec, M. de Falais declared himself in favour of the latter, from whom he received medical advice. He had even written a letter to Bâle in his behalf.

[2] See the preceding letter, p. 312.

[3] The theologians of Zurich, like those of Bâle, did not hesitate to profess adhe-

I can hardly express to you, my dear Farel, how much I am annoyed by their rudeness. There is less humanity among us than among wild beasts. What would happen if we were not surrounded with enemies? What marvellous dulness is it, that when three or four churches are driven together into a corner, they do not recognise each other! In truth, this is worse than dishonourable, because groundless rumours are circulated, by which any brother who may be within the bounds is hindered from showing us any sympathy. The Senate did not consider the pastors worthy of being written to, but to heighten the insult, they limited their communication to the magistrates. Should you be displeased with the general letter of the men of Zurich, let me tell you, that Bullinger's private letter to me was not a whit better, although it is preferable that you should read it and judge for yourself. It is not fair that I should be troubled with his trifles, while he is, at the same time, looking down on our wants with supreme contempt. You will pardon me, therefore, if you do not obtain what you asked regarding the translation of his book. Adieu, very dear brother. May the Lord Jesus guide you, and watch over you continually, together with your brethren and the church! Salute Christopher and the rest in my name. Michael will remain here till the end of the week.—Yours truly,

JOHN CALVIN.

[*Latin copy—Eccl. Archives of Berne*, vol. vi. p. 171.]

rence to the doctrine attacked by Bolsec. "Jerome," said they, "deceives himself and wrongs Zuingle, if he believes that the latter taught that God himself was the cause of man's sinning; for if he appeared to teach something similar to that in his book on *The Providence of God*, we must, at the same time, consult his other writings, where he has plainly established that sin comes by no means from God, but from human corruption and voluntary wickedness." Addressed to the Councils of Geneva by an oversight which the ministers of that church seemed keenly to feel, the answer from Zurich did not appear to Calvin to be a sufficiently explicit condemnation of his adversary. See the letter to Bullinger of January 1552.

## CCLXXXVIII.—To Laelius Socinus.[1]

Refusal to reply to the curious questions proposed to him by Socinus.

[1551.]

You are deceived in so far as you entertain the impression that Melanchthon does not agree with us on the doctrine of predestination. I only said briefly that I had a letter written by his own hand, in which he confessed that his opinion agreed with mine. But I can believe all you say, as it is nothing new for him to deceive in this matter, the better to rid himself of troublesome inquiries. Certainly no one can be more averse to paradox than I am, and in subtleties I find no delight at all. Yet nothing shall ever hinder me from openly avowing what I have learned from the word of God; for nothing but what is useful is taught in the school of this master. It is my only guide, and to acquiesce in its plain doctrines shall be my constant rule of wisdom. Would that you also, my dear Laelius, would learn to regulate your powers with the same moderation! You have no reason to expect a

---

[1] Laelius Socinus, founder of the celebrated sect which bears his name, was born at Sienna of a distinguished family: his father, Marianus Socinus, a professor in the University of Bologna, was one of the most learned juriconsults of his age. Of a bold and active mind, which found pleasure in the most subtle speculations, and which would not stop short of the interpretation of mysteries, Laelius left his native country in 1548, and joined the Reformers of Switzerland and Germany, whose friendship he won by the politeness of his manners, the purity of his life, and his zeal for learning. He resided by turns at Zurich and Wittemberg, and was not slow, by correspondence or conversation, to express his doubts on the common doctrines, which he skilfully advanced rather in the form of questions than as opinions which he was prepared to maintain and to teach. He was beloved by Bullinger, who did not suspect the heterodoxy of his beliefs, and who wrote to Calvin regarding him, "I restrain as far as I can this man's curiosity;" and Calvin himself, after having repeatedly broken off correspondence with Socinus, could not forbear renewing it, and giving a friendly reply to the doubts which he had expressed on the resurrection, baptism, the trinity, &c. (Calv. *Opera*, tom. ix. pp. 51, 57, 197.) The letter, which is published here for the first time, throws valuable light on the relation of the Reformer to the founder of a sect to which even Socinus himself was yet a stranger, and whose doubts were afterwards to be set up as dogmas by his disciples. Laelius Socinus died in 1562, before he had completed his thirty-seventh year.—M'Crie, *Hist. of Ref. in Italy, passim.*

reply from me so long as you bring forward those monstrous questions. If you are gratified by floating among those aërial speculations, permit me, I beseech you, an humble disciple of Christ, to meditate on those things which tend towards the building up of my faith. And indeed I shall hereafter follow out my wishes in silence, that you may not be troubled by me. And in truth, I am very greatly grieved that the fine talents with which God has endowed you, should be occupied not only with what is vain and fruitless, but that they should also be injured by pernicious figments. What I warned you of long ago, I must again seriously repeat, that unless you correct in time this itching after investigation, it is to be feared you will bring upon yourself severe suffering. I should be cruel towards you did I treat with a show of indulgence what I believe to be a very dangerous error. I should prefer, accordingly, offending you a little at present by my severity, rather than allow you to indulge unchecked in the fascinating allurements of curiosity. The time will come, I hope, when you will rejoice in having been so violently admonished. Adieu, brother very highly esteemed by me; and if this rebuke is harsher than it ought to be, ascribe it to my love to you.[1]

[*Latin copy—Library of Geneva.* Vol. 107, *a.*]

## CCLXXXIX.—To BULLINGER.[2]

Thanks for the zeal manifested on behalf of the faithful in France—Complaints of the conduct of the Ministers of Zurich in the affair of Bolsec.

GENEVA, *January* 1552.

You have clearly shown yourself to be what you have always been, by your unremitting endeavours to mitigate the rage of

[1] This letter, without a date, appears to us to belong to the last months of the year 1551. Laelius Socinus was living at that time at Wittemberg.—M'Crie, *Hist. of the Ref. in Italy*, p. 430.

[2] The magistrates of Geneva, after having received the advice of the leading Swiss Churches,—which were unanimous alike in their recognition of the doctrine of election, and in soliciting indulgence for Bolsec,—proceeded with the trial of the prisoner, who, having refused to retract his opinions, was solemnly banished on the 23d December 1551, for having persisted in an obstinate despisal of the judgment

our Pharaoh, and aid our unfortunate brethren. I cannot forget how strenuously and faithfully you have always devoted yourself to this cause. Still, I have good reason to fear that little has been gained by our letters: for the courtiers to frustrate them is nothing wonderful. Indeed, I lately learned as much, in a quiet way, from the royal ambassador when he was here. We would require to send some one, therefore, if we wish to be of any use. The matter was taken up at Baden, I understand, but their deliberations probably came to naught. So confident am I of your watchful attention and faithfulness, that I consider it unnecessary for me to stimulate you by a single word.

Would that we were so well satisfied about another matter, that we could tender our thanks to yourself and your colleagues without any qualification. Inasmuch as we experienced—not without severe pain—considerably less support from you than we had anticipated, I prefer bringing my complaint candidly before you, rather than nourish my displeasure by keeping it to myself. You write that you were astonished why we, annoyed by a vile and impious wretch, should ask your opinion of a doctrine which he was falsely attacking. In this impression you have been greatly mistaken, for when he accused us of holding impious doctrine, we deferred to your judgment out of respect to you. I fail to see why this should annoy you. I certainly did not think you would consider any amount of labour burdensome, which should bring so very great relief to your brethren. You say that it is a serious matter to give an unqualified approval of disputations, especially when they turn upon a matter which, in the reader's judgment, might be handled to better purpose in some other way. And yet, I have never supposed, nor do I yet believe, that you belong to the number of those who are so well pleased with their own performances, that they cannot peruse without aversion anything executed by another; nor, in truth, did I propose dictating a

of the Churches to which he had promised submission.—(*Registers of the Council*, Dec. 1551. Spon and Picot, *Histoires de Genève*.) Calvin did not wish the sentence to be more severe, although he counted on the Swiss Churches taking a more energetic course, and in the ardour of his zeal for what he regarded as sound doctrine, looked upon all hesitation and all weakness as a cowardly abandonment of the truth.

formula to you, to which we desired your unqualified assent. It was enough, and more than enough, to have your approval of a doctrine which we held to be found in the word of God, nor was it our object to discuss it with skill and acuteness; so far from that, the matter, when stripped of all artifice, shows that we wanted nothing more than that by refuting the man's wicked calumnies, you should bear testimony to our teaching only what was drawn from the pure fountain of God.

You ought not to have feared, I think, that any one was accusing you of dishonesty, because I asked you not to think it troublesome, to give an answer to our magistrates, as if on an entirely new subject. For how could they make a public statement regarding a matter, into which no one had made any inquiry, although I readily allow it appeared differently to you? Your charging us with the want of moderation and humanity, was caused, we think, by your placing less confidence in our letter than you ought to have done. Would that Jerome were a better man than our letter declared him to be! Would that he attributed all to the grace of God, as you seem to think. But for you to plead in defence of a man who seditiously disturbed a peaceful Church, who strove to divide us by deadly discord, who, without ever having received the slightest provocation, loaded us with all sorts of abuse, who publicly taunted us with representing God as a tyrannical governor, nay more, that we had put the Jove of the poets in the place of God,—to defend such a man, I say, were the extreme of absurdity. How, moreover, can he attribute all to the grace of God, when he says that grace is offered alike to all, but that its efficacy rests with the free will of every one, when he prates about the heart of flesh, or the susceptibility of grace, being given to all, but so that every one may receive it of his own accord? Altogether, I feel grieved beyond measure that there is not a better understanding between us. Indeed I was astounded, on finding from your letter, that the kind of teaching which I employ is displeasing to many good men, just as Jerome is offended by that of Zuingle. Wherein, I beseech you, lies the similarity? For Zuingle's book, to speak confidentially, is crammed with such knotty paradoxes, as to be very different, indeed, in point of moderation, from what I hold. You are wrong in inferring that I have promised a new work, in which I undertake to demonstrate that God is not the author of sin. When that impostor was vexing me with his calumnies, I stated in refutation what was true, viz., that I had given sufficient evidence in a book which I had published, of my utter abhorrence of such blasphemy. I refer to the book published long since against *Libertines.* The dishonesty of that worthless wretch, however, induced me to publish in addition what remained of my reply to Pighius on *Predestination.* Should I fall into any mistakes, you will be kind enough to set me right. For the rest, I am sufficiently alive to the desirableness of my saying what I have to say with frankness and candour. Jerome has been publicly sentenced to perpetual exile. Certain slanderers have been falsely circulating that we desired a more cruel punishment, and some have been foolish enough to believe it. Our friend, De Falais, whose maid-servant Jerome had cured of cancer, on that account espoused his cause so very warmly, that he seemed almost infatuated. We easily, and from the first, shook ourselves free of this annoyance. But at the request of the neighbouring brethren, we were anxious to remove that plague from the Bernese district. Now that your answer has been ambiguous, the sorry wretch is making his boast that you countenance his error. I only wish I could at present venture to indicate the catastrophe of the tragedy, regarding which you desired to be informed. You will hear, before long, or I am much mistaken, in certain attempts just made, that he has paved the way for making still greater disturbances. Now, if I have laid bare my inmost feelings in making these complaints to you, let that have no weight so far as our reply is concerned. Although you disappointed my expectations, I nevertheless gladly offer you our friendship. I pass by the others just as if I was entirely satisfied. In conclusion, as my brother's sister is anxious about her son who is boarded in your place, I am compelled to trouble you about him. I wish you would inquire at his teacher, in her name, as to what progress he is making, and if you find that he is not realizing the hopes and desires of his father, that you will inform me of it at your earliest opportunity.

JOHN CALVIN.

[*Lat. orig. autogr.—Library of Geneva.* Vol. 107, *a.*]

## CCXC.—To Farel.

*Fresh complaints by Calvin against the ministers of Zurich and Berne—his unpopularity in the latter city—advices to Farel.*

GENEVA, *27th January* 1552.

I received your letter lately, in which you asked me silently to repress the feeling of wrong done me by your neighbours.[1] As for the people of Zurich, the die has been cast three days ago. The remedy was in my hands, indeed, until then. But I have no inclination to recall those letters which I have lately despatched. It was absolutely necessary for me afterwards to write to the theologians of Bâle, with whose answer, apparently so cold and empty, I had good grounds from the first to be displeased. But those things advanced by the others were so very worthless, that they did not cause me much annoyance. You are much mistaken in thinking that the former party are about to see their error. Wait rather till they make an absolute renunciation of the election of God. We have experienced the wonderful providence of God in this matter; for without being at the time aware of it, I, by the formula of our agreement, have so bound them, that they are no longer at

[1] In their reply to the ministers of Geneva concerning Bolsec, the ministers of Berne freely pleaded the cause of toleration :—" We do not believe," said they, " that it is necessary to treat those who err with too much severity, lest while wishing to defend, with too great zeal, the purity of dogmas, we swerve from the law of Jesus Christ, that is, from charity. . . . . Jesus Christ loved the truth, but he loved souls also ; not only those who advanced without declension, but also those who went astray. And it is the latter of which the Good Shepherd, in the Gospel parable, takes the greatest care." . . . . More explicit than the theologians of Zurich and of Bâle on the doctrine which formed the ground of the debate, the ministers of Berne gave a deliverance against the doctrine of predestination :—" To come," said they, " to the subject of dispute with Bolsec, you are not ignorant how much vexation it has caused very many good men, of whom we cannot have a bad opinion, who reading in the Scriptures those passages which exalt the grace of God to all men, have not sufficient discernment rightly to understand the true mysteries of Divine election, attach themselves to the proclamation of grace and of universal benevolence, and think that we cannot make God condemn, harden, and blind any man, without being guilty of the insupportable blasphemy of making God himself the author both of man's blindness and of his perdition, and by consequence of all sin."—See this letter, and those of the Churches of Zurich and Bâle, in the Collection of Professor Alph. Turretin, entitled, *Nubes Testium*, and in Ruchat, tom. v. p. 461, *et seq.*

liberty to do damage to the cause. For, in other circumstances, as I am informed by one, they would have become the patrons of Jerome. Even Bibliander, carried away by a sudden fit of excitement, was within a very little of coming to oppose us. He is at present engaged in writing something or other. However, you will find nothing in my letter, if I am not mistaken, except what is exceedingly temperate. I had, in truth, enough to do in repressing the grief with which I was at that time consumed. You will hear from Christopher what Viret advises to be done with the third. As he has an absolute horror of going to Berne, I have no special counsel to offer. However, the atrocity of the evils by which we are beset, compels us to attempt something. And now new matter for a tragedy has arisen out of mere nothing. For the chief magistrate of Ternier, on false and reckless information, eagerly summoned, as he is accustomed to do, John de Saint André before a public tribunal, charging him with having said before a public assembly, that whoever received the Supper on Christmas-day, received the devil and not Christ.[1] And witnesses were found to give evidence against him. In short, Satan will not lay aside such fanners as these until he has kindled some dreadful conflagration. But I suppose we may rather weep over evils of this sort, than hope to prevent them. At least I do not see what can be done. If I go to Berne, I fear I shall not receive a brotherly welcome from the brethren. Wicked men, who are at present exhibiting so much effrontery, while matters are in a doubtful state, will then be certain to be more insolent in their boasting. And although the pastors hold out some show of friendship, yet I scarcely expect to succeed in inducing them to maintain friendly intercourse with us, except by the permission of the Senate. You know how defective they are in courage and firmness. If they so far comply with our wishes in this matter, they will nevertheless think that they have doubly discharged their duty, when they have indicated in a single word that they have nothing to complain of. There is much talk in the city in the meantime. While revolving these dangers in

[1] This minister was banished shortly after beyond the territory of the Seigneurs of Berne on account of this expression.

my own mind, I can scarcely venture to seek a remedy for evils which vex me all the more from my very desire for their removal. If you hope to find Blaurer of any use to you, you should employ him. But I abstain from writing, lest some might think themselves wronged by my complaining to him. Try him, therefore, and give him advice about what he should do.

In the next place, I have something about which I wish to admonish yourself. For I understand the prolixity of your discourses has furnished ground of complaint to many.[1] You have frequently confessed to us that you were aware of this defect, and that you were endeavouring to correct it. But if private grumblings are disregarded because they do not in the meanwhile give trouble, they may, nevertheless, one day break forth into seditious clamours. I beg and beseech of you to strive to restrain yourself, that you may not afford Satan an opportunity, which we see he is so earnestly desiring. You know that while we are not called upon to show too much indulgence to the foolish, we are nevertheless bound to give them something to allure them. And you are well enough aware that you have to do with the morose and the choleric; and in truth their aversion arises simply from too much pride on their part. Yet, since the Lord commands us to ascend the pulpit, not for our own edification, but for that of the people, you should so regulate the manner of your teaching, that the Word may not be brought into contempt by your tediousness. It is more appropriate, also, for us to lengthen our prayers in private, than when we offer them in the name of the whole Church. You are mistaken if you expect from all an ardour equal to your own.

I have dictated this letter in bed.[2] Adieu, most excellent

---

[1] Farel was a genuine orator. All his contemporaries speak with admiration of his eloquent discourses, of his beautiful exhortations, and of his prayers, so fervent, that no one could hear them without being charmed. But it appears that his discourses were all extempore; none of them have been preserved, but they had a few of the defects of improvisation. Their fault was prolixity. Calvin, in his preface to the Psalms, paid, among other things, a brilliant tribute to the eloquence of his friend, and to those thunders of the Word (*tonitrua*) by which he had been enchained at Geneva.   [2] In Calvin's own hand.

and upright brother. Salute all friends. May the Lord preserve and guide you by His Spirit, and bless your labours!—Yours,

JOHN CALVIN.

[*Lat. orig. autogr.—Library of Geneva.* Vol. 107, *a.*]

## CCXCI.—To MADAME DE CANY.[1]

Rigorous and inflexible spirit of Calvin against heresy—Praise of Theodore Beza.

GENEVA, *January* 1552.

MADAME,—I am very sorry that the praiseworthy act which you did about half a year ago, has met with no better return. This is because no good and true servant of God found himself within reach of such help, as that received by as wicked and unhappy a creature as the world contains. Knowing partly the man he was, I could have wished that he were rotting in some ditch; and his arrival gave me as much pleasure as the piercing my heart with a poniard would have done. But never could I have deemed him to be such a monster of all impiety and contempt of God, as he has proved himself in this. And I assure you, Madame, that had he not so soon escaped, I should, by way of discharging my duty, have done my best to bring him to the stake.[2] Nevertheless, if the good we purpose does not come to pass, it is quite enough that God accepts our service. He commands us to help all those who need, and above all, those who

---

[1] Without date. The end is wanting. We believe that this letter refers to the first month of the year 1552.

[2] Who is the personage to whom these words refer, stamped at once by the inflexible spirit of the time and the stern rigour of the Reformer? The historian can only offer conjectures: can it be Jerome Bolsec? But a regular sentence had banished him from Geneva, and Calvin himself does not appear to have called for a more severe judgment against this innovator whom resentment had transformed into a vile pamphleteer. "That fellow, Jerome, is driven out into perpetual exile by a public sentence. *Certain revilers have spread abroad the falsehood, that we earnestly desired a much severer punishment, and foolishly, it is believed.*"—(Calvin to Bullinger, in the month of January 1552.) In that age of inexorable severity against unsound doctrine, Servetus only appeared at Geneva to expire at the stake, and Gentili only escaped the scaffold for a time, by the voluntary retractation of his opinions. To name Gentili, Servetus, Bolsec, is to recall the principal victims of Calvinistic intolerance in the sixteenth century, but not to solve the mystery which attaches to the personage designated in the letter of Calvin to Madame de Cany.

suffer for His name. If men are often found unworthy of our help, let us be content that the Master acknowledges it all as done to Himself; and that even if men prove ungrateful, He will confer so ample a reward, of which we cannot be deprived. And in this we enjoy a great advantage over those who, in serving their own fancies, persuade themselves that they do God service. For when we follow that which He approves, we are in no danger of losing our labour. Wherefore, let us not weary in well-doing, as likewise St. Paul exhorts us, signifying that we should not fail to find much in men that would immediately discourage us, did we not look beyond them. And, indeed, there is no doubt that our Lord wishes to try our constancy when He allows such temptations to befall us. Accordingly, he who would shield himself behind the ingratitude of mankind, will not be excused. As regards ourselves, there is much need that we should be confirmed against such scandals, for we meet them every day. And I have no doubt, that our Lord has so confirmed you, that you will not cease exerting yourself for His people when the opportunity occurs, and you have the means of doing what your duty requires. For seeing that God accepts and puts down to His account whatever is done to His people, it is to Him that we fall short, and not to men, when we do not fulfil this duty. Now, our Lord presents you by us with an occasion of showing your perseverance, albeit that it is enough for me to have exhorted you in general.

With regard to the present matter, I prefer to entreat you, as I now entreat with all possible affection. It is on the behalf of Monsieur de Bèze,[1] against whom a certain Monsieur de Sunistan, has a lawsuit for the priory of Londjumeau. Upon his retirement, his condemnation was inevitable, for you are aware how things go in our favour. Be that as it may, Monsieur de Sunistan would have been well content with much less, and has

[1] Theodore Beza, then professor of Greek literature in the Academy of Lausanne. Born the 24th June 1549, at Véselay in Burgundy, he had left Paris after a brilliant and dissipated youth, and retired to Geneva the 24th October 1548, giving up the possession of the rich benefices which he held of his uncle, the Abbé of Froidmont. Of this number was the Priory of Londjumeau, which became the matter of a tedious lawsuit between Beza and the new titular, M. de Sunistan, the protégé of the Duchesse d'Etampes.

obtained more than he could have ventured to wish, seeing that the Sieur de Bèze has been found liable for the whole of the costs, with restitution of the rents. Whereupon he (Sunistan) proceeds against the commissioners, who have received them in the name of the aforesaid De Bèze. To remedy this evil, we have bethought ourselves, Madame, of having recourse to you as to a refuge which God vouchsafes to us. We hope, indeed, that Madame[1] will do much for us. And since it has been through her that the said Sunistan has got the benefice, this is a reason why she should have authority to make him relinquish his claim upon the costs. I assure you, in all sincerity, that when he shall have done his utmost, he will not be able to get what he seeks. And therefore, Madame, I again beseech you, that it may please you to write so urgently to the said lady, that she may exert herself warmly to make the aforesaid Sunistan satisfied with the presentation. I do not make this request so much on my own account, as in the name of our Master, who has all credit and power with you as He deserves. I say this, not only to excuse the liberty I take, but also to obtain more easily from you what I ask. Nevertheless, I protest in truth, if I did not all I could to deliver from annoyance the man for whom I speak, I should do wrong to Jesus Christ and his Church. Our Lord has so wrought upon him, that he has withdrawn, notwithstanding the ease which he enjoyed, from the expectation of further advancement. But I let that alone in order to speak as to what I have known. I shall not even touch upon many virtues, which would have won your affections, had you seen them as I have done. I will only tell you, that he has received excellent graces from God, and has so improved them for the general benefit of the Church, that he is truly a pearl. This is why I have said that I less regard in this case the private individual, than my duty to my Master and His whole household, who have so much interest in such a spirit not being quenched by vexations and annoyances. And I am not the only person who think of him thus, but all those to whom the honour of God is dear, love and value this man as a treasure. I believe that my brother

---

[1] Anne de Pisseleu, Duchesse d'Etampes. She was a sister of Madame de Cany.

De Normandie does not write of him to you with less affection than I. We agree in this respect as in everything else, so that I believe that we both equally love him. You may have some taste of his mind by certain passages which he has translated, although he has other gifts which are surpassing and far more valuable. But I hope, Madame, that the reading of the Psalms, which you will receive by the bearer,[1] will of itself be my excuse towards you for so pressingly requesting you to be pleased to be the means of giving him relief, so that he may follow out this work, and also better things besides: and in doing so, you will oblige many worthy persons whom I know you would willingly please. . . . .

[*Fr. Copy—Library of Geneva.* Vol. 107, *a.*]

## CCXCII.—To Bullinger.[2]

*Journey of Calvin and Farel in Switzerland—steps in favour of the Reformed in France—return to the affairs of Bolsec.*

From an Inn at Basle, 13*th March* 1552.

When Farel and I left home, we had resolved to visit you. At Berne we altered our plan, for the following reason:—We

---

[1] Laurent de Normandie. See note 1, p. 296.

This passage seems to refer to an edition of the Psalms, translated into French verse by Theodore Beza, earlier than that which is mentioned by Senebier.—(*Histoire Littéraire de Genève,* tom. i. p. 289.—*Septante-Neuf Pseaulmes mis en Rithme Française, Quarante-Neuf par Clement Marot, avec le Cantique de Siméon et les Dix Commandements,* in 24. Genève, chez Simon de Bosc, 1556.) M. Picot, *Hist. de Genève,* tom. ii. p. 7, mentions an edition of the Psalms, published in 1551. We know that the first complete edition, for the use of the Reformed Churches, appeared at Lyons in 1562, with the "Privilège du Roi."

[2] Despite Calvin's disagreements with the magistrates of Berne and the Helvetic Churches, he did not hesitate to undertake a journey to them in the month of March 1552, which the seriousness of the circumstances demanded, in order to plead the cause, among the Cantons, of the French Protestants, who were then in a most deplorable condition. "This year," says Ruchat, "the King of France carried his persecution of the Reformers, even to the death, so to speak; and those faithful subjects, who wished only to be allowed to serve God in liberty of conscience, were subjected to the violence of his officers, who acted like so many unchained furies. The flames were kindled, the wheel and the gallows were erected at all the tribunals. The Protestant States of the empire, and the four Reformed

stated in the senate that there appeared some hope of relief for our unhappy brethren; because the king lately published an edict, in which he makes unusual concessions to the Germans; for in the first place he puts them on an equality with the natives; and further, by an extraordinary indulgence, he grants them the liberty of living according to their own religion. Besides, the attempts of the Sorbonne to excite cruelty, have less success and favour than hitherto. The death of Chatelain[1] also, who was cut off by an attack of colic, happened seasonably for us. The king seems so bent upon war, that he does not hesitate to prefer his present convenience to the senseless rage with which he formerly burned. There are many things, we think, which at present you may safely concede to them. It is certain, that in a war so changeable and so complicated as this, though there may be no formal compact, they have many common interests involved. Now the miserable condition of our holy brethren admonishes us of the necessity of watching over them, and urgently demands that we assist them to the best of our power. For the king, as if he had exhausted his kindness upon the Germans, ceases not severely to oppress his own. Moreover, as many opportunities might

Cantons, were active in their intercessions with the King, by means of special ambassadors, in behalf these poor persecuted ones; but all their prayers were useless." (*Hist. de la Réf.*, tom. v. p. 479.) The King, on advising the Cantons to abstain from any further approaches to him, declared that he wished to be allowed to remain his own master, and to act as he pleased, and for them to refrain in future, lest those cities continued this business at their own peril; . . . . that they were at liberty to govern their own cities as they thought proper; that, for his own part, he wished, without let or hindrance, to do the same in his own kingdom, because he intended by all means to purge it of those *seditious* men.—(Bullinger to Calvin, tom. ix. p. 68.) This last epithet was a *calumny*. Yet he continued, nevertheless, to persecute the faithful of France as seditious and as rebels, because they desired to serve and to worship God according to His word.

[1] See note 1, Vol. i. p. 415.

"This good bishop," says Beza, "agreeing to persecute those whom he formerly defended as far as he could, was made Bishop of Orleans, whither God attended him on his journey. For on the eve of his *entrée*, he went, as the custom was, to the Monastery called Saint Iverte, and entered a pulpit to preach; there was a very great number of people present, and whilst uttering harsh threats against those termed heretics, he was seized with a colic so sudden and severe, that being carried away he died a miserable death on the following night, and made his *entrée* elsewhere than at Orleans."—*Hist. Eccl.*, tom. i. p. 81.

escape us, from our ignorance of passing events, it had already seemed to us advisable to turn and warn the Bernese to seize a favourable opportunity. But now, being taught by much experience that letters are of little avail, we have besought the Bernese senate to despatch an embassy, to assure the king that the cause was sincerely advocated; and that not only from the entreaties of others, but of your own inclination, and from the deepest feeling of your heart, you are inclined and earnestly desirous to plead it. The senate replied, that the occasion seemed not yet ripe, for that lately letters had been brought from the king, wherein he not only haughtily refused what the four states had sought, but fiercely chid them for not considering him a clement Christian king. It was stated, also, that letters would presently arrive, from which it would appear whether the King's mind were changed. The consul promised, however, that should a convenient opportunity occur, the Senate would by no means neglect this cause. Among other things, also, the Senate dissuaded us from going to Zurich, lest unnecessary expense should be incurred. We were vexed at this, because we would freely confer with you upon other matters, nor would you have been displeased at our arrival; however, that we might not seem too rash, we chose rather to be deprived of the pleasure of seeing you, and the benefit of your conversation, than to attempt anything which might injure the cause. Now both of us beseech you; nay rather all the godly who are suffering in France for the testimony of Christ, humbly beseech you by our mouth to be diligently watchful for all opportunities. Although it is enough to advise you, yet the anxiety under which we know them to groan, compels us to add some vehemence to our entreaties. But as we shall certainly not obtain what we wish, we must exercise moderation, so as not to give offence to the King. The edict has forty-seven heads. If in regard to four or five of the heads some reasonable relief were obtained, the brethren will think themselves not hardly dealt with. One for instance requires, that on holidays each with his family be present at the mass, and not only that he approve that idolatry by his gesture, and defile himself by impious and faithless hypocrisy, but that the articles of the Sorbonne be read aloud at the sacrifice ; and thus all will subscribe to abominable blasphemies. But it is demanded that there be a rigorous examination of this matter. We must beg of the King, therefore, that men who pass their lives quietly, giving offence to none, shall not be eagerly watched, nor be subjected to the captious demands of the priests. The King confiscates the goods of those who betake themselves to us,—to places, as he says, obviously removed from obedience to the Holy See : nay, should their property be sold, he orders the purchasers to be dispossessed. As to this, we must beg that no man shall be considered a criminal, if, having nothing else laid to his charge, he willingly and peacefully migrate elsewhere, because he cannot for conscience sake remain in the kingdom ; provided only that they do not betake themselves to an unfriendly country. But the first thing to be secured is, that an embassy be resolved upon. It will appear afterwards what is to be demanded.

To the letters which I received when already on horseback, I only reply that I had good reason to expostulate, especially to a brother, in a brotherly way. Consider what we expected from you in the troubled state of our affairs. Consider, also, how contrary to our hopes was the answer you gave us ; you may see that we had some cause to grieve. You wonder, because I utter a moderate and gentle complaint, that we were assisted less liberally than we had promised ourselves. However, I make no objection to my letters remaining buried, if they contained anything offensive.

The little book which I send you, will satisfy you, I hope, concerning the whole matter.[1] You may, however, if you choose, convey through me your free judgment. My brother's father-in-law was to have travelled thither with me ; but since God has thrown an obstacle in our way, he writes to his son's master to keep him till the end of the year, for but a short time now remains. In the meanwhile, it will be the master's duty to treat him as a boy who requires a tighter rein and a severer discipline. Farewell, most accomplished Sir, and most

[1] Doubtless the writing published by Calvin and his colleagues, entitled, " Congrégation faite en l'Eglise de Genève sur la Matière de l'élection éternelle." Geneva, 1552, 8vo.

esteemed brother. Salute warmly, in my name, your brethren and fellow-ministers. The Lord guide you by His Spirit, and keep you under His protection! Amen. The Marquis de Vico,[1] and Normandie, and our other companions, desire me to greet you heartily.

Excuse my employing an amanuensis, for I dictate from my bed.

In the name of Farel and myself,

JOHN CALVIN.

[*Lat. orig. autogr.—Arch. of Zurich. Gallicana Scripta,* p. 16.]


CCXCIII.—TO CRANMER.[2]

Agreement to the proposal for assembling a General Synod for the more close union of the Reformed Churches.

GENEVA, [*April* 1552.]

Your opinion, most distinguished Sir, is indeed just and wise, that in the present disordered condition of the Church, no remedy can be devised more suitable than if a general meeting were

---

[1] The Marquis de Vico, a Neapolitan nobleman, retired to Geneva. He was admitted an inhabitant of the city, "after having promised to submit to the laws of the magistrates, and to live in the profession of the Reformed religion."—*Registers of Council,* 15th June 1551.

[2] Thomas Cranmer, Archbishop of Canterbury and Primate of England, took an important part in the Reformation of his country during the reigns of Henry VIII. and Edward VI. He laboured assiduously with the Reformers of the Continent, who esteemed his learning and honoured his character, to establish a bond of union between the foreign churches and his own; and if he did not live to see his efforts crowned with success, he at least left behind him an example worthy of imitation. What is most notable in these endeavours is to be found in Cranmer's Letters to the leading theologians of Switzerland and Germany, reproduced in the Collections of his Works published by the *Parker Society.* They are likewise to be found in the Collection of *Zurich Letters,* 1st series, vol. i. p. 21-26, from which we borrow the following letter to Calvin, which furnishes us with the date of the Reformer's reply to the Prelate:—" As nothing tends more injuriously to the separation of the Churches than heresies and disputes respecting the doctrines of religion, so nothing tends more effectually to unite the Churches of God, and more powerfully to defend the fold of Christ, than the pure teaching of the Gospel and harmony of doctrine. Wherefore I have often wished, and still continue to do so, that learned and godly men, who are eminent for erudition and judgment, might meet together, and, comparing their respective opinions, might handle all the heads of ecclesiastical doc-

held of the devout and the prudent, of those properly exercised in the school of God, and of those who are confessedly at one on the doctrine of holiness. For we see how Satan is attempting, by various devices, to extinguish the light of the Gospel, which, by the wonderful goodness of God, having risen upon us, is shining in many a quarter. The hireling dogs of the Pope cease not to bark, in order to prevent the pure Gospel of Christ from being heard: so great is the licentiousness that is here and there breaking forth, and the ungodliness that is spreading abroad, that religion is become a mere mockery; and those who are not professed enemies of the truth, nevertheless conduct themselves with an impropriety which will create in a short time, unless it be obviated, terrible disorder among us. And not only among the common herd of men here does the distemper of a stupid inquisitiveness alternate with that of fearless extravagance, but, what is more lamentable, in the ranks of the pastors also the malady is now gaining ground. It is too well known with what mad actions Osiander is deceiving himself and deluding certain others.[1] Yet the Lord, as he has

trine, and hand down to posterity, under the weight of their authority, some work not only upon the subjects themselves, but upon the forms of expressing them. Our adversaries are now holding their councils at Trent, for the establishment of their errors; and shall we neglect to call together a godly synod, for the refutation of error, and for restoring and propagating the truth? They are, as I am informed, making decrees respecting the worship of the host; wherefore we ought to leave no stone unturned, not only that we may guard others against this idolatry, but also that we may ourselves come to an agreement upon the doctrine of this sacrament. It cannot escape your prudence how exceedingly the Church of God has been injured by dissensions and varieties of opinion respecting the sacrament of unity; and though they are now in some measure removed, yet I could wish for an agreement in this doctrine, not only as regards the subject itself, but also with respect to the words and forms of expression. You have now my wish, about which I have also written to Masters Philip [Melanchthon] and Bullinger; and I pray you to deliberate among yourselves as to the means by which this synod can be assembled with the greatest convenience. Farewell.—Your very dear brother in Christ,

"Thomas Cantuar.

"Lambeth, 20th March 1552."

Calvin could only subscribe to the wishes so nobly expressed by Cranmer, and which harmonized so well with the most elevated sentiments of the Reformer of Geneva.

[1] Alluding to the unfortunate controversies raised by Osiander in Germany on the doctrine of Justification.

done even from the beginning of the world, will preserve in a miraculous manner, and in a way unknown to us, the unity of a pure faith from being destroyed by the dissensions of men. And those whom He has placed on His watchtower He wishes least of all to be inactive, seeing that He has appointed them to be His ministers, through whose labours He may preserve from all corruptions sound doctrine in the Church, and transmit it safe to posterity. Especially, most illustrious Archbishop, is it necessary for you, in proportion to the distinguished position you occupy, to turn your attention as you are doing towards this object. I do not say this as if to spur you on to greater exertions, who are not only, of your own accord, in advance of others, but are also, as a voluntary encourager, urging them on; I say it in order that, by my congratulations, you may be strengthened in a pursuit so auspicious and noble. I hear that the success of the Gospel in England is indeed cheering; but you will experience there also, I doubt not, what Paul experienced in his time, that by means of the door that has been opened for the reception of pure doctrine, many enemies will suddenly rise up against it. Although I am really ignorant of how many suitable defenders you may have at hand to repel the lies of Satan, still the ungodliness of those who are wholly taken up in creating disturbances, causes the assiduity of the well-disposed to be at no time either too much or superfluous. And then I am aware that English matters are not so all-important in your eyes, but that you, at the same time, regard the interests of the whole world. Moreover, the rare piety of the English King, as well as his noble disposition, is worthy of the highest commendation, in that, of his own inclination, he entertains the pious design of holding a convention of the nature referred to, and offers a place for it also in his own kingdom. And would that it were attainable to bring together into some place, from various Churches, men eminent for their learning, and that after having carefully discussed the main points of belief one by one, they should, from their united judgments, hand down to posterity the true doctrine of Scripture. This other thing also is to be ranked among the chief evils of our time, viz., that the Churches are so divided, that human fellowship is scarcely now in any repute amongst us, far less that Christian intercourse which all make a profession of, but few sincerely practise. If men of learning conduct themselves with more reserve than is seemly, the very heaviest blame attaches to the leaders themselves, who, either engrossed in their own sinful pursuits, are indifferent to the safety and entire piety of the Church, or who, individually satisfied with their own private peace, have no regard for others. Thus it is that the members of the Church being severed, the body lies bleeding. So much does this concern me, that, could I be of any service, I would not grudge to cross even ten seas, if need were, on account of it. If it were but a question regarding the rendering of assistance to the kingdom of England, such a motive would at present be to me a sufficiently just one. Now, seeing that a serious and properly adjusted agreement between men of learning upon the rule of Scripture is still a desideratum, by means of which Churches, though divided on other questions, might be made to unite, I think it right for me, at whatever cost of toil and trouble, to seek to obtain this object. But I hope my own insignificance will cause me to be passed by. If I earnestly pray that it may be undertaken by others, I hope I shall have discharged my duty. Mr. Philip [Melanchthon] is at too great a distance to admit of a speedy interchange of letters. Mr. Bullinger has likely written you before this time. Would that I were as able as I am willing to exert myself! Moreover, the very difficulty of the thing which you feel, compels me to do what, at the outset, I affirmed I would not do, viz., not only to encourage, but also to implore you to increase your exertions, until something at least shall have been accomplished, if not all that we could desire.—Adieu, very distinguished Archbishop, deserving of my hearty reverence. May the Lord continue to guide you by His Spirit, and to bless your holy labours!

JOHN CALVIN.

[Calvin's *Lat. Corresp.* Opera, tom. ix. p. 61.]

## CCXCIV.—To Bullinger.

*Fresh details regarding the persecutions in France.*

GENEVA, *Whitsunday* 1552.

After having resided for some time at Paris, this pious young man retired among you, and, judging from his conduct, I have no doubt but that he has really the fear of God in him, and is of a truly modest character. He studied the humanities with considerable success, has since entered upon theology, and now, that he may make greater progress in this study, he has resolved to enter your College and Church. Although he is not inclined to trouble you, nor, as I trust, any one else, yet as he appeared to me to be a person of pure and simple piety, I did not choose to send him away without this testimony. Our two friends who lately went among you have not yet returned. Would that our pious brethren experienced some relief![1] About two weeks ago, two others were put in chains at Lyons.[2] The faithful in Bretagne and Anjou are being badly treated. One was burnt lately at Bordeaux; others saved their lives by a perfidious recantation. He is venting his rage in other parts of the kingdom also. We must, therefore, be busy while we have opportunity. Adieu, most accomplished Sir and revered brother. May the Lord be ever near you to guide by His Spirit. Salute your fellow-ministers in my name. My brethren salute you earnestly.—Yours,

JOHN CALVIN.

[*Lat. Copy—Imperial Library, Coll. of Dupuy*, 102.]

[1] See the eloquent appeal addressed to Bullinger, *ante*, pp. 304, 326. The latter had written to Calvin, giving him an account of the fruitless efforts of the Cantons with Henry II., and of the haughty response of that monarch: " He lives who delivered His people from Egypt; He lives who brought back the captivity from Babylon; He lives who defended His Church against Cæsars, kings, and profligate princes. Verily we must needs pass through many afflictions into the kingdom of God. But woe to those who touch the apple of God's eye."—*Calv. Opera*, tom. ix. p. 68.

[2] See the following Letter.

CCXCV.—To the Five Prisoners of Lyons,—Martial Alba, Peter Escrivain, Charles Favre, Peter Navihères, Bernard Seguin.[1]

*Information on various doctrinal points, and assurances of Christian sympathy.*

From Geneva, *this* 10*th of June* 1552.

My very dear Brethren,—Hitherto I have put off writing to you, fearing that if the letter fell into bad hands, it might give fresh occasion to the enemy to afflict you. And besides, I had been informed how that God wrought so powerfully in you by His grace, that you stood in no great need of my letters. However, we have not forgotten you, neither I nor all the brethren hereabouts, as to whatever we have been able to do for you. As soon as you were taken, we heard of it, and knew how it had come to pass. We took care that help might be sent you with all speed, and are now waiting the result. Those who have influence with the prince in whose power God has put your lives, are faithfully exerting themselves on your behalf, but we do not yet know how far they have succeeded in their suit. Meanwhile, all the children of God pray for you as they are bound to do, not only on account of the mutual compassion

---

[1] In the month of April 1552, five young Frenchmen, instructed at the school of theology of Lausanne, and devoted to the functions of the ministry, made arrangements for returning to their own country. These were Martial Alba of Montauban, Peter Ecrivain of Gascony, Charles Favre of Blanzac in Angoumois, Peter Navihères of Limousin, and Bernard Seguin of La Reole. After having spent some days at Geneva, they set out for Lyons, and met on the way at the Bourg de Colonges, nigh to L'Ecluse, a stranger, who offered himself as their fellow-traveller. They consented without harbouring any suspicion. Arrived at Lyons, they parted with their travelling companion, who pressed them to visit him at his dwelling of Ainay. They went thither without any distrust, were arrested and led away to the prisons of that jurisdiction. Such was the origin of a long and doleful process, which held the Churches of France and Switzerland for a long time in suspense, and during which, the bloodthirsty cruelty of the judges was only equalled by the constancy of the victims. On the first rumour of the arrest of the five students, the Church of Geneva took the matter up, and lavished upon the captives, by the voice of Calvin, the most lively testimonies of their sympathy.

which ought to exist between members of the same body, but because they know well that you labour for them, in maintaining the cause of their salvation. We hope, come what may, that God of His goodness will give a happy issue to your captivity, so that we shall have reason to rejoice. You see to what He has called you; doubt not, therefore, that according as He employs you, He will give you strength to fulfil His work, for He has promised this, and we know by experience that He has never failed those who allow themselves to be governed by Him. Even now you have proof of this in yourselves, for He has shown His power, by giving you so much constancy in withstanding the first assaults. Be confident, therefore, that He will not leave the work of His hand imperfect. You know what Scripture sets before us, to encourage us to fight for the cause of the Son of God; meditate upon what you have both heard and seen formerly on this head, so as to put it in practice. For all that I could say would be of little service to you, were it not drawn from this fountain. And truly we have need of a much more firm support than that of men, to make us victorious over such strong enemies as the devil, death, and the world; but the firmness which is in Christ Jesus is sufficient for this, and all else that might shake us were we not established in Him. Knowing, then, in whom ye have believed, manifest what authority He deserves to have over you.

As I hope to write to you again, I shall not at present lengthen my letter. I shall only reply briefly to the point which brother Bernard has asked me to solve. Concerning vows, we must hold to this rule, that it is not lawful to vow to God anything but what He approves. Now the fact is, that monastic vows tend only to corrupt His service. As for the second question, we must hold that it is devilish presumption for a man to vow beyond the measure of his vocation. Now, the Scripture declares, both in the nineteenth of St. Matthew and in the seventh of the First to the Corinthians, that the gift of continence is a special grace. It follows, then, that those who put themselves in the position and under the necessity of renouncing marriage for the whole of their life, cannot be acquitted of rashness, and that by so doing they tempt God. The question might very easily be spun out to a greater length, by stating that we ought to consider, first, who HE is to whom we vow; secondly, the nature of that vow; and thirdly, the party making the vow. For God is too great a Master for us to trifle with, and man is bound to consider his own capabilities; for to present a sacrifice without obedience, is nothing but thorough pollution. However, this one point may suffice you to prove to them that the gift of continence is a special gift, and in suchwise special, that for the most part it is only for a season. So that he who possessed it for thirty years, like Isaac, may not do so for the remainder of his life. Hence you may conclude, that the monks, in binding themselves never to marry, attempt without faith to promise what is not given to them. As for their poverty, it is quite the reverse of that which our Lord enjoined upon his followers.

Concerning the nature of a glorified body, true it is, that the qualities thereof are changed, but not entirely. For we must distinguish between the qualities which proceed from the corruption of sin, and those which belong to and are inseparable from the nature of the body. St. Paul, in the third chapter of the Epistle to the Philippians, says that our vile or weak body shall be made like to the glorious body of Christ. By this humble expression or *Tapinosis,* he points out which of the qualities that we at present bear about with us in our bodies are to be changed; those, namely, which are of the corruptible and fading nature of this world. And on this subject St. Augustine says, in *the Epistle to Dardanus,* which in number is the 57th, "*He shall come again in the same form and substance of the flesh, to which certainly he gave immortality; he hath not taken away the nature. In this form he must not be supposed to be everywhere diffused.*" This argument he follows out at greater length, showing that the body of Christ is contained within its own dimensions. And in fact our glorified bodies will not be ubiquitous, although they will have that likeness of which St. Paul speaks. As for the passage of the Apocalypse, the words are these in the fifth chapter: "*And every creature which is in heaven, and on the earth, and under the earth, and such as are in the sea, and all that are in them, heard I saying, Bless-*

ing, and honour, and glory, and power, be unto Him that sitteth upon the throne, and unto the Lamb, for ever and ever." Now you see that it is a childish cavil to apply this to souls in purgatory; for St. John, by the figure which is called *Prosopopœia*, rather conveys that even the fishes blessed God. And in regard to the passages of the Doctors, refer your people to the 27th Epistle of St. Augustine, *To Boniface*, where he states, towards the end, *that the sacraments have a certain similitude of those things which they represent. From whence it comes to pass, that after some fashion the sacrament of the body of Christ may be the body of Christ.* Item, that which he treats of in the third book, *Of Christian Doctrine*, where he says, among other things in the fifth chapter, "*Such is the completely miserable bondage of the soul in conceiving of the signs in place of the things signified, and never lifting up the eye of the understanding above the corporeal creature to breathe eternal light.*" Item, in the ninth chapter.—"*The believer knows by experience, and understands* [agnoscit] *to what the mystery of baptism, and the celebration of the body and blood of the Lord, may be referred, so that the soul can offer religious worship, not in the bondage of the flesh, but rather in the liberty of the spirit. So to follow the literal sense, and in suchwise to conceive of the signs instead of the things sealed or signified by them, is a slavish weakness; that mere symbols should be so unprofitably interpreted, is the result of vague error.*" I do not heap up quotations, because these will be quite enough for your purpose. In conclusion, I beseech our good Lord that He would be pleased to make you feel in every way the worth of His protection of His own, to fill you with His Holy Spirit, who gives you prudence and virtue, and brings you peace, joy, and contentment; and may the name of our Lord Jesus be glorified by you to the edification of His Church!

[*Fr.*—Printed in *Histoire des Martyrs*, lib. iv. p. 225.]

CCXCVI.—To EDWARD VI.[1]

Dedication of a new work, and Christian exhortations.

FROM GENEVA, *this 4th July* 1552.

SIRE,—Although I ought to fear lest my importunity may prove troublesome to your Majesty, and have indeed on that account abstained from writing to you more frequently, nevertheless, I have had the boldness to send you, together with my letters, a short exposition which I have composed of the 78th (87th)[2] Psalm, hoping that you would take pleasure in it, and also that the reading thereof might be profitable to you. As I was one day expounding it in a sermon to the people, the argument appeared to me so appropriate for you, that I was forthwith moved to draw up a summary of it, such as you will see, when it shall please your Majesty to devote to it one hour only. It is very true, that I treat the subject generally, without addressing you personally. But as I have mainly had regard to you in the writing of it, so in the prudent application and appropriation of it, you will find that it contains a very profitable lesson for your Majesty.

You know, Sire, how much danger kings and princes are in, lest the height to which they are raised should dazzle their eyes, and amuse them here below, while making them forgetful of the heavenly kingdom; and I doubt not that God hath so warned you against this evil, to preserve you therefrom, that you are a hundred times more impressed with it, than those

---

[1] Calvin wrote this letter to King Edward VI., when dedicating to him the following little work: Four Sermons of Master John Calvin, treating of matters very profitable for our time, with a Brief Exposition of Psalm lxxxvii. Geneva, 1552, in 8vo, inserted in the *Receuil des Opuscules*, p. 824. These four sermons have been translated at different times into English. In the first, Calvin exhorts the faithful to flee from idolatry; in the second, he encourages them to suffer everything for Jesus Christ; in the third, he shews how highly believers ought to prize the privilege of being in the Church of God, where they are at liberty to worship Him purely; in the last, he shews that this liberty cannot be purchased at too high a price.

[2] An error in the original, it is 87 which we must read.

who have no personal experience of it. Now, in the present Psalm mention is made of the nobleness and dignity of the Church, which ought so to enrapture both great and small, that no earthly honours and possessions should hold them back, or hinder them from aiming to be enrolled among the people of God. It is indeed a great thing to be a king, and yet more, over such a country; nevertheless, I have no doubt that you reckon it beyond comparison better to be a Christian. It is therefore an invaluable privilege that God has vouchsafed you, Sire, to be a Christian king, to serve as his lieutenant in ordering and maintaining the kingdom of Jesus Christ in England. You see, then, that in acknowledgment of such great benefits received from His infinite goodness, you ought to be stirred up to employ all your energies to His honour and service, setting to your subjects an example of homage to this great King, to whom your Majesty is not ashamed to submit yourself with all humility and reverence beneath the spiritual sceptre of His gospel; and if hitherto you have done this, so that we have cause to glorify God for his goodness, the present Psalm will always serve you as a support and a buckler. Meanwhile, I humbly entreat you, Sire, that this short letter may serve as a protest and testimony to your Majesty of the hearty desire I have to do better, if the means were given me.

Sire, after having very humbly commended me to your kind favour, I pray our Lord to fill you with the gifts of his Holy Spirit, to guide you in all prudence and virtue, to make you prosper and flourish to the glory of His name.

Your very humble and obedient servant,

JOHN CALVIN.

[*Fr. orig. autogr.—British Museum. Harl. Coll.* No. 6989, Art. 83.]

## CCXCVII.—To CRANMER.[1]

Calvin exhorts him to prosecute with fresh zeal the reformation of the Church in England, by purging it of the relics of Popery.

[*July* 1552.]

Seeing that, at the present time, that which is most of all to be desired is least likely to be attained, viz., that an assembly of the most eminent men of learning, from all the various Churches which have embraced the pure doctrine of the Gospel, after having discussed separately the controverted topics of the day, might transmit to posterity, out of the pure Word of God, a true and distinct confession; I nevertheless highly commend the plan which you, reverend Sir, have adopted, to make the English frame for themselves, without delay, a religious constitution, lest, by matters remaining longer in an unsettled state, or not being sufficiently adjusted, the minds of the common people should be confirmed in their suspense. And it is the duty of all in your country, who have any influence, to direct their energies with united zeal toward this object, so that your duties may still be special. You see what such a position as yours demands, or rather what God may legitimately require of you in consideration of the nature of the office which He has imposed on you. Supreme authority is vested in you—an authority which your high rank entitles you to, not more than the previously entertained opinion regarding your wisdom and integrity. The eyes of many are fixed upon you, either to second your exertions, or to imitate your lukewarmness. And sincerely do I desire that, under your leadership, they may be advanced to such an extent during the next three years, that the difficulties and contests of the present time, caused by the removing of the grossest superstition, shall have ceased to exist. I, for my part, acknowledge that our cause has made no little progress during the short period the Gospel has flourished in

[1] This letter bears no date, but it refers to the subject set forth in a preceding letter of Calvin's to Cranmer, p. 330, and we have no hesitation in assigning it a place in the course of the same year,—perhaps in *July* 1552.

England. But if you reflect on what yet remains to be done, and how very remiss you have been in many matters, you will discover that you have no reason to advance towards the goal with less rapidity, even although the most of the course has, as it were, been gone over; for I need not inform you that I, as it were, take note of your assiduity, lest, after having escaped danger, you should become self-indulgent. But to speak freely, I greatly fear, and this fear is abiding, that so many autumns will be spent in procrastinating, that by and by the cold of a perpetual winter will set in. You are now somewhat advanced in years, and this ought to stimulate you to increased exertions, so as to save yourself the regret of having been consciously dilatory, and that you may not leave the world while matters remain in so disordered a condition. I say matters are still in a disorganized state, for external religious abuses have been corrected in such a way as to leave remaining innumerable young shoots, which are constantly sprouting forth. In fact, I am informed that such a mass of Papal corruptions remain, as not only to hide, but almost to extinguish the pure worship of God. Meanwhile the life of the whole ecclesiastical order is all but extinct, or at least is not sufficiently vigorous: take, for example, the preaching of doctrine. Assuredly pure and undefiled religion will never flourish, until the Churches shall have been at greater pains to secure suitable pastors, and such as shall conscientiously discharge the duties of teaching. Satan, indeed, opposes his secret wiles to the accomplishment of this. I understand that there is still one shameful obstacle, viz., that the revenues of the Church have been plundered; truly an insufferable evil. But iniquitous as this is, there appears to me to be another vice of equal magnitude, viz., that out of the public revenues of the Church, idle gluttons are supported who chant vespers in an unknown tongue. I shall say nothing farther on this point, except that it is inconsistent for you to approve of such mockery, and it is openly incompatible with the proper arrangements of the Church; besides, it is in itself exceedingly ridiculous. I do not doubt, however, but that these considerations will immediately occur to your own mind, and will be suggested to you by that most upright man Peter Martyr, whose counsel I am exceedingly glad to know you enjoy. Difficulties so numerous and so trying as those against which you are contending, appear to me a sufficient excuse for the exhortations I have offered.—Adieu, most distinguished and esteemed Primate. May the Lord long preserve you in safety; may He fill you more and more with the Spirit of wisdom and fortitude, and bless your labours! Amen.

JOHN CALVIN.

[*Calvin's Lat. Corresp.* Opera, tom. ix. p. 61.]

## CCXCVIII.—TO JOHN LINER.[1]

Thanks for the zeal manifested by him on behalf of the prisoners of Lyons.

*This* 10*th of August* 1552.

VERY DEAR SIR AND BROTHER,—We are all bound to give thanks to God for having made choice of you to assist our poor brethren who are detained in prison by the enemies of the faith, and having so strengthened you by the power of his Spirit, that you spare no pains in so doing. I say that we are bound to give thanks to Him; for we must needs recognise this work as His, and that it is He alone who has disposed and directed you thereto. You have also reason to rejoice at the honour He has done you, in employing you in so worthy and honourable a service, and giving you grace to perform it. For however despised and rejected of men, the poor believers persecuted for the sake of the Gospel may be, yet we know that God esteems them very pearls; that there is nothing more

[1] A letter without address, but evidently, as the date and the contents prove, relating to the trial of the five students of Lausanne.—(See the letter of the 10th of June, and the note at p. 340.) The personage to whom Calvin writes, is doubtless John Liner, a rich merchant of Saint Gall, settled at Lyons, who often visited the scholars in their dungeon, undertook several journeys on their behalf, and was unsparing, during the whole course of the suit, in tokens of most lively affection.—(*Histoire des Martyrs*, liv. iv. pp. 230, 231) John Liner afterwards retired to his own country, where he lived to a very advanced age, and corresponded with Charles de Jonvillers, the secretary of Calvin, a correspondence which has been preserved to our days in the library of Saint Gall. Note, p. 348.

agreeable to Him than our striving to comfort and help them as much as in us lies. The Lord Jesus declares, that whatsoever shall have been done to one of the least of His people, will be acknowledged by Him as done to Himself. How then if we have furthered those who fight His battle? For such are as it were his agents, whom He appoints and ordains for the defence of His Gospel. Yea, He declares that a glass of water given to them shall not be lost. If then you have hitherto had the courage to present so goodly a sacrifice to God, strive to persevere. I know well that the devil will not fail to whisper in your ear on many sides to divert you from it, but let God prove the strongest, as is meet He should. It is said that they who comfort the children of God in their persecutions which they endure for the Gospel, are fellow-labourers for the truth. Be content with this testimony, for it is no light matter that God should uphold and approve us as His martyrs, even though we do not personally suffer, merely because His martyrs are helped and comforted by us. And, therefore, although many tell you the contrary, do not leave off so good a work, or show yourself weary half-way. I feel assured that you did not look to men at the first; follow on then as the servant of Him to whom we must cleave to the end. Reflect, moreover, how many worthy brethren there are who glorify God for what you are doing, who would be scandalized if you altered your course. As for the dangers which they set before you, I have no fear of their coming to pass, for the good brethren for whom you have done so much, feel themselves so indebted to you, that were they at liberty, far from being cowardly enough to betray you, they would expose themselves to death for your sake. You must also consider, that by the support which they receive from you, they are the more confirmed, for they have no doubt whatever that God has directed you to them, as indeed He has. And they have reason to lean still more firmly upon Him, seeing the paternal care He shews them. Be of good courage, therefore, in this holy work, in which you serve not only God and His martyrs, but also the whole Church.

Whereupon, my very dear Sir and brother, after having heartily commended myself to you, I pray our good Lord that

He would increase you more and more with the gifts and riches of His Spirit, for the furtherance of His own honour; and meanwhile, that He would have you in His keeping.

JOHN CALVIN.

[*Fr. copy—Library of Geneva.* Vol. 107.]

## CCXCIX.—To the French Church in London.[1]

Exhortations to harmony—Is it lawful to call Mary the Mother of God, and to pray for the Pope?

FROM GENEVA, this 27th September 1552.

VERY DEAR AND HONOURED BRETHREN,—As I desire your quiet, to the end that, being at peace among yourselves, you may be the better enabled and disposed to serve God, and may do so with the greater courage, I have grieved for the trouble which some inconsiderate people have occasioned you, and grieved doubly because they made a cloak of me and of this Church in order to trouble you. Now, as they did us injustice in that, it appears to me that you ought to have been too reasonable and humane to suffer us to be mixed up and implicated in their follies. One of them, of whom I had heard complaint made, will bear me witness that I have not encouraged him in his fault since his return, but have rather endeavoured to make

---

[1] To the brethren of . . . . , without any further indication. The name of the Polish nobleman, John A Lasco, moderator of the Congregation of Foreign Protestants at London, informs us to what Church this letter was addressed. The Reformed Church of London, next to that of Strasbourg the oldest of the refugee churches, was formed during the first years of the reign of Edward VI., obtained a legal recognition in 1550, had for ministers Francis Péruçel, called La Rivière, and Richard Vanville, and as moderator an illustrious foreign nobleman, devoted to the cause of religious reform, John A Lasco or Laski. Dispersed in 1553, under the intolerant reign of Mary, it reconstituted itself under the reparative reign of Elizabeth, and reckoned in the list of its pastors one of the most distinguished ministers of Geneva, Nicolas des Gallars. In its early commencement, that Church, which has been perpetuated to our own day, and to which the greater part of the French Churches of England, of Scotland, and even of America, owe their origin and their organization, was troubled by theological disputes, which made the intervention of Calvin needful.

him feel and understand it, although M. A Lasco had written to me confidentially that all had been forgiven. I mention this, because I have heard that they have been reproached with wishing to make an idol of me and a Jerusalem of Geneva. I have not deserved that your Church should treat me thus, and even were there twice the amount of ingratitude, I should not cease to seek your welfare. But I am constrained to warn you of it, for such proceedings are calculated rather to ruin than to edify. And however I may seek to bury such matters in oblivion, I cannot hinder many from being offended by them. If those who have stirred up these conflicts have taken occasion to do so from the diversity of ceremonies, as M. A Lasco has informed me,[1] they have but ill understood in what the true unity of Christians consists, and how every member is bound to conform himself to the body of the Church in which he lives. It is true, that if a different form has been seen and preferred, it is quite allowable in communicating first of all with the pastor, to tell him what is thought of it, provided one accommodates one's-self to the usages of the place where one lives, without clamouring for novelty, but peaceably conforming to any order that is not repugnant to the Word of God. Now, how the two persons in question have proceeded I know not, unless I give credit to the testimony which has been furnished me, namely, that there has been a great want of consideration, and that they have neither observed due measure nor modesty. But this I say, because it is well to set such persons right by gentleness, rather than to make matters worse by over-violent remedies. Not that I mean to say that they have been too severely dealt with, but that I have heard it so reported, although I do not believe it. I think that you will not take it ill that I let you know this, as it can do you no harm.

Concerning the other debateable points, I doubt not but there may have been somewhat of ignorance in their reproving the way of speaking of the Virgin Mary as the mother of God, and together with ignorance, it is possible

---

[1] A Lasco had composed a work entitled, *The whole Form and Manner of the Ecclesiastical Ministry in the Church of the Strangers, set up at London by the very faithful Prince, Edward VI.*

that there may have been rashness and too much forwardness, for, as the old proverb says, the most ignorant are ever the boldest. However, to deal with you with brotherly frankness, I cannot conceal that that title being commonly attributed to the Virgin in sermons is disapproved, and, for my own part, I cannot think such language either right, or becoming, or suitable. Neither will any sober-minded people do so, for which reason I cannot persuade myself that there is any such usage in your church, for it is just as if you were to speak of the blood, of the head, and of the death of God. You know that the Scriptures accustom us to a different style; but there is something still worse about this particular instance, for to call the Virgin Mary the mother of God, can only serve to harden the ignorant in their superstitions. And he that would take a pleasure in that, shews clearly that he knows not what it is to edify the Church.

As for the name of the Bishop of Rome, that is a foolish question to dwell upon. We bestow too much honour upon those horned cattle in calling them bishops, for the name is too honourable for them. Neither does the title of Pope any better suit the brigand who has usurped God's seat. In reference to this, I would follow unbiassed that which is commonly received. The chief practical point of difference is about the form of prayer. I know that we must make a due distinction between the individual and the abominable and accursed seat (of the beast). But I do think that those who pray specially for him who bears such a mark of reprobation, have surely much time to spare. I lay down laws for no one, but it were much to be desired that the sobriety of our prayers should shew the reverence we feel for the name of God. I speak with such freedom as you ought to bear from a brother, and I hope, too, that you will bear with it; for I shall be quite ready to suffer the word of admonition from you whenever you disapprove of what I write to you. Moreover, when you have well weighed the matter, and that each is willing, without contention, to submit to the truth, I hope that harmony will easily be established amongst us. Furthermore, if this annoyance has been hard upon you, have some compassion upon us, who have here daily far more rude encounters to sustain. And for my part, I shall continue to pray our good Lord as I do, that it would please Him to increase you more and more in the graces of His Spirit, to make your labours profitable, and to strengthen your hands in the exercise of the rule which He has committed to you. And my brethren will do the same, for I know their mind towards you.

[*Fr. Copy.—Library of Geneva.* Vol. 107.]


## CCC.—To the Seigneurs of Geneva.[1]

Reply of Calvin to the Syndics of Geneva in the case of Trolliet.

*6th October* 1552.

The answer of John Calvin, minister of the Word of God in the Church of God, presented this Tuesday, the 6th of October 1552, to our honourable Lords Messieurs the Syndics and Council, against the writing produced on the Monday preceding, by the Seigneur Trouillet :—

In the first place, Messieurs, as for what he terms his written defence in his disputation against me, I do not understand what he aims at, nor for what purpose he says this, unless to acquire reputation with the ignorant, from having disputed with John

---

[1] On the back, in the handwriting of Calvin : " The case against Trolliet."
Trolliet, of Geneva, a discontented and unsettled spirit, became, first of all a hermit in Burgundy, and lived in affectation of sanctity. Soon tired, however, of playing this part, he reappeared at Geneva, and solicited the functions of the ministry, from which he was warned off by the influence of Calvin, against whom he vowed an irreconcilable hatred. Thenceforward, he made himself remarkable in the ranks of the libertine party, by the violence of his attacks against the Reformer. He arraigned his writings, and offered to prove, that in the book of *The Christian Institution*, Calvin had made God *the author of sin* These accusations, emulously repeated by the adversaries of the Reformer, and speciously tricked up with the authority of Melanchthon, provoked sharp discussions, which were only half appeased by the sentence of the Seigneurs of Geneva, who approved the *Christian Institution*, while at the same time declaring Trolliet, " homme de bien," out of consideration for the party to which he belonged. The whole of the papers relating to the controversy of Calvin with Trolliet, are to be found collected in Vol. 145 of the *MSS. of the Library of Geneva.*

Calvin. And your Excellencies know what the whole procedure was, namely, that he became confused, having no reply to make, except that he did not understand it. Wherefore, it would be well that he should get rid of vain-glory, which has too much incited him already to give unnecessary trouble and annoyance, as well to himself as to others. For had he walked as modestly as he ought, according to his measure, this contention would never have arisen.

But the worst is, that he pretends to sustain his charge against me, and, nevertheless, misrepresents the whole argument. For the point which was debated on the first day of September, was that he charged me with making God the author of sin, which I denied with all due protestation, for it is an utterly execrable blasphemy. Whereupon he attempted to prove it, alleging the passages which he cites in his written representation. So that the main point of our case, as he has maintained in your presence more than ten times over, lies in this,—Whether I have made God the cause of evil and of sin, or not. And but for this, there was no difficulty whatever regarding this first point. For I do not disavow anything that I have written. But I say that we ought to have a horror of applying the word sin, to God; seeing that in Him there is nothing but all equity and justice, even as He is both the rule and the fountain thereof. Wherefore I am amazed that he was not ashamed of denying it. But be that as it may, if he be obstinate in his denial, I require, as right and reason enjoins, that it may please you, before going farther, to order your secretary to give me an act and extract to that effect. For I ought not, and cannot suffer such a reproach to be fastened upon me, without clearing myself as I ought. Moreover, in the sentences which he quotes as extracts from my *Institution*, he does me great wrong, having given them in a detached and garbled form. And he even thrusts in and mixes up with the doctrine which is avowedly mine, the objections which are made to it by blasphemers. He ought to have been much ashamed, when I demonstrated that by such means Saint Paul might be charged with having called God unrighteous. But that he should persist in such a course, is altogether unbearable. Again, that which he brings forward on the first page, from leaf 461, is wrongly stated, and contrary to my true meaning, seeing that he accumulates there what I have said about the wicked, whom I reprove and condemn.[1]

However, I am free to confess, that I have stated that God not only has foreseen, but also foreordained, the fall of Adam, which I maintain to be true,[2] not without good grounds and evidences from holy writ. The opposite party, without alluding to the proofs which I bring forward, says that I have spoken amiss, and at the same time can allege nothing to shew that I have done so, except, indeed, that he is pleased to arrive at that conclusion. Judge, Messieurs, whether this be equitable.

On the second proposition :—

As to his accusing me of having written—That man is by the ordinance and will of God under the necessity of sinning. I much wish, as I have so often said, that people would not attribute to me that jargon of the monks, which I have never used. And indeed it is only those hypocrites who have ever twaddled thus. Let then the doctrine, as I state it, be attentively considered, and I am ready to acknowledge that the

---

[1] "Since we are all corrupt and contaminate by vice, it cannot be but God must hate us, and that not with tyrannical cruelty, but with reasonable equity. . . . . That all the children of Adam come forward to contend and dispute against their Creator, because by His eternal Providence, they were devoted, before they were born, to perpetual calamity. When, on the contrary, God brings them to know themselves, how can they murmur at that ? If they have all been taken out of a corrupt mass, it is no way marvellous that they are liable to condemnation. Let them not therefore accuse God of iniquity, because by His eternal decree they are ordained to condemnation, to which their very nature makes them amenable."— *Institution of the Christian Religion*, edit. of 1554, p. 461.

[2] "The first man fell, because God thought it fit. Now, as to why he thought it fit, we know nothing. Yet it is certain, that he has not thus decided, unless because He saw that it would advance the glory of His name. . . . . Man then falls, according as it has been ordained of God, but he falls by his own vice."— *Ibid.* edit. of 1551, p. 463.

"Although that by the eternal Providence of God man has been created for that state of misery in which he is, yet notwithstanding he has derived the cause of that misery from himself, and not from God. For he perishes only because of his having, through perversity, degenerated from the pure nature which God had given him."—*Ibid.*, p. 464.

wicked, sin of necessity, and that such necessity is by the ordinance and will of God ; but I also add, that such necessity is without constraint, so that he who sins, cannot excuse himself by saying, that he was compelled thereto. And I prove this doctrine so clearly from holy Scripture, that it is impossible for any living man to resist it. And it amazes me, that the adverse party should not display his subtlety in controverting what I have said before you, and that he even conceals the proofs which I have abundantly brought forward in my books. He says that he has maintained contrary opinions, without the will or the power to approve of mine. But were he the most learned personage in the world, it would be too much to insist upon being believed, while simply answering that he neither will nor can consent to what is proposed to him. So much the less reason is there for a man who is scarcely at all versed in the Holy Scriptures, and who is no competent judge in theological matters, to expect that those to whom God has vouchsafed grace to understand them a little better, should be reproved according to his fancy. Now, then, honourable Seigneurs, if the proofs which you have heard are not sufficient, I offer to make them more complete, as often and whenever it may please you. And for the rest, I refer to what is contained in the Book concerning the predestination and providence of God.[1]

On the contradictions which the Seigneur Trouillet has imagined.

The opposing party thinks that I contradict myself, when I teach that a man ought rather to search for the cause of his condemnation in his corrupt nature, than in the predestination of God ; and does not see that I there expressly state, that there are two causes, the one concealed in the eternal counsel of God, and the other open and manifest, in the sin of man. Now, since he confesses that this is true, he condemns himself by his own mouth and sign-manual. And as for me, I willingly accept that confession, which shews plainly that he has never understood a single point of the case which he discusses

---

[1] This is the book : *De Æterna Dei Predestinatione et Providentia.* Genève, 1550, in 8vo ; translated into French the same year.

so boldly. Here, then, Messieurs, is the very core of the whole question : that I say, that all the reprobate will be convicted of guilt by their own consciences, and that thus their condemnation is righteous, and that they err in neglecting what is quite evident, to enter instead into the secret counsels of God, which to us are inaccessible. The Scripture, however, shews us clearly, that God has predestined men to such ends as he chose them to reach. But as to why or how this is done, we must remain ignorant, because it has not been revealed to us.

Touching the contradiction which the adverse party conceits that he has brought forward from the second page of the 463d leaf, it is marvellous, that after having been so disgracefully cast in such a frivolous objection, he should return to it anew. I say, in that passage, that it is perverse to pry into the secrets of God whereto we are unable to attain, in order to search for the origin of the condemnation of mankind, while passing over the corruption of their nature, from whence it manifestly proceeds. However, this does not mean that the counsel of God does not overrule in a sovereign degree the disposal of everything, although proximate causes may strike our eyes. That were as much as to find a contradiction in these propositions, which are all those of holy writ : That man is not nourished by his labour, nor by his industry, but by the grace of God alone. That it is not the heat or influence of the sun which makes the earth fruitful, but the pure grace of God. That it is not bread that sustains and nourishes us, but the strength which God of his goodness puts into us. And on the other hand, that the idle man deserves to starve. Item, that the earth will deny us pasturage. Item, that we are sustained and strengthened by bread. Now the solution is quite easy when we learn to distinguish between the sovereign cause, and those which are secondary, and more upon a level with human understanding.

As to the passages extracted out of the book of Melanchthon,[1]

[1] This is the famous book of the *Common Places* (*Loci Theologici*), translated into French under the care of Calvin : *The Summe of Theology, or Common Places of Melanchthon*, translated from the Latin, by John Calvin. With a Preface. 1546, in 8vo.

I confess that God is not the author of sin. I have even expressly maintained this article of faith in my books, and as warmly as could be required from a faithful servant of God. It is therefore superfluous to set up this as a matter of dispute between us. Notwithstanding, I must confess, as I have formerly declared, that the method of instruction which Melanchthon adopts, is different from mine. I have also, honourable Seigneurs, explained to you the cause of this. It is, that Melanchthon, being a timorous man, has accommodated himself too much to the common feeling of mankind, that he might not give occasion to over-curious people to seek to pry into the secret things of God. And thus, as at last appears, he has spoken of the present question rather as a philosopher than a theologian, having no better authority to rest upon than that of Plato. And then evidently he aims at a middle course, as if he would confess that he swam between two currents, which is what the adverse party ought to take rather more into account.[1]

As for the rest, most honourable Seigneurs, he who would place Melanchthon and myself in opposition, greatly wrongs both the one and the other, as well as the whole Church of God. I honour Melanchthon as much on account of the excellent knowledge which is in him, as for his virtues; and more than all, because of his having laboured faithfully to

---

[1] It is not uninteresting to compare this estimate formed by Calvin of Melanchthon, with the remarkable one contained in the preface to the *Common Places*:—" I perceive that the author, being a person of profound knowledge, has not chosen to enter into subtile disputations, nor to treat these matters with that high degree of skill which it would have been so easy for him to employ. But he has brought himself down as much as he could, having only regard to edification. It is, certes, the style and fashion which we should observe, did not our adversaries constrain us by their cavils to turn aside from this course. . . . . The same about predestination, because he sees now-a-days so many flighty spirits who are but too much given to curiosity, and who go beyond bounds in this matter. Wishing to provide against this danger, he has proposed to touch only on what was needful to be known, leaving all else buried out of sight, rather than by disclosing all he could, to give the reins to much perplexing and confused disputation, from whence arises no good fruit. *I confess that the whole of what God has been pleased to reveal to us in Scripture ought not to be suppressed, whatsoever happens;* but he who seeks to give profitable instruction to his readers, may very well be excused for dwelling upon what he knows to be most essential, passing lightly over or leaving out of sight that which he does not expect to be equally profitable."

further the Gospel. If I find anything to reprove, I do not conceal it from him, as he gives me full liberty not to do so. As for him, there are witnesses more than enough, who know how much he loves me. And I know that he would detest those who sought to shelter themselves behind him, to disparage my doctrine in any way. Moreover, such sort of people only seek to sow tares and scandals to obstruct the course of the Gospel. I shall not waste my time in disproving these propositions, brought forward by the adverse party, in which Melanchthon gives satisfaction to none of the learned, because he yields to too tender a caution, not venturing to say what he knows to be true, because he fears that all may not be capable of hearing it. It suffices that I have produced to you letters under his hand, wherein appears what I have advanced. But even if license were given to the adverse party to form any conclusion he might think proper, and to make what resolutions he liked upon the writings of learned men, you would be at his mercy as to receiving three Sacraments,—among which is the confessional, because, forsooth, Melanchthon receives them. This I merely mention, that he may learn to know himself better, and not be so excessively eager to throw himself into the battle-field.

As for myself, most honourable Seigneurs, having the assurance of my conscience, that what I have taught and written has not been the creation of my own brain, but that I have had it from God, it must needs be that I maintain it, as I think I have fully done, if I would not prove traitor to the truth. And should it seem good to you, I offer anew to reply more fully, until the adverse party be convicted of having falsely accused me, contrary to all truth and reason.[1]

[*The original Minute corrected by Calvin.—Library of Geneva.* Vol. 145.]

[1] Here is the sentence pronounced on this occasion by the Seigneurs of Geneva :—

" *Wednesday, 9th November* 1552.—Having heard in council the worshipful and learned ministers of the Word of God, Master William Farel, and Master Peter Viret, and after them worshipful Monsieur John Calvin, minister of this city of Geneva, and noble John Troillet, also of Geneva, in their depositions and replies, now often repeated, touching the *Christian Institution* of the said Monsieur Calvin, and having well considered the whole, the council has determined and concluded,

## CCCI.—To Farel.[1]

Conspiracy of the Libertines—energy of the Reformer—struggles of Viret at Lausanne.

GENEVA, 26th October 1552.

I occasionally abstain from writing, from having nothing important to write about, but my material is in these days more abundant than I could wish—so much so, that it has kept me from writing altogether. For I think it better silently to repress the very sad cares which torture me, rather than seek consolation by inconveniencing you. Even if I did throw part of the burden on your shoulders, I should rather increase than diminish the evil. The very act of writing, moreover, by awakening the memory, irritates the wound. I was aware that our enemies were making secret preparations for an insurrection, for four months past; the fire was to be kindled at the

---

that all things well heard and understood, it has pronounced and declared, and pronounces and declares the said book of the *Institution* of the said Calvin, to be well and holily done, and his holy doctrine to be God's doctrine, and that he be held as good and true minister of this city, and that henceforward no person dare to speak against the said book, nor the said doctrine. We command both parties, and all concerned, to observe this.

"My said Lords Syndics and Council,

"ROSET."

[1] While Calvin was eloquently pleading among others the cause of the persecuted faithful of France, he was struggling with an ever-increasing energy for the suppression of scandals, and the formation of a new people at Geneva. His efforts, however, seemed powerless before the enormity of the evil, and the furious resistance of that party, which history has justly branded with the name of Libertine. The cabal of the factious gathered strength from day to day, and disorders were committed with impunity. The task of reforming the public morals, courageously undertaken by the ministers, was almost absolutely fruitless. Ashamed of such excesses, but incapable of suppressing them, the Great Council increased the severity of its edicts, but had not the power to impose them upon the multitude who were banded together against the *foreigners*. The French were a particular object of fury to the factions. They beat them in the streets, and subjected them to all sorts of outrages. Most absurd accusations were circulated against them, and were believed by the multitude. The presence of Farel and Viret in Geneva could not quiet these troubles; and it was in vain that these courageous ministers presented themselves before the councils, "to commend to them the care of religion and morals."—*Chronique* of Roset, c. v. pp. 42, 44; Ruchat, c. v. pp. 489, 490.

next election, in the month of November, when it is customary to appoint the chief magistrate. Bernard had given me a hint of it. But we were ignorant of the charge by which they thought to oppress and even overwhelm us. But the Lord has seasonably dragged them forth to the light. They spread a rumour among the petty tradesmen, and then bawled out in the assembly hall, that forty thousand pieces of gold were deposited with three Frenchmen, as a reward for betraying the city. They made indirect allusions to the three guardians of the poor, among whom was Du Tailly, whom the Lord lately called to Himself, and who is very greatly lamented by all the pious. Wendel was not ashamed to allege, in the presence of the Senate, that there were three hundred thousand. This conjecture deceived them, for, when they had hoped, by their atrocious calumny to kindle a fire which should consume us in a moment, the flame by and by ended in smoke. They are, notwithstanding, in the meantime, acting with careless effrontery, seeing, as they do, the inactivity of those who ought to have mended matters, which they could have done with the utmost ease had they possessed a single spark of manliness. For what would not the wicked dare when there is impunity for all evils? But I trust that Christ will ere long prove our deliverer.

He[1] has neglected what he had promised to Viret. I, for my part, am doing all I can to refresh his memory. But he is amusing himself with us. It were better, therefore, for Viret to come of his own accord. The proper time would be, however, before the Martinalia, when despair will drive our enemies to act like the Bacchæ if he does not make his appearance. But he is drawn away elsewhere. And the affairs which he has in hand are to me of so much importance, that I consider it sinful to place any obstacle in his way, or to offer the very least hindrance.[2] On the contrary, I feel exceedingly ashamed that I have afforded him no more comfort under so great difficul-

[1] Probably Amy Perrin.
[2] Placed by his character and talents at the head of the Vaudois clergy, Viret had to maintain a ceaseless struggle against the encroachments and ecclesiastical tyranny of the Seigneurs of Berne.—See Ruchat, c. v. p. 488.

ties, than if I had been buried. Although, therefore, most anxious that you should encourage us with your presence, it must nevertheless be deferred until another occasion, especially as it would be better that both of you should be present at the same time. I scarcely know what to say regarding Garnier's letter.[1] The specimen which I had lately of his character in a private matter, will prevent me in future from having any dealings with him. You will say the public position of the Church is concerned. Pardon my 'timidity, for I fear very much that no men are more insolent and haughty, than those of a servile disposition. Had it been convenient for Viret to come here, nothing could have been more useful and appropriate, than for us to hold a consultation on the leading topics, before the matter had proceeded farther. I fear, however, that it will be scarcely possible for Viret to be here before the completion of the Bernese embassy. Accordingly, I have no one to consult with, unless I lay the matter before my fellow-ministers. I am persuaded, however, that no settlement should be come to until you reach us.

Adieu, most upright and very dear brother. Salute that noble man, the Seigneur de Dammartin, your colleague, and the rest of our friends. May the Lord guard you all by His protection, enrich you with the gifts of His Spirit, and bless you in all things. Amen.—Yours truly,

JOHN CALVIN.

[*Lat. orig. autogr.—Library of Geneva.* Vol. 107, *a.*]

## CCCII.—To VIRET.

### Literary labours of Theodore Beza.

GENEVA, 26*th October* 1552.

After I had written Farel, our friend Gerold undertook, at my request, to make a journey thither. There is, accordingly, a letter designed for both of you, which, having read, you will show to him at your own convenience. I ask no more of you than that you will think of us when it suits you. Your

[1] Minister of the French Church of Strasbourg.

letter was not to be answered until something important had been done, which has not been the case as yet. You will tell Beza not to be anxious about the translating of my discourses,[1] as I have handed over the task to Baduel as if with his permission. Indeed, I felt ashamed, from the first, that his valuable time should be taken up with work so very unworthy of him—time that could and ought to be better occupied. I, on this account, embraced the more gladly the opportunity afforded me of laying the burden on another. He will be urged by and by, by our friend Robert, to engage in a sort of lucubration in which he will be of greater advantage to the Church.[2] —Adieu, brother and very worthy friend. Salute the brethren earnestly, also your wife and little daughters. May the Lord preserve you all; may the Spirit guide you by His wisdom, and sustain you by His might.

JOHN CALVIN.

[*Lat. orig. autogr.—Library of Geneva.* Vol. 107, *a* ]


CCCIII.—TO AMBROISE BLAURER.[3]

Troubles at Geneva—sad intelligence from France and Germany—steady in the promises of God.

GENEVA, 19*th November* 1552.

As I hope that my dearly beloved brother Beza will be with you about the same time that you receive this letter, and as he

[1] *Quatre Sermons traictans des matières fort utiles pour nostre temps.* 1552, 8vo. *Opuscules*, p. 824.

[2] Beza published this year a new edition of his Tragedy of Abraham under the following title :—*Le Sacrifice d'Abraham, Tragédie Française, séparée en trois Pauses à la façon des Actes de Comédies, avec des Chœurs, un Prologue et un Epilogue.* 1552, 8vo.

[3] Ambroise Blaurer, of a noble family of Constance, entered in early youth a convent, which he soon left to become a preacher of reform, for which he had contracted a taste from reading the writings of Luther. Present at the Controversy of Berne with Zwingle, Œcolampadius, Bucer, and Capito, he beheld his preaching attended with the most gratifying success, and saw the Gospel victoriously established in his native town, where he exercised his valuable ministry until the war of Smalkald. Having at that time refused submission to the *Interim*,

will inform you more fully as to my own state and that of the
Church than I can in the longest epistle, I shall at present be
brief. He will tell you the annoyance and disturbance we suffered from some worthless wretches, whose sole power of injuring
us lies in the impunity and license which is allowed them. But
God apparently wishes us to be destitute of human aid, that
Himself alone may protect us. In the meantime, though I
little expected it, I live a survivor of my native town. The
city in which I was born has lately been utterly destroyed by
fire.[1] We are also compelled to hear daily of fearful disasters
throughout all Picardy, but so far is the King's fierceness from
being subdued by them, that never was his pride more insulting to God. I wish that I might at length hear from your
beloved Germany something that might cheer me; yet as nothing now appears but what is saddening, or at least confused,
I scarcely venture to ask what is doing there. And I suppose
you also are filled with alarm whenever any news are announced,
fearing lest some addition be made to the existing evils. Unless the Lord stretch forth his hand to us from heaven, the wise
and far-sighted perceive that these misfortunes, severe and
bitter as they are, are but a gentle prelude to tremendous calamities. But although Satan is going about everywhere with
fearful license, yet if we consider the desperate wickedness of
the world, it is wonderful that God has not given him much
greater liberty. But we who have our anchor fixed in heaven,
must sail amid these troubled storms just as in the peaceful

---

he left Constance, and retired first to Winterthur, near Zurich, and afterwards to
Bienne, whilst his unfortunate city, fallen into the hands of the Imperialists, saw
itself deprived at once of the Gospel and of liberty. Esteemed by Calvin, Blaurer
witnessed his influence at Zurich and at Berne solicited more than once by the
Reformer of Geneva. He died in 1567.—See Beza, *Icones*, and Melch. Adam,
*Theolog. Germ.*, p. 413.

[1] In a letter to an unknown personage, (*Opera*, tom. ix. p. 238,) Calvin mentions
this same event, adding to it a curious detail taken from the letter of an eye-
witness : " Among other things, he informed me of a circumstance which I am
unwilling to withhold from you—that a striking spectacle presented itself to him in
the destruction of our city, viz., that my father's house stood entire after all the
others had been reduced to ashes. Farther on he adds,—'I have no doubt but
that God wished to make this a testimony against all those of our city who, eight
or ten days before, had burnt in effigy Monsieur de Normandie.' "

haven, until the Lord brings us to the blissful rest of His own kingdom.

F―― promised to hand over to you my letters to Beza. If he has not come to you, he will send them to Farel at his earliest opportunity. Robert Stephens has my Commentary on John in the press.[1] As soon as he has finished it, I shall cause a copy to be sent to you.

Adieu, most distinguished Sir, and excellent servant of Christ, deserving of my hearty regard. May the Lord continue to guide you by His Spirit, to shield you by His protection, and to bestow upon you every kind of blessing. Salute your fellow-minister earnestly in my name. My colleagues both salute you, and those who were lately my companions. I desire you to convey my regards to the treasurer of your city, and to the other pious and wise men. I beseech you very earnestly to remember me in your prayers, for I am more in need of this aid at present than words can express. Adieu, together with your wife and family.—Yours sincerely,

JOHN CALVIN.

[*Lat. Copy—Library of Zurich.* Coll. Hottinger, F. 43, p. 464.]

## CCCIV.—To MELANCHTHON.[2]

*Earnest desires for the continuance of their mutual affection—disputes with Trolliet—longing for agreement in doctrine regarding the Communion and Election.*

28*th November* 1552.

Nothing could have come to me more seasonably at this time than your letter, which I received two months after its

---

[1] *Commentarius in Evangelium Johannis.* Geneva, 1553. Fol. Robert Estienne.

[2] See Letter, p. 256. Doubly afflicted by the wars which were desolating Germany, and by the disorders which were rending the Church, Melanchthon had maintained a long silence, which was only broken on the 1st October 1552, by a touching letter to Calvin :—" Reverend Sir and very dear Brother,—I should have written you frequently, had I been able to secure trustworthy letter-carriers. I should have preferred a conversation with you on many questions of very serious

despatch. For, in addition to the very great troubles with which I am so sorely consumed, there is almost no day on which some new pain or anxiety does not occur. I should, therefore, be in a short time entirely overcome by the load of evils under which I am oppressed, did not the Lord by His own means alleviate their severity; among which it was no slight consolation to me to know that you are enjoying tolerable health, such at least as your years admit of and the delicate state of your body, and to be informed, by your own letter, that your affection for me had undergone no change. It was reported to me that you had been so displeased by a rather free admonition of mine—which, however, ought to have affected you far otherwise—that you tore the letter to pieces in the presence of certain witnesses. But even if the messenger was not sufficiently trustworthy, still, after a long lapse of time, his fidelity was established by various proofs, and I was compelled at length to suspect something. Wherefore I have learned the more gladly that up to this time our friendship remains safe, which assuredly, as it grew out of a heartfelt love of piety, ought to remain for ever sacred and inviolable. But it greatly concerns us to cherish faithfully and constantly to the end the friendship which God has sanctified by the authority of His own name, seeing that herein is involved either great advantage or great loss even to the whole Church. For you see how the eyes of many are turned upon us, so that the wicked take occasion from our dissensions to speak evil, and the weak are only perplexed by our unintelligible disputations. Nor, in truth, is it of little importance to prevent the suspicion of any difference having arisen between us from being handed

interest, inasmuch as I set a very high value on your judgment, and am conscious that the integrity and candour of your mind is unexceptionable. I am at present living as if in a wasps' nest. But perhaps I shall ere long put off this mortal life for a brighter companionship in heaven." Full of affection and respect for Melanchthon, whose character he venerated, while he freely blamed him for his weakness and indecision, Calvin made known, in turn, to the German Reformer, the struggles of all sorts which he had to undergo at Geneva, and with which the name of Melanchthon himself is found mixed up, owing to the astute intrigues of the Libertines, who had an interest in involving these two great men in mutual opposition.

down in any way to posterity; for it is worse than absurd that parties should be found disagreeing on the very principles, after we have been compelled to make our departure from the world. I know and confess, moreover, that we occupy widely different positions; still, because I am not ignorant of the place in His theatre to which God has elevated me, there is no reason for my concealing that our friendship could not be interrupted without great injury to the Church. And that we may act independent of the conduct of others, reflect, from your own feeling of the thing, how painful it would be for me to be estranged from that man whom I both love and esteem above all others, and whom God has not only nobly adorned with remarkable gifts, in order to make him distinguished in the eyes of the whole Church, but has also employed as His chief minister for conducting matters of the highest importance. And surely it is indicative of a marvellous and monstrous insensibility, that we so readily set at nought that sacred unanimity, by which we ought to be bringing back into the world the angels of heaven. Meanwhile, Satan is busy scattering here and there the seeds of discord, and our folly is made to supply much material. At length he has discovered fans of his own, for fanning into a flame the fires of discord. I shall refer to what happened to us in this Church, causing extreme pain to all the godly; and now a whole year has elapsed since we were engaged in these conflicts. Certain worthless wretches, after stirring up strife amongst us, in reference to the free election of God, and the sad bondage of the human will, and after creating a public disturbance, had nothing more plausible to urge in defence of their grievous opposition than the authority of your name.[1] And after they had found out how easy it was for us

---

[1] The dispute with Bolsec had hardly terminated, when a new adversary rose up against Calvin in the person of Trolliet of Geneva, a discontented and captious spirit, who had originally been a hermit in Burgundy, and lived in an affectation of sanctity. He soon tired of this life, and having repaired to Geneva, he desired to become a minister, which was refused him owing to the influence of Calvin, against whom he vowed an irreconcilable hatred. He became notorious afterwards, as a partisan of the Libertines, for the violence of his attacks against the Reformer. These invectives, called forth especially by the doctrine of *Predestination*, and specially invested with the authority of Melanchthon, provoked keen discussions,

to refute whatever arguments they adduced, they tried to crush us, forsooth, by this artifice,—by asking, if we were willing openly to disagree with you. And yet, such was the moderation observed by us, that least of all did they extort what they were adroitly seeking to obtain. Therefore, all my colleagues and myself openly professed to hold the same opinion on that doctrine which you hold. Not a word escaped us, in the whole discussion, either less honourable towards yourself than was seemly, or calculated to diminish confidence in you.[1] Meanwhile, nevertheless, such indefinite and reserved expression of opinion cannot but pain me exceedingly; and it cannot but pain me, that opportunity is being left to the evil-disposed for harassing the Church, after our death, as often as they please; while the conflicting parties will array against each other the opinions of those who ought to have spoken, as with one mouth, one and the same thing. It is neither surprising, nor a thing greatly to be lamented, that Osiander has withdrawn himself from us; yet he withdrew only after a violent attack. For you were long ago aware that he belonged to that race of wild animals which are never tamed; and I always ranked him amongst

which were only quieted by a sentence of the Seigneurs of Geneva, who solemnly approved of the doctrine of Calvin, declaring at the same time, out of regard to the party to which he belonged, that Trolliet was "a good man." All the documents relative to this controversy are to be found in Vol. 149 of the MSS. of the Library of Geneva.

[1] We can judge of this from the remarkable memorial of Calvin to the Seigneurie, entitled *La Cause contre Trolliet*, where we meet with these words:—" That party, Noble Seigneurs, which is desirous of bringing Melanchthon and myself into mutual conflict, is doing great wrong to both of us, and in general to the whole Church of God. I honour Melanchthon as much for his superior learning as for his virtues, and above all, for having laboured so faithfully to uphold the Gospel. If I find fault with him, I do not conceal it from him, seeing that he gives me liberty to do so. There are witnesses in abundance on his side, who know how much he loves me. And I know that he will hold in detestation all those who, under cover of his name, seek to blacken my doctrine."—6th Oct. 1552. (Library of Geneva, vol. 145.) Calvin's preface to Melanchthon's *Common Places* may also be consulted. Geneva, 1546, 8vo.

Osiander had published many writings against Melanchthon, in which, by a strange reversing of the orthodox doctrine, he attempted to derive Justification from God the Father, by forgetting the part which belonged to Jesus Christ as the Redeemer. See Seckendorf, and Melch. Adam, p. 229.

the number of those who were a disgrace to us. And assuredly, the very first day that I saw him, I abhorred the wicked disposition and abominable manners of the man. As often as he felt inclined to praise the agreeable and excellent wine, he had these words in his mouth : " I am that I am ;" also, " This is the Son of the living God ;" which he manifestly produced as mockeries of the Deity. Wherefore, I have the more frequently wondered that such a despicable person should at all be encouraged by your indulgence. In truth, I was particularly astonished on reading a passage in a certain preface of yours, where, after the proof of his folly at Worms, you commended him rather more than enough. But let him retire: it is an advantage to us to have got rid of him. I had rather that certain others were retained. Nevertheless,—to pass by these also, —the opposition which is too plainly manifest in our modes of teaching pains me not a little. I, for my part, am well aware that, if any weight is due to the authority of men, it were far more just that I should subscribe your opinions than you mine. But that is not the question ; nor is it even a thing to be desired by the pious ministers of Christ. This, in all truth, we ought both to seek, viz., to come to an agreement on the pure truth of God. But, to speak candidly, religious scruples prevent me from agreeing with you on this point of doctrine, for you appear to discuss the freedom of the will in too philosophical a manner ; and in treating of the doctrine of election, you seem to have no other purpose, save that you may suit yourself to the common feeling of mankind. And it cannot be attributed to hallucination, that you, a man acute and wise, and deeply versed in Scripture, confound the election of God with His promises, which are universal. For nothing is more certain than that the Gospel is addressed to all promiscuously, but that the Spirit of faith is bestowed on the elect alone, by peculiar privilege. The promises are universal. How does it happen, therefore, that their efficacy is not equally felt by all ? For this reason, because God does not reveal His arm to all. Indeed, among men but moderately skilled in Scripture, this subject needs not to be discussed, seeing that the promises of the Gospel make offer of the grace of Christ equally to all; and God, by the external call, invites all who are willing to accept of salvation. Faith, also, is a special gift. I think I have clearly expounded this whole question, involved and intricate though it be, in a book but very lately published. Indeed, the matter is so obvious, that no one of sound judgment can feel persuaded otherwise, than that you are giving out what is quite different from your real inclination. It increases my anxiety, and at the same time my grief, to see you in this matter to be almost unlike yourself; for I heard, when the whole formula of the agreement of our Church with that of Zurich was laid before you, you instantly seized a pen and erased that sentence which cautiously and prudently makes a distinction between the elect and the reprobate. Which procedure, taking into consideration the mildness of your disposition, not to mention other characteristics, greatly shocked me. Accordingly, I do not ask you to endure the reading of my book, or even a part of it, because I think it would be useless to do so. Would that we might have an opportunity of talking over these matters face to face! I am not ignorant of your candour, of your transparent openness and moderation; as for your piety, it is manifest to angels and to the whole world. Therefore, this whole question would be easily, as I hope, arranged between us; wherefore, if an opportunity should present itself, I would desire nothing more than to pay you a visit. But if it shall indeed turn out as you apprehend, it will be no slight comfort to me in circumstances sad and grievous, to see you and embrace you before that I shall take my departure from this world. Here we enjoy least of all that repose which you fancy we enjoy. There is much trouble, annoyance, and even disorder, among us. Full in view is the enemy, who are continually imperilling our lives by new dangers. We are at a distance of three days' journey from Burgundy. The French forces are but an hour's march from our gates. But because nothing is more blessed than to fight under the banner of Christ, there is no reason why these obstacles should prevent you from paying me a visit. Meanwhile, you will greatly oblige me by informing me of your own and the Churches' condition.—Adieu, most distinguished Sir and heartily esteemed brother. May the Lord protect you by His power, guide you by His Spirit, and bless your pious labours. My colleague, and many pious and judicious men, reverently salute you.

JOHN CALVIN.

[*Calvin's Lat. Corresp.* Opera, ix. p. 66.]


CCCV.—To MATHIEU DIMONET.[1]

Exhortation to patience and constancy under persecution.

*The* 10*th of January* 1553.

VERY DEAR BROTHER,—Although I have not at present to sustain the like conflicts that you have, yet you will suffer the word of exhortation from me as if I were your fellow-prisoner, and in truth the zeal which moves me to write to you proceeds from nothing else. Yet I pray you to consider how we ought to refer all to the will and disposal of our heavenly Father, who calls every one of us in the order that He pleases. Sometimes He spares His children, until He has gradually led and prepared them, as we hear it said to St. Peter by the Master's own lips, " When thou shalt be old, they shall carry thee whither thou wouldst not." But it sometimes happens that He chooses novices, or at least such as have not been long disciplined to warfare. However that may be, there is

---

[1] Mathieu Dimonet, a devout Protestant of Lyons, was arrested in that town the 9th January 1553. In his letters to the ministers of Geneva he has himself related the details of his trial:—" On Monday 9 January being in my house in presence of the king's lieutenant and the official, who, after they had searched and visited my books, found nothing, except a little book of spiritual songs set to music. . . . ." Dimonet underwent a first examination, and was then led away to the prison of the officialty. "I have undergone," says he, " great assaults and temptations . . . . for on the one side, they set before me tortures and death, then the shame and dishonour of myself and my relations, the sorrow of my mother, who they said was dying with grief, and many other things . . . . which would have been very hard for me to bear, unless the Lord had strengthened me by His Holy Spirit." The prisoner courageously withstood the threats of the inquisitor Oritz, and the pressing entreaties of his family. The 15th July 1553, quite cheerfully, and praying to the Lord, he endured the torment of death.—*Histoire des Martyrs*, p. 247.

this advantage that He is no less powerful to put forth His strength in the weak, rendering them at once invincible, as to continue it to those who have long experienced it. From what I hear, you have not been one of the first called to His knowledge; yet God has nevertheless put you among the foremost of His witnesses. He has bestowed such strength and steadfastness upon you at the first assault, that the enemies of truth have taken knowledge of the mark of Jesus Christ, which they cannot bear. I feel indeed by the sympathy I have for you (as I ought) that Satan ceases not to give you new alarms; but you must have recourse to Him who has made so good a beginning, praying Him to complete His own work. If you have many trials do not be greatly amazed on that account, even although you feel such frailty in yourself that you are almost ready to be shaken. Rather learn that it is by such means that God would humble you, that His help should be the better recognised by your need of it; and, moreover, that He invites you to call on His name, and to have all dependence on His grace, seeing there is need that we be forcibly driven to do so. I doubt not but that there may also be firebrands from without, who, under cover of friendship and relationship, will prove your worst and most mortal enemies, since to save the body they will do their utmost to draw the soul downward to perdition. And then, men's fancy is a marvellous workshop for forging out foolish imaginations, which disturb the true rest which we ought to have in the holy calling of our God, who commands us to look simply to himself, as indeed we have very good reason to do. Therefore we have need to be armed and accoutred at every point. But you need not be daunted, seeing that God has promised to equip His own according as they are assaulted by Satan. Only commit yourself to Him, distrusting all in yourself, and hope that He only will suffice to sustain you. Further you have to take heed chiefly to two things; first, what the side is you defend, and next, what crown is promised to those who continue steadfast in the Gospel. The service of God, the boundless grace which He has manifested to us in His Son, and all the glory of His kingdom, are such precious things, that no mortal man ought to think it hard to spend his life in fighting against the base corruptions, whose reign throughout the world tends to bring to nought those blessings. And then, we know what will be the end of our warfare, and that He who has bought us will never suffer so dear a price as His blood to be lost, if we be but signed with it. Now we know how He owns as His own, and declares solemnly that He will own at the last day, all those who have confessed Him here below. We do not know as yet what He has determined to do concerning you, but there is nothing better for you than to sacrifice your life to Him, being ready to part with it whenever He wills, and yet hoping that He will preserve it, in so far as He knows it to be profitable for your salvation. And although this be difficult to the flesh, yet it is the true happiness of his faithful ones; and you must pray that it may please this gracious God so to imprint it upon your heart that it may never be effaced therefrom. For our part, we also shall pray that He would make you feel His power, and vouchsafe you the full assurance that you are under his keeping; that He bridles the rage of your enemies, and in every way manifests Himself as your God and Father.

As I hear that our brother, Peter Berger,[1] is in the same prison with you, I beg you to greet him from me, and to give him my letters as common to you both. Let us go forward, until we have arrived at our goal—the being gathered together into the everlasting kingdom.

I had forgotten one point, which is, that you should reply to adversaries reverently and modestly, according to the measure of faith God gives you. I say this because it is not given to every one to dispute. Indeed the martyrs themselves were no great scholars, nor subtile to enter upon profound disputations. Thus humbling yourself under the guidance of the Spirit of

---

[1] Peter Berger of Bar-sur-Seine, burgess of Geneva, was seized at Lyons three days after the scholars of Lausanne, whom he rejoined in the dungeons and preceded to martyrdom. "Having mounted the stake, he said, 'Lord, I commit my soul to Thee.' Then looking up to heaven with steadfast gaze, and crying aloud, he said, 'To-day I see heaven open;' and immediately after, this saint yielded up his spirit to God."—*Histoire des Martyrs*, p. 234.

God, answer soberly, according to your knowledge, following the rule of Scripture, " I have believed, therefore I speak." Yet let not that hinder you from speaking frankly and plainly, in the full persuasion that He who has promised to give you a mouth and wisdom, which all your adversaries shall not be able to gainsay, will never fail you.

[*Fr.*—Printed in *Histoire des Martyrs*, lib. iv. p. 247.]

## CCCVI.—To CHRISTOPHE FABRI.

Congratulations on the subject of his approaching marriage—Calvin's regret that he cannot be present at the ceremony.

GENEVA, 13*th January* 1553.

I am exceedingly glad that you are about to get married, not only because it will be for your own private good, but also because the brethren have considered it to be for the good of the whole Church.[1] And while I do not indeed know enough of the lady, yet I confidently trust, from various conjectures, that each of you will turn out according to our wishes. We have good reason, therefore, to congratulate you, and we feel thankful to God in no ordinary degree. I should gladly have been present at your marriage, had I not been detained at home by the wickedness of those who cease not to bring destruction upon themselves and the community by their madness.[2] I have good reason to call it madness, for they have never exhibited more unbridled licentiousness. I shall say nothing of their mis-

---

[1] Christophe Fabri [or Libertet] was on the eve of his second marriage. We know nothing of his first wife. In a letter of May 1545, to Fabri, then pastor at Thonon, Calvin speaks highly of the entertainment he received from his wife, on his return from a long tour in the German Cantons: " I could never get your wife to treat us in a plain, homely way. . . . She was willing to take advice. She repeatedly requested that I should ask for whatever I chose, as if it were my own; she adhered to her own opinion in this, however, that she entertained us too sumptuously; for there was twice as much food always prepared as there was any occasion for. We felt just as much at home as if you had been present."—*MS. of the Library of Neuchatel.*

[2] In allusion to the efforts of the Libertine party, put forth with increasing violence for the overthrow of ecclesiastical discipline, and which gave rise during the same year to a decisive struggle between the Reformer and his adversaries.

chievous plots for the destruction of the faith, of their gross contempt of God, of their impious conspiracies for the scattering of the Church, of the foul Epicurism of their whole life; and this, not because these are light evils, but because they are not unknown to you. The entire Republic is at present in disorder, and they are striving to root up the established order of things. Had your marriage been a month later, I should have had more leisure. I cannot move a foot at present. I have not been through the city-gates for a month past, not even for recreation. Would that I had less ground for my excuse. Assuredly the season of winter would not have stood in my way. But we shall pray that your marriage may come off well, the effects of which will be felt even here. I would not have thought it labour lost to obtain a conversation with our beloved Farel and your chief magistrate, at the expense of the cold and irksomeness of a three days' journey. But one consideration was sufficient for me, that you wished me to discharge a duty which I was as willing to fulfil, as you were earnest in desiring it. I hope to find it more convenient to visit my friends on another occasion. Adieu, very dear brother in the Lord. Farel will pardon me for not writing him. Present my very kind regards to him. Louis, minister of Veissy,[1] left us lately; I see that his life has been a burden to him for some time past, owing to protracted debility. John Macard[2] supplies his place. We must have a quarrel with Philip.[3] Salute Maturin and the rest of our friends earnestly in my name. May the Lord watch over you and guide you by His Spirit. Amen.—Yours,

JOHN CALVIN.

[*Lat. orig. autogr.—Library of the Company of Neuchatel.*]

---

[1] A village on the banks of the Arve, a few miles from Geneva.

[2] John Macard, originally from the neighbourhood of Laon in Picardy, took refuge in Geneva on account of religion. A man of resolute character, and endowed with a manly eloquence, he rendered eminent service to the Church alternately at Geneva and Paris, and the latter reckoned him among the number of its most distinguished pastors.

[3] The minister, Philip de Ecclesia, deposed on account of his disorderly life.

## CCCVII.—To John Cheke.[1]

Calvin apologizes for silence, and enjoins him to use his influence with the King for the advancement of the Gospel in England.

*Geneva, 13th Feb. 1553.*

I have hitherto avoided writing you, most distinguished Sir, lest I should perhaps seem anxious to obtain what my own inclinations did not prompt. For as the friendships of the world are hollow, and ambition and deception everywhere prevail, so that those who cultivate sincerity are exceedingly few, it is absolutely necessary for us almost to regard all with suspicion whose uprightness of character we have not thoroughly tested. I have at length, however, found an exceedingly just motive for writing you, inasmuch as I have now frequently made bold to write to the King himself, and have never written a single letter to you, which was not at all becoming, seeing that it was owing to your influence (under the grace of God) that myself and the other servants of Christ were permitted access to him. And as for the past my excuse is easy, for I was at the first afraid lest those whom I was writing to exhort might have too little confidence in me if I employed the service of others in presenting my letters; and I was again disinclined to give you any trouble, as no familiarity had passed between us. If I have in any way offended you in this matter, attribute it rather to my shyness than to my negligence. Nay,

---

[1] John Cheke, preceptor of Edward VI., King of England, and distinguished alike in science and in letters, won the esteem and confidence of his royal pupil, who raised him to the rank of knighthood, and who gave him in many ways the most precious testimonies of his affection.—See Fuller's *Church History*, B. vii.; sixteenth cent., 19, 20. Though a man of sincere piety, Cheke was not possessed of a firmness of character equal to the variety of his knowledge and the greatness of his talents. He survived his pupil only to make a deplorable manifestation of the infirmity of his faith under fear of the scaffold and of martyrdom. Arrested in the Low Countries in 1556, by a secret order of Philip II., he was conducted to London, imprisoned in the Tower, and escaped death only by a solemn retractation. He then fell into a profound melancholy, and soon after died, exhibiting sentiments of sincere repentance, asking pardon of God and men for the sin of which he had been guilty. See Strype, *Memoirs*, III., i. 515, and *Zurich Letters*, first series, *passim*.

indeed, it is now a long while ago, that having been led thereto by the fame of your rare piety and excellent learning, I must have worthily esteemed you. Moreover, this one reason is sufficient to win for you the favour of all good men, viz., that England has a king whom you have trained by your labour, not only possessing very superior talents, but also a maturity of moral excellence beyond his years, who is extending a hand to the suffering—I should rather in fact say miserable—Church of God in these very sad times. Certainly, having deemed you worthy of this honour, the Lord has not only endeared you to those who experience the present benefit of it, but to as many as desire to see the Church of God re-established, or at least to see her remains gathered together. If then I bear testimony to that affection which I have so long cherished towards you in silence, I am persuaded this expression of my regard will not be unpleasant to you. And again, while you, in that splendid position of yours, do not require the humble offices of men like me, and I, in turn, content with my own poor state, am averse to impose any burden on you of my own account, let us nevertheless cherish towards each other a mutual good-will throughout this fleeting life, until we find its full enjoyment in heaven. Let us meanwhile, with one accord, make it our study to adorn the kingdom of Christ, and, as far as in us lies, to extend and watch over it. For we see how numerous are its open and malicious enemies, whose fury is already kindled, and is growing greater day by day; and, on the other hand, how few is the number of those who have lent their name to the Gospel, how few are conscientiously labouring for the advancement of the glory of God. We see how much coldness, or rather how much indifference, there is among many men of influence; in a word, how much deadness there is throughout the world. And while I believe you will do so of your own accord, and stand in no need at all of any foreign stimulus, yet, with your accustomed good nature, I have no doubt but that you will take in good part what I have laid thus familiarly before you, and which it becomes every one of us earnestly to call to mind. I have indeed particularly to request of you, that whenever at any time you think that the most serene King could be cheered forward by my exhortations, to advise me thereon, and, according to circumstances, that you will not grudge me your opinion. Adieu, most excellent and heartily esteemed Sir. May the Lord guard you by his protection, continue to guide you by his Spirit, and bless your sacred labours. JOHN CALVIN.

[*Calvin's Lat. Corresp.*—Opera ix. p. 68.]


CCCVIII.—TO THE FIVE PRISONERS OF LYONS.[1]

Exhortations to constancy.—Mention of Oritz, the Inquisitor.

*7th March* 1553.

MY BRETHREN,—We have been for some days past in deeper anxiety and sadness than ever, having heard of the resolve taken by the enemies of the truth. When the gentleman you wot of passed this way,[2] while he was dining very hurriedly, to avoid all delay, I drew up such a form of letters as seemed to me expedient to write. God has given, both to you and all His people, some farther respite; we wait the event as it shall please Him to dispose it, always praying Him to uphold you, and not permit you to fall away; in short, to have you in His keeping. I feel well assured that nothing shakes the firmness which he has put within you. Doubtless, for a long time past, you have meditated upon the last conflict which you will

---

[1] Declared guilty of the crime of heresy, and delivered over to the secular arm by the Judge Ordinary of Lyons, the five students made their appeal to the Parliament ot Paris, while the authorities of Berne strove in vain to save "leurs escholiers." Transferred from dungeon to dungeon, during a trial which lasted for more than a year, brought back at last from Paris to Lyons, to await the sentence of their judges, the constancy of these young men never faltered for a single day. At length, the 1st March 1553, they received the communication of the decree of the Parliament of Paris, which gave them over to the stake.—*Hist. des Martyrs*, lib. iv., p. 230. That melancholy intelligence soon spread around, and brought mourning to Lausanne and to Geneva.

[2] This was the pious merchant, John Liner, of Saint Gall.—See the Letter of the 10th August, p. 348. He was present with the prisoners at the bar of Roanne when they received their sentence of death. He set out immediately for Berne, in order to try a last application on the part of the seigneury of that town to the King of France.—*Hist. des Martyrs*, pp. 230, 231. Various MSS. of the library of St. Gall.

have to sustain, if it be His good pleasure to lead you thereto, and have even so fought hitherto that long practice has inured you to fill up what remains. It cannot be but that you feel some twinges of frailty; yet, be confident that He whose service you are upon will so rule in your hearts by His Holy Spirit, that His grace shall overcome all temptations. If He has promised to strengthen with patience those who suffer chastisement for their sins, how much less will He be found wanting to those who maintain his quarrel,—those whom He employs on so worthy a mission as being witnesses for His truth. You must therefore keep this sentence in mind, that *He who dwells in you is stronger than the world.* We who are here shall do our duty in praying that He would glorify Himself more and more by your constancy, and that He may, by the consolation of His Spirit, sweeten and endear all that is bitter to the flesh, and so absorb your spirits in Himself, that in contemplating that heavenly crown, you may be ready without regret to leave all that belongs to this world.

I have received a certain paper containing some very subtle arguments of that unhappy animal Oritz,[1] to prove that it is allowable to make idols. I do not know whether it is you who have sent it me, and whether you would have me to reply to it. I have not thought it worth while to do so, because I was in some doubt about it, and really I do believe that you have no great need of it. But if you like you shall have an answer to it by the first. There is one thing which I have to request of you: you saw some time ago the letters of a paltry mocker of God in this place, who does nothing but trouble the Church, and has never ceased to deal in that trade for five years past. I wish much that by the first, you would write a word of warning to make known his malice, as there is really no end to him. And this I beseech you, as you love the repose of this Church, which is more teased than you can well believe by internal foes.

---

[1] The inquisitor, Nicolas Oritz, who presided at the trial of the five students. The paper here mentioned still exists in the library of Geneva, 113, with this title:—"*Copy of a paper of the Inquisitor Houriz, given to the prisoners for the Word at Lyons, to be conveyed to M. Calvin to retain.*"

And now, my brethren, after having besought our good Lord to have charge over you, to assist you in everything and through everything, to make you taste by experience how kind a Father He is, and how careful of the salvation of his own, I pray to be remembered in your prayers.

[*Printed Hist. des Martyrs*, L. iv., p. 247.]

## CCCIX.—To EDWARD VI.

Recommendation of a French gentleman, a prisoner for the sake of the Gospel.

FROM GENEVA, *this* 12*th March* 1553.

SIRE,—Although I had a petition to make to you for myself, I should not have the boldness to urge it, yet I think that you will not take it amiss that I should make a request for another, when you are informed of the necessity which constrains me, and the merits of the case, which commends itself to you not less than to myself. It is, Sire, that there is a French gentleman detained prisoner in Paris[1] on account of some intercepted letters written by him to one of our friends, who was the king's lieutenant in the town of Noyon (of which I am a native), and retired to these parts;[2] added to which the said gentleman was already held suspect in the matter of religion. And being a man of some rank they kept an eye upon him, which has been the occasion of his seizure. Now, if my testimony has any weight with your Majesty, I can assure you, Sire, that he is as right-minded a man as you could anywhere meet with, excelling in all honour and virtue, endowed with graces which deserve to be loved and valued, and above all, confirmed in the fear of God. I know very well that this is great praise; but did you know him, Sire, I have no doubt that you would form

---

[1] This gentleman, whose name is not known, corresponded by letter with Calvin, his countryman and friend. Shortly before his arrest he wrote to Calvin on the subject of a fire, which had almost entirely destroyed the town of Noyon, sparing, however, the house of the reformer : " I have no doubt," said he, " that God has left this testimony against those of your town, who eight or ten days before had burnt in effigy Monsieur de Normandie and the rest."—Latin Letter of Calvin of 15th February 1553.

[2] Laurent de Normandie.

a like judgment, and discover that I do not exceed due measure. Now, as he is beloved of all, both high and low, even of Monsieur de Vendosme and other princes, there is nothing save the cause of Jesus Christ on account of which he can be hated or rejected, which cause is so dear to you, Sire, that I hope you will not refuse to help him, if there be any means of doing so. I am aware that your Majesty cannot aid as might be wished, all those who labour and are persecuted on account of the Gospel. But should it be your good pleasure to exert yourself for him of whom I treat, be assured, Sire, that in the person of one man you will console many who are at present greatly dismayed, while the foes of truth are fully intending to triumph if they succeed. But not to be too troublesome to your Majesty, I shall enter no further upon facts, which, if it seem good to you, you can better learn from the statements of the gentleman who delivers this. Only I beseech you, in the name of God, with all possible affection, yea as eagerly as I would on behalf of my own life, that it may please you to grant this request, namely, to ask the King of France to let him depart out of his country, together with his wife, also detained, and with as much of his property as can be withdrawn. In doing which you will not only lay me under obligation more and more to pray God to prosper you, but an infinite number of believers besides.

Sire, after having commended myself as humbly as I can to your kind favour, I pray our good Lord to keep you under His holy protection, and to govern you by his Spirit in all prudence, uprightness, and strength of purpose, and to make your crown to flourish more and more.—Your very humble and obedient servitor, JOHN CALVIN.

[*Fr. copy.*—*Imperial Library.* Coll. Dupuy, vol. 102.]

## CCCX.—To Farel.[1]

Serious illness and unexpected recovery of Farel—Calvin's joy.

Geneva, *27th March* 1553.

When I recently performed the last offices of a friend towards you, as I indeed thought, I was desirous of escaping the remainder of the grief which was incidental to your premature death. I have suffered the punishment which I deserved for my overhastiness. And would that I had been the only one who suffered it. It made the thing worse, that I involved very many good men in the same grief with myself. Consoled, however, now by more joyful news, I am forgetting my folly and disgrace. And it is certainly proper that this wonderful goodness of God should absorb all cause for sorrow. Seeing now that your disease has left you, you must endeavour gradually to recover that vigour of mind which you exercised too actively in the most trying conflicts, and to regain possession of that strength of body which must needs be worn out and exhausted. Since I have buried you before the time, may the Lord grant that the Church may see you my survivor. My own private comfort is joined with the public good of the faithful in this prayer; for my warfare will be the shorter, and I shall not be subjected to the pain of lamenting your death. Yet I am not, in the meanwhile, averse, if it should so

---

[1] The reading of this letter, filled with the most lively and disinterested testimonies of affection for Farel, calls to one's mind the beautiful preface of Calvin's Commentary on the Epistle of St. Paul to Titus, dedicated to Farel and Viret:—"I do not think," says Calvin, "that there have ever been friends who have lived together in such fast friendship and concord, as we have done during our ministry. I have been a fellow-pastor here with both of you. So far from there having been any appearance of envy between you and me, I always regarded us as one. We have since been separated. As for you, Master William, the Church of Neuchatel, which you have delivered from the tyranny of the Papacy, and won over to Christ, called you to be its pastor; and as for you, Master Peter, you stand in a similar relation to the Church of Lausanne. Each of us, however, guards so well the place committed to us, that by our united efforts, the children of God assemble within the fold of Jesus Christ, and are even united in one company."—Dedication of 29th November 1549.

please God, to your life being so long lengthened out, as to allow me yet ten years of labour. But let us now live so for Christ, that we may be daily prepared to die for him; we ought, while we have opportunity to prepare for what will befall us. Make it your sole study, in the meanwhile, to take care of your health, that you may soon recover. My brother will tell you better, orally, than I can here how many friends salute you. Adieu, very worthy brother. May the Lord who, contrary to our expectation, has restored you to His Church, cause you ever to triumph over Satan and the wicked. Much health to your fellow-ministers and others.—Yours truly,

JOHN CALVIN.

[*Calvin's Lat. Corresp.* Opera, tom. ix. p. 69.]


CCCXI.—TO CHRISTOPHER AND TO THOMAS ZOLLICOFFRE.[1]

Last steps in favour of the Prisoners of Lyons.

FROM THE HOSTELLERIE IN LAUSANNE,
*28th March* 1553.

VERY DEAR MESSIEURS AND BRETHREN,—I write you this present letter in much haste, having only just arrived at the town of Lausanne. The occasion of my writing is, that Messieurs of Berne have written so warmly to the king, that if they are ever to obtain anything from him, we hope this appeal may be final. Now, the prisoners have signified that we are to apply to you for the expenses of the journey. We pray you, therefore, to consider and determine speedily what had best be

---

[1] *On the back.*—To my kind brethren and friends, the brothers Christopher and Thomas Sollicoffre, merchants of Saint Gall, dwelling at Lyons. Pardon the mistake as to the names and the haste.

The 21st May 1552. The Seigneury of Berne, informed of the arrest of the five Scholars of Lausanne, had written to the King of France to solicit the deliverance of their "pensionaires." The burgomaster of Zurich, John Hab, obtained an audience of this prince and found him inflexible. The following year, March 1553, the Bernese solicited anew the pardon of the five prisoners, condemned by the official of Lyons and the parliament of Paris. It is to this last intercession, urged forward by Calvin and Viret, that the letter of the Reformer to the brothers Zollicoffre refers.

done. If you have any fitter messenger to send to court, we beg of you to repay him his travelling expenses from Berne to Lyons. If you think that he ought to proceed further be pleased to enjoin that money be furnished him without delay. May God of his infinite mercy prosper the despatch as we hope. I have addressed you privately, according to their instructions, and I believe that you will not object to be employed in an affair of this kind. Whereupon after having affectionately commended myself to you, I beseech our gracious God to have you in His holy keeping, to guide you by His Spirit, and to make you prosperous.

Your humble brother and sincere friend,
JOHN CALVIN.

You can see the copies of the two letters which Messieurs of Berne have written. It might, perhaps, have been desirable that the first, dated the 15th March, should have been kept back.[1] But the thing is done. The remedy is good, inasmuch as the latter is as full as could be desired. Having perused the whole, we beg of you to forward them to the prisoners aforesaid. Our brother, Peter Viret, commends himself most heartily to you.

[*Fr. orig. autogr.—Library of Saint Gall.* Vol. 7, p. 211.]

[1] In a letter to the King of the 15th March, Messieurs of Berne had made strong complaint of the conduct of the Cardinal de Tournon, who, after having promised them to interest himself in behalf of the five students, had, with the utmost rigour, instituted proceedings against them. In a second letter, written three days later, they represented to this prince the innocence of their scholars, arrested at Lyons before they had sojourned there a single day, and condemned to death, although they had neither preached, nor dogmatized, nor excited any disturbance in the kingdom. They concluded by saying,—" We very humbly pray your Majesty to bestow them on us as a pure, royal, gratuitous, and liberal gift, which we shall esteem as great and precious, as if a present had been made us of an inestimable amount of gold and silver." These petitions were of no avail. Inspired by the fatal genius of the Cardinals of Tournon and of Lorraine, Henry II. confirmed the sentence of the parliament of Paris.

## CCCXII.—To Cranmer.

*He entreats his influence in favour of the person already recommended to the King.*

*March* 1553.

When I lately wrote to you my last letter[1]—which may not perhaps be put into your hands until after you have received the present one—nothing was farther from my mind than that I should again trouble you so soon. An unexpected necessity has arisen, however, which compels me, even before I have penned a single friendly letter to you, to solicit you regarding a matter of great importance. A certain man, of a noble family, has been lately thrown into prison, whose kind heart and generous nature render him still more worthy of commendation for his virtues, than for the nobility of his descent. Thinking there was no danger, he had written to a common friend, who came among us as a voluntary exile when the royal prefect was at Noyon, the town in which I was born. Owing to the perfidy of the messenger, the letter was seized. He was arrested by a royal order. The Chancellor, and some others, were appointed judges extraordinary. Seeing that this occurrence has caused many good men to be seized with no ordinary alarm, and that the enemies of the whole Church are ferociously insulting Christ in the person of a man of sincere piety, it is our duty to do all we can to restrain their fury, and bring relief to such a distinguished servant of God. I was not at all afraid, therefore, of any one accusing me of indiscretion in engaging in the pious duty of commending the life of this person to your most serene king. And the same necessity which drove me to this, leads me to exhort you to use your interest, as far as may be lawful, for furthering the end of my petition. And while I am confident that you will be glad to do it of your own accord, I nevertheless ask and beseech of you, most earnestly

---

[1] The letter to which allusion is here made is lost; and one cannot sufficiently deplore the disappearance of documents, which would have shed a fuller light on the relations of Calvin with the Reformer of England.

to do it for my sake all the more speedily. Adieu, most distinguished Sir, deserving in many ways of my hearty reverence.
JOHN CALVIN.

[*Lat. orig. autogr.—Library of Geneva.* Vol. 107, *a.*]

## CCCXIII.—To MONSIEUR DE MAROLLES.[1]

Christian encouragement and consolation.

*12th April* 1553.

MONSIEUR,—I doubt not that you are at present in very great perplexity, seeing that the rage of the enemies is daily kindling, and dangers increasing more and more. Thus you have much need to have recourse to Him who not in vain claims the office of comforting His people in their afflictions. Although it may be difficult to the weakness of our flesh to continue steadfast though we see no end of warfare ; nay more, see that things grow worse ; yet when girt about with the armour which God bestows upon us, we must not fear but that we shall overcome all the devices of Satan. I call " the armour of God," not merely the promises and holy exhortations by which He strengthens us, but the prayers which are to obtain the strength we need. And therefore, Sir, according to your necessity, get by heart what Scripture sets before us, both as to the present condition of Christians, and the miseries to which they must needs be subject, and also as to the happy and desirable issue promised them ; and how, moreover, they shall never be forsaken in the time of their need. I know—long-continued maladies being the most harassing—that it is extremely hard

---

[1] Seigneur of Picardy, no doubt one of the ancestors of that illustrious confessor, Louis de Marolles, who expiated in the galleys of Marseilles the crime of his resistance to the dragooning zeal of Louis XIV. and the pressing solicitations of Bossuet. "The hour of liberty," says M. Charles Weiss, " never struck for that unfortunate one. He died in 1692 in the *Hôpital des Forçats* at Marseilles, and was interred in the Turkish cemetery, the ordinary burial-place of the reformed who died in the galleys, faithful to the last in the religion for which they had suffered."—*Histoire des Refugiés Protestantes de France,* tom. i. p. 101. See also the book entitled *Histoire des Souffrances du bien heureux martyr, M. Louis de Marolles.* La Haye, 1699.

for you to languish for such a length of time. But if the enemies of the truth are thus obstinate in their fury, we ought to be ashamed of not being at least equally steadfast in welldoing; and most of all when it concerns the glory of our God and Redeemer, which, of His infinite goodness, He has bound up with our salvation. And I have no doubt that you put in practice what the apostle tells you about strengthening the feeble knees, and lifting up the hands which hang down. For it cannot be but that the first blows dismay, unless we rouse our virtue to resist temptation. And as I feel well persuaded that you are not slack in bestirring yourself, I am the more brief. It is enough for me to have given you a few words of advice, and at the same time to assure you that you are not forgotten here, but that knowing the difficulties by which you are beset, we have a fellow-feeling of them. I do not mean to say that it is such as we ought to have, but it is at least the testimony of the true brotherly love which we are bound to bear you. Moreover, while praying God that He would strengthen your courage and impart His protection, you will also have to request that He would guide you with his advice, and give you a favourable opening. However scant the means He may offer you, you are free, as I believe, to use them, and that speedily, lest they escape you. As for the road which would be best for you to take, I know not what to say. Although I should be very glad to see you, and to enjoy your good-fellowship, yet I should not repine, knowing that in order to follow after God, and to be the more drawn to Him, were you removed to twice the distance from me. I do not know the advantages of the other place. As for ours, I must not conceal from you that they are so scanty I am ashamed to mention them. I wish much, and it would be desirable, that there had been wherewithal to have drawn you hither. But I ought not to inveigle you by vain expectations, having no other desire than your wellbeing wherever it may be. True it is, that what some promise themselves in retiring hither, rests, as appears to me, on very slender grounds. However, there is this to be said, the Christians here have liberty to worship God purely, which is the chief point of all. For the present, you must commit yourself to Him who has the spirit of prudence, to be guided by Him. Wherefore, in concluding, Monsieur, after having affectionately commended me to your kind favour and prayers, I pray our good Lord to increase you with the gifts of His Spirit, to uphold you with His strong arm that you faint not, to bridle Satan and all his underlings, so that they may not be able to do aught against you, to glorify His name by you even to the end. I desire also that Madame may have her share in these commendations. And should an occasion offer, I especially entreat you to present the like also to Madame, your neighbour.[1] Once more, I pray the gracious Father to have you all under His care, not merely for the preservation of the body, but also for the keeping the soul unpolluted. Your brother and humble servitor,

CHARLES D'ESPEVILLE.

[*Fr. copy.—Library of Geneva.* Vol. 107.]


CCCXIV.—To VIRET.[2]

Extinction of all hope in regard to the prisoners of Lyons.

GENEVA, 22*d April* 1553.

When the present messenger left Lyons matters stood thus: the majority of the judges were disinclined to agree to the condemnation of the brethren, inasmuch as the king had given no express orders respecting it. The Constable, however, stood alone in opposing this.[3] Good men thought accordingly that something would require to be done. To me indeed their

---

[1] This was doubtless Madame de Cany. See note, p. 281.
[2] See the letter to the brothers Zollicoffre, and the notes relative to the last intercession of the Seigneurie of Berne in behalf of the students of Lausanne, p. 378. Viret took the most lively interest in the captives, and wrote them a beautiful letter a short while before their martyrdom, full of Christian exhortations, which may be seen in the *Histoire des Martyrs*, pp. 248, 249.
[3] The Constable, Anne de Montmorency, governor of Lyonnais, shared with Cardinal de Tournon the melancholy honour of having urged on with fury the condemnation of those prisoners who had been recommended to his merciful intercession with the king.—*Hist. des Martyrs*, p. 231., MSS. of the Archives of Berne.

labour appears not only useless, but absurd. For there is no hope of inducing the Bernese, after their insolent repulse, to expose themselves to no purpose to the mockery of the tyrant and his court. Nor in truth would the Lyonnese ask aught of the kind from us, if a copy of a letter which I received three days ago were put into their hands. Should you deem it advisable, you may counsel some of your Bernese friends as to what should be done there. But good men will understand from our letter that they need give themselves no farther trouble. Adieu, very excellent and upright brother, together with your wife and family. Salute Beza, your colleague Ribet, and the rest of my friends. May Christ ever watch over you and guide you.—Yours,               JOHN CALVIN.

[*Lat. orig. autogr.—Library of Geneva.* Vol. 107, a.]

## CCCXV.—To BULLINGER.[1]

*Assurances of respect and fraternal affection.*

*April* 1553.

A letter was shown me lately at Farel's, addressed to himself, in which you informed him that you were gradually recovering from a very severe and all but fatal illness. The life of our brother Farel was at that time despaired of; so much so, that on my return I declared everywhere that he was dead. We have now to offer our sincere thanks to the Lord, who has restored both of you to us and to his Church. I was very glad to find from your letter, three days ago, that you are quite recovered. Although, to speak the truth, the reading of it would have filled me with more joy, had I not ascertained that it was written to prevent me from entertaining any hostility towards you. Certainly such a thing never entered my mind; nor do I think that Ulmius had any reason for saying so. He came twice to me. We conversed together for a long time on various matters, freely and familiarly. Mention was made of yourself,

---

[1] This letter is without a date, but from the allusion to the very dangerous illness of Farel, it must have been written in the month of April 1553.

and the whole of your colleagues, but not a syllable escaped me, so far as I know, calculated to convey an unfavourable opinion of you. On desiring him, however, as he was leaving me, to present my regards to you, I omitted Bibliander, inasmuch as he was openly professing hostility towards us.[1] When Ulmius[2] seemed to regard this with incredulity, and turned away from it as if from an unlucky omen, I briefly explained to him the cause of it :—that having been tormented here by a vile and perfidious character, I led myself to think that we were sure of support from you ; that the issue was not what I had expected ; that, notwithstanding, our brotherly regard for one another remained unchanged, and no token, certainly, of alienation had been given by you. I added, moreover, that myself and my fellow-ministers, while we had not been so fully supported by you as we could have wished, were nevertheless inclined to put a favourable construction on it. Also, that Bibliander was throwing out threats about being engaged on a work against my doctrine, and that he went babbling about concerning it, in some violent way or other, among all without distinction. Our conversation at length concluded, by my saying,—" Bibliander may write what he chooses ; I shall not consider him worthy of a reply."

But, to return to yourself, most excellent and venerable brother, as I would be very far indeed from estimating you by the character of that man, so I was never led to believe that you entertained any hostility towards me whether publicly or privately. If that individual kept up a great deal of offensive babbling, and was, as I have said, boasting about his book, there was really no reason why I should disguise the matter, or make any hesitation about it, for the thing was notorious ; and while I am accustomed to say nothing about it to others, I did

---

[1] Theodore Bibliander, professor of Theology at Zurich. Of an ardent and irritable nature, he could not bear to be contradicted, and it is even told of him that he challenged to a duel the celebrated Peter Martyr, one of his colleagues, owing to some disagreement on the doctrine of predestination. The Seigneurie of Zurich dismissed the warlike theologian.—*Hist. de la Suisse,* tom. xii. p. 87.

[2] Is this John ab Ulmis of whom we read in numerous letters to Bullinger?—*Zurich Letters,* first series, vol. ii. pp. 377, 458.

not think that I required to be silent on it to Ulmius and a select few. This, therefore, I have in the first place to testify to you—and I solemnly declare it—that so far am I from regarding you as an enemy, that I desire to remain bound to you for ever by all ties of brotherly attachment ; and, confidently assured that it will be so, I hail you in no other manner than as a loving and inseparable companion in the work of the Lord. In the next place, I wish you to believe that I never either wrote or spoke anything but what was loving and honourable of that man who has publicly earned so much distinction in the Church, and has been ever my friend in private. If, therefore, you have been vexed at all by this matter, let your mind be hereafter at ease.[1]                   JOHN CALVIN.

[*Lat. copy.—Library of Geneva.* Vol. 107, a.]


## CCCXVI.—TO THE FIVE PRISONERS OF LYONS.[2]

*He exhorts them to steadfastness unto the end, in the assurance of eternal joy reserved in heaven.*

FROM GENEVA, *May* 15, 1553.

MY VERY DEAR BROTHERS,—We have at length heard why the herald of Berne did not return that way. It was because

---

[1] The end of this letter is wanting.

[2] This letter must have preceded by some days the last conflict of the five prisoners. Foreseeing their end near, they wrote, on the 5th May to the Seigneury of Berne, to thank them for the testimonials of affection which they had received from them. "If it has not pleased God," they said, "to preserve life by your means, it has at least been prolonged thereby . . . in spite of the fury of all those who would have desired long ago to put us to death. Since, then, that He is pleased that our blood should soon be shed for the confession of His holy name, we reckon ourselves far happier than if we were set at liberty, for as he is true and all-powerful, He will strengthen us, and will not permit us to be tormented beyond our strength ; and after that we have suffered awhile, He will receive us into His heavenly kingdom, and will bestow upon us eternal rest with Himself. . . . ." It was the 16th May when the five scholars were told to prepare for death ; they received that intelligence with a pious serenity. The stake was set up upon the *Place des Terreaux;* they proceeded thither, singing psalms, and repeating passages of holy writ. "Having arrived at the place of death, they cheerfully mounted on the heap of wood, the two youngest first. . . . The

he had not such an answer as we much desired. For the King has peremptorily refused all the requests made by Messieurs of Berne, as you will see by the copies of the letters, so that nothing further is to be looked for from that quarter. Nay, wherever we look here below, God has stopped the way. This is well, however, that we cannot be frustrated of the hope which we have in Him, and in His holy promises. You have always been settled on that sure foundation, even when it seemed as though you might be helped by men, and that we too thought so ; but whatever prospect of escape you may have had by human means, yet your eyes have never been dazzled so as to divert your heart and trust, either on this side or that. Now, at this present hour, necessity itself exhorts you more than ever to turn your whole mind heavenward. As yet, we know not what will be the event. But since it appears as though God would use your blood to sign His truth, there is nothing better than for you to prepare yourselves to that end, beseeching Him so to subdue you to His good pleasure, that nothing may hinder you from following whithersoever he shall call. For you know, my brothers, that it behoves us to be thus mortified, in order to be offered to Him in sacrifice. It cannot be but that you sustain hard conflicts, in order that what was declared to Peter may be accomplished in you, namely, that they shall carry you whither ye would not. You know, however, in what strength you have to fight—a strength on which all those who trust, shall never be daunted, much less confounded. Even so, my brothers, be confident that you shall be strengthened, according to your need, by the Spirit of our Lord Jesus, so that you shall not faint under the load of temp-

last who went up was Martial Alba, the elder of the five, who had been a long time on both his knees in prayer to the Lord. He earnestly requested Lieutenant Tignac to grant him a favour. The lieutenant said to him : What would you ? He said to him : That I might kiss my brethren before I die. The lieutenant granted his wish. Then the said Martial kissed the other four who were already bound, saying to each of them, *Adieu, adieu, my brother.* The fire was kindled ; the voice of the five confessors was heard, still exhorting the one the other in the midst of the flames : *Courage, my brothers; courage.* . . . These were the last audible words of these five valiant champions and martyrs of the Lord."—*Hist. des Martyrs*, lib. iv. p. 231.

tations, however heavy it be, any more than He did who won so glorious a victory, that in the midst of our miseries it is an unfailing pledge of our triumph. Since it pleases Him to employ you to the death in maintaining His quarrel, He will strengthen your hands in the fight, and will not suffer a single drop of your blood to be spent in vain. And though the fruit may not all at once appear, yet in time it shall spring up more abundantly than we can express. But as He hath vouchsafed you this privilege, that your bonds have been renowned, and that the noise of them has been everywhere spread abroad, it must needs be, in despite of Satan, that your death should resound far more powerfully, so that the name of our Lord be magnified thereby. For my part, I have no doubt, if it please this kind Father to take you unto Himself, that He has preserved you hitherto, in order that your long-continued imprisonment might serve as a preparation for the better awakening of those whom He has determined to edify by your end. For let enemies do their utmost, they never shall be able to bury out of sight that light which God has made to shine in you, in order to be contemplated from afar.

I shall not console, nor exhort you more at length, knowing that our heavenly Father gives you to experience how precious His consolations are, and that you are sufficiently careful to meditate upon what He sets before you in His Word. He has already so shown how His Spirit dwells in you, that we are well assured that He will perfect you to the end. That in leaving this world we do not go away at a venture, you know not only from the certainty you have, that there is a heavenly life, but also because from being assured of the gratuitous adoption of our God, you go thither as to your inheritance. That God should have appointed you His Son's martyrs, is a token to you of superabounding grace. There now remains the conflict, to which the Spirit of God not only exhorts us to go, but even to run. It is indeed a hard and grievous trial, to see the pride of the enemies of truth so enormous, without its getting any check from on high; their rage so unbridled, without God's interfering for the relief of His people. But if we remember that, when it is said that our life is hid, and that we must resemble the dead, this is not a doctrine for any particular time, but for all times, we shall not think it strange that afflictions should continue. While it pleases God to give His enemies the rein, our duty is to be quiet, although the time of our redemption tarries. Moreover, if He hath promised to be the judge of those who have brought His people under thraldom, we need not doubt that He has a horrible punishment prepared for such as have despised His majesty with such enormous pride, and have cruelly persecuted those who call purely upon His name. Put in practice, then, my brethren, that precept of David's, and forget not the law of God, although your life may be in your hands to be parted with at any hour. And seeing that he employs your life in so worthy a cause as is the witness of the Gospel, doubt not that it must be precious to Him. The time draws nigh when the earth shall disclose the blood which has been hid, and we, after having been disencumbered of these fading bodies, shall be completely restored. However, be the Son of God glorified by our shame, and let us be content with this sure testimony, that though we are persecuted and blamed we trust in the living God. In this we have wherewith to despise the whole world with its pride, till we be gathered into that everlasting kingdom, where we shall fully enjoy those blessings, which we now only possess in hope.

My brethren, after having humbly besought your remembrance of me in your prayers, I pray our good Lord to have you in His holy protection, to strengthen you more and more by His power, to make you feel what care He takes of your salvation, to increase in you the gifts of His Spirit, and to make them subserve His glory unto the end.

Your humble brother,

JOHN CALVIN.

I do not make my special remembrances to each of our brethren, because I believe that this letter will be common to them all.[1] Hitherto I have deferred writing on account of the

---

[1] Calvin refers here to other prisoners of Lyons, Mathieu Dimonet and Denis Peloquin, who kept up in prison a pious correspondence by letter with the scholars of Lausanne.

uncertainty of your state, fearing lest I might disquiet you to no purpose. I pray anew our good Lord to stretch out his arm for your confirmation.

[*Fr. copy.—Library of Geneva.* Vol. 107, *a.*]

## CCCXVII.—To Madame de Cany.[1]

Expression of Christian sympathy under trial.

*This 7th of June* 1553.

Madame,—Although I am not so devoid of compassion as not to feel my heart pained, in hearing of the more than ever strict captivity in which you are now held, yet I shall not cease to exhort you to furnish yourself with courage and constancy, according as you feel the trial to be vexatious and hard to bear; for it is just when pressed by Satan and the enemies of the faith to the uttermost, that we ought to make the most of the grace of God. St. Paul glories in this, that although he was chained in prison, nevertheless, the doctrine which he preached was not bound, but having its course, and thriving powerfully. And, indeed, seeing that it is the truth of God which reaches far beyond this world, and upward above the heavens, it is not likely that she should straiten herself acccrding to the fancy or by the tyranny of men. Consequently, the more the devil contrives to torture us by distress, let us strive the more to enlarge our hearts by faith, so as to meet all assaults. Our Saviour, moreover, has formerly afforded you examples of the kind, and gives us all the like daily in divers places; so that we ought to take great shame to ourselves if we are not strength-

---

[1] In the Fellowship Register of Geneva, (*Registres de la Compagnie de Genève*, Vol. A. p. 440,) there is a document entitled, "*Let'er of a Lady persecuted by her Papist Husband,*" from France, 24th June 1552. That lady was of high birth, as these words indicate, "*Knowing the house to which she belongs, and the great lords of the kingdom to whom she is related, and who are in great favour with the king. . . .*" This passage appears to us to point at Madame de Cany; see the Note, p. 281. Persecuted by her husband on account of her belief, that lady found her only consolation in the letters and exhortations which she received in secret from Geneva. Note, p. 391.

ened by them. For were we to grow faint under the strokes of the rod, when others are noways dismayed by death, what excuse should we have for our cowardice? You had not counted on the possibility of meeting with such rude conflicts at home. But you know how the Son of God forewarns us, so that nothing should trouble us, seeing that we have been prepared for it beforehand. Think, rather, that this is not the end, but that God is trying you very gently, supporting your weakness, until you have more strength to sustain blows. But be this as it may, beware of letting yourself be cast down by indifference or despair. Many are overcome, because they allow their zeal to grow cold, and run off in self-flattery. Others, on the contrary, become so alarmed when they do not find in themselves the strength they wish, that they get confused, and give up the struggle altogether. What then is to be done? Arouse yourself to meditate, as much upon the promises of God, which ought to serve as ladders to raise us up to heaven, and make us despise this transitory and fading life, as upon threatenings, which may well induce us to fear His judgments. When you do not feel your heart moved as it ought to be, have recourse, as to a special remedy, to diligently seeking the aid of Him without whom we can do nothing. In the meantime, strive to your utmost, blaming coldness and weakness, until you can perceive that there is some amendment. And in regard to this, great caution is required so as to hold a middle course, namely, to groan unceasingly, and even to woo yourself to sadness and dissatisfaction of your condition, and to such a sense of misery as that you may have no rest; without, at the same time, any doubting that God in due time will strengthen you according to your need, although this may not appear at once. It can be nothing strange to you to see the poor Church of God so miserably afflicted—to see the pride of enemies increase more and more with their cruelty. If your mind is in too great perplexity, this it is that you should find strange, as a proof of your having forgotten what we ought to have rooted in the depths of our heart, the duty of conformity to the image of the Son of God, patiently bearing the ignominy of His cross, until the day of our triumph come. Nevertheless, let not this hinder, but rather induce you to follow on in the way, for we must yet be sifted even more thoroughly.

Had I heard, that, being deprived of the little liberty you had, you did not cease to have your heart set aright, and to persevere in the service of Him who merits well that His honour be preferred to all beside, I should have whereof to rejoice more fully. However, I do rejoice, whatever be the result, in the good hope I have of this: therefore, do not wrong me by disappointment. However, you must consider most of all what you owe to our gracious God, and to the Lord Jesus Christ, who has shown how dear we were to Him, since He has not spared Himself for us; therefore, see to it that Satan and his underlings, who have thought to trample your faith beneath their feet, be confounded. But as so great a victory requires greater strength than your own, take refuge in this kind Lord Jesus, who has been made to us the strength of God his Father, so that in Him we might do all things. And for my part, I shall beseech Him that He would pour out upon you the help of His Spirit, so that you may know by experience what it is to be upheld by Him, and that He may be glorified thereby, praying also that He would take you into His holy protection, against the fury of wolves, and the wiles of foxes. Whereupon, Madame, after having humbly commended me to your kind favour, likewise to your prayers, I shall now make an end.

Your humble brother and servant,

J. DE BONNVILLE.[1]

[*Fr. copy.—Library of Geneva.* Vol. 107.]

---

[1] Pseudonym of the Reformer.

## CCCXVIII.—To the Prisoners of Lyons.[1]

He impresses on them the duty of maintaining their confession of the truth quietly and modestly.

*This 7th of July* 1553.

My Brethren,—I believe you have been informed that I was absent from town when the tidings from your prison arrived, and did not return for eight days after. I need not, therefore, to excuse myself for having so long delayed writing to you. Now, although these tidings have proved sorrowful to the flesh, even in consequence of the love we justly bear you in God, as we are bound to do, yet must we submit ourselves to the will of this kind Father and sovereign Lord, and not only consider His way of disposing of us just and reasonable, but also accept it with a gentle and loving heart as altogether right and profitable for our salvation,—patiently waiting until He palpably shows it to be so. Besides, we have whereof to rejoice even in the midst of our sorrow, in that he has so powerfully aided you, for need was that you should be strengthened by His Spirit, so that the confession of His sacred truth should be more precious to you than your own lives. We all know too well how difficult it is for men to forget self.

[1] The dungeons in which Mathieu Dimonet still pined away, contained several other prisoners, Denis Peloquin of Blois, Louis de Marsac, gentleman of the Bourbonnais, and one of his cousins. It is to the two last, recently arrived at Lyons, that the letter of the Reformer is addressed. The prisoners maintained a pious correspondence with those outside their prison. Peloquin wrote to his relations,—". . . My dear brothers and sisters, . . . do not stay yourselves, I beseech you, upon the judgment of the world, which is so blinded, that it cannot find life in death, nor blessing in cursing. Let us know that the means of being confirmed in Jesus Christ . . . is that we should carry our cross with him, for the servant is not greater than the master. . . ." Louis de Marsac wrote to Calvin:—" Sir and brother, . . . I cannot express to you the great comfort I have received . . . from the letter which you have sent to my brother Denis Peloquin, who found means to deliver it to one of our brethren who was in a vaulted cell above me, and read it to me aloud, as I could not read it myself, being unable to see anything in my dungeon. I entreat of you, therefore, to persevere in helping us with similar consolation, for it invites us to weep and to pray."—*Histoire des Martyrs,* pp. 236, 251.

Therefore it must needs be that our gracious God put forth His strong arm; then, for the sake of glorifying Him we do not fear torments, nor shame, nor death itself. Now, since He has girded you with His power, so as to sustain the first assault, it remains to entreat Him to strengthen you more and more according to your further conflict. And seeing that He has promised us victory in the end, do not doubt, that as He has imparted a measure of His strength, so you will have more ample evidence in future, that He does not make a beginning only to leave His work imperfect, as it is said in the Psalm. Especially when He puts such honour upon His people, as to employ them in maintaining His truth, and leads them, as it were by the hand to martyrdom, He never leaves them unprovided with the needful weapons. Yet, meanwhile, remember to lift up your eyes to that everlasting kingdom of Jesus Christ, and to think of whose cause it is in which you fight; for that glance will not only make you overcome all temptations which may spring from the infirmity of your flesh, but will also render you invincible by all the wiles of Satan, whatever he may devise to darken God's truth,—for I am well assured, that it is by His grace you are so settled and grounded, that you do not walk at a venture, but that you can say with that valiant champion of Jesus Christ, I know on whom I have believed.

This is why I have not sent you such a confession of faith as our good brother Peloquin asked me for, for God will render that which He will enable you to make, according to the measure of mind which He has allotted you, far more profitable than any that might be suggested to you by others. Indeed, having been requested by some of our brethren who have lately shed their blood for the glory of God, to revise and correct the confession they had prepared, I have felt very glad to have a sight of it for my own edification, but I would neither add, nor take away, a single word; believing that any change would but lessen the authority and efficacy which the wisdom and constancy we clearly see to have proceeded from the Spirit of God deserved. Be then assured, that God who manifests himself in time of need, and perfects His strength in our weakness, will not leave you unprovided with that which will powerfully magnify

His name. Only proceed therein with soberness and reverence, knowing that God will no less accept the sacrifice which you offer Him, according to the measure of ability which you have received from Him, than if you comprehended all the revelations of angels, and that He will make effectual that which He puts into your mouth, as well to confirm His own, as to confound the adversaries. And as you know that we have steadfastly to withstand the abominations of the Papacy, unless we would renounce the Son of God, who has purchased us to Himself at so dear a rate, meditate, likewise, on that celestial glory and immortality to which we are invited, and are certain of reaching through the Cross—through ignominy and death. It is strange, indeed, to human reason, that the children of God should be so surfeited with afflictions, while the wicked disport themselves in delights; but even more so, that the slaves of Satan should tread us under foot, as we say, and triumph over us. However, we have wherewith to comfort ourselves in all our miseries, looking for that happy issue which is promised to us, that He will not only deliver us by His angels, but will Himself wipe away the tears from our eyes. And thus we have good right to despise the pride of these poor blinded men, who to their own ruin lift up their rage against heaven; and although we are not at present in your condition, yet we do not on that account leave off fighting together with you by prayer, by anxiety and tender compassion, as fellow-members, seeing that it has pleased our heavenly Father, of his infinite goodness, to unite us into one body, under His Son, our Head. Whereupon I shall beseech Him, that He would vouchsafe you this grace, that being stayed upon Him, you may in nowise waver, but rather grow in strength; that He would keep you under His protection, and give you such assurance of it, that you may be able to despise all that is of the world. My brethren greet you very affectionately, and so do many others.—Your brother,

JOHN CALVIN.

As this letter will, I hope, be in common to you both, I shall merely add, that there is no need whatever for a long exhortation from me; it is enough that I pray God that it may please

Him to impress still better and better upon your heart, what I see by your letter, that you already enjoy. However grievous it may be to pine so long, if you got no other benefit by it than God's showing you that He has not reserved you until now without cause, you have good reason not to grow faint nor wearied out thereby. And as for the sickness, it is well for you to consider, that God in this way wishes to prepare you better for a greater conflict, so that the flesh being entirely subdued, may be more able to resign itself. Thus we ought to turn to profitable improvement everything that the heavenly Father sends us. If you can communicate with the other brethren, I pray you to salute them also from me. May God uphold you all by His strong hand, preserve and guide you, and make His own glory to shine forth in you more and more.

[*Fr.*—Printed in *Histoire des Martyrs*, lib. iv. p. 253.]

## CCCXIX.—To BULLINGER.

Expression of regret for the death of the King of England—sad condition of the German Churches.

GENEVA, 3*d August* 1553.

Paulus an Italian, and a man of tried integrity, on writing lately to our friend Count Celso, stated, among other things, that he had brought a letter for me from the very honourable the Duchess of Ferrara, which he left with you. Seeing that I received a letter from Gualter not long since, in which he makes no mention of such a thing; and seeing, moreover, that John Liner, a merchant of Saint Gall, on passing through this place a short while before, alleged that you had written me through a certain Jew, I am really suspicious that you have been deceived by him. He was not seen by any one here; and indeed I have no doubt but that he has betaken himself to one who is likely to bring him greater gain. If it should turn out accordingly that this letter has been lost, I am anxious that the Duchess should be informed of it. Inasmuch, therefore, as this nobleman, whom she has now employed for many years as a messenger to the French king, was about to make a journey thither, I have requested him to ask you whether anything was done with the packet which Paulus left with you, in order that he may inform his mistress of it.

The messengers regarding the death of the English king are more numerous than I could wish.[1] We are therefore mourning him just as if we were already certain of his death, or rather mourning over the fate of the Church, which has met with an incalculable loss in the person of a single individual. We are held at present in anxious suspense as to whether matters are to go to confusion. It is meanwhile very greatly to be lamented that Germany is being torn by intestine strife, by wounds inflicted by each on the other. But it is nothing wonderful that the Lord should employ violent remedies for such hopeless diseases. All we can do is to pray earnestly and unceasingly that He may not permit his Church to be utterly overwhelmed, but rather that he may guide her safe through the general wreck.

Adieu, most distinguished Sir, and most revered brother in Christ. Salute courteously your fellow-ministers, your wife, your sons-in-law, and your daughters. May the Lord shield you all by His protection and guide you by his Spirit. My colleagues salute you earnestly.—Yours,

JOHN CALVIN.

[*Lat. orig. autogr.—Library of Zurich,* Gallic. Scripta, p. 19.]

[1] King Edward VI. died a very pious death on the 6th of July preceding. See Burnet's *History*. Bullinger verified this mournful event to Calvin in the following words :—" I have received intelligence from England of a very sad occurrence. That most pious king departed to the Lord on the 6th of July; and he departed very happily indeed with a holy confession. The book which I here send you was written by him, and published in the month of May. You will see from it how great a treasure the Church of Christ has lost."—Bullinger to Calvin, August 1553. Eccl. Archives of Berne.

## CCCXX.—To Farel.[1]

Arrest of Servetus, and institution of the process against him.

Geneva, 20th August 1553.

It is as you say, my dear Farel. Although we may be severely buffeted hither and thither by many tempests, yet, seeing that a pilot steers the ship in which we sail, who will never allow us to perish even in the midst of shipwrecks, there is no reason why our minds should be overwhelmed with fear and overcome

[1] We have already read at p. 16, of the present volume of Calvin's first connexion with Servetus, and of the rupture of that connexion as attested by the letter of Calvin to John Frellon (13th February 1546). Wandering by turns in France, Germany, and Italy, Servetus had taken up his residence at Vienne in Dauphiné, where he at once exercised the profession of a doctor, and persisted in his daring attacks on Christianity, for which he aspired to substitute a rational philosophy. Such is the drift of his book entitled *Christianismi Restitutio*, which he published anonymously in 1553, after having two-and-twenty years before directed his bold attacks against the doctrine of the Trinity, in his book *De Trinitatis Erroribus*, published at Haguenau in 1531. Accused by a Genevan refugee before the Inquisition of Lyons, as the author of these writings, Servetus was arrested, cast into the dungeons of Vienne, and condemned by Catholic judges to be burnt, from which he only escaped by flight. Hear how Theodore Beza recounts in his letter to Bullinger, the preparations for the trial of Servetus, of his escape from prison, and of his arrival and arrest at Geneva:—" You have heard doubtless of that impious blasphemer Servetus. He caused a book, or rather volume of his blasphemies to be secretly printed at Lyons. Certain good brethren at Lyons informed the magistrate of this deceitful action. Persons were despatched to Vienne, where he was practising as a physician, to bring him bound [to Lyons]. He was seized, but soon after effected his escape by deceit. At length he came to Geneva, where he went skulking about. He was forthwith recognised, however, by a certain person, and cast into prison. Calvin also, whom he treated very unhandsomely by name in thirty printed letters, pled the cause of the Church against him in the Council, in the presence of a great assemblage of the pious. He continued in his impiety. What will come of it I know not. Let us pray the Lord to purge His Church of these monsters."—*MSS. of Zurich.* Letter of the 27th August 1553. Such was the opening of the process which terminated so fatally for Servetus. Born in an age not disposed to show mercy to errors of faith, he seems, says a historian, to have fled from Spain—the native country of the auto-da-fé—only to see his effigy burnt in a strange land by the torch of a Catholic executioner, and to come afterwards to expire amid flames kindled by Calvinistic justice.—Albert Rilliet. *Relation du Procès Criminel intenté contre Servet.* Genève, 1844. 8vo.—[Translated into English by the Rev. Dr. Tweedie. Edinburgh: Johnstone & Hunter.]

with weariness. We have now new business in hand with Servetus. He intended perhaps passing through this city; for it is not yet known with what design he came. But after he had been recognised, I thought that he should be detained. My friend Nicolas summoned him on a capital charge, offering himself as security according to the *lex talionis*.[1] On the following day he adduced against him forty written charges. He at first sought to evade them. Accordingly we were summoned. He impudently reviled me, just as if he regarded me as obnoxious to him. I answered him as he deserved. At length the Senate pronounced all the charges proven. Nicolas was released from prison on the third day, having given up my brother as his surety; on the fourth day he was set free. Of the man's effrontery I will say nothing; but such was his madness that he did not hesitate to say that devils possessed divinity; yea, that many gods were in individual devils, inasmuch as deity had been substantially communicated to those, equally with wood and stone. I hope that sentence of death will at least be passed upon him; but I desire that the severity of the punishment may be mitigated.[2] Adieu. My colleagues again salute you. Budé does the same, and Normande, who has now recovered. Present my regards to my brother Claude.

JOHN CALVIN.

[*Calvin's Lat. Corresp.* Opera ix. p. 70.]

---

[1] Nicolas de la Fontaine, a servant of Calvin's, was made, conformably to the judicial usages then in operation at Geneva, criminal prosecutor against Servetus. —*Registers of the Council,* 14th August 1553.

[2] It is curious to read on this point the reply of Farel to Calvin :—" In desiring to mitigate the severity of his punishment, you act the part of a friend to a man who is most hostile to you. But I beseech you so to manage the matter that no one whatever may rashly dare to publish new dogmas, and throw all things into confusion with impunity for such a length of time as he has done." In his relentless rigour against heresy, Farel did not hesitate to pronounce himself even to be worthy of death if he should teach any dogma opposed to the faith. His words deserve to be recorded :—" When I read Paul's statement that he did not refuse to suffer death if he had in any way deserved it, I saw clearly that I must be prepared to suffer death if I should teach anything contrary to the doctrine of piety. And I added, that I should be most worthy of any punishment whatever if I should seduce any one from the faith and doctrine of Christ."—8th Sept. 1553. Calv. *Opera,* tom. ix. p. 71.

CCCXXI.—To Denis Peloquin and Louis de Marsac.[1]

*Information regarding various controverted points—exhortation to fidelity, even unto martyrdom.*

*This 22d of August* 1553.

Very dear Brethren,—Although when writing your letter you thought that the enemies of truth were about to sacrifice you soon, I do not omit writing to you, so that if it please God that this should arrive in time, you may again have some words of consolation from me. It is very well and very prudently determined by you to give thanks to God, since you know that He has confirmed you anew in His promises, giving you such constancy as you have lately felt in your last replies. It is indeed of Him alone that you have remained steadfast and unflinching. Hence I feel well assured that this seal, which bears the true mark of the Holy Spirit, will never be effaced. Elsewhere He has wrought so powerfully upon Michael Girard,[2] that his former weakness gives all the greater lustre to the strength which he has received from above. I have no doubt that even the enemies themselves must be convinced that this change did not proceed from man. Consequently there is stronger reason why we should have our eyes

---

[1] Occupying the same cell during the last days of their captivity, the two prisoners were only separated to die. Denis Peloquin was taken from his prison the 4th September, and conducted to Ville Franche, where his heroic constancy at the stake, excited the wonder and tender sympathy of the spectators. Louis de Marsac, with two other victims, Etienne Gravot of Gyen, and Marsac, his cousin, who had followed him into his dungeon, " gave thanks to God for the inestimable honour which he conferred upon them of suffering for His name." At the moment when the three condemned were about to be led to the place of execution, a rope was put about their neck, according to custom. " Louis de Marsac, seeing that they spared him in that particular, out of some regard to his quality, asked in a loud voice if the cause of his two brethren was different from his, adding these words, ' Alas ! do not refuse me the collar of so excellent an order.' The lieutenant agreed to his wish, and the three martyrs, chanting with one voice the song of deliverance, shortly after mounted the pile prepared on the Place des Terreaux, and expired in the midst of the flames."—*Hist. des Martyrs.* Lib. iv. p. 254. *Hist. Eccl.* tom. i. p. 92.

[2] Michael Girard. *In a note in the History of the Martyrs.* This Michael Girard did not persevere.

open to contemplate the hand of God which is here put forth after a wondrous manner, to withdraw his frail creature from the horrible confusion into which he had fallen. At the time that he followed his own devices, he fancied that he had gained much in redeeming for a short period this fading miserable life, by plunging himself into the abysses of eternal death. It is then a Divine work, that of his own goodwill he should have again returned to death, that he might attain to a life of uprightness, from which he had not merely strayed, but absolutely excluded himself as far as in him lay. For the goodness of God has been the more richly displayed, by having raised up His creature out of a fall which seemed fatal, yea, so as even to triumph by it, and to magnify His glory, as He has begun to do, and will I hope carry out to perfection.

I have seen the confession drawn up by him, which is pure and frank, and worthy of a Christian man. Nevertheless, I think it right that he should be warned as to some points, in order that the adversaries may be the more confounded by his making a more distinct reply ;—not that what he says be not true, but because the malignant always lay hold of the slightest occasions to calumniate and pervert what is right.

On being questioned as to whether the body of Christ exist not under the appearance of bread, he answered that this was mere blasphemy, annihilating the death of Jesus Christ. Now there were two things which he ought to have especially reproved in the mass : the one is idolatry, seeing that they make an idol of a bit of bread, worshipping it as God ; the other that they make of it a sacrifice to reconcile men to God. Now as Jesus Christ is the only priest ordained of God the Father, so likewise has he offered Himself once for all, and his death is the sole and perpetual sacrifice for our redemption. Even on the first head, it would have been well to protest his belief, that in the Supper we communicate in the body and blood of Jesus Christ, but that we do so by rising to heaven through faith, and not by making Him descend here below, taking care to add, that this is no argument in favour of their Mass, which is altogether opposed to the Supper of Jesus Christ.

Being questioned as to whether the Virgin Mary and the saints intercede for us, he answered, that there is but one only intercessor and advocate, Jesus Christ; which is true, for there are neither men nor angels who have access to God the Father save by this Mediator alone. But it would have been well to add, that the office of intercession is not bestowed upon the dead, God commanding us to intercede, the one for the other, in the present life: nevertheless, because it is not lawful to pray to God except in assurance of faith, that nothing remains for us but to call upon God in the name of Jesus Christ, and that all those who seek to the Virgin Mary and the saints as their advocates, act extravagantly, and turn aside out of the way.

Being questioned as to free-will, in order to show that of ourselves we have no power of well-doing, he alleges the expression of Saint Paul in the 7th of the Romans: *The good that I would, I do not,* &c. Now it is certain, that Saint Paul does not speak there of unbelievers who are wholly destitute of the grace of God, but of himself and of other saints to whom God had already given grace to aspire after well-doing. On such points he confesses that he felt such a struggle within himself, that he could not attain to a full performance of duty. Accordingly this further statement should have been made: If the faithful feel their whole nature opposed to the will of God, what must be the case with those who are full of pure malice and rebellion? Just as he says in the 8th chapter, that all the affections of the flesh are only so much enmity against God. And in Ephesians ii., he shows clearly what is in man. Item, in the First Epistle to the Corinthians, chapters i. ii., and in Romans iii.; whence it follows, that it is God who works in us to will and to do, according to His good pleasure.

Being questioned concerning vows, he answered, that all our promises are but lies. Now, it would have been well to specify that a part of their vows being impossible, they are nothing but an insult to God; as, for instance, when the monks and priests renounce marriage: and that generally the whole of these vows are nothing but false inventions in order to bastardize the service of God, and that we are not permitted to promise or offer to Him except in accordance with His word. I believe that the said brother will be well pleased to be informed of these things, so that the truth of God may be the more victorious in him.

For the rest, as in the midst of this life we are in death, you have now need to be well persuaded that in the midst of death you are in life. And thus we see that we must not be governed by sense merely in following Jesus Christ, for there is nothing more alien to our nature than to plunge ourselves into disgrace, and abase ourselves unto death, in order to be elevated to the glory of heaven. But in the end we shall feel experimentally, that the Son of God has not disappointed us in promising that whosoever shall lay down his life in this world shall recover it to enjoy it for ever. Wherefore, my brethren, if hitherto you have known by experience the value of the consolations which this kind Lord Jesus Christ vouchsafes to His own, to enable them to welcome all that they suffer in His cause, and the value of the help of His Spirit in giving them such courage that they faint not, beseech Him to continue both the one and the other, and in so praying rest in Him, assured that He will fulfil your holy desire. On our part, while you are fighting, we shall not forget you. All my brethren salute you. The God of grace and Father of mercy have you under His protection; and if it please Him that you should endure death for the testimony of His Gospel, as seems likely, may He show that He has not forsaken you, but rather that while appointing you His martyrs, He dwells and reigns within you, to triumph in you to the confusion of His enemies, and the edification of the faith of His elect; and may He lead us all until He gathers us together into His kingdom.

Excuse me that I have not sooner replied to you, for I only yesterday received your letter which is dated of the twelfth.—Your humble brother,               JOHN CALVIN.

[*Fr.*—Printed in *Histoire des Martyrs*, lib. iv. p. 244.

CCCXXII.—To his dearly Beloved, the Pastors of the Church of Frankfort.[1]

Request for the destruction of the copies at Frankfort of the book of Servetus.

GENEVA, *August* 27, 1553.

Grace to you, and peace, from God our Father, and the Lord Jesus Christ, more peculiarly set apart, and my worshipful brethren.

You have doubtless heard of the name of Servetus, a Spaniard, who twenty years ago corrupted your Germany with a virulent publication, filled with many pernicious errors. This worthless fellow, after being driven out of Germany, and having concealed himself in France under a fictitious name, lately patched up a larger volume, partly from his former book, and partly from new figments which he had invented. This book he printed secretly at Vienne, a town in the neighbourhood of Lyons. Many copies of it had been conveyed to Frankfort for the Easter fairs: the printer's agent, however, a pious and worthy man, on being informed that it contained nothing but a farrago of errors, suppressed whatever he had of it. It would take long to relate with how many errors—yea, prodigious blasphemies against God—the book abounds. Figure to yourselves a rhapsody patched up from the impious ravings of all ages. There is no sort of impiety which this monster has not raked up, as if from the infernal regions. I had rather you should pass sentence

---

[1] The rigour of the judges of Servetus could not fail to extend to the book which served as the basis of the judicial prosecution directed against his person. From the confession of the accused, there had been printed a thousand copies of the *Christianismi Restitutio*, of which a certain number were deposited at Frankfort. Calvin did not forget the latter portion of this acknowledgment, confirmed besides by a letter from the printer at Vienne, but wrote immediately to the Church of Frankfort, desiring the sequestration and destruction of this dangerous deposit. A clerk of the celebrated printer, Robert Stephens, then resident at Geneva, was charged with this mission, which he accomplished with so very great success, that there are only *three* copies of the original edition to be found at the present day. One in the Imperial Library of Paris, another in that of Vienna in Austria, and a third in a private collection.—Rilliet, *Relation du Procès de Servet*, p. 9.

on it from reading the book itself. You will certainly find on almost every single page, what will inspire you with horror. The author himself is held in prison by our magistrates, and he will be punished ere long, I hope ; but it is your duty to see to it that this pestiferous poison does not spread farther. The messenger will inform you respecting the number and the repository of the books. The bookseller, if I mistake not, will permit them to be burnt. Should anything stand in the way, however, I trust that you will act so judiciously, as to purge the world of such noxious corruptions. Besides, your way will be clear,—because if the matter be submitted to your judgment, there will be no necessity for asking the magistrate to interfere. And while I am so persuaded of your integrity that I believe it would be sufficient to inform you of it ; yet the magnitude of the affair demands that I should beseech you, by Christ, faithfully to strive to discharge your duty, lest the opportunity should slip from you.

Fare ye well, most honoured Sirs, and very dear brethren. May the Lord guide you by His Spirit, shield you by His protection, and bless your labours.

JOHN CALVIN.

[*Calvin's Lat. Corresp.* Opera, tom. ix. p. 71.]


CCCXXIII.—To VIRET.[1]

Troubles at Geneva—Berthelier and the chiefs of the Libertins are refused admission to the Lord's Table.

GENEVA, 4*th September* 1553.

I was wishing to maintain silence towards you regarding our affairs, that I might not augment your grief to no purpose.

---

[1] A serious conflict came to be raised between the ministers and the magistrates of Geneva. A chief of the Libertins, Philibert Berthelier, was excommunicated by the consistory for his irregular habits, and appealed to the Council of State, which annulled the ecclesiastical sentence, and gave Berthelier authority to go forward to the Supper. The experiment was decisive ; it was made to know whether or not Calvin would abandon ecclesiastical discipline, or resist the government.

But fearing that you might be more deeply affected by divers rumours, I at length thought it better to inform you respecting the principal point. When Berthelier, a year and a half ago, was interdicted the privilege of the Supper, he complained to the senate, and we, to please the scoundrel, were summoned before their assembly. After having heard the case, the Senate pronounced him to have been rightfully excommunicated. Whether from despair or contempt, he has kept quiet ever since up to the present time. Now, indeed, that the Syndicate of Perrin might not become forgotten, he has wished the Senate to restore him, without consulting the Consistory. On being summoned a second time, I demonstrated in a long speech, that to do so would be to act, not only contrary to what was right, but also contrary to law; nay more, that it was sinful to destroy the discipline of the Church in this manner. During my absence, however, and unknown to the Consistory, an opportunity was afforded him of receiving the Supper. As soon as I got notice of it, I used all my endeavours to get the Syndics to call a meeting of the Senate. I have devoted myself so earnestly to the cause, that, in my mind, nothing calculated to influence their minds was left undone. I endeavoured, partly by vehemence, and partly by moderation, to reduce them to a sound mind. I even took an oath, that I had resolved rather to meet death than profane so shamefully the holy Supper of the Lord; for that nothing was more intolerable than that that individual, mocking and insulting the Church of God by his contumacy, should by raising the standard, so to speak, incite the worst characters, and those like himself, to indulge in the same effrontery. The reply was, that the Senate had nothing to change in its former decision. From which you perceive, that by this law my ministry is abandoned, if I suffer the authority of the Consistory to be trampled upon, and extend

This letter of the Reformer to Viret, shows us with what energetic resolution and heroic constancy he resolved, in this instance, to maintain the honour of Christ. The conflict, which mutually divided the representatives of the spiritual and civil powers, could only be terminated by the solemn intervention of the Helvetian Churches.—*Registers of Council*, anno 1553. See also the various histories of Geneva, Spon, Picot, &c.

the Supper of Christ to open scoffers, who boast that pastors are nothing to them. In truth, I should rather die a hundred times, than subject Christ to such foul mockery. I need not record what I said yesterday in both assemblies, as you will get an oral account of it from many. The wicked and the abandoned may now obtain, therefore, what they have eagerly sought. The calamity to the Church grieves me, as indeed it ought. But if God yields so much power to Satan, as to strip me of the liberty of my ministry by his violent commands, I am satisfied. Certainly, he who has inflicted the wound, will Himself find a remedy. And, indeed, seeing that so much wickedness has now passed with impunity for many years, perhaps the Lord is preparing some judgment which I am not deemed worthy to see. In fine, whatever may happen, it is our duty to submit to His will.

Farewell, most worthy brethren. May the Lord be ever present with you, to guide and protect you. Pray Him, on the other hand, to look down upon this unfortunate Church.

JOHN CALVIN.

[*Calvin's Lat. Corresp.* Opera, tom. ix. p. 74.]

## CCCXXIV.—To BULLINGER.

Deep anxiety on account of the condition of the English Churches—Conference of the Swiss Churches in regard to Servetus.

GENEVA, *7th September* 1553.

With respect to the letter, I had no doubt but that you made a faithful endeavour, so far as it was your duty, to send it to me in safety. That Jew has deceived you however; at least he has not done what you expected of him. He at length arrived here, but alleged that he had been robbed at Fribourg: he could give no definite account of the letter. As circumstances did not turn out here according to his wishes, he crossed over to England. I informed him that matters were in a disturbed state in that country, and endeavoured to deter him from his design. It was of no avail, however; but he may take his own way.

We have good reason to feel anxiety—yea even torment—regarding that nation [England].[1] What is to become of so great a multitude of pious men, who have betaken themselves to voluntary exile in that country?[2] There is danger, also, that we shall hear very sad news ere long, of the many native English who have already embraced Christ, if the Lord do not in His mercy send help to them from heaven. Besides, the same rumour is gathering strength here with respect to Cardinal Pole.[3] Moreover, as I have always heard that she is a very haughty animal who now succeeds to the crown, and cruel withal, there sometimes steals over me a prophetic conjecture, that her audacity will carry her all lengths. You are aware of the rash daring peculiar to her family. She will prove troublesome to almost all parties in the long run. Should she make a weak attempt to alter the existing constitution, she will find opponents not a few. Meanwhile, the Church of God will be in a manner buffeted by manifold tempests. Let us, therefore, as you say, commend this very troubled state of affairs to God.

Our Council will, on an early day, send the opinions of Servetus to your city, to obtain your judgment regarding them.

[1] In a letter to Theodore Beza of 30th August 1553, he gave eloquent expression to his deep anxiety for the Church of England:—" Scarcely has any other thing so much distressed me as this English affair. Let us earnestly implore mercy of God, that He may have pity on us, and upon his most afflicted Church. But where is our Martyr? where John A Lasco? where is Hooper, Bishop of Worcester? where is Cranmer, Archbishop of Canterbury? where is the Duke of Suffolk? where are numberless other excellent men? Lord, have mercy upon them. I cannot easily express how greatly these things distress me."—*Zurich Letters*, 1st series, vol. ii. p. 741.

[2] " The London Church has more than 15,000 foreigners. Where will these miserable ones flee to, should the Pope gain the day? We must pray God therefore. . . ."—Letter of Bullinger to Calvin, of 26th August 1553.—Eccl. Archives of Berne, vol. vi. p. 312.

[3] Cardinal Pole was at that time preparing to leave Rome to return to England:—" An English nobleman was sent lately by Queen Mary to recall that Reginald Pole, who is too well known both to you and myself; for that English Athaliah desires the benefit of his presence and his counsel."—Bullinger to Beza, letter already quoted.

Indeed they cause you this trouble, despite our remonstrances ;[1] but they have reached such a pitch of folly and madness, that they regard with suspicion whatever we say to them. So much so, that were I to allege that it is clear at mid-day, they would forthwith begin to doubt of it. Our brother Gualter [will tell you] more ;[2] for I am compelled to conclude, as there are many here whom I found on returning home from dinner.

Adieu, therefore, most accomplished Sir, and honourable brother in the Lord. Salute your fellow-ministers, your sons-in-law, and your whole family. May Christ preserve, guide, and bless you all. Amen. My colleagues—all very dejected —salute you earnestly.—Yours,

JOHN CALVIN.

[*Lat. orig. autogr.*—*Library of Geneva.* Vol. 107, *a.*]


## CCCXXV.—To SULZER.[3]

Statement of the errors of Servetus, and of the duty of the Christian magistrate to repress them.

GENEVA, 8*th September* 1553.

As Michael Servetus, twenty years ago, infected the Christian world with his virulent and pestilential opinions, I should

[1] At the session of the 5th September, the Council of Geneva had decided, contrary to the wish of Calvin, upon consulting the Churches of Berne, Basle, Schaffhausen, and Zurich, respecting the culpability of Servetus, but this decision was realized just a fortnight too late.—Rilliet, *Relation du Procès de Servet*, p. 84.

[2] Rodolph Gualter, minister of the Church of Zurich, and son-in-law to Bullinger.

[3] The Lesser Council of Geneva, acting upon the preposition made a few days previously, (note 1,) prepared to write to the Churches of Berne, Zurich, Schaffhausen, and Basle, to ask their advice regarding the culpability of Servetus. It was not, however, till the 21st of September, that the messenger, charged with the various papers relative to the trial, had put into his hands the circular letter addressed to the magistrates or pastors of the four towns. These letters were accompanied by a copy of the *Christianismi Restitutio*, a copy of the works of Tertullian, and one of those of Irenæus, as well as the questions put to Servetus, together with his replies, and the refutation of the ministers. In those circulars, the council gave expression to its entire confidence in the intelligence of the pastors of Geneva, but desired, before coming to a decision, to have fuller infor-

suppose his name is not unknown to you. While you may not have read his book, yet you must have heard something of the sort of doctrines contained in it. It was he whom that faithful minister of Christ, Master Bucer of holy memory, in other respects of a mild disposition, declared from the pulpit to be worthy of having his bowels pulled out, and torn to pieces. While he has not permitted any of his poison to go abroad since that time, he has lately, however, brought out a larger volume, printed secretly at Vienne, but patched up from the same errors. To be sure, as soon as the thing became known, he was cast into prison. He escaped from it some way or other, and wandered in Italy for nearly four months. He at length, in an evil hour, came to this place, when, at my instigation, one of the Syndics ordered him to be conducted to prison. For I do not disguise it, that I considered it my duty to put a check, so far as I could, upon this most obstinate and ungovernable man, that his contagion might not spread farther. We see with what wantonness impiety is making progress everywhere, so that new errors are ever and anon breaking forth: we see how very inactive those are whom God has armed with the sword, for the vindication of the glory of His name. Seeing that the defenders of the Papacy are so bitter and bold in behalf of their superstitions, that in their atrocious fury they shed the blood of the innocent, it should shame Christian magistrates, that in the protection of certain truth, they are entirely destitute of spirit. I certainly confess that nothing would be less becoming, than for us to imitate their furious intemperance. But there is some ground for restraining the impious from uttering whatever blasphemies they please with impunity, when there is an opportunity of checking it. As respects this man, three things require to be considered. With what pro-

mation on the point, by consulting the other Churches. The fate of the prisoner evidently depended on the result of this supreme measure. Calvin, addressing Bullinger and Sulzer alternately, insisted strongly on the alleged culpability of Servetus, and on the necessity of a punishment, which should be, as it appeared to him, a solemn consecration of those truths which had been shaken by the attacks of the audacious Spanish doctor. The messenger charged with the letter to Sulzer was the Treasurer Du Pau, one of the most devoted disciples of the Reformer.

digious errors he has corrupted the whole of religion; yea, with what detestable mockeries he has endeavoured to destroy all piety; with what abominable ravings he has obscured Christianity, and razed to the very foundation all the principles of our religion. Secondly, how obstinately he has behaved; with what diabolical pride he has despised all advice; with what desperate stubbornness he has driven headlong in scattering his poison. Thirdly, with what proud scorn he at present avows and defends his abominations. For so far is he from any hope of repentance, that he does not hesitate to fling this blot upon those holy men, Capito and Œcolampadius, as if they were his companions. When the letters of Œcolampadius were shown him, he said that he wondered by what spirit they had been led away from their former opinion. But as I hope you will see to it that the impiety of the man be represented in the character it merits, I shall not add more. Only there is one thing I wish to say to you, viz., that the treasurer of this city, who will deliver to you this letter, takes a correct view of this case, so that he at least does not avoid the issue which we desire. Would that your old disciples were animated by the same spirit![1]

I write you nothing regarding French matters, as I do not think there is anything new here, which is not equally known among yourselves, except that there were three pious brethren burnt at Lyons on Sabbath last; a fourth was sent to a neighbouring town to suffer a similar fate.[2] It is scarcely credible, seeing that they were illiterate men, how they were, as far as it appeared, enlightened by the Spirit of God to the highest perfection of doctrine, and with what courage they were support to maintain an inflexible firmness. One at first, overcome by fear, had swerved from a genuine confession. When the judges resolved upon releasing him, he, having asked forgiveness for his insincerity, eagerly offered himself to the flames.

---

[1] These last words betray Calvin's want of confidence in the Pastors of the Church of Berne, with certain of whom he was found to disagree upon certain points of doctrine, and who had given expression to principles of great toleration in the reply relative to Bolsec.

[2] See letter, p. 400.

Similar fires are kindled, also, in other parts of France; nor is there any hope of relief.—Adieu.

JOHN CALVIN.

[*Calvin's Lat. Corresp.* Opera, tom. ix. p. 70.]

## CCCXXVI.—To a Captive Lady.[1]

He consoles her under her trials, and exhorts her to use every means to secure her retreat to Geneva.

FROM GENEVA, *this* 13*th September* 1553.

MADEMOISELLE AND VERY DEAR SISTER,—I am much grieved by your affliction, not only because the children of God ought to bear each other's burdens, but because I feel the cause for which you suffer to be a common one; for, as I am told, they afflict and detain you captive for having wished to follow Jesus Christ. You have, however, whereof to rejoice in the good testimony which your conscience renders you in the sight of God, that you do not suffer on account of evil doing, but because Satan cannot endure that you should break loose from the bonds of the servitude in which you have hitherto pined. Notwithstanding, you must call upon God, beseeching Him to have compassion upon you, and committing yourself entirely into His hand, to hope for such deliverance as He shall please to send you. Nevertheless, if there were any right and lawful means of escaping out of the hands of him who detains you, you should ask counsel from God, so that by His Spirit He might teach you to take advantage of it. As I am not thoroughly acquainted with the facts, nay, as I do not even know your person nor your rank, I shall write upon the report of the gentlemen who are the bearers of the present letter. They have told me that as you were preparing to come hither, nay, actually on your way, the thing being discovered, some priest

---

[1] Notice in the handwriting of Charles de Jonvillers:—" He wrote this letter to a good young lady, personally unknown to him, who having set out on the way to Geneva, was arrested by a relation of her own, who wished to deprive her of her liberty. Two of her brothers came hither to get letters from him. But fearing lest they might ask them for their own ends, and to the injury of the young lady, he wrote and adopted this style for the express object he had in view."

who is related to you, seized upon you, and now detains you as in a prison, from whence you have no means of getting free, unless you pretend to be willing for a while to live in that neighbourhood. Now, they promise to harbour you in their house, where you will be free to serve God purely, without mixing yourself up with the idolatries which prevail throughout the country. Before giving you any advice as to this, I protest that on no account would I induce you to flinch, or to seek out any by-way which might turn you out of the strait path which God points out to you in His word. Although I have heard that God has endowed you with admirable constancy, for which I bless and magnify His name, I would yet rather strive to increase you still more in such courage than in any degree lessen it. For when we are brought to such an extremity as to have no way of deliverance from the tyranny of the enemies of the truth, save by subterfuges which draw back and estrange us from the right path, there is no doubt but that God calls us to seal with our blood the confession of faith which we owe to Him. For which reason if it were a question as to declining either on one side or the other, it were better to die. And in order that you may not be shaken by threatenings or by anything whatsoever, look to the Son of God, who did not spare His own life for the sake of our salvation, in order that we might not reckon our life too precious when needed to further His glory. Look to that heavenly crown which is prepared for those who have fought courageously. And above all, beware of drawing back, rather than which, we ought to use our utmost endeavours to press forward to the mark which God sets before us. But if the means be offered you of withdrawing with your brethren, who desire with you to worship God with one accord, I do not think that you ought to refuse. In conclusion, you have to pray God, as I shall also do, that He would bestow on you a spirit of counsel and prudence, to decide what is right and fit for you to do ; a spirit of discretion, that you may not be deceived and take evil for good ; a spirit of steadfastness to be constant in wholly conforming yourself to His will.

[*Copy.—Library of Geneva.* Vol. 107.]

CCCXXVII.—To the Believers in the Isles.[1]

Religious counsels, and announcement of the sending of a minister.

*This* 12*th of October* 1553.

Very dear Brethren,—We have to praise God, that in the captivity wherein you are, he vouchsafes you the strength you ask, to worship Him in purity, fearing more the being deprived of His grace, than exposing yourselves to the dangers which may perhaps be about to occur to you, owing to the malice of the adversaries; for the brother who is bearer of the present letter,[2] has declared to us that you have requested him to return to you whenever he could; and that you desire to be by all means exhorted to what is right, and confirmed in the faith of the Gospel; and, indeed, now-a-days, there is greater need of this than ever. It remains that this holy zeal of yours be firm, so that you may continue to advance in the path of salvation. As for the man, you know him; and on our part, seeing he has here approved himself a God-fearing man, has had his conversation among us holy and without reproach, and has also always followed good and wholesome teaching, we doubt not that he will comport himself faithfully among you,

---

[1] "To the faithful dispersed in some isles of France." The peninsula of Arvert on the coast of Saintonge, peopled by fishermen and pirates, received the first seeds of the Gospel from some refugees driven away by persecution from the neighbouring towns. "The seed sown was afterwards fertilized by some monks preaching a kind of half truth, as regarded doctrine, and reproving vices; so that in a little time we saw (in that country) a strange alteration."—Beza, *Hist. Eccl.*, tom. i. p. 101. From the point of Arvert, the Reformation spread into the adjoining islets, and there made numerous disciples, in spite of the rigours of the Parliament of Bourdeaux. A great missionary, Philibert Hamelin, regulated this movement. From Tours originally, he at first preached the reformed doctrine with success at Saintes. Seized in that town, he miraculously escaped death, and sought an asylum at Geneva, where he followed the calling of a printer. But the ardour of his zeal soon led him to betake himself once more to the perilous apostolate, which was to close with martyrdom. He revisited La Saintonge, visited his brethren dispersed among the islands, organized their churches, and taken a second time, he perished at the stake at Bourdeaux, the 18th April 1557. The journal of another glorious missionary of the Reformation, Bernard Palissy, may be consulted as to the ministry and death of Hamelin.

[2] Philibert Hamelin.

and labour for your edification. As to the advice which he has asked of us in your name, this is the order which it appears to us you have to maintain, both as to prayer to God in beginning, and as to being taught by him and others that God shall give you, and to whom he has bestowed grace to minister to you. Thereupon, see that you take courage to separate yourselves from idolatries, from all superstitions, which are contrary to the service of God, and to the acknowledgment and confession which all Christians owe to Him, for to that are we called. When, in course of time, God has so prospered you, that you are, as it were, an ecclesiastical body maintaining the order already mentioned, and that there are some resolved to withdraw themselves from prevailing pollutions, then you may have the use of the sacraments. But we are nowise of opinion that you should begin by them, or even that you should be in a hurry to partake of the holy Supper, until you have some order established among you. And indeed it is much better for you to abstain from it, so that thus you may be led to seek the means which will render you capable of receiving it. That is, as we have already said, that you may be accustomed to meet together in God's name, being as it were one body; and that you may be separated from the idolatries which it is not lawful to mix up with things holy. Nay, it would not be lawful for a man to administer the sacraments to you, unless he recognised you as a flock of Jesus Christ, and found among you the form of a church. Meanwhile, take courage, and devote yourselves wholly to God, who has purchased us so dearly by His own Son, and yield Him the homage of body and soul, showing that you account His glory more precious than all besides; and that you set a higher value upon the eternal salvation which is prepared for you in heaven, than you do on this transitory life.

Wherefore, very dear brethren, making an end for the present, we shall pray this merciful God to complete what He has begun in you, to increase you in all spiritual blessings, and to have you in His holy protection.

CHARLES D'ESPEVILLE,
As well in his own name, as in that of his brethren.

[*Fr. copy.—Fellowship Register of Geneva.* Vol. A.]

## CCCXXVIII.—To Farel.

*Acknowledgment of Farel's care for the Church of Geneva.*

Geneva, 14*th October* 1553.

I cannot find words, my dear Farel, in which to thank you for the extraordinary interest you take in us, and for your equal regard for this Church. I purposely abstained from, or at all events was more sparing in writing you, as I was afraid to take horseback immediately as you have done. Indeed I did not care for troubling you until the very last, as you said that it would not be acceptable to you if I should spare you. I certainly know well enough, and indeed have experienced how you like, yea, desire to undertake labour in behalf of the Church of God, and how prompt you are in rendering us assistance. Of the present state of things here I suppose you have been informed by Viret, or rather by my letter to him, which I wrote with the intention that you should get a reading of it. Our enemies are making general exertions to have some hasty decree passed at the meeting of the greater Council, about the middle of November. I was thinking that it would be well to have Viret here about that time. Yourself, indeed, I am desirous to see here sooner, viz., on occasion of the final sentence of Servetus. This will take place, I hope, before the end of next week.[1] As, however, the son of Claude Bernard has invited Viret to his marriage on Sabbath next, I have no doubt whatever but that Viret will accompany you if you come by Lausanne. Yet I am unwilling, when there is no pressing necessity for it, that you should move a foot unless it suit your convenience.[2] I have no doubt but that Viret will write you his mind on the matter, if he can secure in time a trustworthy messenger, for I asked him to do so. Earnest salutations from

---

[1] See the letters, pp. 404, 409. They were then waiting at Geneva for the reply of the Swiss churches to the circular letters which had been addressed to them concerning the case of Servetus.

[2] Farel arrived at Geneva a few days afterwards, where was reserved for him the melancholy mission of accompanying Servetus to the stake.

all, especially our friend the Marquis,[1] Normandie, and my restored friend. Adieu, most upright and very dear brother. Salute earnestly your fellow-ministers, and your whole family. May the Lord Christ ever guide, preserve, and bless you all.—
Yours, JOHN CALVIN.

[*Lat. copy.—Library of Zurich. Coll. Simler*, tom. 80.]


## CCCXXIX.—To FAREL.[2]

Deliverance by the Swiss Churches regarding Servetus—vain efforts of Calvin to obtain a mitigation of his punishment.

GENEVA, 26*th October* 1553.

Behold what will give you some gratification. Instead of an epistle, here is a summary which will not occupy long time.

---

[1] Galeazzo Caraccioli, Marquis de Vico.

[2] The state messenger charged with the delivery of the documents relative to the trial of Servetus to the Swiss Churches, had visited in succession those of Berne, Zurich, Schaffhausen, and Bâle, and had now returned to Geneva with their replies. The churches were alike unanimous in their judgment of the theological culpability of Servetus, and in their testimonies of affection and confidence towards Calvin and his colleagues. Without giving expression to the nature of the punishment which should be inflicted on the accused, they were unanimous in advising them to rid the Church of a pest, which had already brought ruin to so great a number of souls. Their various replies will be found in *Calvini Opera*, tom. ix. p. 72, *et seq*. The magistrates of Berne, who had counselled toleration to Bolsec, manifested an inflexible rigour towards Servetus, exhorting those of Geneva not to act unworthily of Christian magistrates. The ministers of Zurich were still more decided : " We think," said they, " that you ought in this case to manifest much faith and zeal, inasmuch as our churches have abroad the bad reputation of being heretical, and of being particularly favourable to heresy. Holy Providence at this time affords you an opportunity of freeing yourselves and us from that injurious suspicion, if you know how to be vigilant and active in preventing the further spreading of that poison, and we have no doubt but that your seigneurs will do so." After such replies the sentence against Servetus could not be long doubtful ; and the magistrates in condemning him to death were only the interpreters of the stern thought of an age in which persecution, that sad legacy of the Middle Ages, was the avowed jurisprudence of all Christian communions. The day following that on which Calvin penned these lines addressed to Farel, (27th October 1553,) Servetus was led forth to hear his doom pronounced at the gate of the Hotel de Ville, and mounted the fatal pile erected at Champel, bequeathing a mournful souvenir to the Reformation, and an eternal subject of accusation to the enemies of the

The messenger has returned from the Swiss Churches. They are unanimous in pronouncing that Servetus has now renewed those impious errors with which Satan formerly disturbed the Church, and that he is a monster not to be borne. Those of Bâle were judicious. The Zurichers were the most vehement of all; for they not only animadverted in severe terms on the atrocity of his impieties, but also exhorted our Senate to severity. They of Schaffhausen will agree. Also to an appropriate letter from the Bernese is added one from the Senate, in which they stimulate ours not a little. Caesar, the comedian, after feigning illness for three days, at length went up to the assembly in order to free that wretch from punishment. Nor was he ashamed to ask that inquiry might be made at the [Council of the] Two Hundred. However, he was without doubt condemned. He will be led forth to punishment to-morrow. We endeavoured to alter the mode of his death, but in vain. Why we did not succeed I defer for narration until I see you. Adieu, most upright brother, and distinguished minister of Christ. May God ever guide and preserve you. Much health to all friends. Ours salute you again.

JOHN CALVIN.

[*Calvin's Lat. Corresp.* Opera, tom. ix. p. 71.]

## CCCXXX.—To MADAME DE PONS.

He encourages her to come out of the spiritual bondage in which she is held.

*The 20th of November* 1553.

MADAME AND GOOD SISTER,—If God had given you a husband who had been loyal to you, and had lived in concord with you, there would be need to comfort you at present, and

---

Reformer. The error of Calvin in the death of Servetus was, we may say, altogether that of his age, inasmuch as men of the most conciliating and moderate dispositions, viz., Bucer, Œcolampadius, Melanchthon, and Bullinger, were at one in their approval of the condemnation of the unfortunate Spanish innovator. One may deeply deplore this error without insulting the Reformation, and combine in a just measure that pity which a great victim demands, with respect for those men whom an unhappy time made the accusers and the judges of Servetus.

to exhort you to patience. But since he who ought to have considered you as dear to him as the half of himself, has been, while he lived, a very severe scourge, you have occasion rather to acknowledge that in removing him our gracious God has acted in mercy towards you. Furthermore, the annoyances which you have undergone ought to teach you to humble yourself under the hand of Him who has thought fit thus to try you, n order to make you feel the value of His help, and how His faithfulness never fails His people. But all the ill-treatment under which you have pined away, has been nothing at all compared to that wretched captivity by which you were kept back from the worship of God, and kept away from the Son of God, so as to be unable to keep faith in the holy and sacred marriage which He has contracted with you; and now you must all the more consider, to what end He has set you so much at liberty. Call to mind, I beseech you, the continual sighs you have been heaving for so long a time. Although you had many kinds of grief, I doubt not that your chief regret was that of not being permitted to devote yourself entirely to the service of God. Consider well, whether you have not vowed daily before God, that you wished for nothing but the means of getting rid of the servitude in which you were held. Now that your wish is granted, rely upon it that God holds you to your promise. It is for you to anticipate him, even as your conscience prompts you, without incitements from without. And yet further, call to remembrance that Saint Paul, in saying that married persons are as it were divided, but that widows have nothing to do but to apply themselves entirely to God, takes away from you the excuse which hitherto you could have alleged. It is certain that nothing whatever ought to hinder us from the discharge of what is due to our heavenly Father, and to that kind Redeemer whom He has sent to us; but the better the opportunity of each, so much the more guilty does he become if he does not the more readily discharge his duty. I am well aware that you have regard to your children, and I do not say but that this is right, provided that the sovereign Father of both you and them be not left out. But consider that the greatest benefit which you can confer upon them, is to shew them the way to follow God. However that may be, it will no longer be permitted you to allege that you are under compulsion, and forced to offend, seeing that God has opened a door to you which might have been shut. What remains for you then but to take courage, yea even so as to strive to the very utmost to surmount all the difficulties which keep you back : for I know very well that you cannot without great opposition dedicate yourself fully to our Lord Jesus. But to come to the point, make a right use of the knowledge which He has for a long time past vouchsafed you ; and do not allow the zeal which He has at one time imprinted by the Holy Spirit upon your heart to die away ; and do not knowingly quench the holy desire which has burned within you in bygone times. Behold how God allows those to slip away who grow careless little by little, and how easily He permits them to be so utterly depraved that they go to perdition ; and it is just that the Lord should thus avenge Himself upon those who have preferred the vanities of the world to the treasure of His Gospel. Now, while many allow themselves to be seduced by such examples, let this serve as a warning to you, to keep all the more closely fenced about in fear and solicitude. Finally, let the adversity which you have passed through, during a part of your life, make you ponder all the more seriously that true happiness and perfect glory which is prepared for us in heaven, that we may not beguile ourselves with worldly repose, which can only be fleeting and highly seasoned with never-ceasing care and troubles, and, worse than all, which makes us unmindful of that soul-rest which alone is blessed. But that I may not seem to distrust your good-will, I shall conclude for the present, after having affectionately commended me to your kind favour and prayers, and having besought our merciful God that if in times past He has poured forth upon you the graces and virtues of His Holy Spirit, He would not only continue them, but would increase you therein, and never allow you to decline from the straight path, but advance you therein still more and more, while in the meantime he holds you under His protection. I do not know whereabouts your brother is, or if I should give him pleasure by writing to him, which withholds me from doing so. Nevertheless, I desire that God would hold him with a strong hand, so that he may not be estranged from Him.[1] From what I hear, he is a little gone out of the way in some things, and has much need to be brought back into the straight path; but as I do not know how to effect this, I reserve it for a better opportunity. Once more I commit you to the love of our merciful God.—Your humble brother and servant, CHARLES D'ESPEVILLE.

[*Fr. Copy.—Impl. Library. Coll. Dupuy*, Vol. 102.]

## CCCXXXI.—To Viret.[2]

Recommendation of several English refugees in Switzerland.

GENEVA, 20*th November* 1553.

Those Englishmen, on leaving this place to resort to you, requested me to give them an introduction, in order that by your assistance they might secure suitable lodgings. Indeed they were anxious to live with yourself or M. Beza, but they will not urge this, especially as they were informed that they could scarcely expect it. You will, however, receive them as a good and kind host should; for I understand that they are pious and honourable men, and am confident that they will be easily accommodated. The elder, the father of the young man, is a person of good birth, and was wealthy in his own country. The son merits higher praise for piety and holy zeal; for, under the reign of King Edward, seeing that the Church suffered from want of pastors, he undertook voluntarily the labours of

[1] May not the personage in question be Antoine de Pons, Lord of Marenme. He had taken for his first wife Anne de Parthenay, daughter of M. de Soubise, and had embraced the Reformed faith at the Court of Ferrara. Having afterwards married the lady of Montchenu, he fell away from Protestantism, and even became one of its persecutors —Bèze, *Hist. Eccl.*, tom. i. p. 199.

[2] After the accession of Queen Mary to the throne of England, the Continent was filled with religious exiles, who did not hesitate to sacrifice their country for the free profession of their faith in a strange land. A great many English Churches were established in Germany and Switzerland. Those of Frankfort and Geneva were the most important.—See on the origin and history of the latter, the Memoir published by a Genevese *savant*, M. Heyer, in the *Recueil de la Société d'Histoire et d'Archéologie de Genève*. 1854.

that office. Add to this, that they, with a generous liberality, assisted with their entire property our French brethren, who, on account of the Gospel, had crossed over to England. We must on no account, therefore, deny to these exiles at least a similar friendship. You will also inform our friend Beza of the intended visit of a friend, who will, I expect, be with him to-morrow or soon afterwards. He is brother to Luzarch, whom he had formerly at his house—older than he, however, although not the eldest of the family. Our bold leaders have dined together several times since you left.[1] I have not as yet witnessed any proof of that intrepidity of which they were boasting. Adieu, very worthy brother. Salute M. Beza and the rest of the brethren, also your wife, and little daughters at home. May the Lord guide and watch over you.—Yours,

JOHN CALVIN.

[*Lat. orig. autogr.—Library of Geneva*, Vol. 107, *a*.]


CCCXXXII.—To BULLINGER.[2]

Appeal to the Magistrates of Zurich in reference to ecclesiastical discipline—thanks for the aid afforded by the ministers of that Church in the affair of Servetus.

GENEVA, 26*th November* 1553.

Here is another new labour for you. Those desirous of living a life of licentiousness, have not ceased for the past seven

---

[1] "The whole of the Lesser Council, the gentlemen of justice, M. Calvin, and a great number of the more eminent men of the town, dine together, in order to cement the peace, and it has been decided upon that if any one violate it all the others may oppose him."—*Registers of the Council* for 1553.

[2] See the letter to Viret, p. 405. After having solemnly refused the Supper to Philibert Berthelier, Calvin presented himself before the Council, and demanded a general assembly of the people. The Council could not, he said, annul a discipline which the entire people had sanctioned. Intimidated by this step the Council adopted the course which it had already followed in the case of Servetus, and expressed the intention of consulting the other Reformed Cantons. Charged with a secret mission by the Reformer, his friend John de Budè set out for Zurich, to solicit in that place a decision favourable to the views of Calvin. Bullinger was active in his exertions to gain over the magistrates of his country, as well as in giving Calvin wise counsels of moderation:—" We have laboured with all our

years to oppose the discipline of the Church, which is in a tolerable state of efficiency here. We would not, however, have been so much annoyed by loose-living men among the common people, if there had not been leaders who wished to convert this license into a means of power. It has now come to this, that whatever church order has hitherto flourished will be rooted up if you cannot afford us a remedy. And it is on this account that our very excellent brother, M. de Budè, has not scrupled to undertake a journey to you, at this trying season of the year, in order to acquaint you with the whole business. However, the main point is in brief this: that your most illustrious Senate give as their reply that the form which we have hitherto employed is agreeable to the Word of God; in the next place, that it discountenance innovation. You will learn the rest from the circular letter which I have written; on this condition, however, that should you not deem it expedient to circulate it more widely, you communicate it expressly to M. Gualter. I leave it entirely to your judgment. Should I obtain through you those two chief points, viz., an unambiguous confirmation of our regulations by the suffrages of your Senate, and a discountenancing in our men of their desire for innovation, it will bring peace to this Church for a long time to come. I hope you have received the letter which I sent you lately, in which I thanked you all in my own name and that of my brethren, for the faithful and pious response which you gave in the case of Servetus. The very brilliant commendation with which you honoured us, had its own weight with good men.[1] It has not as yet, as you may perceive, put a check upon the

night," he wrote to him, " to prevent our Seigneurs from acting in any way derogatory to the excellent laws of your Church; we have besides exhorted you to continue faithful, using moderation in all things, lest you lose those whose salvation is desired by the Lord, who does not break the bruised reed nor quench the smoking flax.'—*Bullinger to Calvin.* 12th December 1553.

[1] While giving an energetic deliverance against the errors of Servetus, the ministers of Zurich had paid, in their reply to the Seigneurie of Geneva, a very beautiful tribute to Calvin :—" We trust that the faith and zeal—in a word, the distinguished services among the exiles and the pious—of our brother, your pastor, Calvin, is too illustrious to be obscured by such very disgraceful calumnies, whether in the estimation of your honourable Council, or in that of other good men."—*Calv. Opera*, tom. ix. p. 74.

lawless and the abandoned. However, things will be better in a short time, I trust, if you will come to our assistance. A citizen of yours has conveyed to you the book of Servetus and that farrago which you asked for. Of the sad desolation of England you know too much; I shall stop therefore. Adieu, most distinguished Sir, and venerable brother. Salute earnestly M. Gualter, your wife, your relatives, and the faithful. May the Lord shield you all by His protection, and guide you by His Spirit. — JOHN CALVIN.

[*Calvin's Lat. Corresp.* Opera, tom. ix. p. 75.]

CCCXXXIII.—TO THE PASTORS AND DOCTORS OF THE CHURCH OF ZURICH.[1]

Account of the struggles at Geneva for the maintenance of ecclesiastical discipline—appeal to the Pastors of Zurich for their influence with the magistrates of that town.

GENEVA, 26*th November* 1553.

I feel indeed ashamed, very excellent and sincerely respected brethren, at bringing before you again a new topic of consideration, inasmuch as our Council troubled you lately with the case of Servetus. There is, however, good grounds for excuse in the present instance: for, as the wickedness of certain parties is vaunting itself with a headstrong insolence not to be resisted,

[1] See the preceding letter. The Council of Zurich having received the letter of that of Geneva, and having consulted Bullinger and his colleagues regarding the reply which they would require to make, did not hesitate to give a deliverance in favour of Calvin, and against the demands of the *Libertines*. They accordingly exhorted the magistrates of Geneva to maintain their ecclesiastical laws, "as good and conformable to the prescriptions of the Divine word, and as particularly necessary in an age in which men are becoming more and more wicked." Although the discipline then in operation at Zurich differed essentially from that of Geneva, in being less rigorous, yet the Seigneurs of Zurich pronounced a eulogy upon that of the latter, "inasmuch as it was framed in a manner adapting it to the time, the place, and the persons; and that every Church ought to persevere in those usages which she has received and holily established, according to the word of God."— Ruchat, *Hist. de la Reformation*, tom. vi. pp. 67, 68. The reply of the Seigneurs of Berne was less explicit. They limited themselves to the declaration, that excommunication was not in force among them, but that they had certain regulations, of which they forwarded them a copy.

the pious and upright are forced to apply to you for aid; and while I am assuredly anxious above all things to avoid giving you trouble, I have, nevertheless, from the necessity of the case, thought it my duty not to spare you. From the time of my return to this Church, discipline has at least made tolerable advancement, if it has not been perfect, or such as could have been wished. The Consistory was instituted, and charged with the regulation of morals. It possessed no civil jurisdiction, but simply the administration of rebuke from the word of God; its ultimate punishment was excommunication. Among the other disputes which Satan has been continually stirring up during the past three years, the present one has been a source of extreme vexation to us; for a certain wretch, of abandoned effrontery, having attempted, contrary to the decision of the Church, to force his way to the Holy Table, when he saw that we were prepared to offer a determined resistance to his madness, filled the city with a great tumult. Nor, indeed, had he much difficulty in doing so, seeing that he could make choice of the irreligious faction to act the drama. And because he was not only patronized by those men, who were not ashamed to make a noise in defence of Servetus, but also aided and abetted by them, he, by their assistance, succeeded, after an intense struggle, and by very outrageous behaviour, in prevailing upon the Greater Council rashly to break through the established and hitherto observed order of the Church. We again opposed them. Those who had fallen into the error, have resolved upon consulting the Swiss Churches. And although they have not yet written you, yet because it is certain that the reply of your most illustrious Council will be in accordance with your mind, I have thought that you should be apprised and solicited regarding it in time. Accordingly, a very excellent and eminently judicious man, and my dearly beloved brother, has gladly undertaken a journey to you, in the name of the Church, at the cost of great toil and trouble at this severe season of the year. Let me earnestly beseech you, therefore, in the first place, to reflect, that it should not be treated by you as some ordinary matter; but, that the case proposed for decision concerns the entire welfare of this Church. And because

I consider that it would be perfidious cowardice in me, so long as I occupy my present position, not to contend keenly, even to the utmost, in behalf of a holy and lawful discipline, I have resolved that I should a hundred times rather leave this life —not to say this place—than suffer to be overthrown, that which I am confident is taken from the Word of God. All are not agreed at the present time regarding excommunication. Nor am I ignorant that there are pious and learned men who do not consider excommunication to be necessary under Christian princes. And yet I am confident that there is no person of sound mind, and unbiassed disposition, who would discountenance the employment of it. To me it is clearly the doctrine of Christ. If on any occasion people cannot be got to come under this yoke of Christ, after pastors have exerted themselves to the utmost respecting it, it is their business then, not ours; but it would be exceedingly base for us to stand by and look on, while an edifice which Christ committed to our defence, was being overthrown, and utterly razed to the ground. Nor have I any fear that you will censure my zeal for its pertinacity, when once you have got a thorough understanding of the plan which we have followed up to the present time, and of which godless men are endeavouring forcibly to deprive us. And now, if it shall appear to you to contain nothing but what is consonant with the pure doctrine of Christ, I solemnly beseech you to use your influence, so that your most illustrious Council may bear a similar testimony. For this is of especial importance, in order that our men may understand that they cannot compass that innovation which they desire, without abandoning the example of Christ, or, if this seem too strong, without swerving from it. As for whatever is not sufficiently set forth in this letter, M. de Budè will explain it in your presence. The Lord will be a witness to myself and my colleagues, that for four years wicked men have done all in their power, to accomplish the gradual overthrow of this Church in its present tolerable condition. I saw through their secret machinations from the first; but I did not know what to make of it, unless that the Lord was preparing whips before our eyes, in order that by inspiring us with fear, He might win us back to Himself. For the past two years, we have been precisely as if living among the professed enemies of Christ. The last act is now played; for after many victories, the enemy meditates a splendid triumph over Christ, His doctrine, His ministers, and in a word, over all His members. I shall not speak of how inhumanly, insolently, and barbarously, they have tortured those exiles of Christ who had embraced His faith. And, indeed, the very perpetrators of those wrongs will not be able to deny, with what mildness, modesty, and patience, those who found a ready asylum here, have borne all their indignities. Their profligacy has now reached such a pitch, that having shaken off all shame, they obstinately desire to convert the House of the Lord into a brothel. And, in order that you may know how foully dishonourable they are, they lately, when our brother Farel was here,—to whom they are, as you know, under so great obligations,—and who gave them a free and independent advice, were so inflamed with rage, that they made bold to threaten him with a criminal prosecution.[1]

I am indeed well enough aware, that it is nothing new for factious men, in a free city, to stir up mobs. Yet our Council have been deplorably left to themselves, for they demanded of the people of Neuchatel that they should deliver up to them the father of their liberty, yea, the father of this Church, as accused of a capital offence. I feel constrained to proclaim the infamy of this city, although I could desire to wipe it off with my blood. Farel came: before he entered the city, the officer of the Council delivered an official intimation at my house, that

[1] Farel, while preaching at Geneva, had addressed severe language to the youths of that city; and he said they were "worse than brigands, murderers, thieves, plunderers, atheists." A crowd of young men presenting themselves before the Council, menaced it to its face, and demanded that Farel should be summoned from Neuchatel to give an account of his insolent language. A great tumult followed this proposition. Some made bold to stand up and call to their recollection the services Farel had rendered to the republic, and the shame of an accusation directed against the *spiritual father* of the city. Meanwhile, Farel arrived, calm as usual. The cry got up of Justice! Justice! and the citizens leaving their shops, hastened to rally round the venerable pastor, and preserve him from all disgrace. He had little difficulty in justifying himself, and even Perrin was compelled to proclaim his innocence.—*Registers of the Council*, Nov. 1553; Roset, tom. v. p. 53; and *Hist. de la Suisse*, tom. xi. p. 381.

he was not to enter the pulpit. I shall not dwell upon the rest; for it is sufficient to let you have a taste of this ingratitude, which will stir the just indignation of all good and honest men. And as I have many reasons for not making an open lament over our evils, so, of this be convinced, and that briefly, that unless Satan receive a check through you, he will fling the reins loose altogether. It becomes you, therefore, to make as great exertions, as if the welfare of this Church was entirely in your hands. Nor let it be ascribed to peevishness in us, if we would rather yield up our position than sacrifice our opinions. For all good men know, that we have been hitherto over-accommodating, in order to obviate troubles, even when there could be no doubt at all, that our patience was tried by the wicked. But we must not yield them this victory; nay, we must not knowingly and wilfully surrender the entire liberty of the Church; not only because the authority of our ministry would fall to the ground, but because the name of Christ would be subjected to any the foulest disgrace: an unbridled license for all vices would increase with more and more effrontery: the condition of the pious would not only become exposed to all manner of wrongs, but utterly cast down by suffering,—they would lie in sad prostration. This makes me all the more confident, that you will do your endeavour to assist, by your support, the faithful of this place, so that they may worship God with a little more peace. Adieu, my very excellent and truly revered brethren. May the Lord be present with you, and guide you by His Spirit; may He supply you with an abundance of wisdom, sufficient, not only for maintaining your own Church, but also for upholding that of others. Fare ye well, my very excellent and truly revered brethren. May the Lord be ever present with you, to guide and watch over you.

My colleagues salute you earnestly, and commend this Church, with all possible zeal, to your faithfulness and wisdom. —Yours, JOHN CALVIN.

It will be desirable to conceal this letter, lest our men hear of it.[1]

[*Lat. orig. autogr.—Archives of Zurich.* Gest. vi. 105, p. 515.]

[1] In Calvin's own hand.

## CCCXXXIV.—To Bullinger.

*Fresh details regarding ecclesiastical discipline—hope of speedy realization —announcement of the publication of a book against the errors of Servetus.*

Geneva, 30*th December,* 1553.

The messenger arrived six days after I had received your letter. The people of Schaffhausen give a pious and judicious reply; those of Bâle give a very meagre response; they offer us almost no advice, sending us simply a copy of their edicts, without, however, pronouncing any judgment. Our brother, Sulzer, earnestly apologizes for not having been able to accomplish more. And I can perceive, in various ways, indeed, most upright and respected brother, how strenuously you have exerted yourself in our behalf; nor do I doubt but that our friend Gualter performed his part also. Whatever may have happened, I feel that I owe more to your singular faithfulness and remarkable zeal, than I am able to express. But the Lord, in whose cause you have made such endeavours, will give you his reward. Assuredly my affection for you will not be found wanting. Nothing has as yet been done in the Senate, the letters being still in the hand of the translator. Seeing that we have to do with very base calumniators, they will get up various quarrels with us. I expect, however, either victory, or a satisfactory winding up of the matter. As soon as anything has been effected, I shall see to it that you be informed of it. For it will be a matter of common gratulation to us, if the event turn out according to our wishes. The pamphlet against Servetus, in which I have set forth that argument which you wished me to employ, was published at the late Frankfort Fair.[1]

[1] This is the book against the errors of Michael Servetus.—*Opera*, tom. viii.; and *Opuscules*, p. 230. The Registers of Council contain the following intimation on the subject of this work :—" Calvin has represented to the Council, that at the request of the Swiss Churches, he is about to publish a book, containing an account of the opinions of Servetus; and that he has not been so bold as to commit it to the press without the permission of the Council, assuring it that this book contains nothing not conformable to the word of God, or dishonourable to the city. Agreed to permit Calvin to print it; 11th December 1553." This book, as

With respect to those matters which the men at Bâle are making a clamour about, and of which I complained to you, I resolved to spare their reputation, and have done so, lest the disgrace of a few men should bring dishonour on the whole Church;[1] and certainly they deserve to be overwhelmed in eternal oblivion. The progress of events convinced me of what had not previously occurred to me, viz., that your letter concerning Servetus, should be inserted in the book; and trusting to your kindness, I took the liberty of inserting it. Should you not approve of my plan, however, I shall endeavour to remedy it. Adieu, very distinguished Sir, illustrious minister of Christ, and revered brother. May the Lord continue to guide you by the spirit of wisdom and fortitude, and to protect your Church.

Salute earnestly in my name your colleagues, and your family. My colleagues, MM. Celso Martinengo and Budé, and the other brethren, respectfully salute you.—Yours truly,

JOHN CALVIN.

[*Lat. Copy.—Library of Zurich. Coll. Simler*, tom. 80.]


## CCCXXXV.—To FAREL.[2]

Assistance afforded to the faithful refugees in Switzerland—reply of the Churches on the subject of ecclesiastical discipline.

GENEVA, 30*th December* 1553.

Good men have indeed sent money to be laid out on the banished brethren and the exiles. They have ordered one part to be distributed among us, and they have designed the other

establishing the right of magistrates to punish heresy by the sword, has given place to the most violent controversies.

[1] Calvin had written, what he then suppressed: *De Curione et Similibus*. The condemnation of Servetus was disapproved of by certain of the professors of the Academy of Bâle, among whom is to be found the celebrated Italian refugee, Celio Secondo Curione, and Sebastian Castalio.

[2] Whilst the number of refugees was increasing at Geneva and the other towns of Switzerland, their wants were provided for by liberal charitable donations. This was the origin of the *Bourse Etrangère* founded at Geneva, and whose revenues are applied, even in our own day, to the support of poor students, or to the establishing of new schools.

two parts for the poor of Lausanne and your own city. Our friend Beza caused twenty-five gold pieces to be handed over to them. However, as but few exiles have hitherto gone among you, so far as I know, especially of that sort which is so numerous here, might you not, if you are not in immediate need, expend at your own discretion what would relieve the necessity of others? I do not ask you, certainly, to make a remission to us, but I wished to advise you on the matter, that if it should seem proper to you, you might transmit a certain sum to those who are in urgent need of money. Nevertheless, I do not dictate any course to you, but fearing, as I did, that you might be troubled with some doubts about how to act, I thought it better to anticipate them. The messenger has at length returned from the Helvetian Churches. Our Council will meet with a disappointment to-morrow in their replies. I expect a great deal of quarrelling, the issue of which, however, will perhaps turn out more fortunately than the wicked, who are now beginning to get crestfallen, had previously calculated upon. But there is in the other respect no cordiality. When we shall have completed the contests which are in store for us, I shall write you the whole more fully. Adieu, most upright brother: assist us with your prayers.

The men of Zurich prudently dissuade from making any change. Those of Bâle, without interposing any judgment, send a written copy of their own edicts. The people of Schaffhausen are the most judicious of all. Our neighbours push it coldly aside; a thing which I expected from the first. Salute your brethren and friends earnestly in my name. May the Lord be ever with you to guide you.—Yours,

JOHN CALVIN.

[*Lat. orig. autogr.—Library of Geneva.* Vol. 107, *a.*]

## CCCXXXVI.—To John a Lasco.[1]

*Expression of sympathy under his trials—loud complaints of the intolerance of German theologians.*

*December* 1553.[2]

I have been longer in replying to you, very illustrious Sir and heartily revered brother, than you perhaps expected, as I thought there would be no harm in delaying. For although a young physician set out from this place some time ago for your locality, yet as I hardly expected that a letter would reach you sooner by him, I thought it better not to give it him to be carried to you by a circuitous journey. There was another also a short time afterwards, who likewise purposed making a round-about journey. Besides, M. Secelius, who had brought your letter, went away hurriedly from us, while Messrs. Cheke and Morison, then compelled to retire to Italy, were staying with me. I was accordingly constrained to allow a very fit messenger to go away empty, at least one who would have taken the trouble of delivering to you faithfully and in safety

---

[1] See the note, p. 269, of the present volume. At the death of Edward VI. the congregation of foreign Protestants, under the charge of John à Lasco, obtained permission to quit London and embark for the Low Countries. A storm dispersed their little fleet, and the ship in which à Lasco was, found shelter in the Danish port of Elsinore; but the intolerance of the Lutheran ministers did not long respect this asylum. Received at first with favour by the King of Denmark, Christian III., a mild and pious prince, à Lasco was before long violently attacked by the theologians of the court, Westphal and Bugenhagen, who represented the wandering members of the Church of London as so many infidels, unworthy of the name of Christian, and called them *the Devil's Martyrs*. Led away by their counsels, the King ordered the refugees to evacuate the country, and they were obliged to re-embark during a tempestuous season, and sail through a thousand perils in quest of some more hospitable shore. This shameful violation of hospitality, renewed by the Lutherans of Lubec, Hamburg, and Rostock, excited the lively indignation of the Reformed Churches of Switzerland, which we find eloquently expressed in this letter of Calvin to à Lasco. Having retired to Friesland, where he had founded several churches a number of years previously, à Lasco was not long in directing his steps to Frankfort, where we afterwards find him.—Krasinski, *Hist. Relig. des Peuples Sclaves.* C. vii. pp. 135, 136.

[2] Without a date, but written doubtless towards the end of the year 1553.

whatever I should have written. If you now expect me to pay you with interest for my tardiness, you will be deceived. Nor, indeed, do I suppose you will desire very greatly this sort of favour, as it will take up your time without your gaining much profit. For I have not a subject of a kind like yours, the reading of which, although not at all pleasant, was nevertheless useful and thankworthy to us ; for the narrative of your wanderings so afflicted me with grief and sadness, that I easily perceived that the events were nevertheless exceedingly worthy of being recorded. Nor do I doubt but that many others felt the same. It was therefore in my judgment worth your pains to write a full account of it ; and it may perhaps be useful to give it a somewhat wider publicity. For my own private part, I must not regret what has already been productive of fruit ; but the information respecting the cruelty of the Danes was exceedingly painful and saddening to me. Good God! that the barbarity of a Christian people should exceed even the sea in savageness. When the rumour got afloat here that a signal had been raised by that king to our unfortunate brethren, who, exiled from England, were in search of a new place of retreat, so sudden was our joy that this single act was sufficient to win for him immortal honour. But I now fear that he has brought down upon himself the bitter vengeance of God, no less than kindled the deep indignation of all good men. And I feel it all the more keenly for his mild disposition to have been inflamed by unfortunate instigators, seeing that I had taken such a lively interest in celebrating, yea, in publicly proclaiming his generosity. The perfidy of those who ought even to have smoothed down hostility, was no less detestable than their cruelty. It seems to me, however, that a diabolical fury has seized on almost the whole of that maritime region, and has swept over Saxony and the adjoining countries, so that they show neither bounds nor shame in their mad rage against us. You may rely upon it that it has been a joyful and pleasant spectacle to the Papists. We must therefore strive all the more silently to repress what one cannot make public without at the same time bringing dishonour upon the Gospel. Seeing, however, that I had no doubt at all but that the intemperance of that party was hateful to men of learning and forbearance, I was led to think that I should not be altogether silent; and certainly it was not my fault that some expedient was not adopted by us at the very first for putting a check upon them. It appeared otherwise to our very excellent brother Bullinger, who was placing victory in silence and patient endurance. I desisted from pushing the matter, lest my assiduity might cause trouble or breed mistrust. Tired of the propriety of such a course, he has changed his mind of late, I opine, and has exhorted me of his own accord to repel their foul calumnies in a short tract. This I have promised to do. But as I was busily engaged with Genesis up to the time of the markets, and as I required the general assent of those whose defence I had undertaken, I have done nothing to it as yet. But as soon as I get set about it, I hope to produce a lucubration without much delay. But to return to yourself, revered brother, I think you have set an example doubly praiseworthy, in that yourself and your companions have contended with the savage ferocity and haughtiness of that beast with no less calm discretion than composed dignity, and have besides preserved the same even tenor of moderation as often as others of a similar character have turned their cruel attacks against you. So noble indeed has been your defence of truth, that, already tossed about roughly both by sea and land, you have not thought it a hardship again to undergo a new exile for its cause, and by this steadfastness you have offered alike a sweet sacrifice to God, and set a useful example to all pious men. I rejoice that the Lord has at length looked down upon you, so that you have found a tranquil haven, in which you may not only find rest but also employ yourselves in profitable labour in the cause of God and of his Church. May the Lord enrich that very illustrious lady[1] with every blessing, who has extended her maternal hand to you so kindly and graciously. JOHN CALVIN.

[*Lat. orig. autogr.—Library of Geneva.* Vol. 107, *a.*]

[1] The Countess d'Embden, who, after Calvin's death, engaged in a pious correspondence with Theodore Beza.

# ImTheStory.com

Personalized Classic Books in many genre's

Unique gift for kids, partners, friends, colleagues

Customize:

- Character Names
- Upload your own front/back cover images (optional)
- Inscribe a personal message/dedication on the inside page (optional)

Customize many titles Including
- Alice in Wonderland
- Romeo and Juliet
- The Wizard of Oz
- A Christmas Carol
- Dracula
- Dr. Jekyll & Mr. Hyde
- And more...